Tony Oliva

Tony Oliva

THE LIFE AND TIMES OF A

MINNESOTA TWINS LEGEND

Thom Henninger

Foreword by Patrick Reusse

UNIVERSITY OF MINNESOTA PRESS
MINNEAPOLIS · LONDON

Published by the University of Minnesota Press
111 Third Avenue South, Suite 290
Minneapolis, MN 55401-2520
http://www.upress.umn.edu

Library of Congress Cataloging-in-Publication Data
Henninger, Thom.
Tony Oliva: the life and times of a Minnesota Twins legend / Thom Henninger; foreword by Patrick Reusse.
Includes index.
ISBN 978-0-8166-9489-1 (hc)| ISBN 978-1-5179-0970-3 (pb)
1. Oliva, Tony, 1941–. 2. Baseball players—United States—Biography. 3. Minnesota Twins (Baseball team). I. Title.
GV865.O44H46 2015
796.357092—dc23

                              2014040582

Printed in the United States of America on acid-free paper

The University of Minnesota is an equal-opportunity educator and employer.

25 24 23 22 21 20 19   10 9 8 7 6 5 4 3 2 1

Contents

Foreword . . . . *vii*
PATRICK REUSSE

Preface . . . . *xi*

1. Young Pedro 1

2. Life after Cuba Closes 13

3. The Minor Leagues 32

4. A Fast Start to a Big League Career 50

5. Injured Rookie Wins Unprecedented Batting Crown 69

6. Oliva Leads Pennant Push 80

7. Life's Highs and Lows 99

8. The Great Pennant Race of 1967 113

9. Marriage and Family in the Year of the Pitcher 131

10. Baseball's Summer of Change 144

11. Twins Repeat with a New Bill in Charge 157

12. Family Reunions and the Career-Changing Knee Injury . . . 168

13. The Extremes of 1972 182

14. The Final Years as a Player 198

15. Tony O: The Man 213

Epilogue: The Hall of Fame Question 227

Acknowledgments *251*

Index *255*

Foreword

Patrick Reusse

The announcement that Minnesota was getting a major league baseball team came on October 26, 1960. The excitement here on the prairie was astounding. We wanted to know everything possible about our new ball club.

Yet without such a thing as airfare bargains, there was no migration of newly minted Twins fans to Orlando in March 1961 to check out the ball club in spring training. Instead, we waited to find out what the baseball writers from the Minneapolis and St. Paul newspapers had to offer for information on the previous day's exhibition game. Come the regular season, we listened faithfully to the radio broadcasts, and hardcore fans kept scorebooks at the desk at work or on the kitchen table at home. There are legendary stories of moms and grown daughters exchanging a dozen phone calls in an afternoon to get caught up on what was happening with a couple of batters.

There was no Internet then, so if you wanted to know what was going on in the minor league system, you might find out in Friday's newspaper. It might mention some heroics from a farmhand that had happened on Tuesday with the Double-A team in Nashville or events in the lower minor teams in Charlotte, Wilson, and a place called Wytheville.

During the summer of 1961, we started seeing notes, probably in Sid Hartman's columns, about a young man named Tony Oliva who was hitting over .400 in Class-D ball at Wytheville. He was a Cuban, as were Camilo Pascual, Zoilo Versalles, and others on the first Twins team, and we figured that added to this young man's potential for greatness.

Tony wound up hitting .410—something we probably discovered ten days after the fact by reading the minor league reports in the *Sporting News*. For further insight, "Baseball's Bible" probably let us know he was a lefthanded hitter and played the outfield—but they did not inform us of Tony's OPS or calculate a Class-D version of WAR.

But .410 was enough. We wanted to see this kid.

There was a glimpse in September 1962, after Oliva batted .350 at Class-A Charlotte. There was another glimpse in September 1963, after he batted .304 with twenty-three home runs at Triple-A Dallas–Fort Worth. Finally, in the spring of 1964, it was time. Finally, we were going to see Tony Oliva in right field for the Twins. We knew he was seven for sixteen in those two September glimpses, we had read of his line drives being sprayed around Orlando's Tinker Field and other Florida outposts in exhibitions, but now we would see him in the lineup, hitting third, teamed with Harmon Killebrew, Bob Allison, and the other big bats available to manager Sam Mele.

The Twins had opened with one game in Cleveland, played three in Washington against the expansion Senators, and then came to Detroit to play a scheduled Sunday doubleheader on April 19, 1964.

The first game was on TV. That was a big deal in 1964. I think Twins owner Calvin Griffith was still giving us a total of twenty games on local TV then—sixteen road games and four Friday-night home games in midsummer. If the Twins were going to be on TV in 1964, you circled the date on a calendar (not an electronic note on your cell-phone calendar, but a penciled circle around a square on a real paper calendar).

We were watching this Sunday telecast, and we were watching Oliva more closely than anyone, since he had batted .474 through the first four games. Batting third, Tony singled in a run in the first against Phil Regan, the ill-tempered Detroit starter.

Oliva came around again in the second. Tony dug in, as was his custom, and Regan promptly threw his best fastball at Oliva's helmetless head. Tony sprawled to the dirt of the batter's box to escape being maimed. Then he got up, dusted off the uniform, and hit a pitch over the head of Don Demeter in straightaway center field, which was 440 feet to the fence. Oliva raced to third with an RBI triple. As he raced, and as Demeter chased, Tony Oliva became my favorite Twins player. A decade after that "Take that, Phil Regan" moment, I became the beat writer for the Twins for the St. Paul newspapers.

By 1974, Tony's right knee had been ravaged by annual surgeries. If we had had arthroscopic surgery then, Tony would have played twenty years in the big leagues and had 3,300 hits and five batting titles, and he would have waltzed into the Hall of Fame with 92 percent of the vote in his first year of eligibility. But we did not have such surgery, only the invasive type, so by 1974 Tony O had his three batting titles and was limping through the second of his final four seasons as a designated hitter. If not for the arrival of the DH in 1973, Tony would have been done after being limited to ten games on his ruined knee in 1972, and he would not have had an additional 446 hits on his résumé.

It was sad to cover Tony in those DH days, remembering what he was, but it was also sweet, because you could still see the swing. More important, you could still see Tony. Traveling full time with the Twins, I got to know Tony well during his last seasons as a player and his seasons as a hitting coach. He became "Señor" to me, and I was "Pot" to him, which was either his Cuban twist on my name or a comment on my frame, which is still that way fifty years later.

Now I happen to share four tickets at Target Field in the row directly in front of the tickets that Tony holds. If he is not part of the Spanish-language broadcast for the Twins during a game, there is a good chance he will be in those seats for a few innings. When he is, and when friends of mine are in our seats, I hear this from them after the game 100 percent of the time: "Hey, Pat, Tony O was sitting behind us. He seems like such a great guy."

And I will respond, "You are right. Señor is the best guy I have met in sports."

Truly.

Tony Oliva became my favorite in 1964. Five decades later, that hasn't changed.

Preface

The date was September 26, 1965. In the visitors' clubhouse at Washington's D.C. Stadium, the Minnesota Twins were celebrating the 2–1 victory that secured the franchise's first American League pennant since moving to the Midwest. The youthful Twins, who had put to rest a sixteen-year-long Yankees dynasty dating to 1949, exulted in the moment. Players hugged and laughed, the champagne flowed, and nearly everyone in the clubhouse was soaked in bubbly.

At one point, during the happiest moment in the professional lives of many of these young men, Twins rookie César Tovar discovered Tony Oliva sitting at his locker, tears streaming down his cheeks. Oliva, who had been separated from his family in Cuba for nearly five years, was suffering mixed emotions. Winning a pennant and earning a trip to the World Series brought joy, but at the same time he was saddened, unable to share this high point in his life with his parents and siblings. When Tovar asked his friend what was wrong, Oliva found it easiest to simply say that he was just extremely happy. While he chose not to share his conflicting high and low feelings, his tears were a rare public display of emotion.

Oliva's baseball career, and in fact his life, had unintentionally become entangled in the deteriorating relationship between his native Cuba and the United States. Diplomatic relations between the two countries took a dramatic turn for the worse in the days following his arrival in the United States in April 1961, suddenly making it impossible for Oliva—and many of his countrymen—to return home as long as he hoped to pursue a major league career. The resulting isolation profoundly affected Oliva, who shared those painful emotions only with his fellow Cuban players and those closest to him. Otherwise, few teammates were aware of what Cuba's "closing" meant to him, even five years into Oliva's professional career.

In his earliest days with the Twins, Oliva had won over his teammates with his easy smile and even-keeled approach to his craft. He could mask his loneliness for home even in the worst of times. It did not matter if he was tearing the cover off the ball at the plate or struggling at some aspect of the game; his teammates always saw the same happy-go-lucky manner that made him a delight to be around. To his credit, Oliva could compartmentalize his isolation and stay focused on maximizing his talent. It is difficult enough to be one of the world's top performers in any profession—art, music, business, or baseball—even without the challenges of integrating into a new culture and learning a new language, while also coping with being cut off from loved ones and everything that had been familiar in his life.

One of the great pure hitters of his era, Oliva combined incredible talent with an extraordinary work ethic to win batting titles in his first two seasons (three in eight years) before his ailing right knee forced him to play on one healthy leg for the rest of his career. He, Harmon Killebrew, and Rod Carew were the key run producers for some the best teams in Twins history.

Nearly everyone who has lived in Minnesota during the past fifty years knows who Tony Oliva is, although his life story embraces much more than eight years as one of baseball's best hitters and a devastating knee injury that sabotaged his career in 1971. The Oliva we *do* know has not starred on the baseball field for more than thirty-five years now, but the love affair so many people in the Midwest have with "Tony O" continues. It began during his sensational rookie season in 1964, when the youngster first caught the attention of Twins fans. The team's newest star spoke little English, but fans immediately took to his warm, gold-toothed smile and sunny disposition.

That affection quickly grew beyond the Twin Cities when Oliva became a mainstay of the annual Minnesota Twins Winter Caravan. When baseball was furthest from the minds of midwesterners, a collection of players and coaches traversed the tundra of Minnesota and neighboring states to promote Twins baseball. Oliva began making the wintry excursions as soon as he joined the major league club. Dick Bremer, the team's television play-by-play broadcaster for most of the past three decades, notes that Oliva's appeal to fans was always apparent. "You know you're preaching to the choir," Bremer says of the caravan experience. "People who show up in Bismarck, North Dakota, when it's 22 below, they're baseball fans. But in the case of traveling with Tony, there's just a special charm that he brings. And the ovations are so genuine. He's got a magnetic personality."

Some of that charm surfaces in Oliva's off-kilter storytelling, which both benefits and suffers from his take on the English language. Still, Bremer appreciates a "comedic quality that he has that is really remarkable, given the language barrier. Tony's the only one I've ever met who can tell a joke in which the audience doesn't understand what he's saying, but they still get the punch line and laugh. He's told the same ice-fishing story in the twelve years I've been on the caravan with him. I still have no idea how it turns out, but I still laugh, because it's funny. It's a funny story."

As a player, coach, and goodwill ambassador, Oliva has been a member of the Twins family for more than fifty years. He is a beloved icon in Minnesota. Yet superstar smugness has never been part of Oliva's makeup. Throughout his career and to this day, he has remained steadfastly approachable, rarely if ever turning away an autograph seeker or baseball fan.

Oliva's humble nature and work ethic are byproducts of growing up poor on a small family farm. A family subsisting on its own labor taught Oliva the important lessons of working hard and not taking anything for granted. The Oliva family never had much, but that small plot of land, lush with fruit trees and a variety of crops, was the hub of an idyllic family life. The farm no longer exists as Oliva so fondly remembers it, but the lessons learned there carried him through a Hall of Fame–worthy career and nearly four decades as a coach committed to sharing a lifetime of knowledge.

Although his life has changed dramatically since his humble beginnings, Tony Oliva now travels to Cuba nearly every winter to reunite with his siblings and their families. The family's land has been divided into smaller plots, and the baseball field that his father built is gone, but Oliva never forgets where his story began.

Young Pedro

Long before he faced the fallout of U.S.–Cuban relations and surfaced in the major leagues, Tony Oliva lived quietly in the Cuban province of Piñar del Río (pronounced *pin-yar del REE-o*). For more than a century, Piñar del Río has been famous for growing some of the world's finest cigar tobacco. Today this agriculturally bountiful province on the western tip of the island is just as well known for exporting one of baseball's most gifted pure hitters—a potential Hall of Famer who grew up in the years before the Cuban Revolution of 1959.

The Oliva family farm was nestled in the rural patchwork of Entronque de Herradura, a small village about twenty-five miles east of the seaside provincial capital, also named Piñar del Río. With war threatening Europe at the end of the 1930s—a war that would forever change the world, including Cuba—Pirico Pedro Oliva and Anita Petrona López Oliva started a family, eventually raising five sons and five daughters in that rural setting. On July 20, 1938, Pedro Jr. was born, the third child and oldest son. (He would not be known as Tony until he left Cuba for the United States more than twenty years later.)

Family life revolved around the farm, a plot about a square mile in size with more than one hundred tropical trees, a baseball field, and a river that separated the Oliva family's acreage from that of a neighbor. In one area of the farm, Oliva's father planted fifty orange trees. When the oranges were ready, he would take them to the provincial capital to sell. Mango and guava trees grew wild and flourished without care. The farm was also home to sugarcane plants, as well as grapefruit, banana, and avocado trees. It was a beautiful setting, one that Oliva remembers fondly.

Pedro Sr. worked the farm alone, though with gradually increasing assistance from his five sons as they grew older. The work was hard. Unlike many of the large tobacco plantations in the province, smaller farms in Cuba were not mechanized. Preparing the fields for planting, seeding, weeding, and harvesting were done primarily by hand. The work was year-round, as Pedro Sr. planted various crops, including corn, tomatoes, potatoes, and tobacco, to utilize a number of growing seasons. The Oliva boys had their share of chores and became skillful at various aspects of working the land. Tobacco was among the most labor-intensive crops, and it was one of Pedro Jr.'s annual rituals to prepare the soil for a new growing season. He tilled the fields before planting by pushing a plow hooked up to an old milk cow.

Between school and farm chores, life was busy in the tightly knit Oliva family. The children's community school through the eighth grade was a mile from their home, and they walked to the two-room schoolhouse. A woman taught the younger children in one room, and a man worked with the older ones in another. School let out in May for the summer, but there was plenty to do on the farm to keep the boys busy. When school was in session, class work and chores filled the first six days of the week. Oliva was always there to help his father, and the workload taught him how to apply himself to a task and work hard at a young age. The lessons he learned prepared him to work diligently at baseball later in life.

On Sunday, after church and chores, fathers and sons in western Cuba set aside the tools of the farm to play baseball. The ballfield on the Olivas's land was home to the local country team that played surrounding towns and farm communities on Sunday afternoons. Oliva's father and other men in the community had built the field in the early 1940s, before Pedro Jr. was old enough to go to school. The country teams featured many talented players, from high school age (if a young man was skilled enough) to longtime veterans pushing forty. Pedro Sr. had played on the local country team as a young man. Like his son with the sweet stroke, he was a lefthanded hitter. A catcher and outfielder, Pedro Sr., also much like his talented son, was known for successfully putting the fat part of the bat on the baseball.

On some Sundays, the local team hosted a nearby club. When the local team traveled to play in other towns within the province, such as Consolación del Sur, Los Palacios, and Piñar del Río, the men and boys living near the Oliva farm would strike up their own game—sometimes two or three games—for the afternoon. A typical Sunday ended with some fishing or a dip in the river before the Oliva family sat down for dinner.

Pedro Jr. started playing baseball when he was seven years old. While the farm consumed most of his free time when school let out in May, he and his brothers took to the family diamond every chance they could, playing with bats they made from pieces of tree wood. When they did not have a ball, they cut up a corncob to make one. Baseball gloves and equipment were hard to come by. But Pedro Sr. returned from an early-1950s trip to Havana with bats, catcher's equipment, and nine gloves with which to field a full team.

"I don't know how he did it," Oliva admits, "because we didn't have any money." Sometimes his father might trade a farm animal for something the family needed, and Oliva remembers his father going far beyond what could be expected to benefit his children. "If anyone needed anything, he would find a way to get it for us."

Baseballs were not plentiful either when the Oliva boys were growing up, but the boys would tape over them to make them last. Over time, a baseball might become more tape than anything else. With all the foreign material added to the ball, it often moved in unpredictable ways, providing an early lesson in hitting breaking stuff.

"I was always able to hit," is how Oliva remembers his early days as a ballplayer. "I could hit everything." These two simple truths held true throughout a long and productive career on diamonds across North America.

Already an accomplished hitter at age fifteen, Pedro Jr. joined the local club, playing for the village of Entronque de Herradura. He was among the youngest players in the province on a country team. Despite never having played in an organized league, he quickly demonstrated he could hit against more experienced pitchers. By the time Pedro Jr. had made the jump to the country team, his father was no longer playing, but Pedro Sr. would umpire if work was done and a game was going on.

"I was lucky that my father loved baseball," Oliva says. His father had passed that love on to him. While Pedro Sr. had not had much time to hit grounders or flyballs to his son, he often talked about hitting and how to play the game. The advice proved beneficial when the teenager began playing against stiffer competition. After a year with the country team, Oliva began advancing through more competitive leagues in western Cuba. His ability to hit landed him on a winter league club from nearby Los Palacios when he was nineteen. By then, he was playing against teams from as far away as

Havana, a hundred miles to the east, and some of the players were professionals who had played minor league ball in the United States.

Players who managed to reach the mainland to play baseball came almost exclusively from Havana. It was extremely rare for a rural kid from a faraway province to get noticed as a ballplayer. While no scout had yet seen Oliva play, the chance to take the field with talented players and teams from Havana fueled a dream beyond the realistic possibility of a professional career in the United States. "When you come from Piñar del Río, and you come from a poor family," Oliva says, "you don't have too much of a future." That suddenly changed for Oliva while he was playing for Los Palacios.

One of the men who had reached the mainland and played in the minor leagues was Los Palacios native Roberto Fernández Tápanes. A righthanded hitter with some power, Fernández spent a decade in the Washington Senators and Cincinnati Reds systems and finished his minor league career with the Havana Sugar Kings in 1957, when the club was Cincinnati's Triple-A affiliate. By the time Oliva joined Los Palacios at the close of the 1950s, Fernández was still playing for Latin American clubs during the summer months and his hometown team during the winter.

Fernández and Oliva batted third and fourth, respectively, in the Los Palacios batting order, and the veteran quickly realized that the teenager's tools were special. After seeing Oliva drive pitches in any location to all parts of the park, Fernández recommended him to Joe Cambria, a scouting legend who spent a quarter century mining talent in and around Havana. Papa Joe, as he was called, signed roughly four hundred Cuban prospects for the Griffith family, which had operated the Washington franchise since former star pitcher Clark Griffith joined an ownership group with controlling interest in 1919. When Clark died in 1955, his nephew Calvin Griffith took over and moved the franchise to Minnesota in 1961. Most of the island's key players were on the Twins teams of the 1960s.

Oliva says he was surprised when Fernández asked him if he would be interested in pursuing a professional baseball career. Of course he was interested, but he was caught off guard by the unanticipated inquiry and wanted his parents' blessing before going to the United States.

As it turned out, Cambria was committed to signing Oliva and two others on the Los Palacios club, but only if the players' parents consented to their sons' inking a professional contract. The Olivas would not stand in the way of such an opportunity. In February 1961, Oliva signed with the Twins, beginning an adventure that provided as many lows as highs, at least in the early going. He would leave behind the small world he knew and loved for a much larger one with endless possibilities—but no guarantees. The twenty-two-year-old Oliva spoke virtually no English and his family had little money, yet signing that contract was a chance to chase a dream.

Oliva was to report to Fernandina Beach, Florida, for spring training in early April, for the final two weeks that spring camps were open. However, getting a passport to come to the United States was problematic because Oliva did not have a birth certificate. His younger brother Antonio had one, though, and with so little time to prepare to travel, their parents decided that Pedro would use it. In time, Pedro found that he preferred his brother's name, so when coaches, teammates, and acquaintances began calling him Tony after his arrival in Florida, he took on the new moniker without explaining his real name.

On April 9, 1961, Oliva and twenty-one other young Cubans boarded a plane in Havana headed for Fernandina Beach, a beach town on the Atlantic Ocean roughly thirty-five miles north of Jacksonville. But first there was a stopover in Mexico City to acquire entry visas for the United States. What was expected to be a one- or two-day stay turned into a bureaucratic quagmire lasting eleven days, leaving just three days of spring training when the group reached the Twins' minor league camp.

After a late-night arrival from Mexico City, before ever taking the field in Fernandina Beach, Oliva endured a harsh lesson about life in America. At the front desk of the town's only hotel, Oliva and five others were told they could not stay there because of their skin color. The light-skinned Cubans in the group could get rooms, but the rest were transported to the home of an African American woman who housed black players.

Oliva had not anticipated the institutional racism of American life. There was segregation in pockets of Havana, but all in all, skin color was of little significance in Cuba. It meant nothing in the Oliva family. His mother could have passed for white in the United States, as his grandmother on his mother's side came to Cuba from Spain. His father, whose family was of more mixed ancestry, would have been labeled black. In the early 1960s, Oliva's family would have had trouble sitting down for a meal together in thousands of restaurants across America.

The deep-seated racism sanctioned by law in the South was an affront to Latin Americans. Few endured such bigotry at home. They did not anticipate experiencing it in the hemisphere's most powerful democracy—a country built on a Bill of Rights for its citizens—but racism had a public voice and laws that legitimized it. Latin ballplayers quickly learned that not all citizens shared in the promised rights, and the indignities of segregation further alienated a class of immigrants already isolated by language and social customs.

Oliva soon realized that his initial exposure to racism on his first night in North America would not be an isolated instance. For him and other Latin players of the era, housing in spring training and many baseball cities, particularly in the South, meant living in separate quarters from the rest of the team. When the team traveled, white players stayed in downtown hotels, and the others were driven across town to lodgings that allowed blacks. Legally sanctioned segregation in the South applied to restaurants, buses, gas stations, parks, and even water fountains. Black players often sat on the team bus while the rest of the team dined at a food stop along the road. In Florida during spring training, team golf outings and other public events were usually limited to white players.

Latin players were especially taken aback by racial taunts hurled from the stands during games. Most had never experienced racism on that level at home. For that matter, most had never given much thought to the subject of race or had ever had reason to talk about it, let alone be targeted by such overt bigotry. In North America, race was a subject hard to ignore when it affected everything a player did, wherever he went.

Vic Power, the flamboyant first baseman who was a fan favorite in Minnesota and a mentor to Oliva, arrived from Puerto Rico in 1949, just two years after Jackie Robinson and Larry Doby broke the color barrier. People of all shades of skin color grew up and went to school together in Arecibo, the coastal town where Power was raised in the 1930s. In Puerto Rico people married without paying much attention to color. Power refused to be confined by the prejudice he faced in the United States. He openly dated white women and stood up to racist behavior with a flair that could defuse the situation. Occasionally he ran into trouble in the South, as he sometimes displayed color blindness when using a restroom or sitting down for a meal in a whites-only restaurant. Once a waitress informed him that her restaurant did not serve Negroes, to which Power replied, "That's okay, I don't eat Negroes. I just want some rice and beans."

Power was expected to become the first black Yankee after signing with New York in 1951, but he was not exactly a perfect fit for the staid personality of the franchise. Despite his success as a hitter and his dazzling defensive skills, his career as a Yankees prospect stalled in the minors. After three years in the New York farm system, he was dealt to the Philadelphia Athletics in an eleven-player trade following the 1953 season. He immediately became a big league regular, and in twelve seasons, Power appeared in six All-Star Games and won seven Gold Glove Awards. He was Minnesota's first baseman in 1962 and '63, but the Twins traded him the following summer, after Oliva took over in right field and forced Bob Allison to first base.

In those first few days on the colored side of Fernandina Beach after Oliva arrived in the United States, he began a number of lifelong friendships. He met seasoned Cuban players Minnie Mendoza and Nestor Velazquez, who were staying nearby. Mendoza, who had grown up just outside Havana, was preparing for his eighth season in the minors. He had originally signed in 1954 with the Cincinnati Reds, the only other club with a presence in Cuba. Released after four years in the Reds system, Mendoza signed with the Washington Senators in 1958.

By then, the Senators organization boasted more than forty Cubans, and it was not unusual for Mendoza to host a large contingent of his countrymen in his room during spring training. Black Cubans stayed with families in Fernandina Beach's black neighborhood, two or three players to a room, and Mendoza and Velazquez shared living space. With as many as ten Cuban prospects on hand, Mendoza cooked familiar food and gave them a place to hang out. Mendoza laughs about the risk he took cooking full-scale meals in his room, which was frowned on, but the gatherings were an opportunity for Cuban players to discuss their experiences on and off the field. Getting together also allowed them to relax and forget about the stress of daily life. They often played card games and dominoes, or listened to Cuban music. A baseball career involved a lot of dead time—time many would have spent with family and friends back in Cuba—so gathering in Mendoza's room filled a huge void.

As someone experienced in making the adjustments to a new culture, Mendoza understood the importance of having a comfortable place to address the issues of everyday life. It was difficult enough to reach the majors in this highly competitive environment, and language and cultural differences added to the challenge. Many young Cubans also struggled with financial survival. Mendoza says a number of his poorer friends arrived for spring training with little money. He was in a position to share meals or provide financial assistance until players began receiving paychecks during the regular season.

In the final days of spring training in 1961, Oliva had other concerns. His future in baseball hung on his ability to impress in a tryout that would last just a few days. The new arrivals played in exhibition games during their brief time in Fernandina Beach. Oliva says he played in four games and delivered seven hits in ten at-bats. He struggled catching the ball, something he knew he could learn, but he ran well and showed a strong arm.

At the conclusion of spring camp, eleven Cubans from the group were assigned to minor league clubs. The other eleven were released. Oliva was handed a slip of paper, which he was not able to read. He thought it contained his minor league assignment, so he looked for translation help from another ballplayer, who informed him he had been released. Oliva recalls not being familiar with the word and asking what it meant. The answer was a big jolt. "Released. Go home. They don't want you," he remembers being told. A top Twins official had concluded that Oliva would never hit major league pitching, and it was an understatement to say that his defensive skills were extremely raw. So after only a few days on North American soil, the young prospect faced a return trip to Cuba.

Oliva quickly discovered he had few alternatives. Spring training was winding down, and most minor league rosters were already set. He made the short trip down the Florida coast to Jacksonville, where the Houston Colt .45s had a Class-A affiliate in 1961, a year before joining the National League. After one workout, however, Oliva learned there was no job opening there, either. He says he would have actively pursued a minor league assignment on his own, but he could not communicate in English well enough.

One obstacle to signing Oliva was his color. A major league team had to have a minor league opening in a northern locale to place a black man on a roster. In the case of the Twins, only two clubs remained in Florida when Oliva was released. Both were rookie ball clubs—one based in Erie, Pennsylvania, the other in Fort Walton Beach, Florida. Among the eleven Cubans who were signed, only one was black, and he was assigned to Erie. The others were white enough to play for Fort Walton Beach.

Returning home would have dashed Oliva's dream forever, more because of political realities than baseball talent. Relations between the United States and the fledgling Cuban government had deteriorated rapidly since the Cuban Revolution had ousted dictator Fulgencio Batista in the earliest hours of January 1, 1959. The leader of the revolution, Fidel Castro, had nationalized the American-owned businesses that had flourished under Batista, and President Dwight D. Eisenhower responded by placing an embargo on Cuba. Ike then severed diplomatic relations altogether during the final days of his presidency in January 1961.

Cuban–U.S. relations had taken another downturn while Oliva was on his way to Florida. On April 17, 1961, a band of roughly 1,500 Cuban exiles, trained and financed by the CIA with President John Kennedy's reluctant agreement, invaded Cuba from Guatemala in the early morning hours. With the U.S. Air Force providing cover to take out Cuban Air Force planes, the invasion forces came ashore on the beaches of Bahía de Cochinos, the Bay of Pigs. The plan—conceived by Vice President Richard Nixon during Eisenhower's presidency—was expected to inspire a spontaneous revolt that would overthrow Castro. That expectation was off the mark, for U.S. analysts vastly underestimated public support for the revolution at that point in time. Plus, the Cuban military caught wind of the plan. Cuban fighter planes, targeted for U.S. bombing missions before the exiles reached land, were dispersed and hidden, and air attacks by the Cuban Air Force greeted the new arrivals.

Unaware of the role the CIA and the Kennedy administration had played in the attack, the U.S. ambassador to the United Nations, Adlai Stevenson, faced the press shortly after the invasion and denied U.S. involvement. When he became aware of the U.S. government's role hours later, he publicly called for a halt to this violation of a regional treaty, the Act of Bogotá, in order to avoid international criticism and the risk of a larger war. The exiles' air cover suddenly disappeared and their supply lines dried up. CIA officials had also underestimated the strength of the Cuban military, and without U.S. assistance, the exiles were soundly defeated within seventy-two hours. The two countries were on a collision course, which peaked with the Cuban Missile Crisis in October 1962. Any chance of travel to and from Cuba was quickly snuffed out.

For Oliva, part of the last group of Cubans to receive permission to try out for U.S. teams, there was virtually no chance he would be allowed to leave Cuba again if he went home. All but out of options, however, Oliva was ready to return to Piñar del Río. His first experience away from his family had been a major disappointment, and he missed everyone back on the farm. If he was not going to play baseball, he was going home.

When Oliva told Mendoza he wanted to return to Piñar del Río, the veteran ballplayer had another idea. Mendoza encouraged Oliva to see Phil Howser, the general manager of the Hornets, the minor league team in Charlotte, North Carolina, and a nearly lifelong employee of the Griffith family. Howser and Calvin Griffith had been close friends since the late 1930s, when Howser was beginning his thirty-two-year tenure with the Hornets and Griffith was the team's manager. Howser had helped Mendoza and many other

Cubans settle into North American life, frequently offering young players meal money and a place to stay in Charlotte. He was known to look out for young arrivals who had some talent but were extremely raw and not ready to take on a minor league assignment. Papa Joe Cambria did not want to see his talented find sent home, so he encouraged the general manager to do the same with Oliva.

As it turned out, Howser was intrigued by Oliva's potential. Mendoza says Howser expressed an interest in bringing Oliva to Charlotte, where the young man could work out with his Hornets club and wait for a team to sign him. In the meantime, even though Oliva was not ready to play on his roster, Howser would pay for his housing and meals. Mendoza recalls that Oliva initially said no to going to Charlotte, but he finally convinced him to give it a shot.

This was not the only time Mendoza talked a premier Cuban prospect out of going home. Future Hall of Famer Tony Pérez wanted to return to Cuba when his father fell ill in 1963. Although the twenty-one-year-old Reds prospect had reached the Triple-A level in his fourth pro season that summer, money was tight, and with his father ailing, he wanted to go home at season's end. Mendoza convinced Pérez to head instead to Charlotte, where he and another Cuban minor leaguer, Julio Guerra, shared an apartment. They could offer the Reds prospect a place to stay and meals for the winter.

Mendoza, who had started in the Cincinnati organization, appealed for financial assistance through Dave Bristol, a minor league manager with the Reds. Bristol approached Cincinnati management, which agreed to provide three hundred dollars a month to Pérez over the winter. So Pérez headed to Charlotte and went on to make his major league debut in 1964. Three years later, he became a big league regular and jump-started a brilliant twenty-three-year career by driving in 102 runs for the Reds.

For Oliva, Howser's hunch and generosity delayed a one-way ticket to Piñar del Río. Going to Charlotte provided Oliva an opportunity to work on his game with a professional team and at the same time get acclimated to his new culture. Oliva met with Howser the April morning he arrived in Charlotte, with Mendoza serving as his interpreter. Howser offered to pay for Oliva's housing and three dollars a day in meal money, the going rate in the South Atlantic League.

Both Mendoza and Velazquez played for Charlotte that summer. They were roommates and often hosted Oliva for meals when the Hornets were at home. Mendoza had a car, and the trio drove to the ballpark together. Oliva was not officially on the roster, however, so he was not allowed to play in games or accompany the team on road trips. Consequently, Oliva spent a lot of time alone. When the Hornets traveled, he walked the five miles to and from the ballpark to work out by himself. A taxi ride cost roughly a dollar each way, an expense that would quickly eat up his meal money, so he made the daily trek on foot. Mendoza says that walking to and from the park also allowed Oliva to send a little money home to his family from time to time.

Because Oliva spoke virtually no English, everyday life was an obstacle course, a form of isolation that seemed to grow. He was unable to ask directions, to read menus in restaurants, or to engage in conversation when he was most lonely. So that he could survive the Hornets' first road trip, Howser gave him two pieces of paper, one with "ham and eggs" written on it and another marked "fried chicken." For days on end, that was all Oliva ate.

Even when language was less of an obstacle, food familiar to Latin players was hard to find in many baseball cities and towns. That was true even in cosmopolitan Montreal, where a Puerto Rican prospect named Roberto Clemente spent his only minor league season in 1954. David Maraniss, who penned the revealing biography *Clemente*, described how difficult it was for the future Hall of Famer and his teammate Chico Fernández to find a familiar meal. When their Montreal Royals were playing at home, they spent every morning at the same breakfast spot, ordering the same ham and eggs. They never managed to find a Cuban or Mexican restaurant all season.

After a night game, getting a meal of any kind was problematic for black players and Latinos of color. At many of Oliva's minor league stops, he stayed with a family in a black neighborhood while his teammates roomed in a hotel. He would get back to his room near midnight after night games, and in residential areas, no restaurants were open. Sometimes a member of the host family stayed up late to prepare something for him to eat, but more often players living segregated in residential neighborhoods went to bed hungry. It was the routine, something to which Oliva gave little thought during his minor league years. It was simply the way it was.

The large amount of free time a ballplayer had away from the park magnified the cultural isolation. North American players who were married had families waiting for them at home, but many Latin American prospects traveled north alone and would not see those closest to them for months at a time. "You concentrate and play the game," Mendoza explains. "But after the ballgame, now what? That's the tough part, after the ballgame." With all the time off, it was hard to avoid occasional bouts of longing for family, friends, and familiar food. Sometimes Oliva's homesickness overshadowed what baseball meant to him. Even after he settled in Charlotte, Oliva once again shared with Mendoza and Velazquez his desire to return home. Oliva remembers that Mendoza appealed to him to think about better days and about what life might be like if he eventually found success. It would not be an easy road, but Oliva says he could only follow Mendoza's advice to "listen to your heart." He remained in Charlotte awaiting his visa, often leaning more toward going home than staying.

A few weeks after the Bay of Pigs invasion, team officials told the still-unsigned prospect that the political situation was improving and he would soon be able to return to Cuba via Mexico. But before long, they admitted that negotiations with Cuba had stalled. In time, Oliva realized he would not return home as long as he was committed to a baseball career. For months after the failed military incursion, he was unable to communicate with his family. Being completely cut off from family was painful, but without the breakdown in relations between the United States and Cuba, Oliva might never have had the opportunity to show the Twins that his raw ability was the foundation for a productive major league player.

"The Bay of Pigs saved my career," says Oliva, who believes he probably would have spent his entire life on the family farm if he had not played baseball in the United States. "It was unbelievable what happened to me. It was a miracle."

Life after Cuba Closes

Initially, the Bay of Pigs invasion that turned Oliva's life upside down seemed like anything but a miracle. First exposure to living in a new culture can be disorienting even for a person who speaks the local language. For Oliva, a young man far removed from politics in Cuba and the United States, having an unanticipated political event change the course of his life only magnified his sense of being cut adrift. Suddenly he had no place to call home. He had to take on a complicated new world in which he, like most immigrants, suddenly felt invisible, stripped of the identity he had in familiar surroundings back home. In Oliva's case, having used his younger brother Antonio's birth certificate to acquire a passport, the loss of identify was literal as well. He was now Tony to everyone he met.

The notion that the failed Bay of Pigs invasion and Cuba's eventual closing would open the door to an illustrious major league career was unimaginable to the twenty-two-year-old Oliva. His entire life seemed in utter limbo in the weeks following the unforeseen developments in his homeland. We all may find it difficult to imagine what our lives might be like five years on; Oliva may have found it impossible to conceptualize what his life would be like even five *weeks* down the road. What in hindsight could be recognized as a miraculous twist of fate felt at the time more like a surreal nightmare. Oliva had left behind family and friends to pursue a career, which now was a long shot. Isolated by language and cultural differences, his loneliness for home and loved ones would persist for years. The offseasons were especially tough on him, as the last day of a baseball season meant saying goodbye to his friends in the clubhouse, who were heading home to their families. Oliva would go to Latin America to play winter ball as much to avoid isolation as to work on his game.

As it turned out, the Cubans who had already established themselves in the United States knew they faced an ultimatum even before the first armed exiles landed at the Bay of Pigs. With relations deteriorating between Cuba and the United States, Fidel Castro had decided to end Cuba's professional league, which played from October to February and featured the best Cuban players, including those based on the mainland during the summer months.

The Cuban Winter League, which had existed for eighty-three years, had flourished over the previous decade. Many stars of the Negro leagues, including Josh Gibson, Buck O'Neil, and Cool Papa Bell, played in Cuba when their season ended in the United States. A 1947 agreement with the National Association of Professional Baseball Leagues, the governing body of the minor leagues, allowed prospects and major leaguers with limited experience to play winter ball in the Cuban Winter League. Future Hall of Famers Jim Bunning, Brooks Robinson, and Monte Irvin played in Cuba during the 1950s, as did future Twins Jim Kaat, Jim "Mudcat" Grant, and Bob Allison.

"I loved it in Havana," Robinson recalls. "I played for Cienfuegos. We all played in the same ballpark. It was Havana, Cienfuegos, Marianao, and Almendares. Those four teams played probably five games a week. They had the best players. It was a great experience for me." The year was 1957, and Robinson was twenty years old. His Baltimore Orioles closed that season in Washington playing the Senators, so he joined a caravan of cars headed to Key West. Washington pitchers Camilo Pascual and Pedro Ramos, his teammates with Cienfuegos, had cars, and other Cuban Senators, including José Valdivielso and Carlos Paula, were part of the contingent. From Key West, they took their cars to Cuba via ferry.

During the 1950s, the league drew large crowds to see the local heroes, major leaguers, and Negro league stars. The Cubans who returned home to play were paid well, particularly stars such as Minnie Miñoso and Pascual. Pascual notes that some of the Cuban players, including him during his early years with Washington, made more money playing winter ball at home than they did in the United States.

With the dissolution of the Cuban Winter League, that income disappeared for both Cubans and Americans. For those born in Cuba, so did the opportunity to showcase their skills for baseball fans at home. Cristóbal Torriente, Martín Dihigo, and Silvio García, who were terrific hitters in the first half of the twentieth century, were superstars in Cuba—to this day, icons in the game's history there—but Oliva, arguably the best pure hitter to ever emerge from the island, was never able to play on his country's biggest stage. That was also true for Hall of Famer Tony Pérez, who also debuted in 1964 with the Reds, spent twenty-three years in the majors, and ranked among the major league leaders in hits, doubles, home runs, and RBIs for the decade of the 1970s. Both players regret not having had that chance.

"The Cuban people never had the chance to see me play," Oliva says of the lost opportunity to take the field with the island's best players. "That was the best winter ball league in those days."

Because the league's four teams played their games in and around Havana, roughly a hundred miles from his home, Oliva was never able to attend a Cuban Winter League game. Sometimes he listened to games on the radio, which allowed him to follow Miñoso, arguably the best Cuban player in the majors during the 1950s and one of Oliva's favorites. His favorite team was Cienfuegos, because longtime Senator and Twin Pedro Ramos, another Piñar del Río native, pitched for it. So did Pascual.

In February 1961, at the end of the Cuban Winter League season, a large contingent of Cuban-born major leaguers were playing an informal softball game at a training facility in Havana. Suddenly Fidel Castro unexpectedly appeared. That was not unlike him, according to 1960s Twin Sandy Valdespino, who says that Castro, a baseball fan, might show up in the center-field seats for a Cuban Winter League game or at the door of a team's clubhouse. On this occasion, many of the roughly thirty Cubans who were established in the United States were there, including Mendoza, Valdespino, Pascual, Ramos, Zoilo Versalles, and Miñoso, then a star with the Chicago White Sox. Castro told them he was disbanding the professional league, effective immediately. Suddenly the players faced a decision as big as nearly any in their lives.

"Castro told us," Mendoza recalls, "'If you want to go and continue your career in the United States, you are free to go. But if you stay here, you're going to stay for good.' He said, 'I could give you a job as an instructor as a professional baseball player.' I said, 'No, my career is in the United States.'"

It became more complicated than that for Mendoza. He was in the United States at the time of the Bay of Pigs invasion, but his wife Julia was staying with his parents near Havana, pregnant with their second child. Mendoza was separated from his wife and daughter, and they would not reunite in the United States until February 1965. By then, his younger daughter was nearly three years old and had been isolated from her father by a frustrating and costly bureaucratic process. Cuban officials would not allow Mendoza's wife and children to leave the country unless he returned to sign their passport papers. The United States had severed diplomatic relations with Cuba, but since Mendoza was playing in Vancouver, British Columbia, in 1962, he arranged the trip home via Canada. Although he completed the necessary paperwork, Mendoza returned to Charlotte alone in May 1963.

The family reunited in late 1964 in Nicaragua, where Mendoza played winter ball that year, but not before his wife and daughters had traveled to Spain and spent several weeks there. They managed to get visas for Spain, a country from which many Cuban families had immigrated, and from there completed the paperwork for the Cuban government. Finally in 1965, the family settled in Charlotte, where the Mendozas had two more daughters. They celebrated their fiftieth wedding anniversary in 2010.

Mendoza never again saw his father, who died in 1969. He did not reconnect with his mother for another decade, after Cuba finally reopened its doors to its professional baseball players in the 1970s. Mendoza made a second trip to the island five years later, in 1984, when his mother passed away, but he has not been back since. Although a few siblings and a host of nephews and nieces remain in Cuba, Mendoza's life is firmly rooted in the United States. Following a nineteen-year playing career, he began a twenty-year run working for the Cleveland Indians in various player-development capacities, often in Latin America.

All but sixteen of Mendoza's professional at-bats were in the minors. He was what was called an "organizational guy." At that time, players were under the control of their team's owner for their entire career, and a player like Mendoza, a third baseman who could play all over the infield, was a valuable commodity to an organization. Many franchises kept guys like Mendoza in the high minors, even if they were never needed by the major league club.

For years, the Twins were set with either Harmon Killebrew or Rich Rollins at third and Versalles at short. At second, Bernie Allen gave way to Rod Carew. Players came and went, but Mendoza, an organizational mainstay, finally got a chance to make the Twins roster in the spring of 1970, after batting a career-high .333 for the Triple-A Denver Bears in '69. By then, between the minor leagues and winter ball, he had played more than two hundred games a year for close to fifteen seasons. Winter ball paid well, and he made enough to sustain his family by playing year-round.

Mendoza admits, with amusement forty years after the fact, that the big league opportunity came with a cost. His invitation to the major league camp, which began weeks before the minor leaguers arrived in Florida, meant he had to sacrifice winter ball paychecks. It was a sacrifice he had been waiting his whole life to make, and at age thirty-six, he became the elder statesman of the 1970 rookie class. His major league tenure lasted all of sixteen games, as he got caught in a numbers game when the Twins needed to add a pitcher to the roster in June. He collected just sixteen at-bats, mostly as a pinch hitter, and picked up three hits and two RBIs.

The rookie got his first major league hit on May 2, 1970, a Saturday afternoon in Baltimore, with a pinch single off fellow Cuban Mike Cuellar. The Twins and the Orioles were tied 2–2 when Mendoza slapped a pitch over Orioles shortstop Mark Belanger with one out in the eighth inning. He scored the go-ahead run on Killebrew's double, and the Twins claimed a 4–2 victory for their twenty-game winner, Jim Perry. "I believe I hit seven foul balls before I got the hit," recalls Mendoza. "Elrod Hendricks was the catcher, and he said, 'Hey, when are you going to hit one or strike out? Man, get out of here.' He was a really funny guy."

That day's game between the defending American League division winners was the nationally televised *Game of the Week*. Getting a key hit before such a large audience put Mendoza in front of the microphone after the game. While Mendoza was telling *St. Paul Pioneer Press* writer Bob Fowler that he was happy to see the ball fall in for a hit, Oliva showed up to give his mentor and compatriot some friendly ribbing. "He can only hit when the game is on national television," Oliva joked to Fowler. "Tony, he did what they do to a lot of rookies," Mendoza says. "They ask for the ball when it's your first hit in the big leagues, and then get another ball. After the third out, when I was going to grab it from his hands, he threw it into the stands. 'Oh!' Then the other players said, 'No, no, this is the ball here. He was kidding you.'"

Mendoza never got another big league opportunity. He spent two final seasons with the Charlotte Hornets in 1971 and '72, his ninth and tenth in the North Carolina city. Then, after one last winter ball season in Mexico, he retired to begin a coaching and managing career that led to his current player-development role with Cleveland.

After all these years, Mendoza still talks fondly of Oliva. They first met briefly on a ballfield in Cuba more than a half century ago, and they weathered the adjustment to life in North America, with Mendoza playing mentor. Mendoza notes that Oliva has always been thankful and never forgets his earliest friends on the mainland. "When I made it to the big leagues with Minnesota [in 1970], Tony wouldn't let me pay for anything on a road trip," says Mendoza. "He said, 'You helped me so much. It's time for me to help you.' One of the bigger hearts you will find in a human being belongs to Tony Oliva."

Another Cuban player cut off from his wife following the Bay of Pigs invasion was Julio Bécquer, whom Papa Joe Cambria had signed ten years earlier, in 1951. The 1950s had been a remarkable decade for the Havana native. A part-time first baseman for the Senators during their last four years in Washington, Bécquer led the American League in pinch hits in both 1957 and 1959. It was a time of his life he still treasures. He felt welcome in the city and enjoyed what it had to offer. A block from Griffith Stadium was the Key Club, a jazz venue that brought in the era's best musicians. There he saw Count Basie, Duke Ellington, and many of the genre's icons.

In 1960, the franchise's final season in Washington, Bécquer took part in what came to be called the all-Cuban triple play. The Senators were hosting the Kansas City Athletics on July 23. Pedro Ramos was on the hill for the Senators. Washington took a 3–0 lead in the second inning, aided by Bécquer's RBI triple, but the Athletics threatened when both Bill Tuttle and Jerry Lumpe singled to open the third. The next batter, future major league manager Whitey Herzog, lined a 3–2 pitch back at Ramos. The righthander snared the shot and rifled a throw to Bécquer at first to double up Lumpe. Without a pause, Bécquer tossed the ball to shortstop José Valdivielso, who easily caught Tuttle off second base for the third out.

In the months following the triple play, life took some unexpected turns for Bécquer. Newly married and twenty-nine years old at the end of 1960, he had been selected by the Los Angeles Angels in the expansion draft prior to the 1961 season. That winter, Bécquer had won the home-run and RBI crowns in what turned out to be the final season of professional ball in Cuba. The Bay of Pigs invasion followed a few weeks later. Bécquer was on the Angels roster and the 1961 season was just a few days old when the invasion took place. Suddenly he was separated from his wife Edith in Cuba and further alienated from his homeland. As was the case for Mendoza, the political twists and turns leading to the breakdown of U.S.–Cuban relations created a bureaucratic maze.

Bécquer praises Twins owner Calvin Griffith and Cambria for helping cut through the red tape between governments, something faced by all the Cuban players who were separated from family members in spring 1961. Bécquer says he approached Griffith about the issue, and the owner quickly set the wheels in motion to bring his wife to the United States. Griffith contacted Cambria, who completed all of Edith's paperwork and helped clear hurdles in Cuba. "I have a soft spot in my heart for that man," Bécquer says of the longtime scout. "He helped me a lot. While I was over here, Cambria spent one month [helping out], every day taking my wife to the American Embassy and then putting her on the plane for the United States." The Twins owner, who had been based in Washington for decades, worked his diplomatic contacts to facilitate the process. It took several weeks of wrangling before the newlyweds were reunited in the United States.

Life took another turn toward normal for Bécquer in early June 1961, after his release by the Angels, when he rejoined the Washington franchise, now transplanted to Minnesota and renamed the Twins. He had been buried in Los Angeles behind slugging first basemen Lee Thomas and Ted Kluszewski and had made just nine trips to the plate in two months. Bécquer was now reunited with a host of longtime friends and teammates, though in a completely new setting for major league baseball. He took well to his new surroundings and has lived in the Twin Cities ever since.

With Killebrew and Don Mincher manning first base, Bécquer served mostly as a pinch hitter in what was his final big league season. He was not a slugger, but he flashed some power in his last go-round, collecting five home runs—a single-season high—in just ninety-six plate appearances. A month after joining the team, on July 4, Bécquer stroked a walk-off grand slam to give the Twins a 6–4 victory over Chicago in the first game of a holiday doubleheader.

The Twins were trailing 4–2 in the ninth with White Sox ace Billy Pierce on the mound. Three outs from a complete-game victory, the lefthander retired Killebrew on a long fly before Bob Allison singled to center. Pierce gave way to Russ Kemmerer, who allowed another harmless fly from another slugger, Jim Lemon. Then Earl Battey singled to left, leading to another pitching change. Chicago skipper Al López called for southpaw Frank Baumann to face lefthanded-hitting Lenny Green (the team's first center fielder following the move from Washington in 1961), with two runners aboard. Green drew a walk to load the bases, and Lopez headed to the mound once more to bring out righthander Warren Hacker with righthanded-hitting Bill Tuttle due up.

For the second time in a year, Tuttle became intertwined in one of Bécquer's career highlights. The veteran outfielder, rarely seen without a chaw of tobacco inflating his cheeks, had been the third out of the all-Cuban triple play as a member of the Athletics the previous summer. Now, even though Tuttle had hit a home run earlier in the game, Twins manager Sam Mele pulled him in favor of the lefthanded-hitting Bécquer. Mele was the new man in charge—he had replaced Cookie Lavagetto just two weeks earlier—and Bécquer made him look like a genius. On the first pitch from Hacker, Bécquer, a notorious first-ball hitter, powered a line drive into Metropolitan Stadium's right-field seats for the game-winning slam. The ball got out of the park in a hurry and bounced halfway up in the bleacher seats. It was a memorable day in Bécquer's career, but with his bright, infectious smile lighting up his face during a 2009 interview, he teased, "There's another thing that happened on that day. . . . Killebrew hit an inside-the-park home run!"

It's true: the Hall of Fame slugger legged out the only inside-the-park homer of his major league career on the first Fourth of July in Twins history. In the second game of the twin bill, both clubs were scoreless into the eighth inning, when Twins starter Jack Kralick broke through with an RBI single. Then, with two runners aboard against Cal McLish, Killebrew drilled a shot that looked like it was going into the seats in left-center field. With two outs, the baserunners were off on contact as White Sox center fielder Jim Landis headed to the fence in pursuit of the drive. In a dead run, he leaped high and struck the wire fence violently in an all-out attempt to come down with the ball. The ball bounded toward the infield as Landis landed hard on the turf, suffering a severely bruised elbow. Left fielder Minnie Miñoso reversed field in pursuit of the ball as Killebrew, never known for his blazing speed, wheeled around second base. By the time Miñoso reached the ball and made a hurried throw toward home plate, Killebrew was heading for the dugout, where he was greeted by his laughing, cheering teammates while huffing and puffing from his mad dash.

The franchise's first year in Minnesota proved to be Bécquer's last in the majors, though he played two more seasons in Mexico before retiring. He had trained to be a teacher in Cuba and had picked up English fairly easily on his arrival in the United States, but to prepare for life after baseball, he took some English and business classes before settling into a long career with the Dayton–Hudson Corporation. He had one last fling with the Twins, however, before entering the nine-to-five work world.

In 1963, Bécquer was playing for Veracruz in Mexico, well aware that another trip to the majors was unlikely. He was thinking seriously of retirement when, out of the blue, he received a call from Calvin Griffith, who asked him how quickly he could be in the Twin Cities. The owner wanted to bring the former Senator and Twin back to the club so he could earn the smattering of days he needed to qualify for the major league pension. Bécquer followed up on Griffith's offer and made a final big league appearance as a pinch runner near the end of the 1963 season. "It was unexpected," Bécquer says. "I always had great communication with him, and he always handled all of us from Cuba well. If we needed something, we went directly to Calvin. He was always very receptive."

Bécquer has not returned to Cuba since 1961. Like Mendoza, he never again saw his father, who died early in the 1970s. His mother visited the United States at the end of the '70s, after Cuba began allowing family members to leave for family visits. That day came nearly two decades after the Cuban players in North America were locked out of their homeland.

In September 1961, the final month of his major league career, Bécquer met Oliva. At the conclusion of Oliva's first minor league campaign, he made his first trip to the Twin Cities to spend a month with the major league club. He was not added to the roster, but he practiced with the team before returning to Florida for the instructional league. Bécquer was at the Minneapolis–St. Paul airport when Oliva arrived, and he opened up his St. Paul home to him until Oliva was able to rent space in a rooming house in town. Bécquer, seven years older, drove Oliva to and from Metropolitan Stadium and introduced him to manager Sam Mele and many of the players. Bécquer would also bring Oliva to his home for dinner when the Twins did not have a night game. Oliva still spoke virtually no English and needed assistance to get around and to communicate in public places. Bécquer, who had arrived in Florida alone as a twenty-year-old in 1952, saw a lot of himself in the young prospect—and they became good friends during Oliva's stay in Minnesota.

To this day, Bécquer and Oliva remain close. They have shared Cuban traditions over the years, including an annual Christmastime pig roast. In the early 1960s, Zoilo Versalles, who lived in Bloomington, Minnesota, started the affair, in which a full pig was prepared in his backyard. Versalles hosted Bécquer and Oliva and their families, as well as other Cubans they had befriended in the Twin Cities. Over time, it became common to gather for family celebrations, though they did not need a reason to get together to enjoy the Cuban pastime of roasting a pig. The December pig roast, however, did create the occasional challenge. "I remember one time we roasted a pig in the snow," Oliva says. "We had to open a hole in the snow because the pig had to be a certain height from the charcoal. One time it was so cold, we brought it into the garage. That worked out, too. We got a special pan to put under everything. This way the charcoal didn't burn the floor."

Another challenge was getting supplies that pleased Versalles, who was an exceptional cook and went to great lengths to prepare a meal. Oliva says there was no place in the Twin Cities to buy such key ingredients as black beans, cassava root, or the sweet plantains preferred by Cubans. So he and the chef would jump into Versalles's car and drive to Chicago for what was needed. It did not matter if it was in the days leading up to Christmas or in the middle of the baseball season. Versalles loved to take such road trips.

Since Versalles passed away in 1995, Oliva has frequently hosted gatherings. Bécquer says they are a great opportunity to reminisce and bring families together. The younger generation now outnumbers the older, and for the young ones, the events are a chance to bring to life old customs that the former players and their wives enjoyed in Cuba when *they* were young.

The other Cuban elder statesman whom Oliva met in September 1961 was Camilo Pascual, who, like Bécquer, had arrived on the mainland a decade before. Pascual was all of seventeen, an infielder who had done little pitching before he was signed by Papa Joe Cambria. The Senators scout convinced the teenager that his future was on the mound. Pascual says he could always throw a good curveball, his trademark pitch. In time, his nasty 12–6 curve (named for its sharp, downward break from the position of the number "12" to the number "6" on a clock) was among the best in the business. It rivaled the devastating breaking ball of Hall of Famer Sandy Koufax. To this day, many of the 1960s Twins insist that in that era, no one snapped off a better curve than Pascual.

The young righthander needed only three minor league seasons to reach Washington. His first year in the United States presented enough challenges for a lifetime. He split his first summer as a pro with minor league clubs in New York, Texas, and Oklahoma. He spoke virtually no English, and he recalls the long Greyhound bus rides he made that summer, equipped with only a hand-carried note to get him where he needed to go. He would present the note to bus drivers and anyone else who might keep him moving in the right direction. Pascual did all his other communications by hand signs. For months, he says, he ordered food by pointing.

Pascual and Bécquer became good friends in Geneva, New York, where both started their professional careers in the Border League, a low-level circuit made up of teams from upstate New York and southern Ontario. They were roommates until the league was disbanded in midseason. Pascual, who was fair-skinned enough to play in the South, made one of his long treks by bus to his next assignment, in Big Spring, Texas. Bécquer, who was considered black, had fewer options. The rosters of Washington's minor league teams in northern locales were full, so he returned to Cuba and did not play on the mainland again until the following spring, in 1952.

At that time Havana had a minor league team, the Cubans, in the Florida International League, a Class-B circuit roughly in the middle of the minor league hierarchy. Pascual played on that club for his final two seasons in the minors. He was able to live at home in Havana, with road trips limited to Florida. In 1953, Pascual's final minor league season, he and Bécquer were teammates again for the Havana club. They would be major league teammates as well, of course, but for years they also faced each other as opponents in the Cuban Winter League.

Pascual began his Cuban Winter League career in the 1953–54 season with the Marianao Tigers, where he, Bécquer, and Miñoso were teammates. But Pascual was dealt to the Cienfuegos Elephants in the midst of his rookie campaign. He says he made his Cienfuegos debut a few days later, pitching against his former team. The game remained scoreless and went into extra innings. Pascual pitched a complete game, which ended as a 1–0 loss when Bécquer hit a game-winning home run. Bécquer recalls the showdown as well, though he claims he never fared well against Pascual in Cuba. Of course, few hitters in any league could contend with Pascual's nasty curve. "It was like trying to hit a butterfly," Bécquer says of the righty's bread-and-butter pitch. "This time he didn't throw me a curveball. He tried to surprise me and threw me a changeup. So I hit a home run in the eleventh inning." He laughs aloud and adds, "I hit a mistake." The longtime friends have enjoyed talking about that home run for years.

For much of the 1950s, Pascual and Pedro Ramos were the pitching aces for Cienfuegos. Pascual, one of the circuit's all-time premier pitchers, led his team to the Cuban Winter League pennant and claimed Most Valuable Player honors in 1955–56. Ramos did the same for Cienfuegos and was the MVP in 1960–61, the league's swan song.

Three months after his twentieth birthday in early 1954, Pascual made the Senators roster out of spring training and worked mostly out of the bull-pen. He settled permanently into the Washington rotation in 1957 but posted double-digit losses in five of his first six big league seasons. Although he often recorded respectable ERAs in these years, he would not earn double-digit wins until his sixth season in 1959. In the meantime, he endured on-the-job training on dreadful Senators teams that finished last four times over six summers and averaged ninety-five losses a year. "When I came to the major leagues, I didn't have that much pitching experience," Pascual explains. "I was mostly a fastball pitcher, and I only threw my breaking ball when I got ahead of the hitter. At the beginning of my career, I pitched so often from behind and I couldn't always get my curveball over."

Pascual's career took a positive turn in 1959. Although the Senators finished 63–91, last in the American League for the third straight season, the twenty-five-year-old veteran went 17–10 and finished second in the league with a 2.64 ERA, behind only Baltimore's knuckleballer Hoyt Wilhelm. Pascual fanned 185 batters in 238.2 innings, second in the American League to Detroit's Jim Bunning. Winning seventeen games for the last-place 1959 Senators club was at least as impressive as turning in twenty-win seasons for the much better Twins teams of 1962 and '63.

By 1959, Pascual had learned to consistently locate his fastball low in the strike zone, and his breaking ball had become dominating. He would throw it at different speeds, though the hard, sharp-breaking edition was the most unhittable and the most talked about. Pascual says he often called on a soft curve with less velocity to get ahead in the count—frequently dropping one into the zone for a first-pitch strike—then turned to the filthy version to finish off hitters.

Pascual and his wife Raquel and their children had been living in the United States for a few years by the time the franchise moved to Minnesota in 1961. During the Twins' inaugural week, Cuban exiles landed in the Bay of Pigs for their failed coup attempt. Pascual's immediate family was with him, but his parents and sister were at home in Cuba. It was not until 1964 that Pascual's parents and sister were allowed to leave Cuba for Minnesota. Gaining their release took a long time, but Pascual is quick to credit then U.S. senator Hubert H. Humphrey and Calvin Griffith for making it happen. The good news came that August, when the Twins were in Washington and visited President Lyndon Johnson at the White House before an evening showdown with the Senators.

After spending the first seven years of his major league career in Washington, Pascual took a dismal 57–84 record to Minnesota in 1961. He was 80–51 during the Twins' first five years, and, remarkably, he surpassed the .500 mark for his career during the 1965 championship drive. In those five years, 1961 through 1965, only five pitchers recorded more strikeouts than Pascual, all of them Hall of Famers: Sandy Koufax, Don Drysdale, Bob Gibson, Jim Bunning, and Juan Marichal. Only Koufax, Whitey Ford, Marichal, Drysdale, Bunning, Gibson, and Larry Jackson had more wins.

Pascual recalls the final day of the 1962 season fondly. Gunning to become a twenty-game winner for the first time, he faced the Orioles at Metropolitan Stadium—familiarly known as the Met—on a Sunday afternoon, the final day of September. Center fielder Lenny Green opened Minnesota's half of the first by being walked by Baltimore starter John Miller. Green swiped second and came home on Harmon Killebrew's two-out single to center. The Twins managed just two hits, but Pascual made the first-inning lead stand up with a 1–0 three-hit shutout. He finished the season 20–11, with five shutouts and a league-leading 206 strikeouts.

As an encore, Pascual went 21–9 in 1963, topped the league again in strikeouts with 202, and posted a career-low 2.64 ERA. When back-to-back twenty-win campaigns failed to elicit a noteworthy raise the following winter, Pascual ripped up the contract he received in the mail and returned it to the tight-fisted and hard-bargaining Griffith. "He taped it up and sent it back to me," Pascual recalls, laughing.

Pascual says the owner gave him a hard time when it came to negotiating contracts, but they always settled their differences and got along. Griffith initiated the process of bringing the star pitcher's parents and sister to the United States to live. Pascual says the owner approached Humphrey to set the wheels in motion.

Although Pascual set a personal high with twenty-one victories in 1963, he might have won more games had he not lost six weeks with a midseason shoulder injury. His throwing shoulder continued to act up, forcing him to the sidelines for brief stretches over the next two years and finally requiring surgery during the 1965 pennant race. The righthander got off to a terrific start that spring. The Twins were competing and Pascual started 8–0 with a 2.49 ERA in his first thirteen outings. Then his shoulder troubles returned, and he had to have an operation after the All-Star break. He somehow managed to return in September.

Pascual pitched against the Dodgers in the World Series but had not fully rehabbed his injury and was not at his best. It was a frustrating scenario for a staff ace who had endured terrible years in Washington before developing into one of the game's best pitchers. Although far from fully healthy, Pascual started Game Three of the World Series in Los Angeles. The Twins had won the first two games in Minnesota, but after a day off, Claude Osteen blanked them on five hits and Pascual took the loss in a 4–0 decision.

The aftereffects of the injury continued to be felt long after his only World Series appearance. "After that, I never threw the same," Pascual admits. "I lost all the strength in my arm that year." After a long and frustrating 1966 season,

Griffith dealt him to the new Washington Senators, the expansion team that had joined the American League the same year the original Washington franchise shifted to Minnesota. Pascual rebounded and pitched quite well for two consecutive summers in Washington, posting double-digit victories and winning records in 1967 and '68 for typically lousy Washington clubs.

After brief stints with the Cincinnati Reds, Los Angeles Dodgers, and Cleveland Indians, Pascual retired in 1971 with 174 major league wins—and four fewer losses. He pitched eighteen major league seasons, a little more than fifteen of them in either Minnesota or the nation's capital. After he retired, he began a scouting career that currently has him searching for Venezuelan talent on behalf of the Dodgers. He initially scouted for the Oakland Athletics and signed Cuban-born outfielder Jose Canseco for the A's. Pascual has not seen Cuban shores since 1961, when he left for spring training in the United States following the last season of the Cuban Winter League. His parents, who joined him in 1965, were born in Spain, where most of his relatives still live. Once Pascual's parents and sister departed Cuba, there was less motivation to return.

Another Cuban player who has never returned to his homeland since the Bay of Pigs invasion is Sandy Valdespino, the five-foot-six outfielder who was a valuable rookie for the Twins in their 1965 American League championship season and collected hits off both Drysdale and Koufax in the World Series. Valdespino was twenty-six years old when he made the Twins out of camp that spring. By that time, he had weathered a poor upbringing as a child and eight years in the minor leagues. A native of San José de las Lajas, a small town ten miles out of Havana, Valdespino was forced to grow up quickly. Soon after his father died when he was nine years old, young Sandy went to work in a pipe factory to help support his family. He says his daily life as a teenager was split between three pursuits: school in the morning, work in the afternoon, and a little baseball before the day came to a close.

Valdespino understands what it means to be thrown into a new culture alone. He was signed by the Griffith family in 1956 at age seventeen, but he had to wait until his eighteenth birthday to legally start his career in the United States. By then, of course, he had learned to take care of himself, and he cherished the opportunity. When Papa Joe Cambria had offered him a chance to play in the United States, Valdespino saw it as a ticket to a better life and a better standard of living for his mother in Cuba. Unfortunately, Valdespino's mother died during his first summer in the United States. He still has relatives in Cuba, to whom he has sent money and medicine over the years, but he has not stood on Cuban soil in more than fifty years.

Although Valdespino had learned to survive in the workplace and the world of adults as a young boy, he admits that adjusting to a new culture was a constant challenge. Communicating with teammates was critical to a player's success, he explains, but it was an obstacle for Cuban players trying to establish themselves in a highly competitive work environment. Sometimes the language issue was a source of resentment. "Sandy was a roommate of mine in 1958 in Missoula," says Jim Kaat, recalling one of his early minor league stops. "That's when Joe Cambria began to really sign a lot of the Cuban players. They'd get together and all they knew was Spanish. And [some] guys were kind of harsh with them, where they would say, 'Speak English!' That's where I bonded with Sandy."

Away from the field, players missed family and friends back home and faced day-to-day struggles in new surroundings. Valdespino agrees with his fellow Cubans that food was a big part of that struggle. "Sometimes you want soup and they bring you a steak," he says with a chuckle.

Valdespino remembers the Cuban gatherings in Mendoza's room. He had become friends with Mendoza soon after arriving in Florida in 1957, and Mendoza helped him adjust to his new life. So too did Bécquer, who took him out to dinner and provided rides when needed. In spring training in 1960, the Senators' last year in Washington, Valdespino remembers Bécquer assisting him with his throws from the outfield. Both Mendoza and Bécquer, who were several years older than the Cubans who became fixtures on the 1960s Twins teams, were instrumental in teaching the routines of the pro game and sharing what it took to succeed on and off the field.

By the time Valdespino met Oliva in the final days of spring training in 1961, he had seen Mendoza go out of his way to assist his fellow countrymen for a few years. Nearly three dozen Cubans were in camp that spring, according to Valdespino, and he says Oliva made quite an impression with his hitting in the brief tryout. When Oliva was nevertheless offered nothing but a return ticket to Cuba, Mendoza convinced him to go to Charlotte. There, like many earlier Cuban émigrés, he was helped by Phil Howser. "Phil Howser was a father to all the Cuban baseball players," Valdespino recalls. "He used to help them, keep them in the United States until they matured more and were able to play. So Tony went to Charlotte, and Phil Howser said, 'Don't worry about it. I'm going to send you to a league.' So Tony stayed there, and when the rookie league started playing, they sent Tony there. And he tore up that little park."

Valdespino spent the 1961 season playing Triple-A ball in Syracuse and Indianapolis. Oliva's bat soon launched a rapid rise through the minor leagues, and the two were teammates two years later at Triple-A Dallas–Fort Worth, where Valdespino manned center field and Oliva right. Oliva captured the American League batting title as a rookie the following summer, while Valdespino played his fourth year of Triple-A ball for the Twins affiliate in Atlanta. He enjoyed a career year in 1964, during which he won the International League batting title with a .337 average. The story goes that he was shorter than Atlanta's bat boy, but with his remarkably broad shoulders and some pop at the plate, he drilled sixteen homers for Atlanta.

Despite Valdespino's surprising power, the key to his success at Atlanta was learning to drive the ball to all fields. He had always been more inclined to pull the ball, but after seeing how effectively Oliva sprayed the ball around, he worked hard to perfect the same approach. Valdespino also made himself attractive to the Twins by becoming proficient playing all three outfield positions. His arm, considered a weakness early in his career, improved with work on his mechanics, and he learned to throw well enough to play right field.

As a rookie in 1965, Valdespino picked up some key hits during the pennant chase. Left fielder Bob Allison slumped badly down the stretch, and when the World Series opened against Don Drysdale and the Dodgers at the Met, Valdespino was in the lineup. No one was more surprised than Valdespino, who batted second behind Zoilo Versalles, his nearly lifelong friend going back to their youth in Cuba. The rookie doubled off Drysdale and scored one of six runs in the third inning of Minnesota's 8–2 victory. The Twins also beat Sandy Koufax in Game Two, but he followed up with a pair of shutouts, including a brilliant three-hitter after two days' rest in the decisive Game Seven. The Dodgers ace allowed a total of just seven hits in his final two starts, and one of them was a ninth-inning pinch single by Valdespino during Minnesota's only legitimate rally in Game Five.

Valdespino spent three seasons in Minnesota, including 1967, the year the Twins lost the American League pennant to Boston over the final weekend of the season. He also had brief stints with the Atlanta Braves, the Houston Astros, the Seattle Pilots and Milwaukee Brewers, and the expansion Kansas City Royals before retiring in 1972. Along the way, Valdespino had spent parts of thirteen seasons playing Triple-A ball.

Nearly all of Oliva's Cuban friends in the Twins organization had learned to adjust to cultural differences and had settled into baseball careers by the time the Bay of Pigs invasion led to Cuba's closing. Most of them were married.

That was not the case for Oliva, who arrived in Florida alone in 1961. He stuck it out, even in the worst of times. The young man called his parents during the loneliest times of the offseason. He offered to come home if they wanted him to return to work the family farm, but his mother always encouraged him to stay in North America to pursue an opportunity that was available to so few Cuban athletes. Oliva occasionally sent gifts to his parents, but the packages never reached them.

Oliva stayed focused on baseball during his minor league years, which helped distract him from the feeling of isolation that was sometimes hard to suppress. Staying focused was critical. For Oliva and his fellow Cubans, succeeding between the white lines required overcoming the language barrier. "You don't understand the language," Oliva explains, "and sometimes the coach doesn't understand you. Sometimes coaches or managers go easy on you, but some, after they tell you something a couple of times, they expect you to know. They can be a little bit tough on you. At those times, you felt like they were going to ditch you. Really, they wanted to push you to learn to get better. Then it's a lot easier for you. They wanted you to feel comfortable, but sometimes you didn't feel that way." By the time he was poised to join the Twins in 1964, Oliva had learned the ways of the game and his new surroundings and had even developed some close friendships. Yet he often longed to be in Cuba with his family, particularly when his teammates had all gone home for the winter after a long season.

Oliva's diligence and hard work paid off when he emerged as the American League's Rookie of the Year. His accomplishments in 1964 are well documented, but a chance encounter off the field that spring affected his life as much as anything that happened between the lines. Oliva met a young woman in the lobby of the Hotel Maryland in downtown Minneapolis, where he lived during the baseball season. She was Gordette DuBois, a high school senior from Hitchcock, South Dakota, a small farm community in the eastern part of the state. She and her twin brother Gordon, along with other members of her graduating class of twenty-six, were in Minneapolis for their senior-class trip.

This was the first time out of South Dakota for the twins, the youngest of eight children who, like Oliva, grew up on a family farm. They and their classmates stayed at the Hotel Maryland, from where they toured the local Ford plant, visited the Foshay Tower (then the tallest building in the Twin Cities), and took in a Twins game. Told that a few Twins players lived at the Maryland, they were prepared for autographs while sitting in the lobby after their trip to Metropolitan Stadium. "Tony came in, and Tony being Tony, even though he could only say ten words of English, he still had that charisma," recalls Gordette, who has been married for more than forty years to the man she met in the lobby that day. "He came right up to all of us kids and signed our pieces of ripped-up paper that we gave him to sign. There were about five or six of us in the group, and he stayed and tried to talk to us."

Oliva gave the group a tour of downtown Minneapolis in his new car, which had been loaned to him by a local car dealer. It was part of a memorable weekend for Gordette and her brother, and it included a final meeting with Oliva before they returned to Hitchcock that Sunday. "When we were going to split, he asked me for my telephone number," Gordette says. "I looked at my brother and I said, 'I'm not sure, but I think he's asking me for my telephone number.' And Gordon said, 'What's the difference? He's probably never going to call you anyway.' So I gave it to him. And lo and behold, he called."

"We laugh about it now," Gordette says as a smile crosses her face. She says they still joke about the what-ifs. What if he hadn't asked for her phone number? What if she hadn't given it to him? What if he had never called? She certainly had reason to doubt that a major league ballplayer living in a big city and traveling around the country—someone with whom she could barely communicate—would call a young woman living on a farm in the middle of South Dakota. "I don't know," she adds, "he maybe asked every girl for her phone number in those days."

The relationship was built across telephone wires in its early days, and the couple would date for nearly four years before marrying. They slowly worked through the obstacle of language, which was a two-way street. Tony may have spoken only ten words of English, but Gordette says she spoke only two words of Spanish. Phone calls would last for hours and often little would be communicated. Yet they had reasons to bond. "We certainly found a common camaraderie between the two us," Gordette recalls. "He's a plantation farmer from Cuba and I'm a farm girl from South Dakota. He came from a family of ten children and I came from a family of eight children, so we both have big families to talk about. We just have a lot in common."

Tony called regularly, and they began to date after Gordette moved to Minneapolis to enroll in a business school. The first date was dinner with Gordette's parents when they moved her to Minneapolis, as they wanted to meet him while they were in town. "My parents fell in love with him the first time they met him," Gordette says. "I think my father more than my mother.

We dated for four years, and he just told me that we probably would have some barriers to cross. He just warned me of that." Although language was a struggle, neither Tony nor Gordette took skin color seriously as a potential problem. It was of little consequence in Cuba, where people tended to run the full range of color from white to black. Racial bigotry had no place in Gordette's home. So the young couple considered racism someone else's problem, not theirs. They went out to dinner and attended movies without incident in Minneapolis. Skin color has never been a major theme of their lives together.

The relationship progressed slowly. Oliva was on the road for half the baseball season and traveled to Latin America when it was over, either to play winter ball or to get away to a Spanish-speaking country for some sun and relaxation. Yet they grew closer, and she became aware of how lonely he was for his family in Cuba. She came to realize her family filled a void in his life. "When he came here, he had no idea he was not going to be able to go back home," Gordette explains. "He just loved being around my family, having a family away from his family in Cuba. That was very important to him."

The Minor Leagues

ife remained relatively simple for Oliva during his minor league days. He focused almost entirely on baseball, with music his passion during his free time. He had acquired a record player that moved with him as he changed locales along the minor league trail. Oliva also carried vinyl records to play—a practice not uncommon among Latin players—buying the latest music coming out of Cuba, Puerto Rico, and the Dominican Republic. Even with the record player and the vinyl, Oliva's possessions still did not amount to much. By the time he reached Minnesota in 1964, he could still pack his belongings in four suitcases, which kept him mobile, letting him move from one town to another or head off to Latin America for winter ball.

Oliva's stay at his first professional stop, Charlotte, lasted just six weeks under Phil Howser's guardianship. In June 1961, he joined the Twins' Appalachian League affiliate in Wytheville, Virginia. Technically there was no opening there, but Howser bypassed Twins farm director Sherry Robertson and contacted Red Norwood, Wytheville's manager, to tell him he was sending another player his way. Once Oliva was given some at-bats, the pure hitter in him emerged, and he led all professional baseball with a .410 average in 1961.

Earning three hundred dollars a month and truly being part of a team for the first time picked up Oliva's spirits. For the first time since arriving from Cuba, he was not constantly plagued by loneliness. He was too busy playing and getting to know his teammates to dwell on his personal situation. His success also inspired him, though he remembers one repugnant experience from his first exposure to cross-country travel.

During a long bus trip, the team stopped at a restaurant to eat. After the players had sat down, the restaurant owner informed them that the black players could not eat with their teammates and would have to sit in the kitchen, where they would be out of sight of other patrons. That steamed Oliva, who stormed out of the restaurant and returned to the team bus. It was a firsthand experience of racism, and one of the rare times he let it bother him. A few of his teammates brought food out for him, which still did not take the sting out of the discrimination.

While playing for the Wytheville Twins, Oliva met another first-year pro who would become a lifelong friend and who was for several years a teammate in Minnesota. Frank Quilici, an All-American shortstop at Western Michigan University, spent part of the 1961 season with Oliva in the Appalachian League. Quilici says it was apparent immediately that Oliva was special. He remembers a young, rail-thin prospect who could put the bat on the ball effortlessly and who had the broad shoulders and quick hands needed to drive pitches with authority. On top of that, Oliva was surprisingly fast . . . and there was that throwing arm.

"Tony could throw from the warning track from right field and knock your glove off at third base," Quilici says. "Literally. He had all the tools." At that point, however, Oliva's defensive game was extremely raw. Quilici, who wasted little time moving to second base with Zoilo Versalles planted firmly at short in Minnesota, witnessed Oliva struggling with playing right field under the lights at Wytheville. Oliva had never played night baseball in Cuba, and to make things worse, the light poles at Wytheville's park were too short and the ball frequently sailed above the glare of the lights. A flyball hit his way could be an adventure.

"He would be coming in on a ball and I would be going out for it," Quilici recalls as a wide grin crosses his face. "He would be yelling in Spanish, and I *still* don't know what he was saying. All of a sudden, he'd go 'Whoa, whoa!' and the ball would drop ten feet behind him. He overran it every time. So when I heard him yelling, I would circle him sometimes. If the ball was up in the air far enough, I could actually catch it. He'd say, 'Gracias, gracias!'"

"The guy could hit, but couldn't catch a cold," recalls pitcher Lee Stange, who spent a decade in the majors and met Oliva in Minnesota after his first pro season with Wytheville. Stange remembers Twins pitchers hitting Oliva dozens and dozens of flies that September, when the prospect made his first trip to Minnesota, "and we put a helmet on him when Tony went out there." Oliva admits he provided entertainment to the pitchers who took the time to hit to him.

Numerous players on those early-1960s teams remember longtime Twins instructor Del Wilber hitting an endless stream of flyballs to Oliva. Wilber oversaw the instructional league team after the 1961 season and directed an intensive training program for the young right fielder, a program that continued for a few years. Stange, who was a rookie in '61, saw Wilber's pet project get off the ground when he also attended instructional league that fall to work on his pitches. Twins pitching great Jim Kaat witnessed the drills when he participated in instructional league following the 1962 campaign. Oliva's defensive game still had a ways to go. "I would stand there for long periods of time while Del Wilber hit flyballs to him," Kaat says. "He was still in the process of learning how to catch a flyball. Some flyballs, literally, he wouldn't even get a glove on. And Del just kept hitting him ball after ball."

Wilber also instituted a mechanical tweak to make the most of Oliva's strong arm, a development that instantly made the prospect a better defensive player. The young outfielder was throwing from more of a three-quarter angle when he arrived from Cuba, and Wilber, a former catcher, taught him to throw straight over the top, which immediately made his throws more accurate. Oliva, who had received virtually no instruction in Cuba, also began learning about positioning himself to field the ball, hitting cutoff men, and anticipating what to do before the ball was put in play.

After making light of Oliva's early troubles defensively, Kaat, Quilici, and Stange were all quick to commend him for the hard work he put in to make himself a dependable outfielder. Seeing what a difficult time he had early in his career, Kaat says, made you appreciate how far he came. It's a testimonial repeated by many of Oliva's teammates from the 1960s. And all the hard work paid off. Five years after that first instructional league with Wilber, Oliva won a Gold Glove for his much-improved outfield play in 1966.

It took Oliva a while to develop the defensive side of his game, but few doubted that he could hit, especially once he finished his first minor league season as the only professional in any league to hit .400. It did not matter that at one point Oliva severely jammed a thumb, suffering the first of numerous injuries he would endure. Demonstrating the mind-set that he maintained throughout his years in the game, he played, even with the thumb swollen well beyond its normal size. Oliva could hardly bend his thumb; Quilici says it looked as if it were protruding from his bat when he stood in the batter's box.

Much to their amusement, Oliva and Quilici remember only one instance of playing time lost to the injury. In extreme pain soon after jamming his thumb, Oliva left a game in the middle of an at-bat. Quilici drew the abbreviated pinch-hitting assignment and quickly struck out. He feigns irritation with his friend as he humorously recounts his brief trip to the plate. "I said, 'You lousy rat. You had two strikes on you and you came out of the ballgame!' I got charged with the strikeout."

Despite the thumb ailment, Oliva finished at .410 with thirty-one extra-base hits, including ten homers, in just sixty-four games. During the offseason, he was awarded the Silver Louisville Slugger, an award given annually to the player with the highest average in all of professional baseball. By that time, Papa Joe Cambria, the scout who had signed Oliva, was seriously ill and hospitalized in Charlotte. With Oliva at his bedside, the scouting legend presented the award's silver bat to his last big find. The Italian-born Cambria, who had also owned several minor league teams and the Baltimore Black Sox of the Negro leagues, died several months later.

At the conclusion of Wytheville's season, Oliva joined the major league club for the final month of the 1961 campaign. Although he was not added to the roster, his first exposure to the big league club was invaluable. He was met at the airport by Julio Bécquer, who was nearing the end of his big league career and who became a mentor. With Bécquer assisting him, Oliva found living arrangements and began to learn the ways of city life in the Twin Cities. Bécquer also introduced Oliva to many of his future teammates.

Oliva found the major league clubhouse comforting. Suddenly he had plenty of Spanish-speaking friends: Bécquer, Camilo Pascual, Zoilo Versalles, Pedro Ramos, and José Valdivielso were all on that club. Oliva says that many of the other veterans were welcoming, too, including Earl Battey, who spoke Spanish; Jim Kaat; center fielder Lenny Green; and the club's two sluggers, Harmon Killebrew and Jim Lemon. That September visit was an opportunity to become familiar with both Twins players and the major league setting. Oliva was invigorated on seeing Metropolitan Stadium, easily the largest and most magnificent ballpark he had ever laid eyes on, and on witnessing major league action for the first time. He could not have possibly imagined the experience just five months earlier, when his nascent career was in jeopardy. So much about his new life was still difficult and challenging, but he was not despondent about his fate, as he had been during his first weeks in the United States.

Oliva enjoyed a remarkable first season, but loneliness did set in after Twins players had gone home to families for the winter and the instructional league in Florida had come to a close. He remained in St. Petersburg all winter, renting a room by himself and filling his time by walking around the city for hours. Occasionally he took in a movie, but the only genre that made sense to someone without a working knowledge of English was Westerns, which became an entertainment staple.

As lonely as those two months were leading up to spring training, Oliva received good news that winter. The Twins added him to the forty-man roster in order to keep him from being drafted by another team. His initial spring training in the United States had been a nightmare, but he reported to Orlando and participated in the major league camp in 1962. Although there was virtually no chance Oliva would make the big league club, his spring performance encouraged the Twins to jump him two levels to the Class-A South Atlantic League. He was assigned to the Charlotte Hornets and once again lived in the black neighborhood roughly five miles from the ballpark. But he was in a much better frame of mind than during his initial stint there; this time around, he was signed to a contract and earning a salary. About a month into the season, Oliva and Nestor Velazquez moved into an apartment. Minnie Mendoza had advanced to the Triple-A Vancouver Mounties that summer, but both Oliva and Velazquez had picked up some of his basic culinary skills. Life in Charlotte was now more to Oliva's liking.

Although his mental outlook was much improved, Oliva found the minor league competition markedly tougher in the South Atlantic League. Pitchers were less predictable and their stuff was more polished; after two months he experienced the first batting slump of his life. Oliva struggled with inside pitches for the first time. Everything felt the same at the plate, and he had no obvious mechanical flaws in his swing, yet he was far less successful driving the inside pitch to the opposite field—his preferred approach.

Going the opposite way had always worked well for Oliva, who now found himself jammed when he tried to pull pitches on the inner half. He eventually mastered turning on the ball, but early in his career, he preferred to tag inside stuff to left field. That was not the conventional approach, but the lefthanded hitter excelled at doing things his way, often to the surprise and frustration of pitchers. "He was tough," Stange says. "You could throw a pitch low and away and he'd send it down the right-field line. And throw him inside and he'd hit it down the left-field line. He hit the ball all over the place."

Oliva rarely struggled with the inside pitch as he did in Charlotte. To counter the slump, he showed up early for extra batting practice and asked coaches and pitchers to throw inside and nowhere else. His fortunes turned around when he made a slight adjustment to his stance—moving his front foot even closer to the plate while planting his back foot further away—and soon he found his groove again. With the mechanical tweak in place, Oliva regained a skill that rarely deserted him. And the slump did not stop him from finishing second in the league batting race, trailing Pittsburgh Pirates prospect Elmo Plaskett by the narrowest of margins: .3498 to .3497. Oliva collected 164 hits in just 127 games and delivered 35 doubles, 17 homers, and 92 RBIs. Pete Rose, Don Buford, Roger Repoz, and Dave DeBusschere also played in the league that summer, but Oliva won MVP honors.

Yet the highlight of the season was Oliva's first promotion to Minnesota in September. He was sitting in the clubhouse after Charlotte's final game, knowing that he and his teammates would be going their separate ways for the winter. Suddenly they were coming up to him, shaking his hand and slapping his back. Oliva did not understand the reason for the warm reception until Velazquez told him he was getting his first call to the majors. He debuted on Sunday, September 9, 1962, a day after Plaskett. Pittsburgh's rookie catcher managed just thirty-six plate appearances in the big leagues and played his last major league game the following May. Oliva had a little more staying power. With the second-place Twins closing in on first-place New York, the Twins rookie made his first big league appearance at Detroit's Tiger Stadium. The Twins had won ten of thirteen games to pull within three of the Yankees and were looking to complete a sweep of a three-game set in Detroit.

Minnesota trailed 10–9 in the ninth inning when skipper Sam Mele sent the team's top prospect to the plate to pinch-hit. The Twins had just pulled within a run on a three-run homer by second baseman Bernie Allen, and Oliva would bat with the bases empty and one out. Before stepping into the box to face rookie righthander Bobby Humphreys, Oliva took a look at Tiger Stadium's short right-field fence with its upper deck hanging over the playing field. A home run could make such a difference in the pennant race. Hitting one there seemed entirely possible, but a heroic moment in his first big league at-bat was not in the cards. Oliva struck out, and Humphreys retired center fielder Lenny Green on a grounder to end the game. Boston had beaten the

Yankees soundly that day, so the loss kept the Twins from gaining a game on the American League leader.

Mele informed beat writers that Oliva would be used primarily as a pinch hitter in situations calling for a hit by a lefthanded swinger. First baseman Don Mincher would get the call when a longball was needed, so in the heat of a pennant race, Oliva was not certain to get many at-bats.

Although he did not make his next appearance until five days after his debut, Oliva's second game was a start in right field. The Twins hosted the Cleveland Indians in the Friday-night opener of a weekend series, and Oliva gave left fielder Killebrew a night off, with Bob Allison moving from right to left. Oliva batted third against Cleveland's Dick Donovan, the team's thirty-four-year-old ace, who was 19–8 for a sub-.500 Indians club and looking for twenty wins for the first time in his career.

Donovan didn't last two innings, as the Twins jumped on him for six runs in an 11–1 victory. After Minnesota southpaw Dick Stigman worked a one-two-three first inning, Twins leadoff man Lenny Green blooped a double into shallow left field. Minutes later, number two hitter Vic Power lined a shot into the left-field bleachers just inside the foul pole for a 2–0 Minnesota lead. In his career, Oliva did not make a name for himself by walking, but he drew his first of two free passes that night after Power's homer. One out later, rookie third baseman George Banks made it 4–0 with the second homer of the inning.

Oliva came to the plate again in the second with one out, Green perched at third base, and Power standing at first. Oliva drilled a Donovan offering just inside third base and into the left-field corner for a double. Both Green and Power scored on the rookie's first major league hit, putting the Twins up 6–0, and Donovan was done for the day. Rookie lefthander "Sudden Sam" McDowell came on and pitched well until the Twins erupted for five more runs in the sixth. Oliva singled home another run during the uprising, and finished 2 for 3 with two walks, two runs scored, and three RBIs. The Twins had cooled off that week, but with the win, they crept within four games of New York.

The strong showing earned Oliva another start on Saturday afternoon, but this day was not as memorable. Early in the game, Oliva rolled his right ankle throwing the ball back to the infield after making a catch and limped off the field with assistance from teammates. He made just six plate appearances in six games the rest of the season, but in his first taste of the major leagues, he went 4 for 9 (.444) in nine games, with three walks. Oliva then returned to Florida for the instructional league and batted .347.

Other players had jumped from Charlotte to the Twins roster, and Oliva was confident of his chances to start the 1963 season with the parent club. He was so confident, in fact, that he applied for a Minnesota driver's license. Twins players received cars to drive during the season, so Oliva wanted to be prepared to get around the Twin Cities. He needed a translator to take the written test, yet he managed to pass it—something he finds surprising to this day.

During the 1963 exhibition season, Oliva tore the cover off the ball and played well enough at all three outfield positions. As he had anticipated, he was on the plane to Minnesota when the team left Florida. Once he and his teammates arrived in the Twin Cities, a host of events were on tap leading up to the start of the 1963 season. First baseman extraordinaire Vic Power was Oliva's translator at the Minnesota Twins Welcome Home Luncheon the afternoon before Opening Day, an annual event in Minneapolis that dazzled the kid. That was only the beginning. A few hours later, Metropolitan Stadium was abuzz with sportswriters and photographers when the Twins took the field for a final preseason workout.

All the talk was whether the Twins could catch the world champion Yankees after finishing 91–71 and five games out in 1962. Oliva was not being interviewed, which he figured was because of his lack of fluency in English. Then he realized that the rookies who had made the team were being photographed—and he was not a part of it. Soon after, manager Sam Mele walked in his direction as the rookie waited to step into the cage for a few swings. "I couldn't speak English," Oliva notes, "but it was clear what this message was going to be." Owner Calvin Griffith had decided that Oliva would be better served starting the 1963 campaign with the Triple-A Dallas–Fort Worth Rangers, an assignment that would guarantee plenty of playing time. Mele was the messenger, and he tried to soften the blow by telling Oliva that he could help the big league club. Truthfully, it was simply better to have the organization's top hitting prospect play every day.

Initially Oliva was stunned. He was enjoying the emotional high of realizing his biggest dream in life, traveling north with the team, and suddenly it was sidetracked by an unanticipated trip to the minor leagues. He was angry by the time he reached the clubhouse, convinced he was better off going home to Cuba than heading to Dallas. Mixed with his anger about the cut was his long-standing frustration over issues ranging from language difficulties and cultural differences to on-field matters. Latin players had to internalize that frustration on a daily basis, and on occasion in a trying situation it would bubble over. Luckily Power and Versalles were in the clubhouse when Oliva began talking about turning his life upside down. Oliva's mentors helped him take a longer view. They advised him to go to Dallas, play hard, and have a good season, and to leave the Twins no reason to keep him in the minor leagues. Power, who had taken the lead in the lengthy conversation, told Oliva he would be back in September. And he was.

Living in Dallas, however, meant getting a room in the "colored" section of town. Oliva shared a place with César Tovar, who would become his Twins teammate in 1965. Life was not what Oliva had anticipated when he had flown north from Florida a few days earlier, but it was only a matter of days before he was committed to making the best of the situation. Then he got off to a slow start and was benched. Dallas–Fort Worth skipper Jack McKeon, who was to manage sixteen years in the majors and lead the Florida Marlins to the World Series title in 2003, started playing Tovar in right field about twelve games into the schedule. After Griffith reportedly stepped in, however, Oliva was back in the lineup. He was batting .230 at the time, but he finished at .304 with thirty doubles, twenty-three homers, and seventy-four RBIs in 146 games.

There were two unanticipated occupational hazards playing for that Triple-A club, one more threatening than the other. The team owned its own plane, a Douglas DC-3, which had been in vogue in the 1940s. This particular plane had seen better days by the time Oliva, Tovar, Sandy Valdespino, and their Dallas–Fort Worth teammates were flying between Triple-A destinations in the mid-1960s. Smooth flights were rare, and a few trips were outright alarming. Oliva recalls two or three hair-raising flights that summer, including one between Dallas and Seattle that had players wondering if they might be living out their final minutes. One of the plane's engines developed a problem, and as the decrepit DC-3 sputtered, the pilots warned their passengers that an emergency landing was a distinct possibility. The crew managed to land the plane without incident, but the white-knuckle affair had the young men contemplating their mortality with every turbulent hiccup and dip in altitude.

Even when both engines were working properly, Valdespino says the players called the plane "the Knuckleball" for the way it danced and darted in the air. Even getting back on solid ground could generate anxiety; one touchdown in particular took the phrase "hard landing" to new heights. "I remember a time we were flying to Oklahoma City," Oliva says. "We hit the runway so hard that the plane took off again. We had to go around and get in line to land again."

Jim Rantz, a promising pitching prospect in the early 1960s who went on to oversee the Twins' minor league system, shared many of those scary airborne moments as Oliva's teammate, including the crazy carom on the runway in Oklahoma City. "It was, like, five in the morning, and the explanation was that the pavement was blacktop and it was so hot that the heat made the plane bounce," Rantz reports with a heavy dose of skepticism. He notes that overheated pavement was not the plane's only issue. Weight was often a concern, and luggage and cargo had to be distributed evenly to keep the Knuckleball on course. The players performed a key role in the balancing act. "The DC-3s were a plane where the tail sits almost on the ground," Rantz recalls. "When you got on, you had to walk uphill. When the luggage rack would get filled up in the tail, the twenty-five players would make a human conveyor belt, and we'd have to pass the equipment up the aisle to the front luggage area. So we helped load the plane." Whether it was a matter of weight and its distribution or simply the age of the plane, Rantz says the DC-3 always struggled to gain altitude once it was in the air.

"I remember when we had to go to Denver," says Lee Stange, who mostly pitched for the Twins that summer but made eight starts for the Rangers. "We couldn't get over the mountains, so we used to go in between them. That Denver flight was the scariest one to me. I'd sit up front behind the pilots. You could see the mountains coming at you."

Before long, Oliva and Valdespino had to all but drag Tovar onto the plane for a road trip. Oliva remembers a time after that hellish Seattle flight when Tovar, approaching the plane, got down on his knees and pleaded, "Oh please, oh please, I got three kids in Venezuela. I don't want to get on that plane!" Oliva was often at Tovar's side at takeoff.

"A lot of times, Tony and César, you'd see them sitting in the back," remembers Rantz. "They'd have the blankets over their heads when you'd take off, and they'd have it for the whole flight until you landed." He adds, "I would get a little nervous when the copilot would come down the aisle and it's the middle of the night. He's got his flashlight and he's leaning in front of you, looking at the wings. I said, 'What are you doing?' He said, 'I'm just looking to see if we're picking up any ice on the wings.' Yeah, that's not a comforting feeling."

No one on the team liked to fly on the Knuckleball. Lefthander Gerry Arrigo, who pitched parts of four seasons with the Twins, refused to even set foot on the aircraft. Oliva says Arrigo showed up for his initial team flight, vomited before boarding, and went home instead. "I didn't like to fly to begin with," Arrigo says. "When they started weighing the players at the airport, that was it, I went home. I went back to Amelia, Ohio, and stayed there for a week or so. They called me and wanted to know why I went home. I told them why, and I said, 'I'm not going to fly on that plane, period. Send me to a bus league if you want.' So they sent me to Charlotte, and I played in the bus league there. I only played about ten games and I was sent back to Minnesota."

Another unavoidable hazard of playing in Dallas was the requirement that players dress like Texas ranchers while on road trips. Traveling in Western clothing, leather boots, and ten-gallon hats, they were quite a sight walking through airports. Oliva could only laugh when he first saw Valdespino and Tovar, his Latin friends, in their Western duds. Valdespino says Tony O, amused by the getup they were forced to wear, called the trio the Black Cowboys.

Looking beyond the occupational hazards, one of Oliva's more memorable moments that summer was his mammoth home run at All Sports Stadium in Oklahoma City. A freeway bordered the park, running along the outside wall in right field, and the wind often blew through the park from left field to right. Rantz remembers Oliva defying the crosswind with a towering blast that left the park. He does not recall ever seeing a ball hit as far by a minor leaguer in all his years in baseball. He says the long drive not only sailed over the light stands but completely cleared the freeway beyond the right-field wall.

"I couldn't believe it," Oliva says and laughs. "When I was young, I was very skinny and weighed about 170 pounds, but I hit the ball like someone who weighed 300 pounds. The ball went over the lights."

Oliva returned to the majors in September, first playing on September 9, a year to the day after his big league debut. The Twins were on their way to their second consecutive ninety-one-win season, though this time they were trailing the first-place Yankees by fifteen games when Oliva singled as a pinch hitter in a 7–4 win over Mudcat Grant and the Cleveland Indians. Oliva went on to collect three hits in seven pinch-hitting appearances over the final weeks.

Minnesota's dwindling pennant hopes did not allow Oliva a start in 1963, though he said he was better prepared to play regularly during his second call-up. Not only had his defensive game improved, but he was also better prepared mentally to field his position. After years of just waiting for the ball to be hit and reacting to it, Oliva had learned to anticipate the play before each batter, based on the game's situation. When he made a move on a ball, he had already considered what the baserunners would do and what base he would throw to. His new approach reduced his mental mistakes and allowed him to make the most of his strong throwing arm.

Over two Septembers with Minnesota, Oliva went 7 for 16 (.438), with three walks and four RBIs. His two cups of coffee served as a suitable christening prior to his breakout 1964 campaign. When the '63 season came to a close and the team went home for the winter, the Twins saw no reason to send him back to the instructional league.

Oliva wanted to keep playing—especially with his first opportunity to stick in the major leagues seemingly so close—so he went off to play in the Puerto Rican Winter League. He found it far less lonely to keep playing, and seeing more game action allowed him to fine-tune his skills. His first experience in winter ball was successful, as Oliva finished second to Puerto Rican legend Orlando Cepeda in the batting race. Winter ball was a tremendous tune-up and confidence builder to take to Minnesota's training camp the following spring.

When Oliva arrived in Orlando for spring training in 1964, he was five months shy of his twenty-sixth birthday. But when he had been preparing to come to North America, he had used the birth certificate of his younger brother Antonio to get a passport, so his documentation said he was three years younger, twenty-two going on twenty-three. The practice of using documentation that subtracted years from Latin players' ages went on for decades. This is not surprising, as age figures significantly in a young man's status as a prospect. If two prospects aged twenty and twenty-three share nearly identical sets of tools and skills, the younger man nearly always has a more promising future. So establishing a different date of birth had its advantages, and it was relatively easy to do in much of Latin America.

After all these years, Oliva chooses not to discuss the specifics of his passport and paperwork. Longtime scout Papa Joe Cambria had assisted Cuban prospects in many ways during his years on the island, even going so far as to complete the documentation to get Bécquer's wife out of Cuba after the newlyweds were separated following the Bay of Pigs invasion. Cambria handled most of the paperwork associated with signing young players and probably tweaked Oliva's numbers. Tony's wife, Gordette, admitted as much in a 2011 interview with *Minneapolis Star-Tribune* columnist Patrick Reusse. "That's the way the scouts did it then," Gordette told Reusse when addressing her husband's age discrepancy. "The thought was if a team felt it had a younger player, they were most likely to keep him."

In 1964, just three years after Oliva's arrival in the United States, big league pitchers and managers quickly discovered that he could do it all at the plate. He could bunt for hits, display the power normally associated with sluggers, drive balls to any part of the field, leg out infield hits, and steal bases.

Oliva's stunning assault on big league pitching during the Twins' pennant push in 1965 was equally remarkable. The defending American League batting champion got off to a slow start in his second season and struggled mightily in May, then hit safely in the first seventeen games of July and batted .379 from the Fourth of July through the end of the season. He was a relentless run producer as the Twins surged to the franchise's first Word Series appearance in thirty-two years. In the midst of Oliva's second-half desecration of American League pitchers, Twins hitting coach Jim Lemon praised the twenty-seven-year-old Oliva for his low-maintenance talents. "You don't have to do much work with him," Lemon told *Sports Illustrated* in a 1965 interview. "Everything is so natural." The young Oliva did not follow a hitting theory or think much about who was on the mound. He hardly knew the name of a single major league hurler when he arrived in 1964, and he liked it that way. Simply hitting the ball where it was pitched produced line-drive power and a steady stream of hits.

Teammates were amused that the young man did not know Whitey Ford from Galen Cisco. It may have seemed he was naively going about his business, succeeding on raw skill alone, but Oliva says otherwise. "People gave me a hard time about names, and laughed about this rookie, but I knew what I was doing." When it came to hitting a talented hurler, the pitcher's arsenal and delivery were more significant than his name. The learning process began the first time Oliva faced someone he had never seen before. To get a handle on a new pitcher, Oliva says, "the most important thing was to see how hard he threw. By the time I finished with that guy that day, I had a good idea *what* he threw. You had to learn about a pitcher's motion, his delivery, and what the ball does on his pitches—all that stuff. I learned and remembered."

It helped that Oliva was a terrific curveball hitter when he signed his first contract with the Twins organization and therefore did not need to *think* about seeing one. Young hitters often fall victim to a good breaking pitch, especially when they are behind in the count and must swing at anything close to the plate. But throwing a bender was never a ticket to getting Oliva out. "From the beginning, I was a better breaking-ball hitter than fastball hitter," says Oliva. "I didn't miss the fastball, but I hit the breaking ball better. I worked more at hitting the breaking ball. If you are a good breaking-ball hitter, you don't have to be afraid to get two strikes. That meant the slider or the changeup was coming, but I knew how to hit a breaking ball. I think I hit more home runs off breaking balls than fastballs."

Aided by his ability to hit offspeed stuff, Oliva claimed American League batting titles in 1964 and 1965, his first two major league seasons. He is the only player ever to do this. He led the league in hits in five of his first seven campaigns. The only major league players to lead their circuit in hits more times are Ty Cobb (eight), Tony Gwynn (seven), Pete Rose (seven), Ichiro Suzuki (seven), and Stan Musial (six).

What made Oliva a Hall of Fame–type player went beyond raw skills and the ability to hit a breaking ball. He had received virtually no coaching in Cuba, yet he developed dramatically once he benefited from professional training in the United States. An extraordinary work ethic had as much to do with his production as did raw talent. He had learned to apply himself to a task on the family farm. Nothing was mechanized. Every task was done manually, from planting crops to harvesting them at the end of the growing season. The work could not be taken lightly, something Oliva and his brothers came to understand from their father when they became old enough to help out.

Growing up with little financial security, one learned to take nothing for granted, a life lesson ingrained in both Oliva and Rod Carew, who grew up poor in Panama's Canal Zone. "When God blesses you with an ability like he did with myself and Tony, it meant you didn't let that ability go to waste," says Carew. "We continued to work and get better. We stayed hungry, stayed focused. And what I learned from Tony as a young kid was amazing. I watched the work that he put into what he was doing."

Oliva's work ethic took over even when things were going well on the field. Frank Quilici remembers a July day in either 1969 or '70, at a time he says Oliva was hitting closer to .350 than .300. The Twins were preparing to go on a road trip when Oliva asked Quilici if he would come out to the park the next day, an off day, to throw him batting practice. "I said, 'Tony, what's wrong?'" Quilici recalls. "He said, 'It doesn't feel right.' I said, 'I wish I didn't feel right.'" Quilici laughs at the notion of a guy swinging a hot bat, ranking among the batting leaders, yet taking extra batting practice in the middle of the season. That's the way Oliva approached his job.

Sure enough, Quilici was out on the mound the next afternoon with a basket of roughly a hundred baseballs. As was often his routine in such sessions, Oliva drove pitch after pitch, methodically working his way from left field to right with well-timed swings. "When I'm finished throwing that bunch of balls, you look at the outfield and it looked like it had hailed," says Quilici. "Tony could hit a line drive to left-center field, ten feet off the ground, and hit the fence. He was that strong."

In the 1965 *Sports Illustrated* interview in which Lemon praised Oliva's hitting ability, the Twins coach also credited the newly crowned Rookie of the Year for his commitment to improving his defense after winning his first batting title. "He would take five hundred balls a day in the outfield, just sharpening himself," Lemon said, "and now he can do anything." A year later, in 1966, Oliva captured a Gold Glove.

Complementing Oliva's work ethic was his temperament, which made him a manager's dream. Right from the start, his teammates were taken by his ready smile and easygoing disposition. He was always warm and polite, never in a foul mood despite his loneliness for family, always an even-keeled presence both on the field and in the clubhouse. "Tony never complained," Carew says. "Never threw his helmet. Never threw his bat, even when he made an out in a crucial situation. He just came back to the bench and waited for his next at-bat. And that's a discipline. It's tough to discipline yourself that way." He adds, "Harmon was that way. I would watch Harmon strike out and people would boo. And then he'd hit a home run. I never once saw Harmon come back and get angry. Tony was the exact same way. I learned that from both of them."

Oliva's work ethic also fueled a desire, not uncommon in the 1960s, to play through injuries. Free agency was not an option. Players were bound to their teams as long as the owner wanted them around. They simply did not have the same job security as in today's game, so players frequently did not make their injuries known and did everything they could to avoid the disabled list. "When we played, we played hurt a lot," says Dick Stigman, the early-'60s Twins southpaw who grew up in Nimrod, Minnesota. "Personally, I don't think I ever was 100 percent. You played because you wanted to. We had one-year contracts. You wanted to stick around and get as many years as you can."

Certainly Oliva had job security as one of the team's top run producers, but like his peers, he was driven to keep playing. As a rookie in May 1964, he suffered a significant injury to the big knuckle in his right middle finger, which he did not have surgically repaired until after the 1965 World Series. Despite the discomfort, which contributed to his propensity to launch bats around the ballpark, he won two batting titles before going under the knife.

Over the course of his career, Oliva endured more injuries than most players. He and Tovar were involved in a car accident near the midpoint of the 1966 season, when another driver ran a red light and collided with his vehicle. The collision caused Oliva headaches and chronic neck and back pain for a few years. Despite the nagging aftereffects of the accident, Oliva still managed to compete for the batting title in 1966, though he lost twenty-one points on his batting average over the final two months of the season. He finished at .307, second to Baltimore's Frank Robinson, who hit .316 and won the Triple Crown.

In some seasons, Oliva struggled with an assortment of ailments. The worst was 1967, when he battled through nine different injuries; nevertheless, he played 146 games that year. He was still bothered by problems from the car accident when he arrived in Florida in the spring, and then he pulled a back muscle making a throw from the outfield two weeks before the season began. Oliva was in the starting lineup on Opening Day, but he aggravated the pulled back muscle on a swing before the season was a month old.

The injury bug was not done with him. Before the season was half over, Oliva had suffered bruised ribs and two sore elbows from being hit by pitches. He also jammed the middle finger of his left hand on a slide at second base. On another sliding play at second, he suffered a significant gash on his right middle finger when Yankees second sacker Horace Clarke stepped on his hand. Oliva's right knee acted up for a stretch, as it would more frequently over the years, after he twisted it chasing a flyball.

Somehow, Oliva overcame his injury-riddled, slow start in 1967 to hit .333 and slug .500 over the final two months. It was a remarkable display of perseverance, though the lingering memory for him and his teammates was the frenetic AL pennant race in which the Twins battled the Boston Red Sox and two other contenders to the season's final day before losing out to Boston for the AL crown.

In 1968, a pulled ribcage muscle during spring training lingered deep into May, as Oliva frequently aggravated the tender muscle by swinging the bat. Close to midseason, Oliva suffered an ankle injury and a pulled hamstring, ailments that took a greater toll on his running than his hitting. He was the leader in the AL batting race on the final day of August, when he dove for a ball hit into shallow right field and dislocated his left shoulder.

Despite the run of injuries in 1967 and 1968, Oliva managed to bat .289 each year—the only two seasons in his first eight that he failed to bat .300 or higher. Those .289 averages were impressive nonetheless. Only four AL players hit .300 over those two years—Frank Robinson, Al Kaline, George Scott, and Carl Yastrzemski twice. American League hitters batted .233 in those two seasons combined, meaning that Oliva hit fifty-six points higher than the league average.

Then there were those knees, which endured seven surgeries and eventually required replacement after he retired. George "Doc" Lentz, the Twins trainer, spent his fair share of time working on Oliva during his playing days. In *Tony O!*, a 1973 biography by sportswriter Bob Fowler, Lentz described his first impressions of Oliva, when the young prospect was officially promoted to Minnesota for the first time in 1962. "I had never seen an athlete with a body like his," Lentz told Fowler. "From the hips up, he had a build as good as anyone, although he was skinny. From the hips down, well, his legs looked like those of a newborn colt. He had a deformity in his right leg; his leg from the knee down was bent at a 45-degree angle. He was knock-kneed, but especially in that right leg. I remember thinking then, 'If he makes it to the major leagues, he'll last only as long as those knees hold out.'"

Oliva underwent knee surgery for the first time after the 1965 World Series, when doctors decided to do some cleanup while repairing the knuckle on his right hand. Postseason appointments with the surgeon became an almost annual event after he blew out his right knee on June 29, 1971, diving for a Joe Rudi flyball at the Oakland Coliseum. The 1971 injury accelerated a genetic condition that also plagued his father and a few of his siblings. Bone continually flaked off and irritated nerves. Occasionally a bone fragment lodged in the knee joint and caused it to lock up. Each trip to the operating room reaped a new collection of bone chips.

At the time he was hurt in 1971, Oliva led the American League batting race by a wide margin with a .375 average. After missing the All-Star Game the next week, he continued to play through mid-September. His average dropped to .337, good enough to let him claim his third batting crown. Despite the severely compromised knee, he also led the league in slugging, at .546. Oliva was on course to have his best season as a major leaguer before the injury, which also denied him a lengthy career that seemed certain to land him in the Hall of Fame.

There would be no more career years. There would be no more .300 seasons with twenty-plus homers, which had been a substantial total in the pitching-friendly 1960s. Oliva enjoyed three productive years as a hitter when he returned to regular duty in 1973, but he played out his career on one good leg. His power and speed were dramatically compromised, and he never again played the outfield.

But before his knee troubles took a substantial turn for the worse a month before his thirty-third birthday, Oliva produced eight Hall of Fame–quality seasons and claimed three batting titles. He batted .313 and slugged .507 during those eight years. Oliva collected 1,455 hits in this span—an average of 182 a season—and only Pete Rose, Lou Brock, Billy Williams, and Roberto Clemente had more. No one had more doubles than Oliva between 1964 and 1971, and only Hank Aaron, Williams, and Dick Allen collected more extra-base hits. Brock and Rose placed ahead of Oliva in multihit games, but no big leaguer could top Oliva's 117 game-winning RBIs in those eight years. Next after Oliva were teammate Harmon Killebrew and Willie Mays, each with 115 game winners, followed by Allen and Frank Robinson with 108.

Among the other players mentioned here as statistical leaders during the years 1964–71, only Rose and Allen are not in the Hall of Fame—and certainly Rose's numbers are good enough for enshrinement. Many would say the same is true for Allen. But Cooperstown was the last thing on the mind of a promising rookie in line to join a potent Twins lineup in spring 1964. At that point, Oliva had endured a long, lonely road from Piñar del Río to Orlando, where he arrived from winter ball in Puerto Rico to begin his first major league season. He was unknown by most of his big league peers, but that would not be the case for long.

A Fast Start to a Big League Career

T he offseason leading up to Oliva's phenomenal rookie year was a tumultuous one, beginning with the death of a president. Barely more than a year after negotiating a settlement to the Cuban Missile Crisis, defusing the threat of a large-scale war, John F. Kennedy was assassinated in Dallas on November 22, 1963. The youthful Kennedy had epitomized an era of hope and optimism in the United States. The suspicious nature of the assassination fueled discontent and cynicism, emotions that in time grew and carried over to an unpopular war in Vietnam. And Kennedy's death came at a time when the civil rights movement was beginning to take center stage in America.

This was also the moment when four young men from Britain took the world by storm. On February 7, 1964, as major league players were preparing for spring training, the Beatles stepped off a plane at New York's LaGuardia Airport and onto American soil for the first time. Two nights later, with "I Want to Hold Your Hand" at the top of the charts, the Fab Four made their celebrated debut on *The Ed Sullivan Show*. The music world would never be the same.

Just as the Beatles had exploded onto the scene, so too would Oliva that summer. He seemed to come out of nowhere, competing for a batting title and driving in runs from the start. Few baseball fans tracked the young prospects of their favorite team in the 1960s, and the rookie right fielder had just nineteen big league plate appearances heading into the '64 season. Although he had managed a .438 average and four RBIs, his limited opportunities at the major league level were not enough to forecast one of the best rookie seasons in the game's history.

That kind of breakout performance by a rookie had to be equally surprising to major league veterans, as it was nearly unprecedented for a player to come into the game and perform at the top level. Of course, Oliva had given signs that he would be a great hitter. After all, the young outfielder broke into pro ball with a .410 average—the best mark in organized baseball—in the Appalachian League in 1961. He jumped two levels the next season and hit .350 with Class-A Charlotte. Skipping Double-A ball in 1963, Oliva batted .304 for Triple-A Dallas–Fort Worth and then competed for the batting title in the Puerto Rican Winter League.

When spring training got underway in 1964, the Twins were an optimistic bunch. Just three years after the move from Washington to Minnesota, they had won ninety-one games in each of the two previous seasons, a remarkable feat for a downtrodden franchise that had posted a winning record only one other time in the postwar years (1952). Their success as a youthful club, brimming with talent and promise, fueled hope they could overtake the New York Yankees, winner of the last four American League pennants.

Only two roster spots were up for grabs when training camp opened in February. Fifteen rookies worked out with the big league club, but the only one with a realistic shot at making it was Oliva. In order to play every day, he would have to move a regular to the bench. The twenty-five-year-old rookie found a jersey in his locker when he arrived in camp. The number six on the back was a clear sign that he was expected to make the club. Oliva quickly made a case for a starting job, showing a sweet batting stroke that impressed everyone in camp. In a March intrasquad game, he pounded four hits in seven trips, slashing some pitches to left field and driving others to right. It was a first glimpse of an Oliva trademark: hitting pitches in any location to all parts of the field.

Oliva's performance in that game set the tone for his spring. While players often struggle to get their timing in the early going, he jumped on pitches right from the start. He missed a few days after running into a fence post in the outfield during a late-March exhibition game—causing a bone chip that Oliva says would one day trigger his right knee troubles—but his bat picked up where it left off when he returned. He hit the ball so hard and sprayed it so effectively that the Twins had no choice but to find a spot for him in their outfield. That was no easy task. In 1963, the outfield trio of Harmon Killebrew, Bob Allison, and Jimmie Hall had accounted for 113 of Minnesota's 225 home runs and more than one-third of the team's RBIs. Killebrew was the two-time defending home-run champ, Allison was an established run producer at the peak of his game, and Hall emerged as one in '63. All three had ranked among the American League's top five in homers and slugging.

Getting Oliva into the lineup focused the conversation on who would play first base. The job belonged to Vic Power, one of the game's premier defensive players at the position. The flamboyant first sacker adeptly inflated a wad of gum into an air-filled parachute as he one-handed balls hit his way or scooped up throws from across the infield. Although the charismatic Power enchanted Twins fans, his stylistic leanings were not as entertaining to coaches. Any young boy playing baseball in the 1960s can recall coaches telling kids again and again to catch the ball with *two* hands.

Power would have none of it. His style looked nonchalant, but he was a master at digging out low throws and getting the glove on everything hit in his direction. Power, who was thirty-six years old that spring (but listed as thirty-two), was no longer as productive as a hitter, though there were plenty of big bats in the order to make room for his defensive prowess. "If they can put a first baseman like me on the bench, it has to be one helluva good club," Power told *Pioneer Press* beat writer Arno Goethel in Florida.

A possible move to the bench upset Power, who considered himself the best defensive first baseman in the game. He enjoyed Minnesota, where fans adored him and invited him and his family into their homes for meals. He had been the regular first baseman the previous two seasons, a gig he wanted to keep until he was ready to retire. When Power was mentioned as trade bait during the 1963 campaign, Twins fans deluged owner Calvin Griffith with protest letters. Although Power was frustrated with developments the following spring, he said all the right things about the situation. "I've always been for progress," Power said at the time. "If Allison can play first base well and we can win the pennant, that's fine. But if he can't, then I'll be ready. When we go to spring training, things have a way of settling down." Power even joked that *he* was ready to move to the outfield.

Even though Oliva's arrival was threatening Power's place in Minnesota's lineup, the veteran took the newcomer under his wing, watching out for him and frequently translating for him. That did not mean Oliva was exempt from being victimized by a Power prank. Always looking to get better, the rookie never hesitated to take advice from veterans. The story goes that Power told Oliva that Ted Williams credited shoveling snow for his hitting prowess.

Oliva did not yet own a home, so one winter, he cleared Power's sidewalk and driveway in Edina multiple times.

Big Don Mincher was also in the first-base mix after hitting seventeen homers in just 225 at-bats as a part-time player in 1963, but Oliva's presence pushed Mincher further down the depth chart. Griffith prodded manager Sam Mele to move right fielder Allison to first to make room for Oliva. Allison had played just twenty-two games at the position prior to the 1964 season, and it was conceivable that Oliva would not hit enough in camp to force a decision on Allison. But with Oliva impressing Mele and his coaches in Florida, the experiment was underway.

Griffith thought the athletic and agile Allison, a former fullback for the University of Kansas, was the best fit for first base. The twenty-nine-year-old stayed out of the fray, except to say that he would move if it was in the team's best interests. He downplayed the controversy, noting that he had played eighteen games at the position in 1961. Allison had handled himself quite well there despite his inexperience, making just two errors in 123 chances. Allison's footwork around the bag needed a little work, but he clearly had the necessary athleticism and talent. Still, he was the target of good-natured teasing about his potential move to the infield. Spring training features plenty of dead time, giving teammates ample opportunity to kid each other.

Goethel, covering the Twins in Orlando for the *St. Paul Pioneer Press*, heard a few players suggesting possible nicknames for Allison. One barked "Bobbleson Allison." Another chimed in with "Dr. Strangeglove," a twist on the title of a 1964 film, *Dr. Strangelove; or, How I Learned to Stop Worrying and Love the Bomb*. (The Dr. Strangeglove moniker stuck, but to Boston first baseman and defensive hack Dick Stuart rather than to Allison. Prior to a spring training game when Stuart was with the Pirates earlier in his career, after the stadium announcer gave the traditional pregame warning that anyone interfering with a ball in play would be ejected, Pirates manager Danny Murtaugh quipped, "I hope Stuart doesn't think he means him.")

The nicknames did not stick to Allison, who excelled at both football and baseball and also ran track at Kansas. The Missouri native might have had a future with the NFL's San Francisco 49ers, but instead he signed with the Senators in 1955. He brought a football mentality to the game. "When Bob went into second base on a double-play ball, you'd better get out of the way or he would put you in left field," Oliva says of Allison's running-back approach to baseball. His explosive combination of power and speed also emerged at the plate. After collecting twenty-eight home runs over four minor league seasons, Allison delivered thirty homers and a league-leading nine triples en route to AL Rookie of the Year honors in 1959.

That summer was an encouraging one for the franchise, which was a year away from moving west to Minnesota. Not only did Allison emerge as a middle-of-the-order run producer, but Killebrew arrived as well, hitting forty-two homers to share the AL home-run crown with Rocky Colavito and driving in 105 runs in *his* first full season in the majors.

Killebrew and Allison were the Twins' young versions of Mickey Mantle and Roger Maris. Allison, who hit the first home run in Twins history off Whitey Ford on Opening Day 1961, was twenty-nine and in peak form when the Twins gathered in Orlando in spring 1964. He was in the midst of the four most productive years of his career when he was asked to change positions. He had averaged ninety-nine RBIs a year over the previous three summers and stroked a career-high thirty-five home runs in 1963.

One option that never materialized in camp that spring was to move Killebrew to first base. After his knee surgery in December, the Twins slugger might have been a logical choice for infield duty, but his rapid recovery dispelled any notion of shifting him from left field. Neither Griffith nor Mele wanted to move him. Oliva's spring training performance would determine who would get most of the at-bats as Minnesota's first baseman: Power or Allison. Although the 1963 club won ninety-one games and led the American League in runs, homers, and slugging, team defense was a key weakness. Only shortstop Zoilo Versalles, center fielder Lenny Green, and Power excelled in the field. Mele, concerned about the defensive side of the game, preferred to have Power somewhere on the diamond. Neither Allison at first nor Oliva in right would be assets defensively, so Power was widely considered the favorite to man first base.

Oliva changed all that in Florida, batting .296 while leading the Twins with twenty-one RBIs in twenty-four spring-training games. By Opening Day, he had made his case to start in right field. Two months later, on June 11, Power and Green were dealt to the Los Angeles Angels as part of a three-team trade, bringing infielders Frank Kostro and Jerry Kindall to Minnesota. Kostro was acquired from the Angels. Kindall, a St. Paul native, came over from Cleveland. As for first base, Allison played ninety-three games there and another sixty-one in the outfield. Mincher once again displayed excellent power as a part-timer and made seventy-six appearances at first.

———

Allison was at first when the Twins began the 1964 campaign in Cleveland. Oliva was in right field, batting second behind third baseman Rich Rollins. After Cleveland ace Mudcat Grant fanned Rollins to get things started, Oliva greeted his soon-teammate-to-be with a sharp single to right field, the first of fifteen hits in his first thirty-seven at-bats. Uncertain of his Opening Day status until he saw his name on the lineup card in the dugout, Oliva started fast, hitting safely in his first eight games and batting .405. He set a remarkable pace by getting at least two hits in each of his first five games, and by the time his eight-game hitting streak was over, he had collected three doubles, three triples, and a pair of home runs.

Cleveland jumped on Twins starter Camilo Pascual and reliever Gerry Arrigo in the season opener for four fourth-inning runs. The Tribe's 6–3 lead did not hold up, though, as the Twins scored twice in the fifth and twice more in the sixth, for a 7–6 victory. Oliva started the fifth-inning rally with a two-out single, his second of the day off Grant. Allison drew a walk, and Jimmie Hall followed with a two-run double. In the sixth, with the Twins down by one, Rollins's two-run single put them ahead.

To conclude an impressive 2-for-5 Opening Day performance, Oliva did something he would not do often all season. In the ninth inning, he struck out against Cleveland submariner Ted Abernathy. Oliva whiffed just twice during his eight-game streak, a testament to his uncanny ability to put the bat on the ball, despite facing major league pitching regularly for the first time.

Oliva, who hit thirty-two homers in '64, fanned just sixty-eight times in 719 plate appearances. Among the fifteen players with at least thirty home runs that season, only Kansas City's Rocky Colavito and Boston's Felix Mantilla struck out fewer times than Oliva. Tony O batted more than thirty points higher than either of them, en route to snagging the American League batting title with a .323 average.

After the season opener, Oliva was talking with Power. They were discussing Grant. "That is a funny name, Mudcat," Oliva said to his teammate and interpreter. "Who is this Mudcat?"

"*Who is Mudcat?*" Power replied, startled that the rookie had no idea whom he had faced earlier in the day. "Don't you know who Mudcat is?"

"No," Oliva shrugged, bewildered by Power's response.

"He is the pitcher you got two hits off today," Power informed the rookie.

"Oh," Oliva said and laughed. "But tell me, what is a Mudcat?"

Oliva became better acquainted with Mudcat later in the season, when the Twins acquired the veteran righthander from Cleveland. Usually, Oliva did not care who was on the mound. The idea was to get the best look at every pitch and react to it. Nearly fifty years after Oliva's impressive Opening Day performance, Grant's take on that first encounter is that Oliva "saw it as a contest between him and the ball being pitched, not thinking about who was out there on the mound." Furthermore, if a premier pitcher such as Whitey Ford or Dean Chance was on the mound, ignorance was bliss. Knowledge of a pitcher's prowess could only work against him. He wanted to go to the plate thinking simply about hitting the ball hard.

Names and reputations did not matter. Oliva says, however, that in those early days he was already tracking the type and movement of the pitches those seemingly unnamed men on the mound were throwing to him. They quickly became familiar. "It was very hard to remember names in those days," Oliva says of his language difficulties, "but in my mind, I knew who was pitching."

The learning process was just beginning. After the season-opening win, the Twins traveled to Washington and claimed a 6–2 win in the opener of a three-game set against the Senators. Oliva nearly hit for the cycle in his second game as a big league regular. Jim Kaat went the distance, and Tony O roughed up Senators starter Carl Bouldin for everything but a longball. Oliva was thinking home run in the seventh inning, when he drove a pitch to deep right-center for a triple that scored Rollins. When Washington second baseman Chuck Cottier bobbled the relay from the outfield, Twins third-base coach Floyd Baker waved Oliva home. The play wasn't close; Goethel wrote that "the throw to the plate nailed Oliva by half a mile." With two outs in the Twins' half of the ninth, the rookie had another chance to complete the cycle, facing Senators reliever Jim Hannan. Oliva drilled a pitch to deep right field, sending Don Lock on a mad dash toward the outfield wall. After a long run, Lock hauled in the drive on the warning track.

The following day, the Twins lost for the first time—falling 4–3 to the Senators—but Oliva collected two more hits. He picked up two more in the fourth game of the season, including his first major league home run, a game-winning blast off Washington reliever Steve Ridzik leading off the tenth. He jumped on a first-pitch curveball from Ridzik to put the Twins back in front after they had squandered a 6–2 advantage. They tacked on another run for an 8–6 victory.

Despite collecting two doubles, a triple, and a home run in the first four games, Oliva says his early power did nothing to change his approach. As the number two hitter in the Twins lineup, he understood his role. Mele wanted him to get on base ahead of Killebrew, Allison, and Hall. Oliva was to be a tablesetter. Although the rookie powered thirty-two home runs in his debut season, he also led the league by scoring 109 runs, a career high in eleven years as an everyday player.

After Oliva served up the game-winning clout in Washington, the Twins boarded a plane for Detroit, where a Sunday doubleheader was on the schedule for their first meeting of 1964. Oliva tripled in each game, but in the second game, a 3–1 loss, Detroit pitchers held the fast-starting Twins in check and limited the red-hot rookie to a single hit for the first time in six games. With two men on and two out in the ninth, Oliva flied out to end the game.

Still, Oliva was 12 for 29 in Minnesota's season-opening road trip. The only downside was that Tigers hurlers took umbrage at Oliva's immediate success and rifled a couple of high-and-tight pitches his way—which did nothing to silence his bat. As the 4–2 Twins headed home for their first game at Metropolitan Stadium on Wednesday, April 22, Oliva was batting .414, with three triples and a six-game hitting streak.

The fast start was surprising enough, but what was even more impressive to teammates was Oliva's ability to hit all types of pitches, regardless of location, to all parts of the park. In his season-opening 2-for-5 performance against Cleveland, he pulled a single to right field and drilled another past the shortstop. Among his seven hits in Washington were a pair of doubles down the left-field line and a triple to right-center off an inside curveball.

"Oliva hits pitches instead of pitchers," wrote Max Nichols in the *Sporting News* that spring. "He doesn't even bother to learn the names of the hurlers. His recognition begins with the moment the ball leaves the pitcher's hand." Oliva told beat writers he had never seen Carl Bouldin before, after rapping out three hits against him in the season's second game in Washington, but Bouldin remembered *him* from the Appalachian League three years earlier. "That was the year Oliva hit .410," Bouldin told Nichols after his first start of 1964. "He was at Wytheville and I was pitching for Middlesboro. I used to get him out quite a bit then. But he hit everything I threw him this time."

The rookie right fielder was the hit of the annual Minnesota Twins Welcome Home Luncheon on the Monday afternoon before Tuesday's home opener. Mele told the 1,100 fans in attendance that he had "papered the walls of my den with letters from Power fans. We needed another lefthanded hitter in our lineup and Tony Oliva came along." The luncheon crowd was probably less inclined to protest Power's benching than it might have been a week earlier. Camilo Pascual served as Oliva's interpreter during the rookie's introduction to the crowd. At one point, an attendee asked the veteran how he would pitch to Oliva, to which Pascual quipped, "Now *I* need an interpreter."

The Twins were rained out on Tuesday afternoon, forcing the home opener to Wednesday. Oliva did not rest on his hitting laurels, instead using the downtime to work on his defense with coach Ed Fitz Gerald, who repeatedly drove baseballs into the right-field corner to help familiarize Oliva with the angles of his home park. By then, Oliva was a much better defender, for which he praises Twins instructor Del Wilber. The rookie demonstrated a remarkable combination of arm strength and accuracy after Wilber tweaked his throwing motion. Oliva now rifled low and accurate throws to any base. But because his defensive game was no match for his bat, his strong throwing arm was initially overlooked by his peers, at least until he cut down a few runners and word got around.

Oliva had been asked to work on his defensive deficiencies during the 1963 season, in anticipation of his big league arrival. He dedicated himself to improving, both in the minors and in winter ball, and it showed when he came to camp in 1964. Yet he knew he still had defensive weaknesses. He tended to pick up grounders off balance, and bad-hop balls would skip past him. He also faced the challenge of learning the nooks and crannies of the various major league parks.

Washington was in town to kick off the home slate, and Oliva continued his assault on Washington pitching, which he had victimized with seven hits in fourteen at-bats the previous week. After the Senators scored four times off Jim Kaat in the top of the first, Oliva gave Minnesota's Opening Day crowd something to cheer about in the bottom half, drilling a pitch from Washington starter Howie Koplitz into the right-field bleachers. It was his only hit of the day, though the Twins rebounded for a 7–6 victory.

The Twins lost, 5–4, the following afternoon, but Oliva had two more hits and scored twice. He now had an eight-game hitting streak, including eight extra-base hits. Although Oliva had made quite an impression on veteran teammates, immediate success was no surprise to the confident, young rookie.

"I wasn't surprised about my hitting because I knew I could hit," Oliva says of his earliest days in the Twins lineup. "Since playing in Cuba, I was able to hit everybody. Maybe I surprised them how good I was able to hit against big league pitchers, but I was able to play every day and hit everybody— lefties, righties, twenty-game winners, Hall of Fame pitchers. I had a pretty good idea what I wanted to do at the plate. Sometimes I went to the plate with the idea to hit the ball to the opposite field. Sometimes I went with the idea to pull the ball. I used to pull the lefty better than the righty, but I had a plan of what I wanted to do."

Rookies rarely have a plan at the plate or display the level of quiet confidence that Oliva brought to the game. Even fewer arrive with his natural hitting ability. But Oliva began to pay a regular price for his success.

After the Twins rookie singled and scored in the first inning to extend his streak to eight games, Carl Bouldin, making his second start of the season against Minnesota, threw a high-and-tight fastball on the first pitch to him in the second. Oliva hit the deck to avoid the high hard one, which, in the words of *Minneapolis Tribune* writer Jim Klobuchar, "would have welded Oliva's ears together if Tony hadn't dropped." Two pitches later, Bouldin struck Oliva on the left forearm. Oliva had had four hits in five at-bats against Bouldin in their two meetings, so the Senators starter may not have appreciated getting slapped around by a rookie. If Oliva was going to reach again, Bouldin preferred that he suffer for it.

It was not unusual for a veteran pitcher to throw in tight to a rookie who was hitting well. Rookies were not supposed to feel too comfortable at the plate. Oliva, who loved to step into the ball, had made himself right at home against major league hurlers. Plus, more than a few pitchers were annoyed at Oliva's lengthy digging-in process, which became a trademark. He dug furiously with his left foot to set up a resting place for his back leg, meanwhile holding up his right hand as if to tell pitchers to wait until he was ready. Righthander Lee Stange, who pitched for the Twins in their first four seasons in Minnesota, remembers Oliva as being one of the first major leaguers to hold his hand up to inform the umpire he was not ready. At a time when games rarely lasted much longer than two hours, the whole ordeal could occasionally irritate an umpire, too.

Oliva soon wound up on the wrong end of a lot of brushback pitches. He had been a target in Detroit the previous weekend, when Tigers righthanders Phil Regan and Dave Wickersham put him on his back with pitches thrown at his head. After Bouldin plunked Oliva in Thursday's series finale with the Senators, a few Twins expressed frustration with the head-hunting, but the red-hot rookie kept quiet and kept hitting. Days later, after Mickey Lolich knocked him down, Oliva blew off the hazard of facing disgruntled veterans who did not like to see rookies succeed. "I've been thrown at before," he told beat writers. "Maybe they do it because they think it might scare me. Well, nobody likes to get hit, but I'm not scared, either."

The high-and-inside pitches continued deep into the spring. Mele spoke up in May after Orioles ace Steve Barber hit Oliva in the forehead with a pitch so hard that it punched a hole in the front of his batting helmet. Oliva had delivered a run-scoring single in the first inning of a 6–5 loss to Baltimore on May 22, raising his average to .392. When Oliva stepped to the plate in the third, Barber, always "effectively wild," drilled him with a first-pitch fastball.

Pascual, the ace of the Twins staff at the time, remembers the beaning as one of the scarier and most unusual hit-by-pitches he had ever witnessed. He says he had never seen a batter take a pitch in the middle of the forehead. More often, a batter turns his head and takes it on the side of the helmet. Once Pascual realized his friend was not seriously injured, he could not help teasing him about taking a pitch square on the forehead. "I took him to the hospital after Barber hit him in the head," says Pascual. "I said, 'Tony, you really followed *that* pitch.'" Pascual stayed with Oliva until he was checked into the hospital, where he was kept overnight for observation.

That Oliva was struck in the middle of the forehead indicates how fearless he was at the plate. Despite the run of high-and-tight pitches Oliva was seeing, he stood his ground and did not give an inch to pitchers. Former Twins minor league director Jim Rantz, a Twins pitching prospect in the early 1960s, says Oliva demonstrated the same fearlessness a few years earlier in instructional league. He remembers the hitting prospect getting hit in the head three times one fall. "I know Del Wilber had to sit him down," Rantz says of the longtime Twins instructor who oversaw instructional league. "Tony didn't want to come out of the game. He just shook it off and wanted to stay in the game every time. Tony wouldn't give ground at the plate. He'd hang in there."

Mele, angered by the inside fastballs frequently thrown near Oliva's head, said that Barber was the seventh hurler to knock the star rookie to the ground. He added that their names were noted in the clubhouse for future reference. "We had a meeting in Boston," Mele said of a mid-May visit to play the Red Sox. "I told the pitchers then that whoever knocks Oliva down gets brushed off by one of our pitchers. We've got to protect Oliva. This is the only way we can stop it." Mele went so far as to tell Barber that he was going down, but the Orioles hurler was removed for a pinch hitter the next time he was scheduled to bat.

Speaking through Power, who often interpreted for him, Oliva admitted that inside and brushback pitches were part of the game. It was not a rookie's place to complain, he said, and he addressed the issue calmly as he flashed the charismatic smile that was winning over baseball fans in Minnesota. It helped, of course, that Oliva had not been seriously injured by Barber's beanball.

Even though the incident looked far worse than it turned out to be, Oliva continued to experience dizziness after spending parts of two days in the hospital. He may have been experiencing symptoms of a mild concussion, as concussions were not diagnosed or monitored as they are today. Oliva, anxious to get back on the field, did not discuss his symptoms. Less than forty-eight hours after he was struck in the head, he was back in the lineup and stroked his ninth homer of the young season off Orioles pitcher Milt Pappas in a Sunday doubleheader.

Although Oliva played down the beaning, it stirred plenty of talk, as well as some resentment about a rookie making himself at home in the batter's box. "He digs in for five minutes every time he comes to the plate, planting that back foot on the line," Orioles catcher John Orsino complained. Innings often lasted only five minutes, and games rarely ran two hours in the 1960s. Orsino was not bothered by the lost time. The issue was the ongoing battle between hitter and pitcher. "Pitchers don't like to see a man take that toehold," Orsino said, adding, "Don Drysdale of the Dodgers would deck him every time in the National League."

On the other side of the issue, beat writers covering the Twins began asking why the American League's other power hitters were not being targeted. Harmon Killebrew, Mickey Mantle, and Rocky Colavito rarely had to dodge pitches at their heads, but Minnesota's rookie had sparked the ire of some AL hurlers with his immediate success and his landscaping in the box.

Oliva believes the head-hunting helped him at the plate. "Every time they hit me, I became better," he explains. "I paid more attention. I concentrated more. A lot of times pitchers get people out because they don't concentrate. You have to concentrate to hit the ball good." Regardless of the situation, he was never one to give away an at-bat, especially after a pitcher fired a pitch at him.

Oliva says he used the high-and-tight stuff to his advantage, but Calvin Griffith was concerned about protecting his young star. Two years earlier, catcher Earl Battey had been struck by a pitch and had suffered a broken cheekbone. In 1963 he began wearing a special batting helmet with an earflap to protect his temple and cheekbone. Griffith insisted that one be made for Oliva in 1964, though the Twins right fielder resisted wearing it. The helmet, which looked crude and war ready, was the prototype for what all players wear today to protect the temple area facing the pitcher.

Many managers and pitchers believed that working Oliva high and tight was the ticket to getting him out. Oliva stepped into pitches aggressively and was known for striding toward the plate to jump on outside offerings. By busting him inside, pitchers wanted to make him think twice about lunging over the plate. The idea also was to jam him with pitches, so that he might make hard contact less consistently as he did coming out of the gate. "I think the only way to pitch Tony was high and tight," Jim Kaat says. "Fastballs up and in, and then you had to hope that he'd chase a pitch down and away. He got buzzed up there quite a bit, because that's where pitchers tried to pitch him."

Always pitching Oliva the same way was not a ticket to success, though. He went to the plate with a plan, based on the pitcher's arsenal and tendencies. Even as a rookie, he made adjustments so naturally and effortlessly in the batter's box that he could foil attempts to pitch to his weaknesses. He tweaked his approach or his position in the box based on the game situation and the count. Moving slightly closer to or away from the plate could counter a steady dose of pitches in on the hands or breaking balls fading away from the strike zone. Sometimes Oliva would shift his location in the batter's box to draw a certain pitch from the man on the mound. Working Oliva high and tight failed to cool his bat or deter his approach. He simply could not be intimidated. By the second half of the season, the pitches in his face subsided. Oliva was no longer a regular target.

The day after Oliva suffered his first hit-by-pitch, his eight-game hitting streak ended in Minnesota's first meeting with Detroit at the Met. Oliva was held hitless by promising twenty-three-year-old lefthander Mickey Lolich, who on April 24 tossed a three-hit shutout for his second win in two starts. Only Rich Rollins, Vic Power, and Earl Battey managed hits off the second-year hurler in the 5–0 loss, and no Twin reached third base. Lolich also shut down the hottest hitter in the game. "I just moved the ball around on him," Lolich told a Detroit-area writer after blanking the Twins. "Outside corner, insider corner, here and there." It was one of the earliest of many masterful performances by the talented lefty, who did not overwhelm hitters with velocity. (In fact, Lolich was born righthanded but learned to throw lefthanded after he broke his left collarbone riding a tricycle as a boy. His doctor encouraged it to strengthen the damaged shoulder, and Lolich remained a southpaw.)

Lolich mostly worked away against Oliva on that April afternoon. The rookie did not register a hit in four trips and saw his average slip to a still-robust

.366. Although Lolich was successful pitching away to Oliva, his approach was not a surefire way to retire the rookie. Oliva, like lefthanded-hitting Carl "Yaz" Yastrzemski, the reigning AL batting champion in 1964, could consistently drive the ball hard—and a long way—to left field.

Both Oliva and Yaz drilled extra-base hits to all fields, a skill that put them in direct competition for batting titles throughout the 1960s. Opposing pitchers also faced the challenge of Metropolitan Stadium's left-center power alley, which was conducive to home runs, a fact that benefited both hitters. Yaz was known to park home-run shots over the Met's left-field fence when he played for the Triple-A Minneapolis Millers in 1960.

Oliva's eight-game hitting streak was over, but the debate was just beginning over whether the Twins prospect was the real deal. He certainly was not the first rookie to start fast, and the odds were against him maintaining the kind of success he had enjoyed over the first ten days of the season. But Mele was convinced Oliva would keep hitting, even after pitchers got a second, third, or fourth look at him. Many of the rookie's teammates quickly became believers, too, including former Twins lefty Dick Stigman. "He was one of those guys like Joe Mauer," Stigman says. "You just knew he was going to hit. It was a given. He was that good of a hitter."

Though Oliva had made quite a first impression on teammates, the season was still young. He had demonstrated he belonged in the majors, but what might he contribute over a full season? As the campaign progressed, Oliva increasingly looked like a premier run producer on a club already well stocked with them. "Once you saw him play for about thirty days, he was the talk of the league," says Kaat. "Nobody could figure out a way to get him out. Based on that, it was pretty evident this was not just a young kid in a hot streak—he was a really accomplished hitter. As the year went on, it was not a surprise that he won the batting title." Teammates watched in amazement as the rookie showed remarkable power to left on pitches low and away, then turned on an inside offering for a towering home run the other direction. Talk on the bench was not about *whether* Oliva would hit the ball, but about *where* he would hit it.

That April, however, Oliva may have earned his teammates' respect more for how he handled his early success. The rookie was not boastful or cocky. Nor was he shy or withdrawn, despite language difficulties that limited his ability to express himself. He endeared himself to teammates with his bright smile and even temperament, good-naturedly taking the kidding that goes with being a rookie. He fit in well in the clubhouse and would often play cards with the other regulars before games.

Griffith clearly was enamored with Oliva's prowess at the plate. The owner was always conservative with his praise, which could come back to haunt him when it came time to negotiate contracts, but he did not hold back in the case of his rookie right fielder. After Oliva batted .304 and stroked twenty-three homers in Triple-A ball in 1963, Griffith believed Oliva would hit for average and power and compared his potential to Mickey Mantle's. The owner's greatest concern seemed to be that Oliva should avoid the coaching staff and keep doing it his way at the plate. "I don't want anyone to coach this boy in hitting," Griffith told Max Nichols of the *Sporting News*. "I want him left alone."

Griffith was right about not tinkering with Oliva, who maintained a "see the ball, hit the ball" approach and focused mostly on hitting it hard. Early in 1964, however, more than a few American League veterans doubted the legitimacy of Oliva's fast start. After all, he would be neither the first nor the last rookie to dazzle in the early going before coming back to earth. After Oliva recorded seven hits in three games against Kansas City the second week of May, Athletics manager Eddie Lopat still was not convinced of the rookie's staying power. "We tried pitching him several ways, but obviously nothing worked," Lopat told *St. Paul Pioneer Press* writer Glenn Redmann. "He waits on a pitch real well, then pops it. Right now, everything he hits is finding a hole. He can't keep it up. It's impossible." Lopat was not a believer, and his misguided take on the rookie lives on in the baseball classic *Ball Four*. The book's author, Jim Bouton, a former major league pitcher, quotes an early pronouncement by Lopat that "the kid will never hit in the big leagues."

Oliva was batting .441 in twenty-three games after his assault on Athletics pitching, so he was not going to maintain such a pace. On the other hand, Oliva continued to drive baseballs all over the field and to find holes—and it was impossible to find holes in his swing. Already drawing comparisons to Yogi Berra as a bad-ball hitter, the rookie pounded pitches out of the strike zone as hard as anyone. A few pitches out of the zone left ballparks.

Despite doubts about his early-season exploits, Oliva's eight-game streak to open the season was by no means his last substantial hitting streak of 1964. He hit safely in eleven straight games at the beginning of May and put together a seventeen-game run, his longest of the season, shortly after the All-Star break. The day after his seventeen-game streak stalled, Oliva started a nine-gamer and then hit safely in thirty of thirty-two games from July 16 to August 16, a span in which he batted .353, including eleven doubles and eight homers. In all, he had seven hitting streaks of seven games or more in 1964.

While American League pitchers were waiting for the fast-starting rookie to crash and burn, Oliva countered by hitting safely in twenty-two of the Twins' first twenty-four games. On April 30, when he was held hitless for only the second time in this stretch, his average dipped to .345. It would not drop below .345 until late June.

Oliva opened May by going 2 for 4 and scoring two runs in a 10–5 romp in Kansas City. An eleven-game hitting streak was underway. He recorded the first four-hit and two-homer game of his career on May 2, pushing his average to .388. What that night is remembered for most, however, is a home-run barrage that gave Minnesota a 7–3, eleven-inning victory over the Athletics. After Oliva kicked off the scoring with a two-run homer in the third inning, the Twins tied a major league record by stroking four consecutive home runs in the eleventh.

The game was tied at three when Oliva led off the top of the eleventh and powered a 3–2 pitch from reliever Dan Pfister high over the right-field fence at Kansas City's Municipal Stadium. Bob Allison also went 3–2 against Pfister before drilling a long home run that barely stayed inside the left-field foul pole. Pfister threw three straight balls to the next batter, Jimmie Hall. Then the center fielder turned on the fourth offering for a longball to right. Pfister departed, but Harmon Killebrew, the reigning home-run champ, greeted rookie Vern Handrahan by crushing his first pitch out of the park, beyond the outer wall in left field.

The feat was only the third time in big league history that four teammates had hit consecutive home runs: Eddie Mathews, Hank Aaron, Joe Adcock, and Frank Thomas of the Milwaukee Braves homered consecutively off a pair of Cincinnati pitchers in a 10–8 loss to the Reds on June 8, 1961. And on July 31, 1963, Woodie Held, Pedro Ramos, Tito Francona, and Larry Brown of the Cleveland Indians matched the Braves' quartet's feat. All four Cleveland bombs were hit off Angels reliever Paul Foytack in Cleveland's 9–5 win. Ramos, the former Twin who hit fifteen home runs during his career, stroked two that day.

Oliva, who also had a double to go with his two home runs on that historic May afternoon, tore into Kansas City pitching all season. He batted .457 in eighteen games, going 37 for 81, with seven home runs and eighteen RBIs. The day after his first four-hit game, Oliva went 4 for 4, with another homer, in the second game of a Sunday doubleheader with the Athletics. The Twins were swept, falling to 9–8, but Oliva went 11 for 18 with three home runs in his first visit to Kansas City.

Oliva's second four-hit performance pushed his average to .408. It stayed above .400 for two weeks, as he recorded his third four-hit game four days later, on May 7, in a 9–1 win over the Los Angeles Angels. Once again he hit two homers, including a sixth-inning grand slam off reliever Jack Spring, to break open a close game. Oliva added a solo shot in the eighth and recorded six RBIs—a career high and a Twins rookie record that stood for nearly fifty years, until Oswaldo Arcia equaled the mark late in the 2013 season.

With his third four-hit day in a week, Oliva's average jumped to .427. "He hit a fastball for his first homer (to right) and a curveball for his second homer (to left)," Angels skipper Bill Rigney told *Minneapolis Tribune* writer Sid Hartman after seeing his pitching staff getting roughed up. "He's always ready no matter what pitch you throw him. Even when you get him out, he gives the ball a real good rip. I think one reason for his success is that he has a 'quiet' bat. He has no wasted motion and just hits the ball where it's pitched. . . . Oliva is the finest-looking hitter I've seen since coming into the league."

"He looks like he just came *down* from another league," Twins reliever Bill Fischer said after Oliva's third four-hit game in six days. "They forgot to tell him that Spring was a lefthanded pitcher." Oliva probably did not notice.

There was no slowing down the Twins' leading hitter. A rematch with the Athletics at Metropolitan Stadium followed Oliva's big day against the Angels, and he had seven hits in thirteen at-bats in a three-game set. He had two or more hits in each of the last six games of his eleven-game hitting streak to surpass the five consecutive multihit games he had delivered to open the season.

After two more hits in an 11–1 drubbing of the Chicago White Sox on May 12, Oliva was batting .439. He had a hefty lead in the American League batting race over Boston shortstop Eddie Bressoud and Detroit catcher Bill Freehan, both of whom were on the other side of .400. The Twins rookie also led the league in runs and hits, and only Cleveland's Leon Wagner had more RBIs.

Oliva had already stroked seven homers, though Hall led the team with nine. Both young outfielders, along with Allison, who also had seven in the early going, ranked in the league's top ten.

The only American Leaguer who came close to shutting down Oliva during his surge was teammate Hall. With Oliva perched on first in the Twins' May 12 romp over the White Sox, Hall ripped a line-drive single in the direction of first base that forced Oliva to dodge. "I almost lost my job on that one," Hall told beat writers after the game, when asked about the at-bat. Pressed to explain what he meant, Hall added, "Tony Oliva was on first, wasn't he? And the ball almost hit him, didn't it? Can you imagine hitting a guy who's hitting like Oliva and keeping your job? I can't." Hall's job was not on the line, of course. He had stroked his ninth home run against Chicago to pull into a tie with the Athletics' Rocky Colavito for the American League lead. Hall was leading a Twins club that had pounded forty-four home runs in the first twenty-four games. The Twins were on a record pace for home runs in a season.

Surprisingly, even with the league's most potent offense, Minnesota was just 13–11 after the 11–1 victory over the White Sox. The team ERA was near 5.00, so the Twins had to outslug their opponents to win. Staying over the .500 mark was a season-long struggle for the Twins, who finished in a sixth-place tie with Cleveland at 79–83–1. They went seven games over .500 three times during the first half, but they were never able to build on that margin. The last time they had seven more wins than losses was July 3, when they claimed a 1–0 win over the Yankees on the Friday prior to the All-Star break. An eight-game skid early in the second half dropped the Twins to 47–48, and a 4–18 slide that carried into early August quickly and irretrievably stalled their pursuit of the Orioles and the Yankees in the American League race.

The Twins never established the kind of momentum that Oliva did. Even during that July–August stretch of eighteen losses in twenty-two games, Oliva hit safely in all but three contests. His season-best seventeen-game hitting streak came during this stretch, at a time when his teammates collectively batted .211 and the Twins barely averaged more than three runs a game. The lineup generated plenty of runs in the first half of the season, but the pitching staff was not getting it done. When the pitching came around later in the season, the bats went cold. But all the while, Oliva kept producing.

On May 13, Oliva went 0 for 4 against White Sox lefthander Juan Pizarro. During a forgettable 5–1 loss, Oliva was involved in a statistical oddity in his first plate appearance of the game. Before that plate appearance was over, the White Sox had committed three errors. Oliva lofted a foul ball behind the plate, which Chicago catcher Camilo Carreon dropped; he was charged with an error. Given a second chance, Oliva drilled a hard grounder beyond Pizarro's reach. Shortstop Ron Hansen moved to his left and positioned himself in front of the ball, but it took a high hop and bounced away from him. Hansen quickly recovered and hurried a throw that skipped past first baseman Joe Cunningham, allowing Oliva to move to second. Hansen was assessed two errors on the play. It was the only time Oliva reached base, as he was held hitless for just the third time in twenty-five games.

A few days later, Oliva was held hitless in back-to-back games for the first time all season. The Twins were in Boston, splitting a four-game set with the Red Sox, when Oliva was shut down by Boston hurlers on consecutive days. That happened only six times in 1964, and only once all year was he held without a hit in three consecutive games.

When the Red Sox held Oliva hitless a second time in the first game of a doubleheader on Sunday, May 17, his batting average dropped to .395. He would not see .400 again in 1964, but only for a few days all season did Oliva not lead the batting race. He endured his only rough stretch of the year during a three-week span in June, when he batted .188 in twenty-one games. His average dropped from .389 to .327, allowing others to work their way into the chase for the batting title, though Oliva hit .320 the rest of the way to win AL honors with a .323 mark.

Injured Rookie Wins
Unprecedented Batting Crown

What made Oliva's achievements as a rookie all the more remarkable was that he played all but six weeks of the 1964 season with a hand injury that remained an issue throughout 1965 as well. In fact, he won two batting titles before undergoing surgery to correct the damage, which he had suffered on May 15, 1964, in the first game of the weekend series at Fenway Park.

Oliva was leading the league with a .414 average as Camilo Pascual and Bill Monbouquette squared off in the Friday opener. The rookie collected two hits in three at-bats against Monbouquette, then came to the plate in the ninth to face dominant six-foot-five closer Dick Radatz. With the Twins ahead 1–0, the bases empty, and one out, Oliva attempted to turn on a Radatz fastball but missed, and the knob of Oliva's bat struck the big knuckle of his right middle finger. The pain was instantly severe, but Oliva returned to the batter's box and went the other way with the next fastball, stroking a line drive into the left-field corner and sliding headfirst into second with a double. To add injury to injury, Oliva's shoulder hit the bag hard on his slide, and the hand and shoulder injuries made swinging a bat painful.

The shoulder required a cortisone shot the next day to alleviate the discomfort. The sore knuckle was more difficult to treat. Twins trainer Doc Lentz taped a piece of rubber to the knuckle before each game to protect it, but that did not eliminate the soreness. Oliva quickly discovered that hitting the ball was far less painful than swinging and missing, so he had plenty of incentive to keep making consistent contact.

Even with the two injuries, Oliva did not miss a game, but he went 0 for 9 on Saturday and Sunday for his first back-to-back hitless performances of the season. Then he went on a 23-for-60 surge, batting .383 in a sixteen-game stretch. For the month of May, the rookie posted a .402 average. All that had changed was that Oliva now had trouble hanging on to his bat. Lumber flew every which way, across infields and into dugouts and box seats. If the ball took flight, the bat tended to stay in place, but a painful swing-and-miss might put it into orbit.

Always on the lookout for flying objects was Harmon Killebrew, who usually batted after Oliva in the Minnesota lineup. "Tony hit me twice in the on-deck circle," Killebrew recalled in a 2009 interview. "He didn't like putting pine tar on his bat, and I couldn't hit without pine tar and rosin to hold onto the bat. So, I was kidding him one day. I said, 'Tony, why don't you put that stickum on the bat?' He said, 'Oh no, Killy, I don't like that.' I said, 'Okay, let's do this. Let me get a little rope and I'll tie it around your wrist and then tie the other end to the bat.' He goes, 'Oh no, that's no good.'"

Oliva continued to hit, but otherwise the news in Twins territory was less promising. The team failed to win more than two games in a row throughout June, when the errors and mental miscues started to pile up. Owner Calvin Griffith had watched his club win ninety-one games in consecutive seasons, so its 1964 start sparked his ire. He lit into a number of players, and he did not limit his criticism to performance on the field, accusing players of "carousing around at night and closing up some of the restaurants around town."

Only manager Sam Mele was spared Griffith's wrath, though the owner couched his support for his skipper by saying "maybe Sam's too nice. . . . I've talked to Mele about fines, but Sam is against that." In time, the owner got his way. Fumbled fundamentals, missed signs, and assorted brain cramps could take more than fifty dollars out of a player's pocket, a substantial penalty at a time when many major leaguers made roughly the same money as the average American worker. Despite the threat of a thinner wallet, from the start of the crackdown through the end of the season, the Twins were seven games under .500.

Griffith made changes. On June 11, he dealt two of the club's top defensive players, first baseman Vic Power and center fielder Lenny Green, to the Los Angeles Angels. Then Griffith picked up a key arm four days later at the June 15 trade deadline. He traded swingman Lee Stange and highly touted third-base prospect George Banks to Cleveland for Mudcat Grant. The twenty-eight-year-old righthanded pitcher had won sixty-seven games in six-plus seasons with the Indians, but he had yet to have a breakout season. In Minnesota, he hit his stride. The trade's big payoff came the following season, when Grant went 21–7 for the American League champions.

Otherwise, the only good news for the Twins was that Oliva, Killebrew, and Allison would be All-Star starters for the American League at the New York Mets' brand-new Shea Stadium on July 7. Since players at this time voted on All-Stars, Oliva's selection showed that his big league peers were believers. Oliva got the call over future Hall of Famer Al Kaline, whose all-around game made him one of the rookie's favorite players. It was an honor to start over "the best right fielder in both leagues," Oliva told reporters when the All-Star assignments were announced on June 20.

Allison, in the thick of the AL batting and home-run races, earned his first All-Star start at first base following two previous appearances as an outfielder. Killebrew joined the All-Star starting lineup as an outfielder for the first time after making the AL team five times as either a first or a third baseman. They were the sluggers the Twins built around when the franchise moved to Minnesota. They were close friends and had been longtime road roommates during minor league stops in Charlotte and Chattanooga before reaching the majors. Allison was outgoing and social—the guy who might call a players-only meeting in the clubhouse. Killebrew was quiet and reserved; he let his bat do the talking. Both had exploded onto the scene in 1959, and Killebrew had claimed three home-run titles by the time they and Oliva headed for New York. For Oliva, the midseason favorite to claim AL rookie honors in 1964, starting the All-Star Game at Shea Stadium with the franchise's premier run producers was heady stuff.

Collectively the trio went 1 for 11 facing the likes of Don Drysdale, Jim Bunning, and Juan Marichal, and the National League claimed a 7–4 decision. Phillies right fielder Johnny Callison put an end to the 1964 game with a three-run, walk-off homer off Red Sox closer Dick Radatz—with two outs in the ninth. Oliva went hitless in four trips, appearing opposite Hall of Fame right fielders Roberto Clemente and Hank Aaron. More than 50,000 fans attended the game at the Mets' new park, the largest crowd Oliva had ever seen in a baseball stadium. A highlight of the rookie's first All-Star appearance was the autographed ball that Willie Mays signed "to Pedro."

The All-Star Game also proved to be a turning point in the Minnesota clubhouse. Although Oliva had been treated warmly by teammates and fit in well, he had mostly been called "Rook" or "Rookie" during the first half, but by now, he was "Tony" to everyone.

Although the Twins were not fated to make a competitive challenge for the American League pennant in 1964, Oliva's rookie season and pursuit of the American League batting crown made worthy storylines. An AL rookie had never won a batting title, but Oliva took a substantial lead over his peers with his fast start. He was batting .356 at June's midpoint, good for a twenty-five-point edge over the Washington Senators' Chuck Hinton. By then, the rookie had convinced nearly everyone he was for real, especially those facing him on the mound.

"The pitchers didn't know him, but they knew he could hit after the first time around," recalls Jim Perry, who joined the Twins in a 1963 trade with Cleveland. "Tony was hitting the high pitch, the outside pitch, the low pitch. He hit every kind of pitch up there." Oliva had won over Perry and his teammates from the beginning.

"You could just see the ability he had," notes Gerry Arrigo, a lefthander who had also been Oliva's teammate briefly in Dallas in 1963. "A real good hitter. Anybody who's a pitcher or a hitter, if someone has got that ability that's going to be better than anybody else, it shows. It really does."

After Oliva tore the cover off the ball for two months, the gap in the AL batting race closed markedly when he ran into a three-week June swoon. Two hot hitters, Bob Allison and Yankees star Mickey Mantle, were in pursuit. Allison moved to the top of the AL leaderboard briefly, hitting .387 in June to push his average to a league-leading .340 on June 28. Oliva regained the league lead by a single point the next day. When the Twins traveled to New York to close out the season's first half against the Yankees over the Fourth of July weekend, Allison sat at .342, followed by Oliva (.338) and Mantle (.323). With Mantle in the midst of a twelve-game hitting streak, the weekend provided competition beyond the Twins' long-shot push to stay close to the AL contenders.

The Yankees slugger was rapidly closing the gap. With two hits on Friday night, Mantle was the only one of the three to hit safely in Minnesota's 1–0 ten-inning victory. He had half of the four hits allowed by Twins lefty Dick Stigman, who went the distance. The Yankees swept the July 4 doubleheader on Saturday, with Mantle going 4 for 8 and providing an eighth-inning three-run homer to secure a 7–5 win in the opener. When New York had claimed the nightcap, a 2–1 decision behind Al Downing, Allison, Mantle, and Oliva were separated by one percentage point: Allison and Mantle were at exactly .333 with Oliva trailing at .33233.

After the Fourth of July sweep, Yankees skipper Yogi Berra was moved to make two predictions to beat writers covering the series. His Yankees had been battling injuries, but with the team now within three games of first-place Baltimore, he forecast another AL pennant in the Bronx. That was not exactly going out on a limb for the four-time defending champs, but the lovable Berra went a step further and predicted a batting title for his star slugger and longtime teammate. "If Mantle stays healthy, no one can beat him out for the batting title," the first-year manager said. Berra did not get this one right. Although Mantle was at his best heading into the All-Star break, going 7 for 16 against the Twins, Oliva prevailed down the stretch. At season's end, another legendary Yogiism might have been appropriate: "The future ain't what it used to be."

Not only did Oliva win the AL batting crown in his rookie season, but he led the majors in total bases—with a little help from Mantle on that Fourth of July. In the fifth inning of the first game, Oliva drilled a Jim Bouton pitch over the center fielder's head. Mantle broke back and to his right and closed in on the ball, but he only got a bare hand on it before it bounded beyond his reach and headed toward Monument Park in deep center. Left fielder Héctor López finally retrieved the ball as Oliva headed home. "By the time López got the ball near the monuments, I was ready to sit and drink a cup of coffee," Oliva jokes.

Other than the short right-field porch down the line, Yankee Stadium was cavernous in the 1960s. The fences in the power alleys were more than 400 feet from home plate, and it was 461 feet to dead center, with the monuments honoring Yankees greats in play. Oliva loved hitting there. He says he liked to move closer to the plate and was much more of a pull hitter with the short porch just 296 feet down the right-field line. But his inside-the-park home run to deep center, his eighteenth homer of the season, was a footrace.

On July 16, with the Washington Senators at the Met, Oliva kicked off his longest hitting streak of the season. He went on a seventeen-game run in which he took a substantial lead in the AL batting race. The Twins lost eight in a row and fourteen of seventeen in this stretch, but Oliva was relentless with the bat. He had two or more hits in seven of the last eight games of the streak. On July's final day, in a 4–3 win over the visiting Yankees, the hot-hitting rookie extended his run to sixteen games with a two-strike, two-out single that was classic Tony O. He threw his bat at the ball and sent it into right field for the base hit.

After hitting safely in his seventeenth straight game on August 1, Oliva was batting .339. He had opened a sixteen-point lead over Mantle, his closest competitor, and had moved twenty-eight points in front of Allison, who endured a 2-for-26 skid the last week of July. Only two other AL players were within striking distance: Jim Fregosi, the Angels' twenty-two-year-old shortstop, hitting .315 in the midst of a breakout season in which he stroked eighteen home runs, and Baltimore third baseman Brooks Robinson, who was hitting .310.

Oliva maintained his torrid pace by demonstrating an uncanny ability to adjust to the way big league pitchers worked him. That was the case with Detroit at the Met on August 11. The Twins fell behind 3–0, but Oliva doubled and scored in a two-run fourth inning. He also struck out twice against Tigers southpaw Hank Aguirre, but in the seventh, with two outs, no one on base, and the score 3–3, Oliva was 0–2 in the count when he teed off on a slow curve from Detroit's curveball–screwball specialist. He drove the pitch on a line into the right-field bleachers, putting Minnesota in front en route to a 5–3 win.

The home run, his twenty-sixth, showed how dangerous the rookie could be, no matter how foolish a pitcher might have made him look in a previous at-bat. Oliva had taken the same slow curve *twice* for strike three earlier in the game, but he was not fooled a third time. Aguirre found too much of the plate and, as usual, Oliva did not miss a mistake. He admitted he had been looking for the bender and had guessed right. "You look good sometimes and look bad sometimes," Oliva said after the game, taking a matter-of-fact approach talking to *Pioneer Press* writer Glenn Redmann.

The thirty-four-year-old Aguirre, pitching in his tenth big league season, was less inclined to play down what Oliva did that day. Talking with *Minneapolis Tribune* staff writer Dwayne Netland, the lefthander heaped praise on the Twins rookie. "Nobody stands in there and slashes at the ball like Oliva," Aguirre said, adding, "Sure, I struck him out twice. But I had two strikes on him on both his double and home run. I really respect that guy. He battles the pitcher. . . . He's the best lefthanded hitter in the American League since Ted Williams."

The comparison to Williams, the "Splendid Splinter," came a day after Mele, his friend and former teammate in Boston, had written him a letter telling him about the new kid on the block. "Ted always liked to see a kid stand in there like that and battle those lefthanders," Mele declared. No doubt Oliva's first manager was a believer. "I'm convinced this boy is not just a hitter having a hot year. He's hit too many good pitchers this summer for that."

On August 18, the team met President Lyndon Johnson and Senator Hubert H. Humphrey during a tour of the White House before opening a series with the Washington Senators. Although less than two weeks later Humphrey would become Johnson's running mate in the 1964 presidential election, the Minnesota senator was at the White House that day as a Twins fan.

Everyone in the Twins' party shook hands with the president, including rookie pitcher Gerry Arrigo, whose second encounter with the commander in chief went better than his first. In mid-June, when both the Twins and LBJ were in Cleveland, Arrigo had come across the presidential motorcade and had had an opportunity to approach Johnson. The Twins hurler was carrying a package containing a lamp for his daughter's bedroom, causing the always-vigilant Secret Service to quickly step in and restrain him.

One of the happiest members of the Minnesota contingent was Camilo Pascual, who had arrived from Cuba in 1951 and was playing his eleventh major league season with the franchise. The Bay of Pigs incident three years earlier had isolated Pascual from family members in Cuba, but during the Washington visit, State Department officials informed him that his parents were scheduled to arrive in the United States within a week. They and four other relatives had reached Mexico City and were awaiting clearance from the U.S. embassy. The Twins pitcher had been working with Humphrey for more than a year to facilitate his family's release. Pascual's celebratory mood carried onto the field that night, as he went the distance and scattered eight hits in a 6–1 win that was close until the Twins tallied five runs in the seventh inning. In the midst of a season-high six-game winning streak, Minnesota had returned to .500 at 60–60.

With a single in the win over Washington, by August 18 Oliva had hit safely in thirty-one of his previous thirty-three games. But the long season was taking its toll. The knuckle injury he had suffered in May was a constant source of pain. The region around home plate was a danger zone, with Oliva inadvertently throwing bats more frequently as the season wore on. While making contact was not a problem, swinging and missing was extremely painful. The discomfort was obvious on a late-August Sunday afternoon in Detroit. Oliva literally had the bat knocked out of his hands three times by Mickey Lolich. The lefty worked into the eighth inning and struck out ten, though Oliva delivered a run-scoring single against him in the fourth. He had driven in Minnesota's only run until Don Mincher powered an eighth-inning grand slam off Fred Gladding to tie the game at 5–5. In the ninth, Oliva singled, driving in winning pitcher Al Worthington with the go-ahead run.

Injured or not, Oliva kept hitting. He closed August with a dramatic eighth-inning home run to clinch a seesaw 5–4 victory over Washington. He had committed two costly errors earlier in the game, but he escaped goat status by pulling an eighth-inning pitch from reliever Al Koch into the right-field bleachers to break a 4–4 tie. After Oliva nailed down the win, reporters asked if he was thinking about making up for his fielding mistakes when he stepped to the plate. "Nada," Oliva said and laughed. "I don't think about anything when I'm hitting." The strategy worked for him. Plenty of distractions can get in the way—a slump, a bad at-bat, a key miscue, or personal issues off the field—and keeping such things out of mind can be difficult for a prospect in his first major league trial. Not for Oliva.

The Twins wanted Oliva to be a tablesetter as a rookie. He gave them that, and power, too. With thirty-two home runs, he was one of only nine American Leaguers to reach the thirty plateau. He delivered his twenty-ninth and thirtieth in the Friday opener of a Labor Day–weekend series with the Red Sox at the Met, where the home team put fourteen on the board in a lopsided win.

Number thirty was an inside-the-park job that highlighted a five-run eighth inning. Oliva drilled a scorching groundball through the legs of second baseman Eddie Bressoud and took off as the ball rolled to the wall in right-center. With right fielder Lee Thomas and center fielder Carl Yastrzemski in hot pursuit, Oliva wheeled around the bases looking for three. The ball was finally retrieved, but it was sent back toward the infield with a weak relay throw, so Oliva ran through a stop sign at third and came home with his second inside-the-park homer of the season.

Oliva added another memorable moment to an extraordinary rookie year on Labor Day, when a doubleheader was planned, though an evening rain limited the Twins and Yankees to a single afternoon matchup on what was the final day of summer for kids going back to school. With Jim Bouton on the mound, the Yankees enjoyed a comfortable 4–0 lead going into the eighth inning. Bob Allison connected on a two-out two-run homer, and Bouton was pulled when Rich Rollins followed with a single. Zoilo Versalles doubled off righthander Pete Mikkelsen, bringing Berra back out to make another pitching change. With New York still in front, 4–2, and two outs, Berra called for six-foot-six lefthander Steve Hamilton to face Oliva with both Rollins and Versalles in scoring position.

After Oliva had thrown the bat twice while failing to connect, he went a foot outside the strike zone to make contact on a Hamilton slider that was breaking away from him. Once again the bat left Oliva's hands, but this time the ball blooped over the head of shortstop Tony Kubek into left-center field, scoring both runners to tie the game.

This remarkable piece of hitting certainly looked like a thrown-bat single, which is how it was reported in newspaper accounts. Yet Oliva maintained he still had one hand on the bat and had not actually thrown it at the pitch. Yankees catcher Elston Howard saw it differently. "I don't know how he ever hit that pitch in the eighth inning," Howard told beat writers after the game. "He's either good, lucky or both. He threw his bat at the ball!" Did it matter if Oliva was in possession of his bat when he made contact? The answer still would not explain how the talented rookie put the ball into play so artfully.

With barely more than two weeks left to the season, Baltimore's Brooks Robinson was the only contender still in the AL batting race. The Orioles third baseman had a September to remember, batting .381 and driving in runs in bunches. Although Killebrew and Oliva had a chance to take all three Triple Crown categories—Oliva the batting championship and Killebrew the homer and RBI crowns—Robinson overtook Killebrew for the league RBI title, with twenty-four in his last seventeen games.

Despite Robinson's strong finish, he could not close the gap on Oliva. Tony O hit safely in thirteen of fourteen games to close the season, batting .373 to keep Robinson from claiming two of the three Triple Crown categories. But Robinson, with a .317 average, 28 homers, and 118 RBIs, was named the American League's Most Valuable Player at season's end.

Oliva won his first batting title with a .323 average, the highest mark posted by a rookie since fellow Cuban Minnie Miñoso hit .326 for Cleveland and the White Sox in 1951. "I finished second to Tony that year," Robinson recalls. "I was the MVP, but for a rookie to come into the league and win the batting crown, that just doesn't happen. To come into the league and be that kind of hitter, it doesn't happen."

After hitting safely in his final seven games, Oliva had accumulated a major league–leading 217 hits. To that point in the modern era, only two rookies had recorded more hits in a season: "Shoeless" Joe Jackson, who collected 233 for Cleveland in 1911, and Pittsburgh's Lloyd Waner, with 223 in 1923. Jackson's total stood as the record for ninety years, until Ichiro Suzuki surpassed it with 242 in his Seattle Mariners debut in 2001.

On the season's final day, with the first AL batting title by a rookie already secured, Oliva capped a brilliant coming-out party with a triple in three trips. While the Twins concluded a disappointing summer with a 3–0 loss to the Angels at the Met, Oliva's ninth three-bagger of 1964 gave him 374 total bases, a major league high. To this day, he and Hal Trosky, a slugging first baseman who batted .330 with thirty-five homers and 142 RBIs for Cleveland in 1934, share the rookie mark for total bases.

Oliva not only stroked thirty-two homers but an AL-leading forty-three doubles. The power display was unanticipated, but Oliva's ability to make hard contact consistently was equally impressive. He accumulated four four-hit games, seven hitting streaks of seven or more games, and four two-homer performances. The American League's Rookie the Year also drew attention as an MVP candidate. He finished fourth in the vote behind Robinson, who won AL honors convincingly, and Yankees stars Mickey Mantle and Elston Howard.

Oliva secured nineteen of twenty first-place votes in AL Rookie of the Year balloting. But ranking among the league's top rookie vote getters in 1964 might seem to have been a curse. The three AL rookies pulling down the highest point totals—Oliva, Baltimore's Wally Bunker, and Boston's Tony Conigliaro—had careers significantly compromised or shortened by injury. Oliva, of course, had his knees to blame.

Baltimore righthander Wally Bunker, second in the voting, won his first six starts, the first a 2–1 one-hitter over Washington on May 5. The nineteen-year-old rookie was at his best at the end of the season, going 6–1 in September to finish 19–5 with a 2.95 ERA for the 97–65 Orioles. Only Cy Young Award winner Dean Chance of the Angels (20–9) and White Sox lefthander Gary Peters (20–8) won more games than Bunker in the American League, though the Orioles rookie topped the league with a .792 winning percentage. He claimed the one first-place vote not cast for Oliva.

After a breakout season as a rookie, Bunker developed a sore arm the following summer. He worked just one two-hundred-inning season after his rookie campaign—with the expansion Kansas City Royals in 1969—and two years later, recurring arm woes forced him to retire with a 60–52 lifetime record.

Another teenager, Boston prospect Tony Conigliaro, ranked third in the rookie balloting. The nineteen-year-old outfielder, blessed with an abundance of talent and desire, was a Boston-area native who became the darling of Red Sox fans with a terrific rookie season. He batted a career-high .290 and belted twenty-four homers in just 111 games, as he lost six weeks to injury.

Those numbers might have been good enough to secure rookie honors in a year without a player as spectacular as Oliva.

The slugging righthanded hitter seemed a perfect fit for Fenway Park. In 1965, Conigliaro, all of twenty years old, became the youngest player to win a home-run crown with thirty-two dingers in an otherwise disastrous season for the Red Sox. Boston lost one hundred games in Conigliaro's second season—a year sandwiched between ninety-loss campaigns—but the budding star, paired in the lineup with Carl Yastrzemski, gave the Red Sox faithful hope.

Two years later, in the heat of the 1967 pennant race, Conigliaro took a pitch square in the face in a mid-August contest with the Angels. Bleeding profusely from his nose and with his left eye swelling shut almost immediately, Conigliaro was carried off on a stretcher by teammates. He spent the rest of the season in the hospital and did not return until 1969. Despite now being blind in his left eye, Conigliaro was a productive hitter for two seasons, including a career year in 1970, when he set personal bests with thirty-six home runs and 116 RBIs. Injuries and worsening sight forced him out of baseball soon after—at age twenty-six. A futile comeback effort in 1975 lasted twenty-one games.

Life seemed to have set its milestones prematurely for Conigliaro, including his passing. He experienced major league success as a teenager, retirement before reaching his prime, and an incapacitating heart attack the month he turned thirty-seven. Tragically, he required around-the-clock care for the final eight years of his life and died seven weeks after his forty-fifth birthday in 1990.

Oliva Leads Pennant Push

ost Minnesotans were not thinking about baseball in spring 1965. Instead, the forces of nature were foremost in their minds, as news of extreme weather dominated the airwaves and hijacked attention. After a bitter, cold winter that laid layer upon layer of snow on the north country, March floods on the Root and Zumbro Rivers in southeast Minnesota began a cycle of destruction and misery that beset dozens of towns along the state's main waterways. Heavy snowfall continued well into March, and a late thaw prolonged the inevitable flooding. Then spring came with a vengeance.

By early April, when ice jams on the rivers began to melt, waters rose to dangerous levels across the eastern part of the state. The Vermillion River near Hastings was the first to overrun its banks in April. Soon after, communities along the Minnesota, Blue Earth, Crow, St. Croix, and Mississippi Rivers were struggling to stay above climbing water levels. Some towns were deluged by floodwaters from more than one source. Newspapers and TV newscasts daily featured images of anxious residents piling sandbags and building dikes. Thousands of homes and buildings were under water, and some flood victims had to navigate city streets in boats. At least 22,000 Minnesotans were forced from their homes during the worst flood season in the region's recorded history.

While those near the river were awaiting the onslaught of floodwaters, the Twins were out of harm's way in Florida, training after a disappointing 1964 season. News out of the Twins' camp that spring had little impact on flood-ravaged Minnesota, though one story may have been interpreted as a bad omen.

New third-base coach Billy Martin had been working all spring with twenty-five-year-old shortstop Zoilo Versalles, whose lack of focus and maturity had baffled the Twins since 1961. That year, Martin and Versalles had been double-play partners, and now the retired second baseman played mentor. Versalles had responded well to Martin's coaching in Florida, but the two hit a bump in the road before the team broke camp. During a game in the final week of spring training, skipper Sam Mele believed that his short-stop had failed to give maximum effort on a routine grounder that got past him and led to two runs in a loss to the New York Mets. Mele replaced Versalles one pitch later with rookie infielder Bill Bethea. Pulled off the field, Versalles headed to the outfield to finish his running for the day, but Martin confronted him when he returned to the dugout.

When Mele stepped in and told Versalles to sit on the bench on the chance he might learn something, Versalles angrily replied that he would sit on the bench for Martin, but not for his manager. His display of loyalty to Martin quickly became costly, as *St. Paul Pioneer Press* writer Arno Goethel recounted from his spring-training beat in Florida:

"That'll cost you $100," said Mele.
"Why not make it $200?" Versalles countered.
"Okay," said Mele. "It's $200."
Versalles persisted. "Why not make it $300?"
"That's what it is," Mele agreed.

And so it was. The skipper freed his insubordinate player of three hundred dollars. In an effort to recoup some of that lost cash, Versalles had a face-to-face chat with ever-stingy owner Calvin Griffith, but it proved futile.

Interestingly enough, the incident was *not* an omen for the kind of season Versalles or the Twins would have in 1965. However, it *did* illustrate the way mass media shaped the image of Latino players in that era. Cubans, especially those without a working knowledge of English, received little coverage and were quoted in Twin Cities newspapers less often than their teammates. The attention they did receive often mimicked the media coverage afforded most Third World countries: we only hear about them if they suffer a natural disaster or are at the center of a controversy.

Versalles struggled with English and rarely talked to reporters. His first year as a major league regular was 1961, the year Washington's Senators moved to Minnesota. The twenty-one-year-old rookie was reserved and sometimes moody, and the challenges of establishing himself in the majors were complicated by the Bay of Pigs fiasco that spring. He had lost contact with his family, including his young wife Maria Josefa, pregnant back in Cuba with Ampy, the first of six children. Diplomatic efforts to get Maria to the United States repeatedly hit snags, causing Versalles to become increasingly lonely and distraught.

The youngster had been a popular attraction at the inaugural Minnesota Twins Welcome Home Luncheon prior to Opening Day in 1961, and by the start of June, he was batting .308 with a team-high twelve doubles. He found media attention, though, only when his frustration with the political process boiled over. After the Twins swept a Fourth of July doubleheader from the Chicago White Sox, Versalles emptied his locker and announced he was going home to his family in Cuba. He did not show for a game against the Angels at Metropolitan Stadium the following evening, and Griffith immediately suspended him and fined him $500—a substantial chunk of Versalles's roughly $7,000 salary. Even a lengthy meeting with Griffith the following afternoon could not convince Versalles to change his mind. Although he said that Griffith had treated him well as a member of the organization, the young man still insisted on going home.

"When I left for the United States two years ago, my mother didn't want me to go," Versalles explained to reporters. "I told her I'd make good money for her. She died and I never saw her again. Now I'm tired and want to go home." He must have spoken those words with a touch of despair; as much as he wanted to return to Cuba at that point, he did not have the cash to purchase an airline ticket.

Versalles, who battled health issues throughout his life, developed an ulcer during his three-week absence from the Twins. His life took an upturn, however, when a wealthy Minneapolis family read of his plight and invited him to stay at their home. The generous offer from investment counselor Farrell Stiehm proved a big assist to the impoverished Versalles. Mrs. Stiehm, already busy raising eleven children, said she would "mother" the newest family member. When Maria, still a teenager, was finally allowed to leave Cuba during her husband's time away from the team, they lived with the Stiehms until solidifying their financial situation.

Going AWOL in 1961 and getting into a public spat with his manager four years later made some observers see Versalles as "temperamental." He

Tony Oliva with the Charlotte Hornets in 1962. Courtesy of the Minnesota Twins.

Minnie Mendoza, who befriended Oliva and directed him to Charlotte general manager Phil Howser when Oliva had nowhere to go but back to Cuba. Bob Jackson/*Denver Post.*

Julio Bécquer, a mentor to Oliva, was the elder statesman of the Cuban contingent that moved from Washington to Minnesota in 1961. Bécquer and Oliva remain close friends today. Courtesy of the Minnesota Twins.

Frank Quilici, one of Oliva's first teammates in the United States and a longtime friend. Courtesy of the Minnesota Twins.

Oliva receiving his Silver Louisville Slugger in the Charlotte hospital room of scout Papa Joe Cambria in 1961. They were joined by Phil Howser *(second from left)* and a Louisville Slugger representative *(far right)*. Courtesy of the Minnesota Twins.

Fellow Cuban José Valdivielso, who made the move from Washington to Minnesota in 1961. Courtesy of the Minnesota Twins.

Oliva sits in his room at the Chicago Sheraton before a night game against the White Sox, less than a month into his first big league season in May 1964. Photograph by Bud Daley, *Chicago Daily News.* Courtesy of Sun–Times Media.

Oliva settles into the batter's box, digging a foot into position as he prepares his hands to hit. More than a few pitchers thought the process took too long. Courtesy of the Minnesota Twins.

Oliva's bat is airborne during a game with the Kansas City Athletics on May 8, 1964. Keeping the bat in hand became difficult after he injured the big knuckle on his right middle finger that season. Courtesy of the Minnesota Twins.

Twins owner Calvin Griffith ordered a specially designed flap for Oliva's batting helmet after the rookie was beaned by Baltimore's Steve Barber in May 1964. Earl Battey (*right*) also began wearing one after a 1961 beaning. Courtesy of Sporting News Collection.

American League president Joe Cronin presents Oliva with the Silver Bat Award for winning the American League batting title in 1964. Courtesy of Sporting News Collection.

Oliva won Rookie of the Year honors and the American League batting title in 1964, only four years after leaving his family farm in Cuba. He repeated as batting champion in 1965 and remains the only major leaguer to claim titles in his first two seasons. Courtesy of the Minnesota Twins.

Oliva has a reputation for pleasing autograph seekers, and his generosity with fans continues to this day. Courtesy of the Minnesota Twins.

Camilo Pascual *(right)*, the Twins' original ace and a Havana native, chats with Minnesota's first catcher, Earl Battey, a fellow Spanish speaker. Courtesy of the Minnesota Twins.

The Cuban stars of the 1965 American League champion Minnesota Twins, Zoilo Versalles *(right)* and Tony Oliva. Both won postseason recognition: Oliva took the batting title and Versalles the MVP trophy. Courtesy of the Minnesota Twins.

Oliva and Sandy Valdespino *(left)* were teammates with the Triple-A Dallas–Fort Worth Rangers in 1963. Oliva arrived in Minnesota the following spring and Valdespino a year later in 1965. Courtesy of the Minnesota Twins.

Manager Sam Mele *(left)* piloted the 1965 Twins to the AL pennant, despite numerous injuries among players. Role players and rookies, including Frank Quilici *(right)*, aided the club's push to its first World Series in Minnesota. Courtesy of the Minnesota Twins.

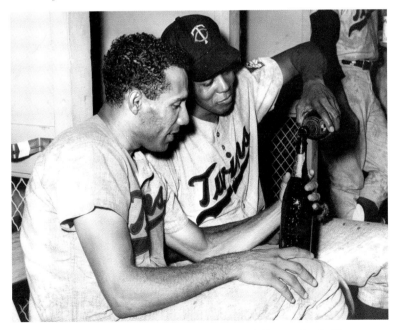

Zoilo Versalles *(left)* and Oliva share champagne in the clubhouse after the Twins clinched the American League pennant on September 26, 1965, in Washington, D.C. Courtesy of the Minnesota Twins.

Oliva tumbles after completing a running shoestring catch during the first inning in Game Seven of the 1965 World Series. UPI Photo Files.

American League president Joe Cronin presents Oliva with his second consecutive Silver Bat Award for winning the batting title in 1965. Twins owner Calvin Griffith watches the ceremony. Courtesy of the Minnesota Twins.

From left, Venezuelan native César Tovar, Zoilo Versalles, and Oliva take in the view from the Twins dugout. Courtesy of the Minnesota Twins.

Oliva hit a walk-off home run leading off the ninth inning on September 25, 1966, securing Jim Kaat's league-leading twenty-fifth win. Courtesy of the Minnesota Twins.

Oliva and future Hall of Famer Frank Robinson look down the barrel of a bat before a Twins–Orioles matchup. Courtesy of the Minnesota Twins.

Before a game at Metropolitan Stadium in 1967, Oliva is presented his Gold Glove by Rawlings representatives. Twins prospects Jim Ollom (*second from left*) and Rich Reese (*third from left*) were also honored for impressive minor league seasons in 1966. Courtesy of the Minnesota Twins.

certainly could be that when criticized by his manager or a coach, especially in front of others. He was likely to face both challenges and criticism with the same brash air, although later in life Versalles admitted that his apparent confidence and occasional cockiness masked a deep insecurity.

Media coverage also presented a distorted and incomplete picture of a complicated and intriguing man. Versalles grew up in a one-room shack on Havana's outskirts. He did not complete grade school and taught himself to read his native language. He was eighteen when the Senators signed him before the 1958 season. Like so many of his fellow Cubans, Versalles was devastated when political tensions between the United States and the Castro regime worsened after the failed Bay of Pigs invasion. The youngest of the six Cubans on the Twins' 1961 roster, Versalles faced the pressure of trying to establish himself in the majors while separated from family.

Family meant everything to Versalles. His oldest daughter, Ampy Versalles-Curtis, remembers him as "a very loving, caring and emotionally sensitive person" who doted on his children. He was perpetually concerned to make sure they had whatever they needed; he had often gone without shoes and other basics while growing up.

Versalles's warmth and generosity were apparent to his friends, as well, including fellow Havana native Julio Bécquer, who first met Versalles on a baseball field in the late 1940s. "I played with Zoilo when I was seventeen," Bécquer recalls. "I was with Zoilo all the time. Zoilo wasn't that difficult. He was a free spirit. A lot of people took it the wrong way. Zoilo was very, very nice, and he had a big heart. You asked Zoilo for anything, he gave it to you without thinking about it." At home, Versalles was so softhearted that disciplinary duties fell to Maria. She took charge of running the house, of course, when he and the Twins traveled during the baseball season.

Versalles-Curtis says that when her father was home, music was a fixture of everyday life. "My dad sang all the time," she says. "Music was a huge part of our household. And we all sang. My dad would have friends over and eventually it would all end with music. Everybody would grab an instrument. I can play the spoons to this day. You'd have to have something. Or you'd hit the side of a glass or something, and everybody would get into whatever it was. My uncle Ramón played the guitar. So did my grandfather Zoilo and his brother Ramón. They'd all play guitar and we'd sing old songs, more of the Buena Vista Social Club kind of music." Versalles's passion was opera, an art form that might seem incongruous for a man who grew up dirt-poor in Cuba. He skillfully sang the music he adored, and it was not unusual for teammates to hear his powerful voice emanating from the club-house shower after a game. The same was true at home. "He'd just break into song," Versalles-Curtis recalls fondly, "especially Giacomo Puccini's 'Nessun Dorma.' Luciano Pavarotti singing it was his favorite."

Another of Versalles's passions was food, something often in short sup-ply when he was growing up in Cuba. Though he grew up eating simply, he became masterful and creative in the kitchen, cooking with a flair that drew raves from family and friends. His approach to food seemed to match his chaotic, sometimes erratic approach to life: he cooked without recipes and frequently made something of nothing. "He would put things together that you would never imagine would go together," says Versalles-Curtis, "and it would taste great."

Versalles regularly prepared a more traditional meal that made a lasting impression on his daughters, though his timing was a tad unconventional. When their father arrived home from a team road trip, usually late at night after an afternoon game earlier in the day, the girls knew he would greet them with a feast. "We knew he was home because we would smell pancakes and hear opera music," Versalles-Curtis says with a laugh. "We'd pop out of bed in our pajamas. 'Poppy's home! Poppy's home!' and he'd made pancakes and bacon and sausage and eggs. We'd listen to opera music and have orange juice and eat pancakes."

Versalles-Curtis says that growing up in Bloomington was anything but traditional. Her parents did not speak much English and were new to Amer-ican culture, so they and their children had to navigate unfamiliar social customs in the then-lily-white Minneapolis suburb. She adds that her father also grappled with obsessive-compulsive issues. "It made him a very nervous person," Versalles-Curtis explains. She believes his predisposition to com-pulsive behavior and anxiety was magnified by "things that happened in his life and how rough it was—being somebody who didn't know the language, whose mother had passed away, whose wife was pregnant in another coun-try. And then you have the Bay of Pigs and all these things going on. You put all those things together and you can have a lot of anxiety issues. It can affect your relationship with people who don't know you very well. It can affect how people take what you do and why you're doing it. People misinterpreted what was going on."

Versalles's obsessive-compulsive tendencies sparked a deep-seated desire to give his children what he had never had. It also fueled wild spending habits. If Versalles saw something he liked, he bought it. A frequent stop was a clothing store in Cleveland that was popular among players. Oliva says that Versalles tended to buy two or three of everything, whether shirts, shoes or accessories. "Zoilo dressed like a million dollars all the time," Oliva recalls. "Everything he'd wear was perfect. His suit, his pants, his shoes, his shirt all looked perfect. He was a nice dresser."

Then there were the impulsive road trips, often to buy food products preferred by Cubans but not easily found in the Twin Cities. At a moment's notice, Versalles would jump into his car and head to Chicago to buy the ingredients he needed for Cuban dishes. He was often accompanied by Oliva, who says, only half-jokingly, that his friend might drive from Minneapolis to Miami to get a haircut. Versalles-Curtis says that those last-second road trips, often to visit relatives in Miami, continued long after her father's baseball career concluded.

But soon after Versalles left the game, he fell on hard times. He certainly was neither the first nor the last professional athlete to struggle after retiring, but Versalles's employment options were especially limited and generated little income. He had never become fluent at reading or writing English, and a back injury suffered in 1968 while he was with the Dodgers led to chronic pain during his retirement years. The back ailment eventually prevented him from performing physical labor, forcing him to give up a well-paying job as a cargo loader for Northwest Airlines. He worked a series of menial jobs, and in time, he lost his house to foreclosure and sold off his 1965 MVP trophy, his All-Star rings, and his Gold Glove Awards. Sadly, Versalles's overall health also took a downturn. He suffered two heart attacks and endured stomach surgery before dying of heart disease at age fifty-five in 1995.

But thirty years earlier, a confident Versalles had been at the very top of his game. The wiry, 150-pound shortstop displayed an impressive blend of power and speed. He had powered twenty homers in 1964—then a rare feat for a shortstop—and ran as well as anyone in the majors.

Versalles was one of his era's premier defensive shortstops, fluid and graceful with an artful flair. He made quite an impression on another promising shortstop, Frank Quilici, an All-American at Western Michigan who signed with the Twins in 1961. He recalls getting his first look at the Twins' defensive whiz and immediately knowing what it meant for him. "The Twins told me that they didn't think I could play shortstop in the big leagues, so they wanted me to move over to second base," Quilici says. "Of course I was a little cocky until I went to spring training with the Twins and I saw a guy working out at shortstop. I said, 'Who's that?' And a teammate said, 'Zoilo Versalles.' I said, 'Where's second base?'"

Like Versalles, Oliva endured a difficult spring in Florida. The knuckle injury in his right middle finger, which he had suffered in May 1964, bedeviled him from the start of spring training. The reigning batting champion suffered all season from a floating bone chip in that knuckle. He also ran into an outfield fence during spring training in 1964, which led to a sore right knee that he struggled with later in the year. A bone chip would occasionally settle into the knee joint, causing great pain. But the finger was especially problematic.

To minimize the risk of further injury to Oliva's already painful knuckle, the Twins had asked their new star to bypass winter ball for the first time in his brief pro career. Oliva says the layoff came with a price. He lost his swing and his timing at the plate, and he gained twenty pounds eating well during an extended visit to Puerto Rico. His weight ballooned to nearly two hundred pounds, compromising his efforts to regain his swing. The pain in the knuckle did not help.

Twins trainer Doc Lentz had designed a ring cushion made of rubber for the finger, which Oliva began wearing when the knuckle became troublesome in '64. The cushion absorbed some of the discomfort from swinging, but the knuckle swelled the next spring after a March spring training game. Oliva even tried using a bat without a knob in an effort to reduce the soreness in the finger. The source of the months-long discomfort was not diagnosed until late March, when the bone chip made its first appearance on an X-ray. Since surgery to remove the chip would sideline Oliva for ten weeks, all parties agreed to delay it until the end of the 1965 campaign. While the rubber cushion would help Oliva get through the season, the best remedy for the pain was to hit the ball on the money. "My finger doesn't bother me when I make contact with the ball," Oliva told writers in Florida. "Only when I swing and miss, then the finger hurts." Talk about an incentive to win another American League batting title.

Repeating would not come easy. The Twins started fast, but it took Oliva nearly two months of the season to regain his timing. Hitless in his first twelve at-bats, he did not clear .250 to stay until May 31. By the end of June, Oliva was batting .268 and trailed the league leader, Boston's Carl Yastrzemski, by seventy-four points.

Oliva still believed he was going to rank among the league leaders by season's end. He recalls Bob Allison, who had vacated right field to make room for him the previous spring, trying to take some pressure off him when things were not going well. Allison told him not to worry because young hitters do struggle, and a down year does sometimes happen. The second-year player was not ready to concede, as Oliva recounts. "I told Bobby, 'By the time the season's over, I am going to be hitting .300.' I knew I could still hit .300." And he was right. From July 1 through the end of the season, a stretch of seventy-eight games, Oliva hit .374, and he overtook Yastrzemski in September.

"I remember he would get on tears where it didn't make any difference whether it was Jim Palmer or Denny McLain, they could not get him out," says Dick Bremer, the Twins' longtime broadcaster. "Major league hitters have those periods, I suppose, where they just are locked in. For Tony, it seemed like those periods lasted longer than for most ballplayers."

Despite Oliva's slow start and Versalles's spring rebellion, manager Sam Mele steered the 1965 club to a first-place finish with virtually the same talent that had disappointed the year before. The Twins claimed 102 victories and the first American League pennant the Senators-turned-Twins had achieved in thirty-two years, spearheading the demise of the mighty Yankees. The Twins got off to a good start and were in the race from the beginning. Their early success proved to be a good buffer, as the club endured a host of injuries, perhaps more than any other AL club that summer.

Ace righthander Camilo Pascual tore a muscle in his back in late July and was out until September. Harmon Killebrew went down in August with a dislocated and fractured elbow and missed forty-eight games. Also missing substantial time were Bob Allison, who fractured a small bone in his wrist; rookie hurler Dave Boswell, out for a month with mononucleosis; and catcher Earl Battey, who was sidelined thirteen times by assorted injuries.

A key to Minnesota's success was Billy Martin, who made the Twins far more aggressive on the bases. Martin's penchant for stealing and taking the extra base gave the power-laden Twins lineup an added dimension. Martin's pet project was refining the skills and boosting the confidence of the young infielder. "Zoilo Versalles can win the Most Valuable Player Award," Martin proclaimed prior to the '65 campaign. "He has all the tools. Someone just has to teach him." That someone was Martin, who worked constantly with Versalles on bunting and base stealing.

Much has been written over the years claiming that Versalles turned in one of the poorest-ever MVP performances, compared to other MVP winners. Many thought Oliva, with his strong second half, deserved the honor in 1965. But while Versalles lacked impressive hitting percentages, he led the American League with 126 runs, 76 extra-base hits, and 308 total bases—and it is hard to imagine the Twins winning the AL pennant without him. He always seemed to figure in late-game rallies, either getting on base to start trouble or driving in a key run in a clutch situation. Versalles also played one of the more demanding defensive positions and excelled at it. "Billy knew how to get the best out of his players," says Oliva. He credits Martin with knowing how to successfully and respectfully work with Versalles, an intelligent and proud man who often lacked confidence. He wholeheartedly plugged into what Martin told him.

In fact, Martin had the entire Twins lineup running more aggressively, and the difference was immediately apparent. The club ran off six wins in its first seven games, including a dramatic eleven-inning Opening Day victory over the five-time defending American League champion Yankees at the Met.

The season began on a typically blustery day for early April. Starting pitcher Jim Kaat, third baseman Rich Rollins, and reliever Dick Stigman, who were housed in an apartment complex in nearby Burnsville, had to be flown to the ballpark by helicopter because a bridge on their route was still under water from recent floods. Oliva, on the other hand, did not have to contend with the Mississippi to get to work. He was still at the Hotel Maryland in downtown Minneapolis, which like the Met was west of the raging river. Floodwaters had threatened but spared the downtown area when they crested the week after the season opener.

Tony O had his own troubles. He had collected seven hits in his first thirteen at-bats to kick-start his stellar rookie season. Now he needed thirteen at-bats to secure his first hit of 1965—a seventh-inning single to left field off Indians reliever Sonny Siebert in the third game. Oliva's bat did show some spark when the Twins traveled to the Bronx to open New York's home schedule. He always liked taking shots at Yankee Stadium's short fence in right field.

There was also something special about playing in New York, Oliva recalls. A large contingent of Cubans came to the park, and some of them would pick up Oliva and his fellow Cubans and drive them around the city to show them the sights. Sometimes they took Oliva, Versalles, and Pascual to their homes and cooked them familiar favorites such as rice, black beans, and pork. The opportunity to speak in Spanish with people sharing common interests and experiences comforted the Cuban players, most of whom still had limited contact with family and friends.

Those off-the-field excursions provided a nice break from the daily routine and ate up a lot of dead time on road trips. When the Twins were home, Oliva lived alone at the Hotel Maryland, an early-twentieth-century apartment hotel on the corner of LaSalle Avenue and Grant Street in Minneapolis, two blocks from Loring Park. The five-story brick building was U-shaped, with a courtyard in the middle and a café on the first floor. Oliva's room had a small kitchen, and like a lot of Latin players at the time, he learned to cook some of his favorite dishes from home, including rice and beans. He had grown to like porterhouse steaks, and he often prepared them in his apartment.

Nearly all the Twins players, including the other Cubans, were married. A few might reside temporarily at the Hotel Maryland at the start of the season until they found a place to live in the Twin Cities, but Oliva, as a single man, lived there for a few years. He grew tired of living alone and cooking for only himself, so the interaction with other Cubans on road trips was exhilarating.

There was nothing like New York, and it did not take much to get juiced about playing the Yankees. Despite his early troubles at the plate in 1965, Oliva was always ready for a trip to the Bronx. This time, the Twins claimed two victories, spoiling New York's home opener on April 21 with a 7–2 romp and thumping the Yankees 8–2 the following day. Twins hitters powered three homers each afternoon.

The Bronx Bombers drew 39,082 fans to Yankee Stadium on Opening Day, the largest home-opener crowd since 1952, but the big turnout went home with less-than-fond memories of two-run homers by Oliva, Rich Rollins, and Jimmie Hall. Oliva slipped a pitch from Yankees starter Mel Stottlemyre just inside the left-field foul pole, giving Minnesota a 3–2 edge in the third inning. The opposite-way shot was just his third hit of the season, but connecting on the game-winner reduced the sting of a 3-for-21 start.

Oliva drilled two more homers the next day, stroking a pair of impressive two-run shots down the right-field line. The first came off Yankees reliever Hal Reniff in the seventh inning. Then, in the ninth, Oliva jumped on a slider from fellow Piñar del Río native Pedro Ramos. Oliva had been fooled by the same pitch earlier in the count, missing by not a few inches but a few feet. Fooling Oliva more than once never came easy, and he hit the second slider on the money into the seats.

Versalles generated the most excitement in the second game of the series, however, with an inside-the-park homer off Ramos. With two out in the ninth, Versalles lined a shot between left fielder Mickey Mantle and Tom Tresh in center. As the ball rolled to the wall nearly 450 feet from home plate, Versalles turned on the jets and easily beat the relay home. The young speedster flashed a dazzling slide across home to complete a three-hit, three-RBI day.

Those three April victories over the Yankees set the tone for the 1965 pennant race. In their first four seasons in Minnesota, the Twins had never won a season series from the Yankees, but this time they claimed thirteen of eighteen matchups and unseated the only club to win the AL flag since their move to the Midwest.

For most of the season, the Yankees floundered near .500. They were in sixth place, 12.5 games behind the first-place Twins, when they arrived at the Met for four weekend games leading up to the All-Star break. On the eve of the series opener, New York ace Whitey Ford told *St. Paul Pioneer Press* writer Glenn Redmann that he believed his 40–43 Yankees could still emerge victorious in the 1965 pennant race. While he conceded that the Twins had the most potent offense in the circuit, he added, "We still think we have the best team in the American League. Once we get over that .500 mark, I think we'll be OK and ready to move." Although Ford and the Yankees had history on their side, the first-place Twins, with a seven-game winning streak and with Cleveland, Baltimore, Chicago, and Detroit struggling to keep pace, took three of four from the fast-fading Yankees.

Attendance topped 138,000 for the four-game set, and those on hand for Sunday's finale witnessed a dramatic walk-off win. New York took a 5–4 lead in the ninth, but in Minnesota's half of the inning, Rollins drew a one-out walk from Yankees reliever Pete Mikkelsen. Oliva was retired for the second out. Then Harmon Killebrew, on a 3–2 count from the righthander, drilled a liner into the left-field bleachers for a stunning 6–5 victory. A few of the more than 35,000 ecstatic fans at the stadium leapt onto the field as Killebrew, in typical fashion, stoically made his way around the bases with his head down. The modest slugger's blast gave the Twins a five-game bulge over both Cleveland and Baltimore heading into the All-Star break.

Although the Yankees were not officially dead in the 1965 pennant chase, with one swing of the bat they had fallen 14.5 games behind the front-running Twins. If a single moment marked the fall of the Yankees' sixteen-year dynasty, it might have been Killebrew's walk-off shot that signaled a new day in the American League.

The final day before the break had been remarkable for Oliva as well. American League president Joe Cronin honored him for his 1964 batting title before the game, presenting Oliva with the Silver Bat Award. Two days later, despite struggling for much of the first half, Tony O appeared in his second consecutive All-Star Game.

On July 13, a sunny Tuesday afternoon, Metropolitan Stadium hosted Minnesota's first Midsummer Classic. If Killebrew's home run hadn't generated enough buzz heading into the break, the news that six Minnesota players had been chosen to play before the home crowd further fueled Twins fever. Killebrew and catcher Earl Battey were in the American League's starting lineup. Killebrew, who got the start at first, was having a typically productive year. Battey, despite missing time with a multitude of nagging injuries, was batting .313 and had been on a tear since returning from a dislocated finger at the start of July. Mudcat Grant, Zoilo Versalles, and Jimmie Hall were AL reserves, and when injuries sidelined both Mickey Mantle and AL batting leader Carl Yastrzemski, Oliva was added to the roster.

A sellout crowd of 46,706 packed the Met, which took on the air of a World Series venue. Red, white, and blue bunting adorned the facades of each deck in the three-tiered stadium. The stands and the press box were filled to capacity, and even standing-room tickets were a hot commodity. This was the largest crowd yet to see a baseball game in Minnesota.

The game featured a host of power-hitting future Hall of Famers, including a starting National League outfield of Willie Stargell, Willie Mays, and Hank Aaron. Two other future Hall of Fame outfielders, Roberto Clemente and Frank Robinson, were on the bench. Five home runs were hit that day, including a 410-foot bomb into the left-field seats by Killebrew, tying the game at 5–5 in the fifth inning. Killebrew, with his head down, circled the bases to a rousing standing ovation.

In the end, a crazy-hop infield single in the seventh pushed across the game-winning run. Cubs third baseman Ron Santo drilled a ball into the dirt in front of home plate. The ball bounced and did not touch down until it cleared Cleveland's Sam McDowell on the mound as Giants star Willie Mays crossed the plate in the National League's 6–5 victory. Oliva doubled off Cardinals ace Bob Gibson leading off the ninth but was stranded when the righthander fanned Killebrew and Yankees first baseman Joe Pepitone to preserve the win.

While the Twins were setting the pace in the American League early in the season, Oliva's batting average hit rock bottom on May 22 in a 6–2 loss to the woeful 8–24 Athletics. After going 0 for 5 and grounding out to end the game, the AL batting champion, mired in a 5-for-38 slump, was hitting just .227 in thirty-four games. Even six late-May contests with last-place Kansas City could not ignite a turnaround. Oliva had batted .457 and executed a pair of four-hit games against Athletics pitching in 1964, but he collected only four hits in the first six Twins–Athletics matchups of 1965. With June approaching, he was still looking for his first extended hot streak.

Despite Oliva's struggles, Sam Mele still put the right fielder's name on the lineup card each day. Oliva was among the walking wounded, playing with a bruised right knee and the knuckle problem that had been bothering him for an entire year. But he was on the field. He began his turnaround when the Twins departed Kansas City to start an East Coast trip in Boston on May 25. They roughed up Red Sox pitchers for eight homers and twenty-six runs in the first two games of a three-game set, with Tony O powering homers in each win. After a few weeks of taking extra batting practice, Oliva suddenly was spraying the ball all over the field again, a sign that his timing was coming around. Oliva hit .371 and drove in ten runs in Minnesota's eight games on the East Coast.

Even today, Oliva appreciates not having been pulled from the lineup, which a second-year player might have expected after struggling for several weeks. Mele's show of confidence took pressure off him. He believes that not having to worry about landing on the bench after a hitless performance allowed him to turn his season around. Oliva hit safely in twenty-four of twenty-nine games in June. He was on an 11-for-27 tear in the midst of a twelve-game hitting streak when the Twins swept a doubleheader from New York on Sunday, June 20, before a disappointed Bat Day crowd of 71,245 at Yankee Stadium. Oliva hit safely in both victories, yet one of the more lasting memories of his red-hot run involved a swing-and-miss.

The loose bone chip in the middle finger of Oliva's right hand continued to bother him, and his teammates were always on guard for flying bats when he was in the batter's box. On this day, he inadvertently pitched his bat into the New York dugout during the fourth inning of the second game. It was quickly airmailed back to him, and he had to skip rope to avoid being hit by it. Players advanced to the steps of both dugouts, but the incident went no further.

Oliva finished June at .268, more than seventy points behind the new AL batting leader, Carl Yastrzemski. But that was fine with him; he had found his stroke with the Twins in the thick of a pennant race. He kicked off July with a fourteen-game hitting streak in which he batted .424. He scored a dozen runs while the Twins cruised to nine wins in ten games leading up to the All-Star break. And though the Twins stumbled out of the gate following the break, losing seven of twelve, Oliva's bat was immune from slumping.

In time, the Twins got back on the winning track and took charge of the AL pennant race. All the while, Oliva swung a hot bat. "Tony Oliva was one of the best players I ever saw when the team was winning," says Sandy Valdespino, a rookie on the 1965 club. "He never gave up. When he came out of that slump, he started hitting the ball all over the place, just like the first year. We were winning, and he got better and better and better."

Oliva and Zoilo Versalles were at their best down the stretch, when the Twins put away the other contenders. From August 1 through the end of the season, Versalles batted .346 and scored fifty-three runs in fifty-nine games. In sixty-seven games following the All-Star break, Oliva hit .368, tallied fifty-one runs, and drove in fifty-two.

That run production proved critical. On August 2, four days after the Twins lost Camilo Pascual to shoulder surgery, Harmon Killebrew suffered a gruesome injury during a 6–5 win over Baltimore. In the sixth inning, Orioles center fielder Russ Snyder dropped a bunt down the third-base line. Third baseman Rich Rollins charged, fielded the ball, and rushed a throw that tailed into Snyder running down the line. Killebrew, playing first base, reached across the baseline for the ball a split second before Snyder collided with him. The loud "crack" coming from Killebrew's elbow was audible to his teammates in the dugout. "It completely dislocated my elbow around the ulnar nerve area," Killebrew said in 2010. "It felt like I broke my arm off. I was afraid to look at my arm because it was so painful. It was one of the worst injuries I'd ever had in my life." The Hall of Fame slugger added that it was not long before he recognized another downside of the injury. "After all those years that our ball club had not played in the World Series, it finally looked like we were going to play in the World Series. And it didn't look like I was going to get a chance to play."

Having Killebrew carried off the field that August afternoon was a sobering experience for the first-place Twins. They would have to do without their top righthanded power threat for forty-eight games, and they were likely to see more lefty starters with three lefthanded hitters—Oliva, Don Mincher, and Jimmie Hall—in the middle of the batting order.

But the Twins kept winning, running up a 30–18 mark without Killebrew. Mincher stepped up, knocking in a team-high thirty-four runs in that stretch. The Cuban connection—Versalles and Oliva—was as productive as ever. Zoilo batted .335, stole thirteen bases without getting caught, and scored forty-five runs in those forty-eight games. Oliva put wood on almost any pitch worthy of a cut and hit .356 with Killebrew out. In fact, he did his best imitation of Killebrew; the free-swinger reached base nearly half the time, drawing walks at a remarkable rate because pitchers would not give in to him. He still drove in thirty-one runs in forty games before Killebrew's return in late September.

During his second-half surge, Oliva also delivered a pair of five-hit performances. In the first game of a July 21 doubleheader, he collected hits in his first five at-bats. He beat out two infield singles, and some Tony O hustle and flair on the bases produced a pair of doubles. With Zoilo Versalles on second base in the sixth, Oliva rapped a routine grounder toward Boston second baseman Chuck Schilling. When the ball took a weird hop past Schilling, Oliva was off to the races and reached second while Versalles came around to score. Oliva legged out his second double leading off the eighth, after lofting what appeared to be a single into left-center field. When Yastrzemski threw behind him at first base, Oliva scampered into second. He pumped his average to a season-high .297 and left Boston at .299, though still forty-six points behind Yastrzemski.

In an 8–1 win over Washington on July 28, Oliva pushed his average over .300 to stay with his second five-hit game in eight days. He paced a fifteen-hit attack with five singles and raised his average to .308.

Oliva crept within fifteen points of Yastrzemski in August, during Minnesota's three-game sweep of Yaz's Red Sox at the Met. Tony O went 4 for 5 in the August 8 finale; meanwhile Twins pitching had stifled Yaz in all three games, limiting him to a solo homer in twelve at-bats. Yastrzemski's average had dropped to .322, and only two others now ranked between him and Oliva on the leaderboard: Boston second baseman Felix Mantilla (.310) and Oliva's teammate, Jimmie Hall (.307).

Only an injury could slow Oliva. During a 4–1 Minnesota loss to 1964 Cy Young Award winner Dean Chance and the Angels on August 22, a first-inning pickoff throw by Chance to second base struck Oliva on the head and cracked his batting helmet. The hot-hitting right fielder left the game for precautionary X-rays. When no skull fracture was found, Oliva traveled home with his teammates and was back in action the next day.

While a cracked batting helmet spared Oliva from serious injury in Los Angeles, he was not quite so lucky in the second game of a fourteen-game homestand that would carry into September. In a 2–1 loss to the Yankees on August 24, he slid home headfirst on an infield grounder and jammed his ring finger on the plate. Oliva stayed in the game and recorded another hit, but the knuckle swelled markedly overnight and forced him out for a week. The time off came in the midst of a 24-for-63 tear, a .381 clip that pushed his average to a season-high .311.

Wearing gloves to protect *two* tender knuckles, Oliva returned on September 1 to spark a 5–2 win over Detroit with two doubles and a single. When Tony O followed up his three-hit performance with a 2-for-4 effort against the Tigers, his average climbed to .316. Then he went 3 for 3 in the opener of a Labor Day–weekend series with the White Sox, giving him eight hits in eleven at-bats since returning. He also drove in four runs in a 6–4 victory over second-place Chicago.

Oliva was nine points behind Yastrzemski when the Twins arrived at Fenway Park on Friday, September 10. Tony O contributed a pair of two-baggers and went 2 for 5 in an 8–5 victory, but he lost ground in the race, as Yastrzemski went 2 for 4. In the three games, however, Oliva collected six hits and finished at .318, five points off the lead.

But on September 14, a rainy night at the Met, with Kansas City in town, Oliva's pursuit of a second straight batting title took a hit. Running out a groundball, he stretched for the first-base bag and felt something pull behind his right knee. The knee was already problematic because of a floating bone chip, and now he had strained a muscle. Despite that, he had no intention of sitting out with the pennant race approaching its climax. The Twins took a seven-game winning streak into the second matchup with the Athletics on September 15, a downright frosty night on which 9,354 hardy fans braved temperatures in the forties to see the Twins secure a 7–5 win. After Oliva drove in the first run of the night with a first-inning single, his knee forced him from the game.

His average had climbed to .318, with Yastrzemski at .322, but Oliva wondered if his reign as the AL batting champ was coming to end. Retaining the title would be difficult, as he would be playing hurt and might not play every day. He would have to be productive when he got the chance.

Oliva rarely played back-to-back days over the final three weeks, and despite his concern about playing time, took over the AL batting lead while planted in the dugout. On September 19, he watched his teammates drop their magic number, the number they needed to clinch the AL pennant, to three with an 8–1 cakewalk over Washington. He had trailed Yastrzemski by sixty-five points barely more than two months earlier on July 9, but when the Boston outfielder went hitless in four trips that Sunday afternoon, Oliva, hitting .317, led by two points. "That's good, but it would be better if I was playing," Oliva responded to *St. Paul Pioneer Press* writer Glenn Redmann when informed that he had jumped ahead of Yaz.

Oliva never relinquished the lead. Just as he had when he returned from his finger injury in late August, he found his stroke immediately after rejoining the lineup on September 21. He had eight hits in his final eighteen at-bats (.444) leading up to Minnesota's pennant-clinching victory on September 26. With the AL race decided, Oliva rested his ailing knee over the final five games and finished with a .321 average, beating Yaz by nine points to win AL batting crowns in his first two seasons.

The pennant clincher on September 26 took place in Washington, where fans had celebrated the franchise's last AL flag as the Senators, thirty-two years earlier. Owner Calvin Griffith could not travel with the team. Injunctions filed against Griffith when he moved the team to Minnesota would have forced a lengthy stay in the nation's capital had he even stepped foot there, so he was forced to track his team's progress from his office at Metropolitan Stadium. But Harmon Killebrew and Camilo Pascual, the premier power bat and pitching ace when the Twins began play, were back on the field. Both had made remarkable recoveries from severe injuries, allowing them to be part of the franchise's biggest moment in decades.

Lefties Jim Kaat and Pete Richert went at it that Sunday afternoon. Both were masterful and went the distance, and an RBI single from Washington slugger Frank Howard had tallied the game's only run through five innings. In the sixth, Versalles drove a liner into the left-center gap for his league-leading twelfth triple and later scored on a wild pitch. With the game still tied in the eighth, Frank Quilici slashed a leadoff double past Senators third baseman Ken McMullen. Quilici advanced to third on a wild pitch that sailed past catcher Don Zimmer, a career-long infielder who had been asked to catch in his final big league season. Moments later, Quilici slid home safely with the go-ahead run on Versalles's short fly to strong-armed Don Lock in center field.

Trailing 2–1, Richert put the Twins down one-two-three in the ninth, ending his night with a three-hitter. Kaat, who had scattered eight singles and allowed only an unearned run, retired Lock on a fly to right to start Washington's ninth. After Kaat struck out first baseman Dick Nen on three pitches, up stepped Zimmer, in the final days of a twelve-year career highlighted by World Series titles with the 1955 and 1959 Dodgers. Zimmer swung at and missed Kaat's first pitch, lofting his bat in the vicinity of the Twins dugout. He took strike two from Kaat and then fouled back the lefthander's third offering. Down 0–2, Zimmer started to swing at the next pitch and then checked it. Before he could turn around to look for the call, he heard umpire John Flaherty call him out. Minnesota had clinched its first American League pennant.

The Twins headed for their clubhouse, where Oliva uncorked the first bottle of champagne. Earl Battey shook a bottle and sent the cork and the first spray across the room. Soon the beverage of choice for baseball celebrations was everywhere. Two rookies rewarded manager Sam Mele for his team's fine season. Sandy Valdespino quickly gave the gray-haired skipper a champagne shampoo, and soon after, as the party heated up, Quilici unloaded a shaken bottle in his face. Mudcat Grant wrapped an arm around the neck of third-base coach Billy Martin and poured champagne freely over the former Yankee's head. Anyone who stepped into the clubhouse was likely to get a shower. "This is one of the wildest celebrations I've seen," said Martin, part of six such pennant clinchings with New York. Perhaps the ritual had become old hat in the Bronx; this young Minnesota club was showing its youthful vigor.

Oliva sat at his locker watching the celebration, thinking about the key veterans who had waited so long for this moment and about his family back in Cuba. Overwhelmed by both happiness and a touch of sadness, he began to cry. Rookie César Tovar found his teammate sitting alone. So did fellow Cuban Sandy Valdespino, who had roomed with Oliva on road trips during the championship season. "I said, 'Tony, what's wrong with you? Everybody is having fun. Everybody's happy. Why are you not happy?'" Valdespino recalls. "He said, 'Sandy, I'm thinking of my family in Cuba. They should have shared this thing with me, but they are not here. This is very sad for me.'"

A mix of conflicting emotions. Four years earlier, struggling with a new life and culture, Oliva could never have imagined playing in the World Series—the high point of a major league career. So many had retired without ever appearing in one, but he was living every ballplayer's dream in his second big league season. Oliva's baseball career had changed his life dramatically, and was cause for celebration, but no one he grew up with could be part of it. Nearly five years had passed since he had left Piñar del Río. As devastating as it could be to be isolated during bad times from the ones he loved, he found it equally melancholic without family to share his happiness.

At season's end, Oliva's torrid second half thrust him into the MVP discussion with his good friend Zoilo Versalles. Twins fans speculated which Cuban would be named the American League's Most Valuable Player. Local newspapers noted that Oliva had been MVP-worthy for four months of the season, particularly when Killebrew went down in August, but Versalles had been on top of his game nearly all year.

Versalles had fueled the Twins offense with his habit of stretching singles into doubles and doubles into triples. The fleet-footed shortstop had adopted a simple approach to advancing to the next base. "If you get to one base and you can see the ball on the ground in the outfield," Versalles explained to *Sports Illustrated*'s William Leggett in 1965, "run to the next base." It worked like a charm. Zoilo led the circuit in total bases, having ignited rallies and late-inning comebacks all season long. Running with reckless abandon, he easily topped the league with 126 runs. The only other AL player to record triple-digit runs in 1965 was Oliva, with 107.

Despite his slow start, Oliva closed the season with 185 hits, most among all AL hitters and three more than Versalles. Tony O ranked third in the league with 98 RBIs, and only Cleveland's Rocky Colavito (108) and Detroit's Willie Horton (104) had more. At one point late in the summer, Oliva was quoted as saying, "Let Zoilo have the Most Valuable Player Award. I'll settle for the batting title and the pennant." All three came to pass. And when Oliva had wrapped up his second straight batting title, the Yankees' dynasty was dead and the Twins were on their way to the World Series.

Life's Highs and Lows

A s Oliva sat in the Twins clubhouse, experiencing life's emotional highs and lows simultaneously during the pennant celebration, he anticipated his first taste of the World Series. It was a moment that presaged the year of highs and lows that lay ahead. Oliva faced surgery following the World Series, and midway through a disappointing 1966 season for the Twins, he suffered neck and head injuries in a car accident. The collision caused headaches and neck pain that lingered for a few years.

The days leading up to the World Series, however, were a time of great joy and pride. Oliva had reached his sport's pinnacle in just his second season as a regular, and he and the Twins were optimistic as they awaited their matchup with the National League champion Los Angeles Dodgers. Not only did the Twins have one of the game's most dynamic offenses, but they also avoided Sandy Koufax, arguably the game's best pitcher, in the opener. Game One was scheduled for Wednesday, October 6—Yom Kippur, the holiest day of the Jewish calendar. Koufax chose to observe the solemn holiday and pitch in Thursday's Game Two.

Koufax's decision appeared to be a lucky break for the Twins, who seemed likely to see him only twice in a seven-game series. With Koufax out, the opener pitted Don Drysdale against Mudcat Grant, who led the league in wins and finished 21–7 with a 3.30 ERA.

On a windy Wednesday afternoon at Metropolitan Stadium, rookie Frank Quilici figured prominently in roughing up Drysdale in an 8–2 victory. He led off the third and jump-started a six-run rally by driving a two-strike pitch over the third-base bag for a double. A short time later he tied a World Series record by recording his second hit of the inning: a run-scoring single to right to make it 7–1 and end Drysdale's outing. The big blast of the inning, though, was Zoilo Versalles's three-run homer off the big righthander, who was lacking his best stuff and could not locate his pitches.

While Grant effectively scattered ten hits and went the distance, Oliva was the only Twin to go hitless. Following the pennant-clinching victory in Washington, he had sat out the final week to rest the muscle pull in his right leg. After an incredible second half, he wondered whether sitting might have been a bad idea. But Oliva's concern was minimized by the Twins' convincing win against a pitcher as difficult to hit as Drysdale. Despite his off day at the plate, Oliva tied a World Series record by handling seven putouts in right field. The most memorable was a leaping, backhanded catch in the right-center gap that robbed Dodgers center fielder Willie Davis of an extra-base hit in the first inning. Oliva also earned the honor of throwing the first bat of the series: in the sixth, he launched one into the first-base coaching box.

In Game Two, Koufax and Jim Kaat put zeroes on the scoreboard for five innings. By then, Koufax—who had allowed just a single run over his previous thirty-two innings—had fanned eight Twins. Minnesota finally rallied in the sixth after Dodgers third baseman Jim Gilliam failed to come up with Versalles's hard-hit inning-opening two-hopper. When the ball caromed off Gilliam's body into short left field, the speedy shortstop never broke stride as he rounded first and slid safely into second. Then rookie Joe Nossek set up an ideal opportunity to push across a run by bunting Versalles to third.

Oliva, who had gone hitless in his first six World Series at-bats, quickly fell behind when he swung through a pair of explosive fastballs from Koufax. Suddenly Oliva understood the frustration that the hard-throwing southpaw triggered in National League hitters. "Koufax was hard to face," Oliva says and laughs heartily, forty-five years after the encounter. "To hit the ball, you had to *see* the ball." Picking up Koufax's fastball was difficult enough; getting good wood on it was the ultimate challenge. Oliva knew that striking out with Versalles on third and one out could be a rally killer. With the count 2–2, however, Oliva's third swing was the charm.

Anticipating another fastball from Koufax, Tony O hit the next one into the left-field corner. He had noticed left fielder Lou Johnson playing deep, so, like Versalles, he had second base in mind as soon as the ball cleared the infield. Oliva was still bothered by the pulled muscle suffered late in the season. Despite a heavily wrapped and taped right leg, he sprinted hard and beat Johnson's throw to second base for a run-scoring double. The Twins were up 1–0.

A day earlier, sportscaster Byrum Saam, on NBC radio, had praised Oliva for his ability to go the other way, adding that numerous big league managers had told him that Oliva was "the finest two-strike hitter they had ever seen." With his opposite-field double after falling behind, the American League's two-time batting champion was true to Saam's word. Joe Garagiola, Saam's partner in the booth, had countered that strikes did not matter to Tony O. "This youngster knows no strike zone," was the former catcher's take. "He's an aggressive hitter, and whenever a pitcher releases the ball, he feels he has a license to hit it—and he does!"

The next two hitters, Harmon Killebrew and Earl Battey, greeted Koufax with first-pitch singles to left. The rallying Twins rolled to a 5–1 victory, with Kaat shutting down the Dodgers for nine innings. Later, Koufax admitted that he had struggled with location. He said the pitches to Killebrew and Battey were supposed to be high and in but came in too low. Location had not been the issue, however, on Oliva's RBI double. "That pitch Oliva hit for a double to left to score their first run was a good pitch, a fastball," Koufax told Jim Klobuchar of the *St. Paul Pioneer Press*. "He hit it on the end of his bat and pushed it to left."

Scoring on Koufax was big news, but equally critical to the win was Bob Allison's diving catch to thwart a Dodgers rally in the fifth. The outfield was still a soggy mess from heavy rains the previous evening. Dodgers right fielder Ron Fairly laced a leadoff single to right field for his team's first hit. Up stepped second baseman Jim Lefebvre, who drilled a liner down the left-field line. The ball began to tail away from Allison and was going to land in fair territory. It had "extra-base hit" written all over it, but the hard-charging outfielder made a spectacular diving catch, snagging the ball about a foot off the ground with a backhanded stab before sliding into foul territory on his right hip. He came out of his long slide holding his glove high to show he had the ball.

The importance of Allison's defensive gem became apparent moments later when the Dodgers' Wes Parker stroked a single off the outstretched glove of first baseman Don Mincher into right field. If not for Allison's catch, the Dodgers might have had a lead with two runners aboard and no outs, but the game remained scoreless when Kaat quickly induced a pair of foul pops to kill the rally. Koufax could make a single run stand up for nine innings, so not falling behind the Dodgers in the fifth was a boost to the home team.

After the Twins pulled off the unthinkable, beating both Drysdale and

Koufax, the Series moved west to Los Angeles. Twins hitters were certainly familiar with Dodger Stadium in Chavez Ravine, which was home to the expansion Los Angeles Angels for four seasons, beginning in 1962. Oliva remembers the park as a difficult place to score runs, even though the Angels were not particularly good. The ball never carried well, he recalls, and the hitter's background was a light green that made it difficult to pick up the ball coming out of the pitcher's hand. Plus, the mound was widely believed to be at least a few inches higher than the era's maximum legal height of fifteen inches. Oliva says pitchers appeared to be throwing from a mountaintop.

Of course, *this* visit to Los Angeles was unlike any other. The Twins were playing the National League champion Dodgers, in October, facing one of the game's great pitching staffs. And whereas the Angels rarely drew more than 12,000 fans to Chavez Ravine in those days, the Twins and Dodgers would square off before a full house, hoards of reporters, and a host of Hollywood stars. David Janssen, Milton Berle, and Doris Day were among the Hollywood elite sitting near the playing field for Game Three on a surprisingly overcast afternoon. The sun eventually appeared, but it never seemed to shine on the Twins. The Los Angeles pitching staff, which had surrendered just seventeen runs in the Dodgers' season-ending 15–1 surge to the National League pennant, took over the series.

The Twins scored just two runs at Dodger Stadium, on home runs by Killebrew and Oliva in a Game Four loss to Drysdale. That defeat was sandwiched between shutouts by Game Three starter Claude Osteen and by Koufax in Game Five. The five-foot-eleven, 160-pound Osteen was far less imposing than the Dodgers' flamethrowers, but he was masterful in a critical 4–0 win when the Dodgers were down two games to none.

Minnesota manager Sam Mele called on Camilo Pascual to pitch the first game in Los Angeles. The thirty-one-year-old righty had endured several years with the dreadful Washington Senators before the franchise move to Minnesota. He had been the team's best pitcher for most of them. Pascual was the manager's sentimental favorite to work Game Three, even though he had not been at his best following August surgery to repair muscle tears behind his throwing shoulder. Pascual missed only six weeks, but it was impossible for him to have his best stuff and stamina. It was remarkable, in fact, that he had returned at all. He worked five innings and gave up three runs in the only World Series appearance of his career.

Backup catcher Jerry Zimmerman was called into action when Earl Battey left with a frightening injury in the seventh. On a foul pop near the Twins dugout on the first-base side, Battey and Don Mincher both gave chase. Only Battey had a legitimate play on the ball, and while tracking its flight, he slid to his knees as he approached the wall. His slide ended abruptly when his throat struck the metal rail atop the wall. Aided by teammates, Battey left the field with a severely bruised neck. Although swallowing was difficult and he was unable to speak, Battey was back in the lineup for Game Four. His neck would be a source of discomfort throughout the series, and the Dodgers looked to capitalize on the injury. They attempted eleven stolen bases in the final four games, yet the strong-armed catcher thwarted five of them. He checked into a hospital for treatment only after the series ended.

The Twins saw the real Koufax in Game Five. He impressed Oliva with his ability to throw all his pitches with the same over-the-top motion, which made it nearly impossible to read the pitch type until it was too late to react. Despite the southpaw's arthritic elbow, his fastball had good life, and he used an exceptional changeup to match. If snapping off his curveball caused an extra surge of pain in his tender elbow, Koufax did not let it get in the way of locating the pitch effectively. He struck out ten and stifled every attempt by the Twins to get something going. The Twins never advanced a runner beyond first base until the ninth inning, and Koufax closed out the four-hit shutout by inducing a double-play liner to Dodgers shortstop Maury Wills, who, in addition, had as many hits as the Twins did in Game Five.

The Twins flew home that Monday night, October 11. When the players stepped off the plane, they were met with cheers by more than a thousand fans who had braved temperatures in the midthirties. It was a warm welcome home for a team with bats as cold as the chilly October air. Except for Versalles, Minnesota's regulars were slumping. Oliva was 3 for 19 (.158), with a double and a home run. The American League batting champion had managed a hit off each of the three Los Angeles starters in the series, but he was not happy with his production. "I don't think the pitchers make the difference," Oliva told Associated Press writer Lew Ferguson after the Twins had been swept in Los Angeles. "If you are hitting the ball, you can hit against any pitcher."

Although he refused to make an excuse for his lack of hitting, Oliva and his teammates had faced two of the game's premier pitchers in four of the first five contests. In an attempt to reach base for Harmon Killebrew, Oliva had even tried to bunt his way on in the first inning of Game Five against Koufax, but the Dodgers ace fielded his bunt attempt cleanly and threw him out. If the pulled muscle in his right leg was a factor in his performance, Oliva was not talking about it.

The home team had won all five games so far, so the Twins were not ready to concede the series. In a must-win situation, Mele turned to Mudcat Grant on just two days' rest. The staff ace all season long, he would be asked to extend the Twins' season for another day. Pitching before a standing-room-only crowd of 49,578 on a sunny fall day, Grant was sharp from the start and shut down the Dodgers. He did not allow a hit until Ron Fairly led off the fifth inning with a single. A Fairly home run in the seventh was the only damage done, and the Twins tied the series with a 5–1 win. For good measure, Grant himself provided some insurance with a two-run homer off Dodgers reliever Howie Reed.

Dodgers manager Walt Alston faced a critical pitching decision heading into Game Seven. He could go with Game Four winner Drysdale on three days' rest, typical for pitchers in that era. Or he could come back with Koufax after only two days off. The two aces arrived in the Dodgers clubhouse before Game Seven not knowing who would be the starting pitcher. Alston chose to go with his sore-armed lefty, keeping Drysdale as his first option out of the bullpen.

Kaat also got the Game Seven nod on short rest. Kaat and Koufax had squared off twice already in the series, and each had won once. While the southpaws were warming up for the finale, the Twins squeezed an extra thousand fans into the crevices of the park, setting a single-game high at the Met of 50,596.

Koufax, who struggled to locate his breaking ball in the early innings, issued two-out walks to Oliva and Killebrew in the first, but he struck out Battey to end the threat. The lefty also dodged trouble in the third and fifth innings, and it took a terrific diving stop by third baseman Gilliam on a hard one-hopper by Versalles to keep the Twins off the scoreboard in the fifth.

Gilliam's play was the biggest of Game Seven. By then, the Dodgers had scratched for two runs, and that was enough for Koufax, who blanked the Twins on three hits, 2–0, for the clincher. "Koufax was so good," Oliva recalls. "He was in trouble the first few innings, but he was able to make the big pitches when he needed. The only guy who handled him pretty well was Zoilo Versalles. He smoked the ball over third base and Junior Gilliam made a big play. If that ball had gone through, we probably had a chance to win the game, or at least score two runs on the play. Maybe that was the difference in the game."

When Koufax fanned Bob Allison to close it out, he had struck out ten Twins for the second straight start. Mobbed by teammates before a quiet Metropolitan Stadium crowd, Koufax strode passively toward the visitor's clubhouse as he was offered congratulations. Game Seven marked the twenty-second time he had recorded double-digit strikeouts in 1965, and he did not appear excited about this October performance as he headed down the third-base dugout's steps. "I started out with a bad curveball," Koufax explained to *St. Paul Pioneer Press* writer Jim Klobuchar in the winning club-house after the game. "I never really did get it over. So I laid off it after the fifth or sixth inning, and then I felt myself get stronger."

Few pitchers can win a big game with one of their premier pitches off. Koufax did it in the biggest game a pitcher can work, and against one of the game's most dangerous lineups. Of course, his fastball was a special pitch, too.

"His fastball was different," Oliva explains. "The ball came out straight, but at the last moment, it looked like it rose higher. He was throwing ninety-six, ninety-seven, ninety-eight miles per hour, and the ball was jumping from his hand. With his delivery, you never knew if a fastball or curve was coming. That made him tougher. He threw me only two pitches in the World Series: a big curve and fastball. He threw me a curve in Los Angeles, and I hit it so far, but it was a foul ball. After that, he threw me fastball, fastball, fastball. I'd swing at them and never touch the ball." He laughs. "I had a double off him in Game Two. After that, I was history. He got me out all the time." Oliva was right; he finished one for ten against the game's best pitcher.

The Twins, shut out only three times during the regular season, were blanked three times by the Dodgers in seven games. As a team, Minnesota batted .195 in the series. Even making contact was problematic, as the Los Angeles pitching staff posted double-digit strikeouts four times. Oliva collected just five hits in seven games, batting .192 with a double, a homer, and two RBIs. He regrets his failed attempts to come through when he stepped to the plate with runners on base. In a World Series that went the full seven games and was tight to the end, one or two more hits might have made the difference.

Soon after the World Series, with the sting of losing the final game still fresh, Oliva had his first close encounter with a surgical knife. Doctors planned to remove bone chips from his right middle finger—from the injury suffered in May 1964—which had eventually made it difficult to swing or even grip a bat without pain. Surgeons had also decided to remove floating bodies from his right knee. Oliva had tweaked the knee running into a fence pole during spring training two years earlier, and while the knee had not given him much trouble, it occasionally locked up. The cleanup was first of seven knee procedures Oliva would undergo over the next decade. Following his initial Mayo Clinic visit, he spent his first full winter in Minnesota. Not only could he rehab under the watchful eyes of doctors, but he also could join the annual Minnesota Twins Winter Caravan traversing Minnesota and neighboring states to promote Twins baseball.

With the club coming off its first World Series appearance, the caravan was a big draw, and wherever it stopped, Tony O was a crowd favorite. Audiences were taken by the two-time batting champion's easy, pleasant disposition. He genuinely seemed to enjoy the fans, and he willingly signed autographs for whoever wanted them. Language still got in the way of communicating for Oliva, but he also played up his difficulties with English to entertain the crowds.

Frank Quilici, outgoing, funny, and always comfortable in front of a crowd, worked a few comedic routines with Oliva, which drew hearty laughs. Quilici explained to caravan crowds that he and his teammates had taught their Cuban teammate some basic English. When Quilici asked Oliva to share some of what he had learned, Tony responded with, "Please . . . thank you . . . ham and eggs . . . girls . . . money . . . car . . . girls . . . money . . . girls . . ." In another routine, Quilici asked Oliva a lengthy question in English, to which the Cuban native countered with a lengthy answer in Spanish. After explaining that the audience did not understand Spanish, Quilici asked Oliva to respond in English. Quilici again asked the long-winded question, to which Oliva, after a lengthy pause, simply answered, "Yes" or "No."

Oliva has been a caravan mainstay and a big draw for decades. To this day, whether on a caravan stop, at a Twins function in the Twin Cities area, or at the stadium, Oliva does not say no to an autograph seeker. Former Twins farm director Jim Rantz, in his fifty years as a player and then as a team executive, has seen Oliva's penchant for satisfying fans firsthand. "If you don't have an autograph from Tony Oliva and you live in Minnesota, you're not a baseball fan," Rantz explains. "Because he's given one out to everyone. He never turns anyone down. He's an ambassador."

After a brief holdout over his 1966 contract, which he negotiated directly with Calvin Griffith, Oliva arrived in Orlando expecting big things. He had won two batting crowns playing with a middle finger so stiff that he could not make a fist. Neither his finger nor his knee swelled in Florida that spring, so with the bone chips removed and the pain gone, an even better season seemed entirely possible. Ty Cobb had been the last major leaguer to win three straight batting titles. The combative Hall of Fame outfielder claimed twelve in his career and last won three in a row for the 1917–19 Tigers. Cobb needed three years to win his first, but Oliva, twenty-seven that spring, had a chance to win in each of his first three major league seasons.

This was a good time in Oliva's life. He had negotiated a substantial raise from Griffith, giving him financial stability. While he lived modestly and did not spend much money, he had a comfortable apartment at the Hotel Maryland. After two years in Minnesota, he had made friends and was suffering fewer bouts of loneliness. And now he was beginning a new season completely healthy after having played injured the two previous summers.

Oliva started fast and was productive for long stretches of the season. After going hitless in the season opener, a 2–1 win in which the Twins managed just four hits off Kansas City ace Catfish Hunter, Oliva went on a five-week tear. He stroked home runs in his next four games, including an eighth-inning, three-run shot off the Athletics' Paul Lindblad to secure a 5–3 win in the season's second game. An Oliva home run made the difference again the very next day. His two-run bomb off Athletics righthander Fred Talbot in the fourth inning of a 4–2 victory secured a Twins sweep of the season-opening series. Oliva seemed to have developed the power stroke of a bona fide slugger. He had homered forty-eight times in 1964 and 1965 combined, a total exceeded by only eight American Leaguers, and now he clubbed four in the season's first week.

Though Oliva's healed right hand pulled his bat through the hitting zone with authority, he shot down suggestions that he was becoming a slugger. He countered that he was pulling pitches not because he was healthy but rather because pitchers were working him inside. "Last year, everybody pitched me outside, outside, outside," he explained to *Sporting News* writer Max Nichols. "So far, I just get more pitches I can pull, that's all."

On April 16, Oliva powered a two-run homer and two singles in a 3–2 loss to Dean Chance and the recently renamed California Angels. After the game, Chance told reporters that Oliva, who had had three of Minnesota's four hits, was "the best player in the American League, by far." He quipped, "I'm convinced the only way to pitch Oliva is about four yards behind him. . . . I should have walked him. There isn't any sense in fighting City Hall. . . . He hit two pitches about two feet off the ground to right field. I jammed him with three straight pitches, then gave him a ball on the outside corner, and he hit a home run to left field."

Oliva's ability to adjust to a sudden change after a steady diet of one pitch or location astounded Chance, a former Cy Young Award winner, but Tony

O's teammates had seen him do it many times. Harmon Killebrew, who batted next to Oliva in the Twins lineup for more than half his career, admired his teammate's uncanny knack of adjusting to an abrupt about-face in a pitcher's approach or pitch selection. "A pitcher could throw him ninety-nine fastballs and one changeup, and he'd lose it," Killebrew explained in 2010. "He was just a great hitter, the best offspeed hitter I ever saw. He was a Rod Carew–type hitter with power." Suddenly Chance knew what Killebrew had known for some time.

The home-run surge put Oliva near the top of the league leaderboard with George Scott, a twenty-two-year-old Boston rookie. At Metropolitan Stadium on May 6, Scott stroked solo homers off Dave Boswell and Al Worthington, including a game-tying blast in the top of the ninth. Oliva had hit a two-run bomb off former teammate Dick Stigman early in the game, and he drilled a two-out ninth-inning shot off Dan Osinski to secure a 5–4 win. Oliva teed off on a 3–1 changeup from Osinski. The veteran righthander had thrown three straight fastballs away and did not expect Oliva to anticipate anything offspeed, but Oliva powered the ball out of the stadium in a hurry. Former Twins hurler Lee Stange remembers the home run well. "I was with Boston and Dan Osinski was my roommate," says Stange. "I told him before the series, 'Whatever you do, don't throw Tony any changeups.' He threw him a changeup, and he hit it about three-quarters of the way up the scoreboard in right-center. That ended the game real quick."

Tony O batted a major league–leading .407 through his first hundred plate appearances, with nine homers and twenty-four RBIs in twenty-four games. Former Twins slugger Jim Lemon, the team's first-base coach and a hitting instructor in 1965, told *Minneapolis Tribune* columnist Sid Hartman that it was apparent Oliva had fully recuperated from the offseason surgical procedure on his finger. Lemon said he had never seen Oliva hit the ball as hard as he was that spring. A June slump brought Oliva's batting average back to earth, and after a torrid July, his bat went cold again in August. While Oliva did top the American League with 191 hits in 1966, another American Leaguer posted a higher batting average. It took a newcomer to the league, Frank Robinson, to displace the two-time champ.

Robinson had batted .303 and averaged thirty-two home runs and 101 RBIs a season over ten years with Cincinnati. But after the 1965 campaign, Reds general manager William DeWitt deemed the thirty-year-old slugger "an old thirty" and traded Robinson to Baltimore for veteran righthander Milt Pappas and two fringe players. Robinson responded by winning the

Triple Crown in 1966. Oliva finished strong, but Robinson batted .395 over his final ten games to top Oliva in the only Triple Crown category up for grabs down the stretch. The first Triple Crown winner since Mickey Mantle in 1956, Robinson was named MVP for his stellar American League debut, five years after taking the National League's trophy as a member of the Reds. No other player has been so honored in both leagues.

The newest Orioles star (.316) and Oliva (.307) were the only AL qualifiers to hit as high as .300. The game turned in favor of the pitcher during the 1960s, the most pitcher-friendly time since the dead-ball era at the start of the twentieth century. Between 1964 and 1966, only eleven qualifying AL hitters batted .300. Oliva did it in all three seasons; no other AL player hit .300 more than once. Across both leagues, only Oliva, Roberto Clemente, and Dick Allen batted .300 each of those three seasons.

Like Oliva, the Twins finished second in 1966. Nearly everyone from the 1965 club returned, but the defending AL champs were a major disappointment, struggling to stay above .500 well into August. They rarely scored runs in bunches as they had in 1965, and winning three or four in a row was nearly always followed by a run of consecutive losses. The Twins won twenty of their last thirty games to finish 89–73 but were never in the pennant race. With Frank Robinson, Boog Powell, and Brooks Robinson leading a potent Orioles offense, Baltimore cruised to the franchise's first pennant since 1944, when it was the St. Louis Browns.

In a season light on highlights, the Twins did set an American League home-run record on June 9, 1966, in a 9–4 victory over Catfish Hunter and the Athletics. The Twins were down 4–3 in the seventh. Earl Battey led off with a walk. After Hunter retired Bernie Allen, pinch hitter Rich Rollins drilled Hunter's first pitch into the Met's left-field seats to put the Twins ahead. Then Zoilo Versalles hit a Hunter fastball in the same vicinity for a two-run lead. With three straight lefthanded hitters due up, Athletics manager Alvin Dark replaced Hunter with lefty Paul Lindblad, who gave up a grounder from Sandy Valdespino. Then Oliva jumped on a curve and drilled it into the bullpen in right-center. On the very next pitch, Don Mincher clubbed Minnesota's fourth homer of the inning.

Three National League teams had powered five home runs in a single inning, but none had done so in the American League. With Mincher's shot, the Twins tied a mark they already shared with Cleveland, having stroked four consecutive home runs in a wild eleventh inning against these same Athletics on May 2, 1964.

After Mincher's blast, Harmon Killebrew stepped up with a chance for number five. First, Dark pulled Lindblad for righthander John Wyatt. With the entire Minnesota team perched on the dugout steps for Killebrew's at-bat, the slugger went 3–2 against Wyatt, then pounded the hurler's next offering into the left-field bleachers to set a new AL record. And the inning was not over. The next batter, Jimmie Hall, also had his teammates' full attention as he settled into the batter's box. Hall turned on a Wyatt pitch and drove a liner deep to right. The ball had a chance, but it was hit so hard on a line that it missed clearing the fence by a foot or two. When Bernie Allen dribbled a ball in front of the plate to end the inning, the Twins had missed setting a new major league record by inches.

One of the final highlights of the 1966 season for both Oliva and the Twins was Jim Kaat's brilliant four-hit performance on September 25. On a beautiful Sunday afternoon at the Met, the redheaded southpaw limited Detroit to four singles en route to his league-leading twenty-fifth victory. Both Kaat and Tigers righthander Earl Wilson pitched gems. The game was scoreless until Oliva, leading off the bottom of the ninth, teed off on a 2–2 pitch and sent a walk-off homer deep into the right-field bleachers. Wilson had nearly reached the Detroit dugout by the time the ball landed. Oliva hit some memorable home runs in his career, but his blast off Wilson is Kaat's favorite. It ended a game that capped a career year for the lefty: 25–13 with a 2.75 ERA in 304.2 innings—career bests for innings, wins, and ERA.

Although Oliva's cleaned-up middle finger and right knee provided no problems, 1966 was by no means injury free. Just after the All-Star break, Oliva was driving home with Twins rookie César Tovar after a game at the Met. He was pulling away from a light that had just turned green when a vehicle on the cross street ran the red light and nearly totaled Oliva's gold Mustang. Oliva suffered whiplash, which caused constant neck pain, severe headaches, and some blurred vision. Concussions were not diagnosed as effectively then as they are today, and he wonders if he might have suffered one.

Twins trainer Doc Lentz treated him the rest of the summer and kept him on the field. As a result, Oliva missed only three games, but the discomfort hindered his ability to swing freely. The headaches and vision issues probably compromised the acute focus required to hit a baseball squarely. Oliva wonders if the accident cost him a third straight batting title. Nothing could control Oliva's severe headaches, which he says persisted for a few years before they eventually disappeared. An offseason trip to the Mayo Clinic, where

Oliva underwent a battery of tests, could not pinpoint the exact source of the headaches. Until they ran their course, he just had to live with them.

Yet the year ended happily when Oliva won a Gold Glove as the American League's best right fielder. Five years earlier, his defensive game had been enough of a liability that the Twins were not interested in signing him. Now he made a difference with more than his bat.

In the finale of a three-game sweep in Cleveland on July 6, he delivered a two-run double in the eighth inning to put the Twins in front, 4–2. The Indians threatened in the ninth when Johnny Klippstein walked the bases loaded. Then rain delayed the game for twenty-three minutes. When play resumed with two outs, lefthanded-hitting first baseman Fred Whitfield lined a base hit toward Oliva in right. Chuck Hinton easily scored to close the gap to 4–3, and speedster Chico Salmon darted around third with the potential tying run. Oliva charged, plucked the ball cleanly from the wet grass, and rifled a bullet on the fly to catcher Jerry Zimmerman. The throw easily beat Salmon to the plate, and Zimmerman applied the game-ending tag.

"I got a good jump," Salmon insisted after the game. "Then I come home and the ball's there." Although the conditions seemed to favor Salmon, Oliva played down that angle in amusing fashion. "I didn't have time to see if the ball was wet," he said. It was the second time that season that Salmon had fallen victim to Oliva's strong arm. He was just one of several baserunners surprised to find the baseball awaiting them. Oliva had gunned down eight runners by the All-Star break, after collecting just five assists as a rookie in 1964 and five more in 1965.

The steady climb in Oliva's assist totals was another sign of his diligence and work ethic. His throws were more accurate, missing the cutoff man less often, and he was hitting long-distance targets in the air. Prior to Oliva's surgery, his swollen middle finger affected his ability to keep the ball down and hit cutoff men, though he did not use the injury as an excuse. After his run of assists in the first three months of the 1966 season, Oliva threw out only three more runners after the All-Star break—perhaps a sign that his arm had earned the respect of his peers. As Oliva's reputation grew, baserunners did not challenge him as often.

Teammates and coaches took notice of the strength and accuracy of Oliva's arm. After Oliva threw out Salmon to end the July 6 game, Mele called his right fielder "the best all-around player in the American League today." Oliva's peg also caught the attention of Twins pitching coach Johnny Sain.

"Tomorrow we're going to have Oliva throw batting practice from right field," Sain quipped to the *Sporting News's* Max Nichols. Oliva, of course, already had a day job.

Oliva took great pride in developing into a dependable major league outfielder. Players selected the Gold Glove winners at the time, and being recognized by his peers made the award extra special to Oliva. Being honored for skills that did not come nearly as easy as swinging a bat is something he cherishes to this day.

The Great Pennant Race of 1967

I n the wake of the Twins' struggles in 1966, owner Calvin Griffith retooled a young team that a year earlier had seemed poised to capture a few more American League pennants. By year's end, he had dealt several cornerstones of the 1965 World Series team to improve the pitching staff.

In December 1966, Griffith made a bold move to pick up a number one starter, trading center fielder Jimmie Hall, slugging first baseman Don Mincher, and pitching prospect Pete Cimino to the California Angels for Dean Chance. The righthander had won Cy Young honors in 1964 with a 20–9 mark, but in 1966 he had had a disappointing 12–17 year.

The day after picking up Chance, Griffith dealt Camilo Pascual, the staff ace since the franchise had arrived from Washington in 1961. Pascual had spent thirteen big league seasons with the organization, including some of the worst in its history. Griffith shipped Pascual back to Washington, dealing him and second baseman Bernie Allen to the expansion Senators for top reliever Ron Kline. With one of the best curveballs in the game, Pascual had posted a pair of twenty-win seasons and 145 victories pitching for the Griffith family. He had not been the same since undergoing shoulder surgery during the 1965 season, however, and Griffith felt he could move him with Chance coming aboard. Pascual, at thirty-three, made adjustments and regained his effectiveness in Washington.

With the release of Johnny Klippstein after the 1966 campaign, the thirty-four-year-old Kline, coming off four excellent seasons with the Senators, was slated to team with Al Worthington to anchor Minnesota's relief corps. The deals left the Twins with three starters—Chance, Jim Kaat, and Mudcat Grant—each of whom had posted a twenty-win season in the preceding three years.

Even with Hall and Mincher exiled to California, the Twins still had the power trio of Harmon Killebrew, Bob Allison, and Oliva. Killebrew had manned third base in 1966, but Mincher's departure moved him back to first, his position of choice. With Hall gone, Ted Uhlaender was in line to be the primary center fielder if he could hit enough, with utilityman César Tovar as the fallback option. In 1967, the versatile Tovar played more than a few games at every position except pitcher, catcher, and first base.

The 1967 addition to have the biggest impact was Rod Carew, the last great position player the Twins developed in the 1960s. The Panamanian-born prospect grew up in the Canal Zone before moving to the Washington Heights area of New York City as a teenager. He never played baseball in high school, but Twins scouts discovered him playing semipro ball in the Bronx in 1964. Griffith had lobbied to make room for the unproven Oliva in 1964; three years later, he did the same thing in spring training with the twenty-one-year-old Carew. As he had with Oliva, Griffith sang the praises of his latest top prospect, telling reporters in camp that Carew "could be the American League All-Star second baseman if he puts his mind to it." Of course, the rookie would have to perform well enough in camp to justify a starting role before worrying about an All-Star berth, but he had the owner on his side. Although manager Sam Mele was less enthusiastic about giving the second-base job to an untested rookie, Carew took care of business in Florida and won the assignment.

When the Twins broke camp, Carew and Oliva had adjoining lockers in the clubhouse. After rooming with Zoilo Versalles for two of his three seasons and with Sandy Valdespino in 1965, Oliva paired with Carew for 1967. When the team went north following spring training, the veteran gave the rookie a tour of the Twin Cities and steered him through the other American League cities. The two spent a lot of time together, talking baseball, eating meals, hanging out, or walking to the ballpark. On the bench, Oliva was always discussing pitchers, their arsenals, and their tendencies.

Carew says he was a loner when he first reached the major leagues, so Oliva's reaching out to him was vital to his new life off the field. Oliva and his wife Gordette often had him over for dinner when the Twins were home. "I just liked being around him because he always had a smile on his face," says Carew. "He always had a good word to say about everybody. Never spoke bad about anybody. I was just amazed, because I'd never met someone like that. That was Tony O. Today he's the same person. He always has a kind word. Always has time for people."

To this day, Carew speaks fondly of the way Oliva befriended him in 1965 during his first spring training with the Twins. He says there was no pretense or star-quality air about Oliva, who became mentor, teacher, and big brother. The veteran made himself available to the extremely shy Carew, and when the rookie joined the big league club two years later, Oliva included him in the daily card games with Earl Battey, Sandy Valdespino, and other veterans. "Learning from Tony as a young kid was just amazing," recalls Carew. "I watched the work he put into what he was doing. And we became friends, fast friends. He took me in as his roommate on the road, and we were roommates for ten years. For an established player to do something like that for a kid was just an amazing thing."

The two met during Carew's first time on a field with the Twins in 1964, when the front office was looking to sign the eighteen-year-old. During a Twins stop at Yankee Stadium that summer, the skinny young man was brought in to take pregame batting practice. He was given one of Oliva's jerseys, and fans called "Oliva!" when he stepped onto the field. To Carew's surprise, they were addressing *him*. Oliva introduced himself to the awe-struck Carew in English, though they quickly switched to Spanish. "Just go hit and run and take groundballs. Don't be afraid," the major leaguer told the anxious teenager. Carew certainly appeared fearless. He put on a show, blasting balls all over the stadium before Mele rushed him off the field, afraid that someone connected with the Yankees might see the hitting display.

Although Oliva was successful in easing Carew's first spring training as a big leaguer, his own spring was difficult from day one. Despite an offseason of rest and treatment, the neck pain and headaches brought on by his car accident the previous summer quickly returned. Oliva then pulled a back muscle two weeks before Opening Day. He missed ten days of spring training action, and even after he returned, the back injury continued to hamper his swing.

For Oliva, spring training was not so much about getting in shape physically as it was about fine-tuning reflexes and his timing at the plate. Playing winter ball usually gave Oliva a huge head start in his spring prep, but at the Twins' request, he did not play following the 1965 and 1966 seasons. After a winter of inactivity in Minnesota, Oliva—always a perfectionist about being ready—reported early with the pitchers and catchers, but he could not seem to get healthy. Although Oliva's spring routine included regular visits to the trainer's room, he was in the starting lineup when the Twins began 1967 in Baltimore against the defending World Series champions.

Neither Oliva nor the Twins began well. For the first time since the franchise moved west in 1961, the Twins lost their first two games of a new season. They posted back-to-back wins only once in April, a month marred by poor defensive play, baserunning blunders, and other mental mistakes. After closing April by losing three of four to the lowly Senators in Washington, the Twins occupied the American League cellar with a 5–10 record. Minnesota barely averaged more than three runs a game in April, with a number of players suffering slow starts. Oliva stroked two hits and doubled home two runs in Minnesota's season-opening loss to Baltimore, but he collected just eight hits in eleven April contests. Even his best day of the opening month was tarnished by a once-in-a-lifetime blunder that epitomized the team's early struggles.

At Tiger Stadium on April 21, César Tovar singled to center to lead off the third inning of a scoreless game. Detroit righthander Denny McLain, a twenty-game winner in 1966, struck out Rich Rollins before Oliva sent a towering fly to right-center. Right fielder Al Kaline backtracked to the wall as the ball sailed in his direction. Instead of going halfway to second base, Tovar retreated toward first, thinking the ball would be caught. Oliva and first-base coach Jim Lemon watched the ball land in Tiger Stadium's upper deck, which hung over the playing field. As he rounded first base, Oliva heard Tovar shout in Spanish, "Don't pass me on the bases!" It was too late. Detroit first baseman Norm Cash quickly alerted umpire John Stevens, who had his back to the infield as he followed the flight of the ball. Tovar was allowed to score, but Stevens called Oliva out for passing his teammate.

Tovar said Lemon had called him back to the bag to tag up. Mele, convinced that Kaline's strong arm made tagging up impossible, thought Tovar should have been able to judge on his own that going halfway was the right move. Tired of his team's mental mistakes, Mele fined Tovar for the lost run. But well into May, a steady stream of mishaps and mistakes tried Mele's patience. In a stretch of twelve games from April 27 through May 9, his players committed eighteen errors. With management unhappy, several Twins were being mentioned in trade rumors.

The day of Tovar's baserunning miscue was a dreadful one all around. Although Oliva hit another long homer in the ninth inning and Carew had clubbed the first of his career on a 3–2 fastball from McLain two innings earlier, the Tigers jumped on Twins pitching for seven runs in the fourth en route to a 12–4 victory. The frustrated manager held a brief team meeting during a seventh-inning rain delay and another after the game.

Oliva's two upper-deck shots in the lopsided loss came despite his lingering back injury, which caused him pain every time he swung a bat. A week later, on April 27, he aggravated the pulled back muscle fouling off a pitch from Cleveland's "Sudden Sam" McDowell. The muscle pull, which sidelined Oliva for two weeks, was the first of several injuries to hamper his performance during the season's first two months. He suffered bruised ribs and sore elbows when plunked by pitches from southpaws Dave McNally, Al Downing, and Sam McDowell. Oliva also jammed the middle finger of his left hand on a slide at second base and severely bruised his right foot fouling off a pitch. His right knee also acted up for a stretch after he twisted it chasing down a flyball.

Oliva played through the injuries, except for the nagging muscle pull. But he was forced out for five days in early June after Yankees second baseman Horace Clarke stepped on him during a stolen-base attempt. Clarke went high into the air to handle the throw from catcher Jake Gibbs. He came down on Oliva, who needed stitches in his right middle finger.

After missing two weeks because of his back, Oliva returned to action against Kansas City in mid-May. When the Athletics took three of four at Metropolitan Stadium, the Twins were 11–15 and shared the AL cellar with the Orioles, who had started slowly after sweeping the Dodgers in the World Series seven months earlier.

Oliva had played in only half of Minnesota's first twenty-six games and was hitting .205, with just four RBIs. Killebrew had also started slowly, and a few days after Oliva returned from his recurring back ailment, Mele decided to move Oliva behind Killebrew in the batting order. Oliva had nearly always been the third-place hitter, with Killebrew following at cleanup, but now he would bat fifth. In the first twenty-three games after the switch, Killebrew went on a home-run binge and soon ranked near the top of several American League leaderboards. Managers do not mess with success, though Mele's move did not spark a turnaround in Oliva's hitting.

Carew, on the other hand, was finding his way. After recording just nine hits in his first eleven major league games, he jump-started his bat with an eight-game hitting streak in early May. Midway through the streak, on May 8, the rookie collected the first of seven five-hit games he would record in nineteen seasons. After posting consecutive three-hit performances in mid-May, he was batting .340 in his first hundred at-bats.

Only new arrival Chance kept the Twins from slipping into an extended losing streak. The twenty-five-year-old righthander lost his first start for the Twins on the second day of the season before reeling off seven straight wins, including three shutouts. He improved to 9–2 with a 4–0 win at Boston on June 1.

The Twins, a game under .500 following Chance's third shutout, returned to the Met for two weeks. In a less-than-stellar homestand, Killebrew generated the most on-field excitement. On June 3, a breezy Saturday afternoon with the Angels in town, Killebrew drilled what is regarded as the longest home run ever hit at Metropolitan Stadium. Facing forty-year-old Lew Burdette in the fourth inning, the Twins slugger turned on a pitch and drove it several rows into the stadium's upper deck in left field. "It was a knuckleball, of all things," Killebrew said of the pitch from Burdette, a longtime Milwaukee Braves righty who won three World Series games for the 1957 world champions. "He told me later it was the only knuckleball that he threw all year."

The scoreboard's Twins-O-Gram quickly listed the homer as a 430-foot shot, measuring it to the point it landed. Considering the second deck stood more than seventy feet about ground level, the ball would have traveled some 520 feet, according to a projection from Twins executives Bill and Sherry Robertson. The Twins acknowledged the first home run to reach the Met's upper deck by painting the seat red. Whether it was the longest one ever hit at Metropolitan Stadium became a point of contention the very next day.

When Killebrew stepped to the plate in the second inning against Angels righty Jack Sanford, Twins public address announcer Bob Casey informed the crowd that the previous day's home run was a 520-foot blast and that the seat it struck would be retired. Before Casey had finished speaking, Killebrew stepped into Sanford's first-pitch slider and drove it off the facing of the upper deck in left-center field, one section over toward center from the ball he had hit the day before. The point of impact was measured at 434 feet, four more than Saturday's home run, and projections estimated that the two homers would have traveled nearly the same distance. Teammates debated which would have gone the greatest distance. "I think the second one would have gone farther," Killebrew said. "It was actually hit harder."

Killebrew's two monster home runs provided Mele with the last memorable moments of his managerial career. On June 9, with the 25–25 Twins lodged in sixth place, Calvin Griffith fired Mele, less than two years after the forty-five-year-old skipper had steered the team through a host of injuries to the franchise's first pennant in four decades. The Twins' slide in 1966 and mediocre start in 1967 led Griffith to swing the ax.

The firing caught most of the players by surprise, including Oliva, who says, "I think they fired him too quickly. Most of the time, a good team that starts slow will pull it all together." By this time, Oliva had developed a strong sense of loyalty to Mele, who had given him his first chance. The two grew close as Oliva's English improved. Oliva had also befriended Mele's young son Steve, and the two often played catch before games. To this day, Oliva appreciates the faith Mele showed in him as a young player. He says that not only did Mele take a chance on his still-developing defensive skills, but the manager also never benched him when he slumped. "Managers watch their players very carefully," Oliva adds, "and I think he saw me work so hard every day that he knew I wanted to get better." Mele knew Oliva never needed a motivator.

The new man in charge was Calvin Coolidge Ermer, a forty-three-year-old baseball lifer who had spent a decade in the minors and played his one and only major league game in Washington for the Griffith family in 1947. For much of the next two decades, Ermer had played or managed in the organization. Now Griffith promoted him from Triple-A Denver to become the Twins' third manager. Nearly half the 1967 roster had played for Ermer in the minors.

Ermer's tenure with the Twins got off to a rough start as the Orioles stuck Chance with only his third loss, coming away with an 11–2 win. Still, the Twins soon surged back into the pennant chase. The next day, Saturday, June 10, Jim Kaat went the distance and allowed just six hits in an 8–1 victory over the Orioles. The big lefthander, who had struggled with his control all season, did not walk anyone in claiming his first win since April 22. Kaat, now just 2–7, would rebound to be one of Minnesota's best pitchers during the season's second half.

The other key figure in Saturday's win was Oliva, now hitting fourth. Mele had been batting Zoilo Versalles third, followed by Killebrew and then Oliva, but Ermer dropped the shortstop down in the order and put Killebrew, the longtime cleanup hitter, into the three spot. Oliva responded by driving in six of his team's eight runs. The highlight was a three-run shot into the bullpen in right-center off knuckleballer Eddie Fisher, just Oliva's second homer of the season.

After his return in early June from the finger injury suffered in his collision with Horace Clarke, Oliva had begun to find his groove. With his six-RBI performance against Baltimore, he had an eight-game hitting streak. But the injury bug bit again a week later. With the Twins in Cleveland on June 16, Oliva ran deep into the right-center gap in pursuit of a Joe Azcue drive. As he sprinted onto the warning track, he leaped for the ball and crashed hard into the fence. His head struck the metal railing at the top of the wall and punched a hole in the cyclone fence behind the protective tarp. Briefly knocked unconscious, Oliva was carried off on a stretcher by several teammates.

Frank Quilici, who had seen his friend repeatedly play through injuries, was taken aback at seeing Oliva prone and in need of a stretcher. Later Quilici, known for giving friends and teammates the business, could not resist giving Oliva a hard time about being carried off the field. "We had to haul him back from center field on a stretcher and bring him down into the clubhouse," Quilici recalls. "We had to go down these steps coming to the clubhouse, and then up the stairs and into the clubhouse. I says, 'Tony, if you ever do that again, you're going to have to lay out in center field!'"

In addition to suffering facial cuts and bruises, Oliva also came away with two slipped vertebrae, which pinched nerves and caused neck pain. After Doc Lentz worked the vertebrae back into place, Oliva was hospitalized for observation. The neck injury was another in a long list of nagging ailments. But his violent collision with Cleveland's outfield wall did not keep him out long. Less than forty-eight hours later, and only a few hours after being released from the hospital, Oliva pinch-hit in the Sunday finale of the Cleveland series. He still had a stiff neck and says his vision had not been right earlier that day. But Lentz worked on his neck prior to the first pitch, and Oliva was back on the field.

Two lefties, Jim Kaat and hard-throwing Sam McDowell, were painting a scoreless masterpiece. The Twins loaded the bases against McDowell in the top of the eighth, with two walks sandwiched around a single by Kaat. McDowell walked Killebrew with two outs to force in the game's first run, leading Cleveland manager Joe Adcock to summon righthander Steve Bailey to face pinch hitter Oliva. Tony O jumped on an 0–2 offering from Bailey, driving it to right for a bases-clearing double. The Twins came away with a 4–2 victory, but not before Sandy Valdespino climbed Municipal Stadium's left-field wall, reached over the top, and robbed Larry Brown of a grand slam to end the eighth. Longtime Indians general manager Gabe Paul called it the greatest catch he had ever seen at Cleveland's park.

The following night in Baltimore, in the first of two games, Oliva broke up another scoreless affair in the sixth with a two-run homer off Orioles starter

Tom Phoebus. Dave Boswell tossed a three-hitter to claim a 4–0 victory. Two days later, Boswell and Oliva would be at the center of a team squabble.

The twenty-two-year-old Boswell had earned the nickname "Flakey" for his clubhouse chatter and antics. Known for his imitations of animal, bird, and insect calls, he once had a team bus driver searching under the seats for a cricket. Less amusing was Boswell's propensity for carrying guns on road trips. On the team bus, traveling from the Detroit airport to the hotel after a flight from Baltimore, Boswell took out one of his handguns, unloaded, and started pulling the trigger. According to Rod Carew's 1979 self-titled autobiography with Ira Berkow, Oliva was the most upset with Boswell and confronted the young pitcher about flashing his arsenal on the team bus. "Don't be playing with that thing on this bus," Oliva angrily responded to seeing the gun, according to Carew. Boswell quickly countered, "Well, you guys can play with guns in Cuba; why can't we play with guns here?" Mudcat Grant and Ted Uhlaender piped in and the argument escalated quickly, with sides taken along racial lines, noted Carew. The fray was Ermer's first touch of internal strife as manager. He threatened fines when the argument turned noisy, and the bus went silent. That wasn't the end of the incident. Money did exchange hands, as Ermer reportedly fined Boswell, Oliva, and Uhlaender $250 each for their roles in the dispute.

Though a bit poorer, Boswell turned in another fine performance on June 28, working a four-hitter and striking out thirteen in a 3–2 win over Boston at the Met. The victory kicked off an eight-game winning streak that included doubleheader sweeps of Washington and New York. With a 43–34 record, the Twins were working their way into what was shaping up as a four-team race for the AL pennant. The offense had come alive. Oliva collected a team-leading twelve hits and batted .364 during the streak. His biggest hit was a walk-off ninth-inning single against Yankees lefthander Steve Hamilton to secure a 7–6 comeback win in the second game of a Fourth of July doubleheader. The hit gave the Twins sole possession of second place behind Chicago. Minnesota closed the first half by winning twelve of fifteen games to move within 2.5 games of the White Sox.

The surging Twins placed four players in the American League's starting lineup at the 1967 All-Star Game in Anaheim, California. Despite his slow start, Oliva made his fourth straight All-Star appearance and was selected as a starter. The AL lineup lacked a true center fielder, so Orioles manager Hank Bauer asked the Twins right fielder to man the position. Oliva played the entire game in center with Boston's Carl Yastrzemski and Tony Conigliaro playing the corner spots. Oliva batted third between teammates Rod Carew, a leading Rookie of the Year contender, and Harmon Killebrew. Minnesota's fourth starter was its biggest offseason acquisition, Dean Chance.

The game was a coming-out party for Anaheim Stadium, which the Angels had opened a year earlier. For the game to be aired in prime time on the East Coast, it had to start in the late afternoon in California, so hitters faced the game's best pitchers at twilight. Oliva says it was difficult to pick up the ball coming out of the pitchers' hands. The hurlers dominated a 2–1 affair that took fifteen innings to decide. Oliva collected a pair of singles, joining Yastrzemski and the Cardinals' Tim McCarver as the only players with multiple hits. What may have made a bigger impression than Oliva's two hits, however, were the two bats he launched during the first inning.

After Giants ace Juan Marichal retired Brooks Robinson and Rod Carew for the first two outs, Oliva rifled a bat in the direction of the National League dugout, sending a number of All-Stars scurrying. Before the players had settled back into their seats, Tony O fired another bat their way. The second projectile did not carry as far, but nonetheless, a few NL players tossed white towels from the dugout, signaling either displeasure or surrender.

Solo homers accounted for all three runs. Phillies third baseman Dick Allen greeted Dean Chance with a leadoff shot to straightaway center to open the second inning. Orioles third baseman Brooks Robinson tied the game in the sixth with a homer off Cubs ace Ferguson Jenkins. The zeroes and strikeouts then stacked up for nearly nine full frames before Reds star Tony Pérez powered a Catfish Hunter pitch deep into the left-field seats for the game winner.

The American League race became a dogfight after the break. The White Sox began the second half leading Detroit by two games, with the Twins trailing the Tigers by a half game and the California Angels not far behind. The Angels did not stick around long; the fifth-place Boston Red Sox took their place as the fourth challenger in one of the wildest races in major league history.

Boston was the dark horse. Coming off a ninth-place finish in 1966, the rejuvenated Red Sox were six games off the pace at the break. But under the direction of rookie manager Dick Williams, they posted a league-best 51–31 second-half record in pursuit of the franchise's first pennant since 1946. All four teams remained in the race until the final weekend of the season.

The Twins dropped seven straight soon after the break but used a mid-August seven-game winning streak to once again close ground on the first-place White Sox. When they completed a three-game sweep of Chicago on August 13 before more than 42,000 fans at the Met, the Twins improved to 62–50, a season-high twelve games over .500, and took over the top spot.

The pennant chase became a game of musical chairs. The Twins soon relinquished first place, then reclaimed it briefly when Dean Chance fired a no-hitter in Cleveland on August 25. The Twins fell to the Indians the following day, and the Red Sox beat up White Sox ace Joe Horlen to take over the top spot. The lead over the Twins was a mere half game, but it marked the first time that Boston had led the American League since the final days of the 1949 season. After such a long wait, sole possession of first place lasted a single day.

The contenders stayed neck-and-neck into September, and a week into the final month, the four contenders were virtually tied for first place (Table 1). The AL race could not have been tighter. At this point, the Twins headed to Baltimore for five games with the defending World Series champions, who were out of the race and failed to play spoiler. The Twins captured four of five and reclaimed the league lead.

Table 1. American League standings through Wednesday, September 6, 1967

	Wins–Losses	Win percentage
Chicago	78–61	.561
Minnesota	78–61	.561
Boston	79–62	.560
Detroit	79–62	.560

Oliva delivered fifteen hits in twenty-one at-bats during the series, including five doubles and a triple. He also drew three walks to reach base eighteen times in five games; the only way to keep him from hitting the ball hard was to walk him. "Guys like Brooks Robinson and Jim Palmer, who pitched against him, still remember that and talk about that series," Harmon Killebrew said in a 2009 interview. "It was just a once-in-a-lifetime series."

In the middle of it all, Oliva collected a team-record nine consecutive hits. After stroking two doubles in the opener, a 4–2 win, Tony O went 8 for 9, with two more doubles in a Friday-night doubleheader. In the first game, a 7–2 Twins victory, he was 3 for 4, with hits in his final two plate appearances. Then he went 5 for 5 in the second game, a 5–3 loss, with five singles, giving him seven straight hits. His average jumped to .284, good for fifth place in the AL batting race, though he was twenty-seven points behind the leader, Carl Yastrzemski. The streak of consecutive hits continued the next day, as Oliva led off the second inning with a single off Orioles rookie Bill Dillman. After Killebrew powered his thirty-eighth home run to give the Twins a 1–0 lead in the fourth, Oliva singled again off Dillman for his ninth straight hit and a new Twins record.

The score was still 1–0 in the fifth when Jim Kaat and César Tovar both singled, and Killebrew drew a two-out walk to load the bases. Oliva came to the plate looking for his third hit of the day. The count went 3–2, putting the runners in motion with two outs, but the twenty-two-year-old Dillman threw a fastball past the game's hottest hitter, ending the threat and his streak. Only two Minnesota players have matched Oliva with hits in nine straight plate appearances: Mickey Hatcher in 1985 and Todd Walker in 1998.

Despite Baltimore's fine pitching in those years, Oliva excelled against the Orioles. In 157 career games, roughly the equivalent of a full season, he batted .331 and slugged .490, with twenty-nine doubles, eighteen homers, and eighty-six RBIs. Brooks Robinson, Baltimore's Hall of Fame third baseman, says, "Tony was probably the toughest out that the Orioles had to play against." He explains, "You had no place to pitch this guy. He was the type of hitter that you just tried to keep the ball down, but he was going to get his base hits no matter who pitched against him. I don't care if it's Palmer or Cuellar or McNally—you're going to have to deal with Oliva. He's just a great hitter. Absolutely in the top two or three guys I played against, hitting-wise."

Despite setting a team record, Oliva still fell three hits short of tying the major league mark for consecutive hits, set by Cubs catcher Johnny Kling in 1902. Two others have tied Kling's record: longtime Red Sox third baseman Pinky Higgins in 1938 and Detroit first baseman Walt Dropo in 1952. Oliva believes that stroking twelve consecutive hits falls into the same rarified class as batting averages over .400—Ted Williams being the last .400 hitter in 1941—or Joe DiMaggio's fifty-six-game hitting streak. He is convinced that none of these milestones will ever be matched because of the pitching specialization that now provides fresh arms in the late innings.

After collecting fifteen hits in the Baltimore series, Oliva was batting .290.

Suddenly hitting .300 again was plausible, and another batting title was not out of the question either. He considered himself a strong finisher, though he had considerable ground to gain in the batting race. The league's two leading hitters were Red Sox stars Carl Yastrzemski (.312) and George Scott (.305). To overtake them, Oliva would have to add roughly twenty-five points to his average, seemingly impossible with just eighteen games remaining. Then again, he had lifted his average by thirty-five points in his previous thirty-three games. The two-time batting champ would have to keep hitting at a torrid clip to catch Yaz. Oliva continued to inch closer, as his assault on Orioles pitching was only the start of a nine-game hitting streak in which he batted .543.

On September 11, Oliva and the Twins moved down the turnpike to Washington, where the hitting streak continued, and they took two of three from the Senators. Tony O collected hits in all three contests, and it seemed that nothing could slow him down—except perhaps a violent collision with another outfield wall.

Jim Kaat took a 3–0 lead into the ninth of the rubber game, but Washington opened the frame with a pair of singles that put runners on the corners. With no outs, Senators outfielder Fred Valentine sent a drive to deep right field, and Oliva, in full pursuit, crashed hard into the fence attempting the catch. The ball fell in for a double, scoring pinch runner Ed Stroud for Washington's first run. Despite the jarring collision, Oliva got back on his feet quickly, retrieved the ball, and rifled it back to the infield, which kept catcher Paul Casanova from scoring.

By then Oliva was bleeding from his left eye. A cut across the top of his eyelid would require two stitches. Sandy Valdespino, who had helped carry Oliva to the clubhouse on a stretcher earlier that season in Cleveland, thought his friend's chance meeting with the right-field fence at D.C. Stadium was far scarier. He marvels at how lucky Oliva was and at how close he came—in a game of inches—to losing an eye. He left the game, having had eighteen hits in his last thirty-two at-bats. Despite the collision and the stitches in his eyelid, Oliva barely skipped a beat at the plate. He was back on the field the next day, hit safely in fifteen of the last seventeen games, and batted .345 over the last month.

The Detroit Tigers scrambled to the front of the American League pack on September 17 with a dozen games yet to be played. The Tigers were a half game up on the White Sox and a full game ahead of Minnesota and Boston, with the Red Sox coming to Tiger Stadium for two games. It was the last day the Tigers held sole possession of first place, as Boston beat them twice. From that point on, only the Red Sox and Twins held down the top spot. At the start of the final week, the White Sox looked positioned to win it all. Their final five games were against the American League's two worst teams: Kansas City and Washington. But the Athletics swept a September 27 doubleheader from Chicago, and the reeling White Sox journeyed home and were swept by the Senators, dropping their final five games.

In a strange scheduling quirk, Minnesota and Boston had two days off before closing the season at Fenway Park with Saturday and Sunday matchups. The Tigers, still in the hunt, were to face the Angels in Detroit on Thursday and Friday, but consecutive rainouts forced the two clubs to play doubleheaders on both Saturday and Sunday with the AL pennant on the line. Heading into the final weekend, the Tigers were tied with first-place Minnesota in the loss column, but they probably needed to win at least three of four from the Angels to have a chance. The Twins could clinch the pennant with a single win (Table 2).

Table 2. American League standings through Friday, September 29, 1967

	Wins–Losses	Games back
Minnesota	91–69	—
Boston	90–70	1.0
Detroit	89–69	1.0
Chicago	89–71	2.0

Jim Kaat drew the Saturday afternoon assignment at Fenway Park. The Red Sox had roughed up southpaws at home all season, but Kaat, with seven straight wins in September, had dominated after the All-Star break. His fastball was breaking down and away against righthanded hitters, a good formula to avoid having pitches launched toward the Green Monster.

Red Sox fans, starved for a World Series appearance after two mostly disappointing decades, came out in full force. A World Series atmosphere took hold at the old ballpark. "I had never heard a crowd holler like that," recalls Twins relief pitcher Al Worthington. "They hollered from the first inning through the whole night. I think that might have bothered us some. We always scored a lot of runs when we went into Boston, but we didn't score those two games. The noise was deafening."

The two-game set started well for Minnesota. Zoilo Versalles opened the game with a single to left, advanced to second when Harmon Killebrew drew a walk, and scored on a single up the middle by Oliva. Kaat, who had already worked more than sixty innings in September, looked as though he might repeat his pennant-clinching success of two years earlier. Four of the first seven outs he recorded were strikeouts, but when he threw a third strike past Boston starter José Santiago to open the third inning, he felt a pop in his throwing elbow.

Kaat was forced to leave the game. The innings had piled up over two seasons—568 combined in 1966 and '67—and his ninth start that September was the breaking point. For Kaat, poised to complete Minnesota's four-month surge to the pennant, the elbow injury was crushing. Nearly forty-five years later, however, he fondly recalls pitching well in a historic pennant race. "I think probably the most satisfying month of pitching I ever had was September of '67," he says. "It was far and away my best month of pitching." His elbow did not really hurt, so he kept pitching and never underwent elbow surgery, which was far less successful at the time. The compromise was that he would not be nearly as effective until his elbow rebounded on its own years later.

The Red Sox scratched for two runs off Jim Perry in the fifth, taking the lead on Carl Yastrzemski's infield single. Yaz all but put the game away in the seventh, when he jumped on a 3–1 fastball from Jim Merritt and launched it into the right-field bullpen for a 6–2 Boston lead. With two runners aboard, Yastrzemski's major league–leading forty-fourth of the season was arguably the biggest blow in a year in which he pulled Boston's wagon. Yaz, who like Oliva could hit for both average and power, won the Triple Crown in 1967. In the five seasons from 1963 to 1967, either Oliva or Yastrzemski led the American League in hits, doubles, and batting average, except for 1966, when Frank Robinson took the Triple Crown. This was Yaz's summer.

Boston's lead stood up, although Killebrew hit his forty-fourth as well, a two-run shot into the netting above the left-field wall with two outs in the ninth. The late comeback ended abruptly when Oliva, facing Red Sox reliever Gary Bell, lined a hard shot that third baseman Jerry Adair speared at the bag for a 6–4 final.

The loss dropped the Twins into a first-place tie with Boston. Meanwhile, in Detroit, the Tigers split their Saturday twinbill with the Angels, though they could still control their own destiny. If the Tigers swept Sunday's doubleheader, they would face the winner of the Minnesota–Boston finale in a three-game playoff to determine who would face the St. Louis Cardinals in the World Series.

The Sunday afternoon affair at Fenway Park featured two of the league's three twenty-game winners: Jim Lonborg, who finished 22–9 in his only twenty-win season, and Dean Chance, a two-time twenty-game winner in pursuit of a career-high twenty-first victory. The Twins again got on the board in the first inning, as Killebrew drew a two-out walk and Oliva drilled his league-leading thirty-fourth double off the Green Monster. Minnesota added an unearned run in the third, but the Red Sox struck back in the sixth. With Lonborg leading off the inning, many managers might have turned to a pinch hitter in an elimination game. But Red Sox skipper Dick Williams sent his ace to the plate.

Acting on his own, Lonborg laid a bunt down the third-base line. César Tovar had not been anticipating a bunt. He charged the ball and juggled it for a split second, allowing Lonborg to leg out a hit. Then everything unraveled for the Twins. The next three batters—Adair, Dalton Jones, and Yastrzemski—all singled, and Yaz's shot over second base chased home Adair and Jones to tie the game. Chance did not survive the inning. Before it was over, the Red Sox had scored five runs, aided by a botched fielder's choice, two wild pitches from Worthington, and an error by Killebrew. "Biggest disappointment in my life was losing that last game of '67 to the Red Sox," Chance says. "I beat them four times, shut them out twice, and then that inning they get five runs. It was like a nightmare."

That was all Boston needed, as Lonborg went the distance for the pennant-clinching victory. The Twins, trailing 5–2, took one last shot in the eighth when Killebrew and Oliva singled with two outs to put runners on the corners. The season now hinged on Bob Allison, who came through by pulling a pitch down the third-base line that headed for the left-field corner. With Oliva at first, the Twins could have closed the gap to a single run if the ball got by Yaz and caromed around the corner. But Yastrzemski, who had been patrolling left field at Fenway Park since Ted Williams's retirement seven years earlier, instinctively dashed for the foul line to cut the ball off. Yaz got a good jump and backhanded the ball just as he reached the grandstand along the line.

In his 1968 autobiography *Yaz*, Yastrzemski noted that he often used the base of the grandstand wall to brace his foot before throwing. Normally he would throw home on a play like this, but as he planted his right foot firmly against the wall, he saw the speedy Oliva already approaching third. Instead of throwing home, Yastrzemski pivoted and rifled a perfect throw to second base, where Mike Andrews tagged Allison out. Killebrew had crossed the plate, making the score 5–3, but the rally was over. Within fifteen minutes, the Twins' season was over, too. Yastrzemski had made sure of that. Not only did he go 4 for 4 in the pennant clincher, but he capped his MVP season with a perfect throw that cut down the potential tying run and all but eliminated the Twins.

Back in Detroit, the Tigers won the first game of their Sunday doubleheader with the Angels but failed to force a three-game playoff with Boston. The Angels jumped on Denny McLain and three Detroit relievers for eight runs in the first four frames of the nightcap. The AL race finally came to an end when the Angels wrapped up an 8–5 victory.

Oliva remembers the flight home to Minnesota as one of the quietest he ever endured. It was supposed to be a celebratory return to prepare for Game One of the World Series against the Cardinals at Metropolitan Stadium, but for the Twins, the two losses at Fenway Park brought a sudden end to one of the greatest pennant races in baseball history. It was hard to not think of the what-ifs on the plane and for days after, Oliva says. There were a couple of games before the Fenway Park losses that stuck with him, and he recalls them to this day.

"We lost one day in Chicago when we were winning with two outs in the ninth," Oliva says, referring to a critical September 16 contest at Comiskey Park. The Twins were up 4–1 to start the ninth, but the White Sox strung together a series of hits. They also capitalized on a Dean Chance error and a Jim Kaat wild pitch before claiming a 5–4 victory on a two-out RBI single by Pete Ward.

"We lost another game to the Washington Senators," Oliva recalls. "We were winning 7–0 in the seventh, and we played all night long and then lost." In that August 9 loss at the Met, the Senators tied the game with a seven-run seventh inning. A leadoff homer by Washington third baseman Ken McMullen broke the deadlock in the twentieth, and the Senators added a run for a 9–7 win.

The Twins had still looked like the team to beat heading into the final weekend at Fenway Park. They needed one win and had beaten the Red Sox in six of the previous eight matchups, but Yastrzemski made sure the Twins would win neither of the last two.

Yaz is most remembered by Red Sox fans for his 1967 performance. He almost single-handedly carried the club down the stretch, batting .417 from September 1 through the end of the season. Over the final two weeks, when the Red Sox won eight of their final twelve games to win the pennant, he was 23 for 44, with five home runs and sixteen RBIs. He claimed the Triple Crown and MVP honors, batting .326, with forty-four home runs and 121 RBIs.

Oliva's season ended with a long flight home from Boston, but he had played valiantly despite two violent outfield collisions and a host of injuries. He had hit safely in fifteen of his final eighteen games, though the steady stream of multihit games came to end in September and he finished eighth in the batting race at .289. He failed to hit .300 for the first time in four major league seasons, but he again led the league with thirty-four doubles and ranked in the league's top ten for hits, triples, extra-base hits, total bases, RBIs, batting, and slugging.

Marriage and Family in the Year of the Pitcher

After a disheartening finish to the 1967 season, the following year began with a celebration. On January 6, 1968, Gordette DuBois and Tony Oliva married in the bride's hometown of Hitchcock, South Dakota, a farm community some 350 miles west of the Twin Cities.

Although they could barely communicate when they first met in spring 1964, the two soon realized that their childhoods had had much in common. Both bride and groom had grown up on family farms with a large contingent of brothers and sisters. Gordette had seven siblings, including her twin Gordon; Tony had nine brothers and sisters. Both had daily chores on the farm, a labor-intensive operation that required a contribution from everyone in the family. At the same time, they enjoyed the simple pleasures of farm life.

For all the similarities in their upbringings, Hitchcock's winters were wildly different from Piñar del Río's. On the couple's wedding day, the blizzard of the season raged, and temperatures plummeted below zero. On a day bestowing the worst of winter, roughly seventy-five people gathered for the ceremony at Hitchcock Methodist Church. Tony had invited a few teammates, but the extreme weather kept them away. His best man was Johnny Harper, one of the first friends he had made on his initial trip to Minnesota in 1961. Otherwise, the wedding was witnessed only by Gordette's family and friends, which meant nearly all of Hitchcock. By then, nearly seven years had passed since Tony had seen *his* family.

The snowstorm ended the following day, allowing the newlyweds to return to the Twin Cities for a flight to Puerto Rico. They had planned to honeymoon there for a few weeks, but after a few days, Tony received a phone call from an executive of the Águilas Cibaeñas, a winter league team in Santiago de los Caballeros, Dominican Republic. The team wanted to add Oliva to its playoff roster. The Twins star did not want to interrupt his honeymoon, nor did he like to risk offending a team owner by refusing to play.

Calvin Griffith did not like his key players risking injury in winter ball and had insisted that Oliva take recent winters off. So the newly married ballplayer told the Águilas executive he would play only if the Twins owner gave his permission. This seemed like an easy way to avoid an early departure from Puerto Rico, but to Oliva's surprise, Griffith granted the Águilas club's request to sign him for the playoffs. Oliva felt obligated to play, so the couple spent the rest of their honeymoon in Santo Domingo.

The couple returned to Minneapolis a few weeks before spring camp opened. They were living in an apartment but began looking for their first house. Before Tony headed to Florida, they agreed to buy the Bloomington home of Sandy Valdespino, who had been traded to the Atlanta Braves that winter and had moved his family to Miami. Conveniently, the Olivas now lived just minutes from Metropolitan Stadium. They remain in Bloomington to this day.

Both the Twins and Oliva made a lot of changes that winter. Griffith did not sit still after losing the final two games of 1967 and the American League pennant to the Boston Red Sox. That November, he traded two key members of the 1965 American League champions: twenty-one-game winner Mudcat Grant and league MVP Zoilo Versalles. They moved to the Los Angeles Dodgers, the 1965 World Series winners, in exchange for catcher John Roseboro and relievers Ron Perranoski and Bob Miller.

Grant had feuded and fallen out of favor with new skipper Cal Ermer, who had arrived the previous June and had soon demoted the former staff ace to the bullpen. Grant mostly worked as a reliever for the rest of his career. He closed in Oakland, his final stop, where he tutored a young prospect, Rollie Fingers, who took over ninth-inning duties from him in 1971.

Versalles had been the only starting shortstop fans in Minnesota had ever known. After improving steadily at the plate in his first five years with the Twins, leading to his MVP season, his offensive production dropped sharply the next two summers. In 1967, Versalles endured his worst big league season, batting .200 and scoring just sixty-three runs in 160 games.

Two months after the trade, in late January, Versalles appeared with new American League MVP Carl Yastrzemski at the annual Twin Cities baseball writers' dinner. Although stung by the trade, the veteran shortstop did not lash out at the Twins, instead giving a heartfelt talk in which he thanked Griffith for kindnesses to him and his family. He said he realized the trade was part of the business of baseball, but it was clearly difficult for him. "I'm sorry I can't give you my best last year," Versalles told the crowd. "One thing I will tell you: I can bounce back, and I will this year." He struggled to get the last sentence out, and when he did, he left the podium to loud and sustained applause. Even Griffith was moved. He later paid tribute to Versalles's remarkable contribution in 1965, saying, "Zo's heart is too big for his body." Yastrzemski also recognized the former Twin in his presentation. "It took a lot of courage for Versalles to come here and talk to you after being traded."

In Roseboro, the Twins acquired the frontline catcher they needed, as Earl Battey, whose skills were in decline, was given his outright release over the winter and retired. Miller and Perranoski were expected to fortify a relief corps coming off a mediocre season. The Twins had finished only one game behind the Red Sox, and a better bullpen could have made the difference. Even with an upgrade behind the plate and a better pen, however, the 1968 club staggered to a 79–83 finish. As much as anything else, what doomed the Twins to a losing record was their poor defensive play. They committed a major league–high 170 errors and posted the majors' worst fielding percentage.

Pitching dominated the game in 1968, now known as the Year of the Pitcher. Cardinals ace Bob Gibson posted his record-setting 1.12 ERA that summer, still the lowest in the last ninety-plus years of baseball, and Denny McLain won thirty-one games for the World Series champion Tigers. Major league hurlers collectively posted a 2.98 ERA, the lowest mark since 1918. That major league–wide ERA still stands as the lowest since the dead-ball era, which ended when Babe Ruth pounded fifty-four home runs in 1920. Raw numbers suggest the Twins offense took one of the bigger downturns when run production dropped off dramatically in 1968. For the first time since 1961, the franchise's first year in Minnesota, the Twins did not rank among the league's top run-scoring clubs. The pitching staff received far less run support than in 1967, and a porous defense sabotaged its work.

The season opener in Washington was a meeting of old friends. Former Washington Senators slugger Jim Lemon, who had moved to Minnesota with the franchise in 1961 and was the Twins first-base coach in 1965, was making his debut as a big league manager with the new expansion team Senators. Another old friend, former Twins ace Camilo Pascual, got the Opening Day nod in his second season after returning to Washington.

Pascual and current Twins ace Dean Chance worked five scoreless innings before Harmon Killebrew and Bob Allison greeted their former teammate with home runs. Oliva touched the Cuban righty for three hits in four trips and stole a base. Pascual pitched effectively for eight innings on Opening Day, but Chance, coming off a twenty-win season, tossed a four-hitter for a 2–0 victory.

Oliva and Pascual did not go face-to-face often, which was fine with Oliva. He says Pascual threw the nastiest curveball he ever confronted, and you could not sit on the hard-breaking version. "You saw the fast curve," Oliva explains, "and the slow curve he used mostly like a changeup. Both were very devastating. He had a good fastball and he threw strikes. He was a small guy, but a mean pitcher. You weren't going to play around with Camilo. He could smoke you in a minute." In head-to-head matchups between one of the era's best breaking-ball hitters and the owner of one of its best curveballs, Oliva went 8 for 20, batting .400 with a double and triple, according to the Baseball Cube Web site. Still, Oliva did not cherish facing Pascual's signature pitch.

The Twins won their first six contests, but it marked the only time all season they were six games over .500. They often struggled to string together hits and score runs. They managed neither hit nor run on May 8 in Oakland, where the Athletics had moved for the 1968 season. The new fan base witnessed a historic event when twenty-two-year-old Catfish Hunter worked a perfect game and struck out eleven in a 4–0 win—the first AL perfecto since Don Larsen's against the Brooklyn Dodgers in the 1956 World Series. The Twins scored more than three runs only once in a twelve-game stretch near the start of June, and they reached a new low, scoring just six times in losing four games to the White Sox to open June.

The only thing on fire in Chicago was broadcaster Halsey Hall's jacket. On June 2, the day after Chance took a no-hitter into the bottom of the ninth before losing a 1–0 decision, the cigar-smoking Hall set his coat ablaze in the broadcast booth. Hall later noted that he must have dropped ashes onto some ticker tape beneath his feet. While stamping out that fire, he discovered his coat was burning. His partner in the booth, Merle Harmon, who watched the seventy-year-old Hall battle the blaze, later noted, "That's what's known as operating under fire." Twins catcher Jerry Zimmerman weighed in: "Halsey's the only man I know who can turn a sports coat into a blazer."

The 3M Company, the Minnesota icon known for a wide array of home and industrial products, presented Hall with an asbestos suit.

Even if the team's fate had not been completely decided by the time Hall set his jacket ablaze, it was sealed in the third inning of the All-Star Game in Houston's Astrodome on July 9. Harmon Killebrew, the AL starter at first base, stretched for a throw from Angels shortstop Jim Fregosi with Cardinals star Curt Flood speeding toward the bag. Killebrew ruptured his left hamstring muscle and had to be carried off the field. He missed nearly two months and only returned in September.

Oliva was in Houston as well that day, making his fifth All-Star Game appearance in five seasons. For only the second time, though, he was not in the starting lineup. He had not generated his typical numbers, and Washington slugger Frank Howard, enjoying one of his best seasons, got the start in right. Howard gave way to Oliva in the middle innings. In his only at-bat in the seventh, Oliva collected one of only three American League hits—a long, two-out drive to left-center off Mets righthander Tom Seaver. The ball nearly carried into the seats at the Astrodome but instead hit high off the wall and Oliva had to settle for a double.

The National League had tallied the sole run of the game on a double-play grounder in the first inning, and pitchers like Don Drysdale, Juan Marichal, Steve Carlton, and Tom Seaver made the lead stand up. Oliva was stranded in the seventh, and the National League continued its All-Star dominance with its sixth straight victory, 1–0, a befitting score in the Year of the Pitcher.

When the Twins were floundering in the early going, Oliva was in no position to carry the load. He had pulled a ribcage muscle in spring training and missed two weeks of preparation for the season. Oliva frequently aggravated the injury by swinging the bat, and the malady lingered well into May. When he did make contact, he lacked power. He managed to bat .277 in April, but his average dipped to .242, with only three homers, by late May.

There were signs of a turnaround when Oliva closed May with a seven-game hitting streak, but in early June he hurt his right ankle. Although the injury had no effect on his hitting, Oliva, who had ten stolen bases in fifty-two games prior to the injury, stopped running and did not swipe another base all season. Then, in late July, Oliva pulled his left hamstring muscle running to first base in a lopsided win over the Angels. He had played through the ankle injury, but the hamstring pull forced him to sit for ten days.

Nevertheless, as the season progressed Oliva worked his way into a crowded American League batting race. It was not easy. Even after closing May with a hitting streak, he was batting just .249 and trailed Washington's Frank Howard, the league's leading hitter, by nearly a hundred points. With a .343 average, nineteen homers, and forty RBIs, Howard led all three Triple Crown categories heading into June.

Tony O began hitting the ball on the money more frequently. Hard contact finally had a bigger payoff in a June 2 doubleheader at Chicago. Although the Twins scored just five runs and dropped both ends of the twinbill, Oliva went 6 for 8, collecting six straight hits and going 4 for 4 with solo homers off Chicago's Joe Horlen and Hoyt Wilhelm in the second game. One of them was a tape-measure blast deep into the upper deck in left field. The two longballs indicated that Oliva's ribcage injury was no longer affecting his performance. Oliva and the Twins moved on to New York, where they won three of four from the Yankees and where Tony O went 5 for 12, with two doubles and two more home runs. On June 6, his two-run shot into Yankee Stadium's upper deck provided the scoring in a 2–0 win.

Now batting .275, Tony O had powered four homers in five days. He continued to hit, batting .337 and stroking a league-leading nine home runs in June. There was the upper-deck shot at Yankee Stadium, and two weeks later, on June 21, Oliva teed off on Yankees ace Mel Stottlemyre, delivering a 462-foot blast to straightaway center at the Met. The home run was the longest he had hit to that point in his career.

After powering a double and two homers in a 6–4 loss to Baltimore on June's final day, Oliva was batting .280 and had moved within thirty-three points of the American League's latest batting leader, Boston's Ken Harrelson, who was hitting .313. Heading into July, Oakland Athletics center fielder Rick Monday (.304) and reigning Triple Crown winner Carl Yastrzemski (.300) were the only other .300 hitters, but Oliva was determined to rejoin the fraternity with a strong finish.

Oliva batted .329 in July and continued his push up the AL leaderboard. Soon after the All-Star break, he assembled a season-high eight-game hitting streak that pushed his average to .291 on July 22. He had moved into third place in the batting race, nine points behind the new league leader, the Athletics' Rick Monday, and five behind Ken Harrelson. Teammates Rod Carew (.288) and Ted Uhlaender (.285) were not far behind, but Yastrzemski, mired in a 3-for-27 skid, had fallen to .279.

The day after Oliva's hitting streak stalled, on July 24, the Twins erupted for twenty hits, tying a team record in a 12–1 win over the Angels. Minnesota was playing without Harmon Killebrew because of the ruptured hamstring at the All-Star Game; Oliva now joined him on the sidelines when he suffered his left hamstring pull. Without Killebrew and Oliva, the Twins fell further out of the pennant chase. At the same time, the batting race tightened. Uhlaender, Carew, and Harrelson took turns leading the league, though Carew, who was in the U.S. Marine Corps Reserve, missed three weeks in June to meet his military obligation and lacked enough plate appearances to qualify for the batting title.

The Twins began a seven-game road trip in Baltimore on August 6, and Oliva returned to the lineup with a hit in three trips in a 5–4 win. With six hits in the four-game set, including two in the August 8 finale, Tony O pushed his average to .298 and took over the top spot in the AL batting race for the first time all season. With three hits in consecutive mid-August contests with Washington, Oliva's average surged over the .300 mark for the first time since the early days of the season. He was on one of his classic tears, running his average to a league-leading .307 on August 16. Carew was still close at .302, but otherwise, the closest competition was Harrelson at .294. Uhlaender and Monday had slipped into the .280s, and Yastrzemski was hitting just .272.

Soon the batting race became a two-man competition between Oliva and Yastrzemski. While the others stumbled, Yaz turned it up. He hit safely in seventeen of his final twenty games in August and used a nine-game hitting streak to bump his average to .290 on August 29. He had gone 2 for 3 that day against Oakland. Oliva had also stroked two hits in Cleveland, but in five trips, and Yaz took a one-point lead over the Twins star.

Oliva took a four-point lead on August 31, but the day ended dreadfully for the AL batting leader. In the sixth inning of a 4–3 Twins win, White Sox center fielder Ken Berry lofted a shallow fly toward the foul line in right field. Oliva charged hard but did not appear to have a legitimate shot at catching it. When the ball seemed to hang up longer than anticipated, he dove for it, landing on his elbow and dislocating his left shoulder as he rolled. He still got up and chased the ball down. After Oliva threw the ball back to the infield, the pain took over. He was helped from the field and headed to suburban Fairview–Southdale Hospital with his shoulder still out of joint. "They put the shoulder back in place at the hospital and put a cast on it for almost a month," Oliva recalls. "I was lucky there was no permanent damage to my arm. The next year it was fine."

Oliva was hospitalized for only a few days, but his season was over. There was nothing he could do. Oliva held out hope he might return for the final week of the season, but he knew it was a long shot.

In the days following the injury, manager Cal Ermer and a number of Twins coaches and players noted the irony that Oliva was hurt diving for a ball in the outfield. The consensus was that no one had ever seen him leave his feet to catch a ball, and Oliva himself verified that fact from his hospital bed. "I never did it before," Oliva told Sid Hartman of the *Minneapolis Tribune*. "I watched Ted Uhlaender and César Tovar dive for balls, but I always believed that you could do as well reaching out for a ball." Although he had seen Tovar and Uhlaender dive and make seemingly impossible catches, he was convinced the risk was not worth it. If you dived and missed and the ball got past you, it meant extra bases. If you stayed on your feet, the result was nothing more than a single.

Oliva's dislocated shoulder abruptly ended a frustrating season. The spring ribcage injury had slowed his preparation and stunted his power stroke. Then the June ankle injury stalled his running game, and the July hamstring pull shelved him for ten days. Just when he was on course to secure his third batting title in five seasons, he wound up in a hospital bed. Even after his brief slump in late August, he was convinced he would have made a strong finish if he had not been injured. He had history on his side. To that point in his career, he had been a .330 hitter in September and October. He had a track record of finishing strong. As it was, he had enough plate appearances to claim the batting title, but with a .289 average, he was sure it would not be good enough.

Yastrzemski moved ahead of Oliva after going 4 for 5 in a 10–2 Red Sox romp over the Twins in early September, and he trailed Oliva only one day the rest of the way. At season's end, Yaz, who had batted .369 over his final forty-five games, finished first in the league at .301. He displaced Hall of Famer Elmer Flick of the 1905 Cleveland Bronchos as the batting champion with the lowest AL average in major league history (.306). That distinction, of course, does not take away from Yaz's accomplishment. Major league hitters collectively batted a meager .237 in 1968, still the lowest single-season overall average in big league history. In claiming his third batting crown in a span of six seasons, Yaz topped Oakland's Danny Cater, who finished with a flourish to hit .290. Oliva placed third by hitting .289 for a second consecutive season.

Injuries limited Oliva to 138 games, during which he recorded just twenty-four doubles, eighteen homers, and sixty-eight RBIs. In the Year of the Pitcher, however, those were more than decent numbers. Oliva finished twelfth in the league in RBIs and first on his team, despite missing the final month. He tied for thirteenth on the AL leaderboard in both doubles and homers.

It was a disappointing season for the Twins. They had started the season promisingly but ended in seventh place, twenty-four games behind the AL champion Detroit Tigers. A bright spot in 1968 was César Tovar, who played all over the diamond and scored eighty-nine runs, only six fewer than the league leader, Detroit's Dick McAuliffe. Appropriately, the 155-pound Tovar may be most remembered for playing all nine positions in a 2–1 win over Oakland on September 22.

Oakland shortstop Bert Campaneris had done the same in September 1965, as a publicity stunt, and Tovar followed in his footsteps, taking the mound to start his own defensive trip around the diamond. Tovar kept Athletics hitters off stride, or unnerved, with a triple or even quadruple pump as he went into his windup. He opened the game by getting Campaneris to pop out to Ron Clark at third. The highlight of Tovar's only big league mound stint was striking out the second batter he faced, a young outfielder named Reggie Jackson. Tovar then walked Danny Cater and balked him to second, but he kept the Athletics off the scoreboard by getting Sal Bando to fly out to Twins rookie Graig Nettles at first base. Tovar had not allowed a fair ball beyond the infield. Oliva says Tovar threw nothing but "garbage" from the mound, but he got people out. "Tovar was tough."

The slight Venezuelan moved behind the plate for the second inning. He did not have a catcher's build, which amused Oliva. Oliva, laughing at the thought of his friend walking onto the field in full equipment, says the shin guards and chest protector looked supersized. The chest protector all but touched the ground when Tovar went into his crouch.

After getting out from behind the plate, Tovar shifted to first base and worked his way around the infield. Then he did a tour of the outfield. When it was over, he was 1 for 3, with a stolen base, five putouts, and a nifty dive to his right to snag a hot grounder at first base in the third. When he recovered to flip the ball to pitcher Tom Hall covering first base, he had retired Jackson again. Tovar also tallied the game's first run. The only thing he *did not* do was collect the win or the save in the one-run victory.

For Oliva, the baseball season ended prematurely with a dislocated shoulder. Life was more upbeat at home, where he and Gordette had settled into the house they had purchased from Sandy Valdespino. Gordette immediately engineered a makeover of the interior. She was pregnant, and changes were necessary with a baby on the way. Before a busy summer came to a close, Tony and Gordette became parents. Tony managed to be home for the birth of their daughter Anita. She was due in the days leading up to the All-Star break, when the Twins were playing in Boston. But it was not until Oliva, Rod Carew, and Harmon Killebrew were on a flight home following the All-Star Game in Houston that Gordette began experiencing labor pains. Anita was born that evening.

After seven years of isolation from his parents and siblings, Oliva had a family of his own. Less than three years later, in January 1970, the Olivas welcomed their first son, Pedro Jr. Ricardo arrived in 1975. The children filled a huge void. "He was a very, very lonesome man," Gordette recalls of their earliest days together. "I personally do not know anyone closer to their family, their siblings. His mother and father are gone now, but he just can't do enough for them or be with them enough. He's still not happy he can't be with them more."

In the 1970s, traveling to Cuba finally became a reality for Cubans living in the United States. Over the years, it has become increasingly easier, and Oliva has visited frequently. But that decade of complete isolation from loved ones, a source of lingering sadness through the years, instilled a deeper appreciation of what his own wife and children meant to him.

Oliva's profession required an abbreviated version of forced separation from family. Through the spring and summer months, he was on the road as much as he was at home. Even when the Twins were in town, night games kept the young father away when the kids were home from school. He frequently missed dinnertime and bedtime. "Mom's family was our extended family, and Dad was gone a lot," recalls Anita. "We went to church with some of our cousins. We'd get together almost every Sunday afternoon with cousins. They were kind of a nucleus that helped Mom raise us when we were really young."

For many years, baseball was a year-round affair. If Oliva was not playing winter ball, he was on a plane bound for Mexico or Colombia to coach or manage a team, departing roughly a week after the major league season. He was preparing for a career beyond his playing days, a commitment that meant long stretches away from his family. The tasks of raising the children mostly fell to Gordette during Tony's playing days. "It was hard," Gordette admits, "but I met other wives that were married to businessmen. Businessmen have to travel, too. When I'd get down, Tony would always say, 'Honey, you know what? Life is full of sacrifices and this is a sacrifice we have to make now.'"

Anita says her mother was a take-charge parent, well suited to running a household. Mom also was the rules enforcer, one of many hats she wore raising three children. "She's kind of a tomboy, very crafty, very self-sufficient," Anita says. "She was the carpenter, the plumber, the painter. She always saved major projects for the winter ball season, because that would help pass the time." One winter, Anita notes, Gordette installed a floor in their Bloomington home. She ordered the materials to lay a brick floor, cutting the bricks and completing the job herself. "She replaced our entryway, hallway, and kitchen flooring that winter."

Winter ball sometimes meant celebrating Christmas in Latin America. Anita warmly remembers "my mom traveling with three kids and nine suitcases to some small town in the middle of Mexico or Colombia." The baseball life provided unique challenges, though Gordette is quick to point out, "It paid off. Now the children are grown. I don't have to stay home any more. I can travel with him."

"We truly lived the baseball schedule, so that we could have time with him," Anita adds. "When it was spring training, he'd be in Florida. When Peter and I were younger, my mom would take us out of school and put us in school in Florida—so that we could be there a little longer." The Olivas and Carews rented homes near each other there, and Anita remembers playing with Rod and Marilyn's three daughters. Baseball activity kept her brother Pedro busy.

Although the Oliva boys spent summer afternoons running around the Twins clubhouse when they were young, the perks and quirks of growing up children of a pro baseball player were simply part of everyday life. Their parents—hard-working, down-to-earth people—never bought into an ostentatious lifestyle. "So, where a lot of people would expect the family of Tony Oliva to live in the big house on a hill, we always lived in a very humble but nice neighborhood," Anita says. "My parents have always been people who lived below their means, because they wanted to be sure they were saving."

In 1972, with the family growing, the Olivas moved into a larger home in Bloomington. Forty years later, Tony and Gordette still live in that house, which holds a lifetime of memories for the kids. They remember their father as someone who unconditionally reached out and talked to everyone. "My father is passionate about people," Anita says. "Encouraging them. Motivating them. And getting them to think positive. That's his mantra. He's always telling people, 'Lift your head up. Give everything your best all the time.'"

Oliva taught his children to approach life the same way. Anita and Pedro, along with the Versalles girls, were among the few young people of color attending Bloomington's public schools in the 1970s. As children of a professional athlete, they were mostly embraced by their peers. But regardless of circumstances, their father set an example in how to deal with others and put their best foot forward, which served them well. "We were brought up in a diverse culture and environment, where we thought everybody was a potential friend," Anita explains. "That's how he brought us up. You are no better than the person on the corner who may be homeless. At the core of it all, he has a heart for people. He has a capability of forgiveness and understanding like nobody I've ever met in my life."

The three children have taken distinctly different paths in life. Anita earned a business degree from St. Thomas University in St. Paul, with an emphasis on international business. Her mother describes her as a hard worker who has done well in her field. Today Anita runs two graphic design companies, M Design Interactive, Inc., and Oliva Management, LLC.

Pedro, who also goes by Peter, followed in his father's footsteps and pursued a baseball career. He was a power prospect who, like his father and his father's father, hit lefthanded and threw righthanded. Tony notes that his son was blessed with both good instincts and the ability to hit, qualities that a prospect must have to succeed professionally. Pedro stroked a home run in the Metrodome during his high school years, but he suffered a major knee injury that stalled his pro career.

Ric, a graduate of the Berklee College of Music in Boston, is a songwriter and an accomplished guitarist. He has released a compact disc of his own compositions. He also teaches guitar and songwriting, both privately and as a faculty member of a St. Paul music school. He frequently appears in Twin Cities clubs with rock bands and occasionally performs "The Star Spangled Banner" at Target Field.

Their personal pursuits vary greatly, but all three children live within a few minutes of their parents' home in Bloomington. Gordette and Tony see them all the time, along with their four grandchildren.

Oliva also has a son, Damion Oliva, from a relationship he had prior to meeting Gordette in 1964. Damion, who is married without children, spent roughly a decade in the military and has settled in Virginia. He has never lived near the other Oliva children, but despite the physical distance, Gordette says all of the kids are close and stay in touch.

Tony and Gordette travel together more now, whether to Cuba or Florida. They spend at least a few weeks in Florida each winter. In January, Tony participates in the Minnesota Twins fantasy camp, which takes place at the team's complex in Fort Myers. They remain there for spring training, as Tony continues to serve as a hitting instructor with the club. As nice as it is to ditch Minnesota's cold weather, he says they try not to stay away as long when they travel in winter months because of their children and grandchildren. "I know we miss them when we're not around for a week or so," Tony explains. "We miss them. It's nice to be around the kids."

Baseball's Summer of Change

C hange was in the air in spring 1969. In response to the game's slow but steady tilt toward the sparse run production of the dead-ball era, Major League Baseball owners looked to level the playing field between hitters and pitchers by lowering the mound to a maximum of ten inches. For decades, the maximum height had been fifteen inches, though a few mounds, including Dodger Stadium's, were rumored to be closer to twenty. But for 1969, everything would be different.

A new round of expansion added two teams to each league and, for the first time, divided each league into two divisions of six teams each. The Twins joined the American League West, along with the White Sox, the California clubs in Oakland and Anaheim, and the new Kansas City Royals and Seattle Pilots. The new alignment added a round of playoffs to determine the World Series matchup.

Another dramatic change took place closer to home. After the team's 79–83 finish in 1968, owner Calvin Griffith fired Cal Ermer and gave Billy Martin his first big league managerial gig. A stubborn owner and a combative former player were an improbable pairing to run the club, but Griffith had seen Martin motivate Zoilo Versalles to capitalize on his talent and win MVP honors in 1965. As Minnesota's third-base coach that summer, Martin had made the slugging Twins multidimensional, running more and forcing opponents to respond. With Martin in charge in 1969, the Twins stole more bases, executed the hit-and-run, and almost recklessly took the extra base.

Oliva liked Martin's gambling nature, which gave him, Rod Carew, César Tovar, and the other speedsters the green light to run if they thought they could steal a bag. Oliva appreciated that Martin never second-guessed an attempt. As long as a player hustled and played hard, the skipper did not mind if a gamble failed. Martin had the respect of his players because he was fair with them, Oliva said, and that made them want to play hard.

"Billy did a great job," Harmon Killebrew recalled in a 2010 interview. "The thing I think that he was best at was trying to keep the guys from making little mistakes. He was really big on fundamentals and the little things to win games. He knew as much about the game as anybody that you want to be around."

When the Twins gathered in Florida prior to the 1969 season, what had *not* changed was having Killebrew and Oliva anchor the Twins lineup. Killebrew had averaged forty-two homers and 108 RBIs over seven seasons before rupturing his hamstring in Houston at the 1968 All-Star Game. Remarkably, he was in camp ready to play the next spring. Oliva had led the American League in hitting when he dislocated his shoulder on the last day of August 1968. He missed the rest of that season and lost the batting race to Carl Yastrzemski, but he still led the Twins in extra-base hits and RBIs during the club's dismal 79–83 campaign.

In 1969, his sixth season, Tony O batted .309, led the league in hits for the fourth time and in doubles for the third time, and recorded one hundred RBIs for the first time in his career. Yet his performance was overshadowed by stellar seasons from Killebrew and Carew.

Killebrew topped the majors with forty-nine home runs and a career-best 140 RBIs. With Martin running the show, the slugger also set a personal high by stealing eight bases. His new running game included a pair of steals in a single inning against the Yankees on June 4. At season's end, Killebrew claimed the American League's MVP trophy. "1969 was my best year," Killebrew said forty years later. "I don't know why, because 1968 is when I got hurt in the All-Star Game and I missed half a season. Some of the doctors said I was through playing, that I wouldn't recover. I worked real hard that winter and came back and had the best year I ever had in baseball. Why? I don't know."

Carew blossomed into a star during the first two months of Martin's tenure. Heading into June, Carew was hitting .403 and held a seventy-point lead in the batting race. He cruised to his first of seven batting crowns with a .332 average, and he electrified baseball fans by stealing home seven times that summer. Before the 1969 season, Martin tutored Carew in the art of stealing home. Carew says Martin taught him to time a pitcher's delivery and start for home from a walking lead when he knew he could make it safely. The student mastered beating a pitch to the plate, though he fell one short of Ty Cobb's major league record of eight steals of home in 1912.

With Killebrew and Carew divvying up the Triple Crown categories, and with Killebrew winning the league's ultimate prize, it was easy to overlook Oliva. But Tony O again ranked among league leaders. In addition to posting a league-leading 197 hits and thirty-nine doubles, he finished third in the batting race at .309, one of only six AL players to bat .300. With 101 RBIs, he was one of just eight in the league to reach the century mark.

For much of Oliva's career, Killebrew was the face of the Twins franchise—the prodigious slugger and run producer who was among the biggest home-run threats of his era. That was always fine with Oliva, who witnessed his friend's best season in 1969 while sharing the third and fourth spots in the Twins lineup with him. Oliva was equally excited to see Carew, his friend and roomie, develop into a batting champ and thrill crowds with his mad dashes to the plate. With Martin at the helm, the Twins improved by eighteen wins and finished atop the AL West with a 97–65 record. Oliva says the fiery Martin deserved a lot of the credit for leading the 1969 Twins into the playoffs. He views that club as a collection of older players—some of them castoffs from other organizations—who produced beyond expectations.

The elevation of Rich Reese into the starting lineup in June paid off. After Killebrew agreed to shift to third base to make room for Reese, the lefthanded-hitting first baseman had his best year, batting .322 with sixteen home runs and sixty-nine RBIs—all career highs.

Reese was not the only Twin to have a career year. Cuban shortstop Leo Cárdenas, who had come over from Cincinnati in an offseason trade that shipped promising lefty Jim Merritt to the Reds, led all big league shortstops in putouts, assists, and double plays in 1969. He was nicknamed "Mr. Automatic" for his sure-handed glove work. "Leo Cárdenas did a beautiful job for us," Oliva says of his fellow Cuban, a native of the northern port city of Matanzas. "He was a great shortstop and could hit. He had a great year that year." Indeed, he did. Cárdenas had one of his best offensive seasons, batting .280 with ten homers and a career-high seventy RBIs.

César Tovar, who took over leadoff duties in the course of the summer, enjoyed a breakout year. He set personal highs with a .288 average, eleven home runs, ninety-nine runs, and forty-five stolen bases. Tovar, twenty-nine years old and in his prime, enjoyed the first of three consecutive seasons as a top tablesetter and run scorer. He tallied 313 runs in this three-year stretch, most among AL players.

Pitchers Jim Perry and Dave Boswell joined the twenty-win club for the first time in their careers. Perry stepped up as a starter in Minnesota's 1965 championship run after Camilo Pascual had midseason surgery, but he was not a rotation mainstay until Martin took over. The righthander went 20–6 with a 2.82 ERA in thirty-six starts and ten relief appearances.

Boswell, who had shown occasional flashes of brilliance over his first five seasons in the majors, put it all together in 1969. The righthander finished 20–12 with a 3.23 ERA. The aggressive, combative Boswell pitched through bone chips that caused severe pain and occasional swelling in his pitching elbow. One of the game's true characters of the 1960s, the free-spirited righthander's eccentricities amused teammates and sometimes overshadowed his performance on the field. Even in his best season, Boswell may be best known not for his playing but for a run-in he had with Martin in a Detroit bar in August 1969. By then, his tender elbow had swollen well beyond normal size, but after sitting out two weeks to recover from his bar-fight injuries, Boswell won eight of eleven decisions down the stretch. The time off had to have helped.

When Oliva hit, the Twins usually won in 1969. After losing the first four games of Billy Martin's big league managerial career, the Twins won sixteen of their next nineteen, a stretch in which Oliva assembled a thirteen-game hitting streak and scored fourteen runs.

Tony O began his hottest stretch of hitting in a June 22 doubleheader in Oakland, against the Twins' chief rival in the AL West chase. The Athletics led by only a few percentage points, and it stayed that way when the clubs split the Sunday twinbill. Oliva went 6 for 10, with four doubles in the two games. One of those doubles led off the thirteenth inning of the second contest, and Oliva tallied the game-winner on Jim Perry's successful suicide squeeze.

Oliva's big day kicked off a torrid ten-game hitting streak in which he was 25 for 45, with eleven doubles and five home runs. Two of those homers came a week later, in the second game of a June 29 doubleheader with the Kansas City Royals. After collecting two singles and a double in the opener, Tony O capped the twinbill by going 5 for 5, leading the Twins to a 12–2 victory. It was Oliva's fourth five-hit game and the tenth by a Minnesota player, but only Oliva had more than one. This time he collected each hit off a different Royals pitcher.

Although Oliva finished a triple shy of the cycle, his day's work demonstrated the range of his offensive skill. In addition to hitting the two homers, he beat out a bunt in the first, drilled a line-drive single, and stroked a 410-foot double that just missed clearing the wall in left-center field for a third homer. The ball hit the railing on the top of the wall and bounded back onto the field.

The big blast, a towering three-run homer in the second, sailed over the right-field upper deck and onto Brooklyn Avenue outside old Municipal Stadium. Kansas City starter Dave Wickersham had given Oliva trouble when he was a mainstay with the Tigers during the mid-1960s, but on this occasion, Tony O turned on a slider for the longest ball he ever hit in the major leagues. Wickersham had "a little slider, a little sinker," remembers Oliva. "I don't know how he got me out so easy. There's always someone who's got your number. He had my number—him and Marcelino López—but that day I smoked that ball." As a prolific breaking-ball hitter who usually found sliders to his liking, Oliva finally teed off on Wickersham, one pitch after the Royals righthander had put the red-hot hitter on his backside with an inside offering.

"Tony got up and hit it out of the stadium," recalls Rod Carew. "There's a house up on a hill in right field. This lady came out and was waving a towel because the ball had hit the house." Royals officials left the stadium to measure the home run's distance and determined that it had traveled 517 feet. The ball—only the thirteenth to clear the right side of Municipal Stadium since the Athletics had departed Philadelphia for Kansas City in 1955—was retrieved and returned to Oliva.

Oliva finished the game with five RBIs, giving him seventeen during his ten-game hitting streak. He had collected hits in his final three at-bats of the first game, and by the end of the day he had hit safely in his preceding eight trips. He might have had a chance to make it nine straight hits in the ninth inning of the second game, which would have tied the team record he had set against the Orioles in 1967. But Martin removed him after his eighth-inning single, hoping to protect the slugger's back. Rookie Charlie Manuel ran for Oliva and batted in the ninth, when the Twins rallied for three more runs.

"We tried everything except a shotgun," Royals manager and Hall of Fame second baseman Joe Gordon told sportswriters after Oliva's assault on his pitching staff. "Wickersham knocked him down and that only got him mad. We tried sliders, changeups and curves, and nothing worked. When a good hitter like Oliva gets hot, it doesn't matter what you throw up there." And Gordon was right: Oliva was hot. He was hitting everything in sight and spraying the ball with authority.

Walt Dropo of the Tigers holds the American League record for consecutive hits, with twelve, achieved over two days in July 1952. Oliva's chance of approaching Dropo's mark ended quickly on June 30 in Chicago. Facing righthander Joe Horlen in the first, Tony O hit a hard one-hopper that looked destined for center field, but White Sox second baseman Rich Morales made a diving stop and threw him out from his backside. Oliva went hitless that day, but two days later he kicked off a fifteen-game hitting streak. That coincided with Minnesota's 18–2 run at the start of July, which put the Twins in charge of the AL West race.

Harmon Killebrew's bat boomed during the surge. He was the league's most fearsome run producer, at one point drilling nine homers and driving in nineteen runs in a ten-game stretch. He powered four shots into the Met's seats in a Fourth of July weekend sweep of the Athletics. Oliva stroked nine hits and scored five runs in the three wins. Both Killebrew and Oliva stuck it to Oakland all season long. Killebrew batted .435 with eleven homers and thirty-four RBIs in eighteen games; Oliva hit .417 with ten doubles, six homers, and twenty-one RBIs. With the duo driving the offense, the Twins won thirteen of eighteen games from their only competition for the AL West title.

On July 14, Oliva's hitting streak reached fourteen games in a dramatic 4–3 victory over Chicago, secured when Leo Cárdenas singled Oliva home in the thirteenth. Tony O had two hits in the game, but he felt ill and missed the rest of the Chicago series, which closed out a stunning 14–1 homestand by the Twins. By the time the club flew to Seattle, Oliva had a 104° fever and bumps had broken out over his entire body. He had come down with chicken pox, probably contracted from his infant daughter Anita. The illness, which knocked him out of action for ten days, could not have come at a worse time. Oliva, 25 for 50 in his preceding twelve games, had seen his average climb to .339 in the midst of the Twins' 18–2 run.

He also missed the All-Star Game ten days later at Washington, D.C.'s RFK Memorial Stadium. Oliva had appeared in all five Midsummer Classics since his 1964 arrival, and it took chicken pox to keep him off the field when the game's best players gathered at RFK. The lost opportunity also ended Oliva's bid to match Joe DiMaggio for consecutive All-Star Game appearances to start a career. The Yankee Clipper had played in six straight after taking his place in New York's outfield in 1936.

The final day of the first half, July 20, was Oliva's thirty-first birthday, though hardly anyone knew he had reached the big three-oh. Because he had used his younger brother Tony's birth certificate to obtain a passport in 1961, the man who did not look a day over thirty was thought to be twenty-eight. On that day, Oliva was home recovering from the chicken pox. The virus took its toll, as it often does on adults. Oliva, weakened by fever, lost a lot of weight. To keep other Twins from contracting the virus, he stayed away from the clubhouse and had been home for a nearly a week when his birthday rolled around.

Oliva's birthday also fell on the day that Apollo 11 executed the first moon landing. As the Twins were engaged with the Seattle Pilots in the first-half finale and Oliva was recuperating, astronauts Buzz Aldrin and Neil Armstrong executed a last-minute maneuver to avoid a rocky crater and landed their spacecraft on the moon's Sea of Tranquility. Armstrong climbed down onto the lunar surface before a worldwide television audience watching grainy satellite images. As he descended onto the moon's powdery surface, Armstrong described the historic moment with those immortal words: "One small step for man, one giant leap for mankind."

The Apollo 11 crew splashed down in the Pacific Ocean on July 24, the day the second half of the baseball season began. Although Oliva had lost eight pounds and had not hit a baseball in ten days, he returned that night in Cleveland. He had been swinging a hot bat before the chicken pox outbreak, and with his July surge, he was hitting .339 at the All-Star break, matching Boston's Reggie Smith and twenty-five points behind Rod Carew.

The layoff proved costly. Not only had Oliva been weakened by his illness, but his timing was now off at the plate. He doubled in his first appearance against Cleveland righthander Luis Tiant, extending his long-dormant hitting streak to fifteen games, but he then went hitless over his next sixteen at-bats. A 6-for-35 slide before regaining his stroke put another batting title out of reach.

The Twins floundered in August, though they maintained a lead in the AL West race heading down the stretch. The race came down to how the Athletics fared against the Twins in their six September matchups. The Twins took three of four in Oakland over the Labor Day weekend to stretch their lead. Ten days later, they all but clinched the AL West title by sweeping the final two games of the season series behind their righthanded aces, Jim Perry and Dave Boswell.

Minnesota finally wrapped up the West in Kansas City with a 4–3 win on September 22, moments after Oliva threw out the potential tying run at second base with one out in the ninth. When pinch runner Scott Northey rounded second base on Buck Martinez's RBI single to right, Oliva rifled a perfect strike to shortstop Leo Cárdenas waiting at second. The throw caught Northey off base and left Martinez perched at first with two outs. Relief ace Al Worthington got Paul Schaal to slap a grounder to Harmon Killebrew near the first-base bag. The slugger stepped deliberately on first to nail down the division title.

Billy Martin and the troops celebrated in the usual way, dousing each other with champagne, but the postseason that loomed was like no other. The Twins would be preparing for the first American League Championship Series, with the Baltimore Orioles on the docket. Before the ALCS got under way on October 4, a few Twins had unfinished business. Perry and Boswell became twenty-game winners following the clincher in Kansas City—the first time the Twins had two twenty-game winners in the same season. And on October 1, the second-to-last day of the season, Killebrew drilled his forty-ninth homer, off White Sox rookie Billy Wynne, to claim his sixth and final home-run title. After a slow start in the power department, he overtook both Reggie Jackson and Frank Howard in the season's final days.

That first day of October was memorable for Oliva, too. He had not driven in a run after collecting his ninety-ninth RBI on September 22, a stretch of ten games, but he had three hits and singled home a run in the seventh inning of Minnesota's 4–3 loss to the White Sox. For the first time in his career, Oliva had hit the century mark in RBIs. "That was a big thing because a few times I had been close," Oliva recalls, though he is quick to spread the credit around. "To have a hundred RBIs, you have to have some people on base in front of you. We had César Tovar and Rod Carew."

In Minnesota's finale the following afternoon, Oliva drilled a long home run off lefty Danny Lazar—a tailing shot that hit high off the Met's right-field foul pole. Tony O finished the season with twenty-four home runs and a career-high 101 RBIs.

The 97–65 Twins finished nine games in front of Oakland, though with twelve fewer victories than their American League Championship Series opponent. With 109 wins, the 1969 Orioles, widely considered among the best teams of all time, were steeped in both power and pitching. The 1969 club was the foundation for Earl Weaver's managerial philosophy of winning: pitching, fundamentals, and three-run homers. With Frank Robinson, Boog Powell, and Brooks Robinson providing the power, Baltimore could slug with the best of them. The pitching staff featured twenty-game winners Mike Cuellar and Dave McNally, plus up-and-coming righthander Jim Palmer, who won sixteen games in a breakout campaign.

The Orioles had won eight of the twelve games between the two division winners in 1969. Lefty Jim Kaat had been the most effective starter against the Orioles, claiming two of Minnesota's four wins and posting a 1.80 ERA in three starts, but the key issue for manager Billy Martin was deciding which twenty-game winner, Perry or Boswell, would start Game One of the best-of-five ALCS. Regardless who pitched the opener, the Twins needed to beat one of the Orioles' twenty-game winners in Baltimore, where the ALCS kicked off and where the Orioles had gone 60–21. By defeating Cuellar or McNally, the Twins would not have to win three straight games against a team that rarely lost three in a row.

Perry got the Game One nod against Cuellar. Both twenty-game winners had solid outings, but home runs marked the game. Both teams were limited to a single through the first three frames, but in the fourth, Frank Robinson turned on a Perry pitch and dinged a hard liner off the left-field foul pole for a 1–0 Orioles lead.

Barely five minutes later, Oliva led off the fifth with a double to right field and wheeled into third when Frank Robinson allowed the ball to get by him. Bob Allison lined a Cuellar offering to Orioles left fielder Don Buford, allowing Oliva to dash home with the tying run. But the Orioles went back in front in the bottom of the fifth, 2–1, when number eight hitter Mark Belanger lifted a 2–0 pitch from Perry into the first row of seats in left field. The Orioles' light-hitting shortstop had hit just two home runs all season.

The Twins rebounded in the seventh, when Harmon Killebrew walked with one out and Oliva tagged a 400-foot home run to right-center to give them their first lead. That 3–2 edge stood until Powell opened the bottom of the ninth by jumping on a 3–2 pitch and depositing it into the right-field seats. Perry had come within three outs of beating Cuellar and the Orioles.

Twins closer Ron Perranoski entered the tied game and retired the Orioles to force extra innings. After the lefthander worked out of a jam in the eleventh, the Twins loaded the bases but failed to score in the twelfth. Then Belanger led off the Baltimore twelfth with an infield single off Killebrew's glove at third base. The ball deflected directly to shortstop Leo Cárdenas, but too late for him to make a play at first. After Perranoski retired the next two men on a sacrifice bunt and a ground out, Belanger stood at third with two outs. Baltimore center fielder Paul Blair, a speedster and an excellent bunter, laid one down in the direction of third base. Catcher John Roseboro could not get to the ball quickly and Belanger sped home with the winning run. In a postgame interview, Blair said his plan had been to take one cut at driving in Belanger. If that failed, he would bunt. After admittedly looking "pretty bad" on a swing, he worked the plan to perfection.

The ALCS opener stood as a testament that baseball is a game of inches. The Orioles scored on a home run that just caught the foul pole, another that barely cleared the wall, and a perfectly placed fifteen-foot bunt that settled into no man's land between the pitcher, catcher, and third baseman.

It was more of the same in Game Two the following afternoon, with Dave Boswell on the hill. Boswell, a Baltimore native, squared off against lefty Dave McNally, and the pair pitched masterfully: neither team scored through the first ten innings. Both dodged occasional trouble, but the Twins managed just three hits and only twice advanced a runner to second.

Boswell walked seven Orioles—compared to five free passes by McNally—and worked out of a few jams. Who knows how many pitches either starter threw? The most damaging walk opened Baltimore's eleventh, as Boswell put Powell aboard. Brooks Robinson deftly moved Powell to second with a sacrifice, inspiring the Twins to intentionally walk second baseman Davey Johnson in order to face Belanger. The move paid off, as Belanger fouled out to Killebrew at third for the second out.

Lefthanded-hitting catcher Elrod Hendricks was up next. Martin called on the lefty Perranoski, and Orioles skipper Weaver turned to righthanded-hitting Curt Motton. On a 1–1 pitch, Motton slashed a liner that nicked the glove of a leaping Carew and bounded into right field. Oliva charged the ball hard, backhanded it, and rifled a strong throw to the plate. It was already a nearly impossible play, but it was further complicated by the fact that the ball arrived at the same time Powell reached home. The throw was slightly up the line, and the Orioles slugger plowed into catcher George Mitterwald and sent him sprawling. Powell missed the plate, but with the ball skipping to the backstop, he got to his feet and stomped on home to end the game.

Once again the Twins had dropped a one-run affair by a matter of inches, this time 1–0 in eleven innings. Boswell had pitched impressively, but his teammates had not been able to push across a run. "We had a chance to win those first two games, but didn't have the clutch hit at the right time," Oliva concludes. "The pitching was there. I remember Boswell said, 'Give me one run,' but we didn't give it to him." As it turned out, Boswell's impressive performance was the last one left in his right arm.

On the final pitch of the tenth inning, Boswell struck out Orioles star Frank Robinson with a slider. "It felt like my shoulder went right into my jawbone," Boswell told the *Fort Myers News-Press* years later. "The arm would actually turn black and run all the way down the elbow."

That day proved to be a bittersweet. Boswell was never the same. He pitched just two more seasons and retired at age twenty-six after a brief stint with his hometown Orioles. That October afternoon in 1969, departing a scoreless game with two outs in the eleventh, he did not know his career had taken a drastic downturn. But the hometown kid walked off the mound to a standing ovation from the Baltimore crowd—a tribute he always treasured.

The Twins headed home down two games to none; they would have to win three in a row at the Met. For Game Three, Martin chose another righthander, Bob Miller, instead of Kaat, who had won two of his three regular-season starts against Baltimore. Martin held Miller in high regard for his role in aiding the Twins to a postseason berth, but his decision to go with the righthander in Game Three did not pay off. Miller did not survive the second and was shelled for three runs before giving way to Dick Woodson. Two of the runs were unearned after Oliva slipped trying to catch a fly hit by Davey Johnson. Woodson got out of the second without further damage, but not much else went well for Twins pitchers.

After two close wins, the Orioles erupted for an 11–2 romp. Jim Palmer went the distance in the clincher that vaulted the Orioles into the World Series. The afternoon was equally difficult for Oliva, who had injured his shoulder on the throw home on the final play of Game Two. The pain started in the clubhouse soon after the game and escalated throughout the night. By morning, he had trouble lifting his arm and could not throw, but he pressed Martin to play him in Game Three because of its importance—and the manager relented. Oliva sat out pregame fielding drills, hoping to keep the Orioles in the dark about his sore shoulder, but he was in the starting lineup. The Orioles were apparently well aware of Oliva's injury, as Johnson hit the fly to right in the second inning and Belanger also went the opposite way leading off the fourth, drilling a Woodson pitch into right-center and legging out a triple on what normally would have been a double.

Although Oliva played through the pain and collected two hits, the injury took its toll in the ninth inning. With the Orioles up 9–2, Johnson led off the final frame with a single to left. Perranoski relieved Dean Chance, and Elrod Hendricks greeted him with a double down the right-field line. Oliva retrieved the ball and fired his relay directly into the grass in front of Carew, who was less than fifty feet away. The ball skipped past the second baseman, allowing Hendricks to circle the bases and score. The Metropolitan Stadium crowd of 32,735 unleashed its anger on Oliva, taking out its frustration for the team's failure in the ALCS.

Belanger then singled to right and Oliva made another throw to the infield with nothing on it. The boos grew louder. He was greeted with another Bronx cheer when he stepped into the on-deck circle in the bottom of the ninth with two outs, and the roar grew even louder when Carew grounded out to end Minnesota's season.

Baltimore's sweep and the poor showing in Game Three were frustrating enough, but such a verbal assault had never happened to Oliva in his years with the Twins. Under the circumstances, it was difficult to take. "I'm mad," Oliva told Sid Hartman after the game. "They boo me and don't even know what is wrong with me." The fans could not have known what caused the errant throw, of course, and Oliva was the victim of his own desire to play at all costs.

The experience was a bad way to walk off the field with a long winter ahead. Oliva's shoulder did not require surgery, but the recovery time was a constant reminder of the disappointing end to a wonderful season. "I shouldn't have played, but I wanted to play," Oliva says in retrospect. "I had a cortisone shot and I was able to hit, but I had to play right field and I wasn't able to throw the ball."

The Twins' inability to push across runs was the real culprit in the ALCS. They scored only five runs in the series and batted just .155. Oliva, who had gone 5 for 13 with two doubles and a homer, was the only Twin with more than two hits in the three games. The lack of scoring punch, however, was not what had the media talking. Martin's decision to start Bob Miller in Game Three was a constant source of speculation. The second-guessing began even before the first game of the World Series (in which the New York Mets would pull off one of the biggest upsets in World Series history).

Why hadn't Kaat, who had pitched impressively and allowed a total of five earned runs in three 1969 starts against the Orioles, worked Game Three? Martin did not take kindly to the talk, replying that Miller had been a stopper for the Twins all season. "What if Miller had won today and what if Kaat had started and lost?" Martin retorted, growing increasingly irritated with all the chatter. At one point, someone asked Martin what he thought the Twins needed to produce a better result in 1970. A new manager, he said, with a straight face. And that's what they got, as Griffith fired Martin during the World Series. The decision to start Miller over Kaat may have been the last straw for the owner. The story goes that Griffith had wanted the lefthander to start Game Three, but the manager stuck with *his* choice.

By then, Griffith had a host of reasons to cut loose the guy who had led his team to ninety-seven wins and a division title. When the decision was announced on the off day after Game Two of the World Series, Griffith cited Martin's propensity to ignore organizational policies and guidelines. Undoubtedly the friction centered on Martin's clash with Boswell, as well as on an angry mid-May confrontation between the manager and farm director George Brophy regarding the minor league assignments of Twins prospects Charley Walters and Bill Zepp. By no means was his dismissal a complete surprise.

What was *not* anticipated was the intense outcry from Twins fans. Telephones rang incessantly for days in the team offices at Metropolitan Stadium as fans voiced their displeasure. Callers also flooded the switchboards of the sports departments of local newspapers, and Griffith was hung in effigy at the University of Minnesota campus following Martin's dismissal. In the weeks that followed, fans bought more than 10,000 bumper stickers imploring the Twins to "Bring Billy Back." Hundreds of Twins fans swore off the team. Regardless of whether they actually stayed away, fans saying they were done with the Twins was a common retort for years after Martin was gone.

A number of players also spoke out against the firing, including Rod Carew, who credited Martin with making a big difference in his career. Nearly every Twin, including Oliva, was shocked at the firing. "I was surprised because the most important thing was winning," Oliva explains. "And we won with Billy Martin managing. He did a beautiful job, and Minnesota loved him." The Twins had won nearly a hundred games and had a chance to repeat, but change was in the air once again. Nothing the players might do or say would bring Billy back, of course, and the Twins would defend their 1969 AL West crown with a new man in charge.

Twins Repeat with a New Bill in Charge

Forty years ago, baseball did not generate nearly as much offseason buzz as it does today, but the long Minnesota winter leading up to the 1970 season was different. Twins fans were not talking about the team's triumph in winning the first American League West title or the disappointing postseason. Instead, they were consumed with Calvin Griffith's canning of manager Billy Martin after a ninety-seven-win performance.

Martin's firing also made it a less-than-typical winter for new manager Bill Rigney. The fifty-two-year-old Rigney, who had spent twelve-plus seasons managing the Giants and the Angels, accepted the unenviable task of replacing Martin, whose popularity seemed to grow after he lost his job. When he saw "Bring Billy Back" bumper stickers all over Minnesota, Rigney quipped that he thought the message was addressed to him.

Both Bills were excellent teachers, though the white-haired Rigney projected a more fatherly image than Martin. He had the air of a gentleman less likely to vent about team issues or players to the press. The outgoing and incoming skippers took different approaches to earning the respect of their players, but both had little trouble commanding it.

In the Twins' spirit of instituting major change following an outstanding season, Oliva began using a new hitting stance in spring 1970. The thirty-one-year-old veteran was coming off a terrific year in which he had ranked among the league leaders in several categories, but he believed he needed to adjust to pitchers' ever-increasing tendency to work him inside. Oliva abandoned his trademark stance, a low crouch with his feet spread far apart.

Beginning in 1970, he moved his feet closer together and stood more upright than he ever had.

Despite Minnesota's quick exit from the 1969 playoffs and the rough treatment he had received from fans in the year's final game, Oliva arrived in camp refreshed and ready. Best of all, his shoulder was healthy, free of trouble after the injury in the American League Championship Series. Oliva had found the remedy on a trip to the mountains of northern Mexico.

After the 1969 season, Oliva had agreed to play for the Mexican winter league team based in Los Mochis, a coastal city on the Gulf of California. When he arrived there, he was still unable to throw. Team officials sent Oliva to an elderly woman who lived in the mountains near Navojoa, a town roughly forty miles north of Los Mochis. She had a history of successfully treating similar ailments, though not with Western medicine. Oliva was ready to try almost anything to rid himself of the pain and get back on the field. "She put an ointment on my arm and rubbed it in," Oliva says of the woman, whose name he no longer remembers. "She massaged and stretched my arm, put a patch on the sore spot, and then wrapped my arm in a bandage. She told me I should do nothing for five days before I remove the wrap. I was able to throw after the five days, and a couple days later I was able to play. Somebody tried to score from second base on me in a game, and I made a perfect throw from right field to home to get him out. I was throwing BBs. My arm never hurt again. It was a miracle."

While the medical solution was an unforeseen benefit of playing for Los Mochis, a possible family reunion had spurred Oliva's commitment. He had considered playing for Águilas in the Dominican Republic, as in previous offseasons, but encouraged by former teammate Sandy Valdespino, Oliva went to Mexico instead. Los Mochis owner Martín Estrada was a relative of Mexican president Gustavo Díaz Ordaz, and Valdespino was convinced that Estrada could help Oliva reunite with his family. By then, nearly nine years had passed since the Bay of Pigs incident, and nothing could have made Oliva happier than a family reunion.

Estrada told Valdespino he could make a reunion happen. Oliva's mother Anita and sister Felicia planned to join him and his family in Mexico, but the process of getting visas dragged on. Gordette was pregnant with their second child, Pedro Jr., and eventually she and Tony had to head home to Minnesota without a reunion. It was a frustrating ending after weeks of anticipation, but at least Oliva's shoulder was sound going into the new season.

With a new skipper and new batting stance in place, the Twins and Oliva started hot. The Twins demonstrated that they were the team to beat in the AL West with an explosive 31–13 start, and the three-team race came down to September matchups with the California Angels and the Oakland Athletics. The Twins pulled away down the stretch, finishing nine games ahead of second-place Oakland at 98–64. Bill Rigney's club had won one more game than Billy Martin's.

Oliva not only opened the campaign with a seven-game hitting streak, batting .438 with ten RBIs, but he hit safely in fifty of his first fifty-six games. He produced hitting streaks of eleven and seventeen games during Minnesota's 31–13 run, and he was held without a hit only once in May, when he posted a team-leading twenty-eight RBIs. At times, Oliva could provide all the offense the Twins needed. He almost single-handedly secured an 8–5 victory at Tiger Stadium on May 5, getting a single, a triple, a home run, and six RBIs off Detroit lefty Mickey Lolich. It was one of twenty games in 1970 in which Oliva had three or more hits.

But Tony O was not doing it alone. The front end of the Twins lineup—César Tovar, Rod Carew, Oliva, and Harmon Killebrew—was on its game right from Opening Day, and all four made a difference during the club's early surge. As the season moved into June, Carew was batting a league-leading .394, and both Oliva (.330) and Killebrew (.329) were on the leaderboard. Tovar had scored forty-five runs in forty-four games. The top of the order set the tone in the season opener, a 12–0 romp over the White Sox in Chicago. Tovar kicked things off with a triple and scored one of three Twins runs in the opening frame. Carew and Oliva both had two hits and combined to score five times. Jim Perry, a first-time twenty-game winner in 1969, blanked Chicago on six hits to jump-start a 24–12 campaign that culminated in Cy Young honors in 1970.

The foursome could also turn a few scratch hits into a win. In a 5–4 victory at Kansas City on May 19, Tovar forced extra innings with a two-out RBI single in the ninth. After Carew bunted his way on to open the tenth, Oliva laid down a bunt to the left side and beat it out, putting two runners on with no one out. The rally nearly died when Killebrew struck out and Rich Reese lined out to center, but Carew advanced to third on Reese's out and scampered home with the game-winning run on Tom Burgmeier's wild pitch.

Oliva piled up hits at a remarkable rate well into June, enjoying one of those long stretches in which he was nearly every pitcher's nightmare. More often than not, Tovar, Carew, and Killebrew were just as productive, each seemingly feeding off the others' success and taking turns coming through with the clutch hit.

The Twins' pennant hopes took a huge hit in Milwaukee on June 22, when Carew tore a ligament in his knee and suffered cartilage damage on a hard slide by Brewers first baseman Mike Hegan at second base. Killebrew, playing third, had fielded a classic double-play ball off the bat of Milwaukee's Mike Hershberger. He rifled a good throw to Carew, who pivoted and threw to first baseman Rich Reese as Hegan waylaid him with a rolling block. Carew was not likely to return until September, if he could come back at all. At the time of the injury, the defending American League batting champ led the AL batting race at .376, more than thirty points ahead of the rest of the pack.

But by late June, the Twins had stumbled. They still scored runs in bunches, but not as frequently as they had during their fast start. And manager Bill Rigney was legitimately concerned about his pitching staff. Jim Perry and Jim Kaat were struggling, but his bigger worry was who would follow the two Jims in an unsettled rotation. Dave Boswell, a twenty-game winner in 1969, no longer had his fastball after the shoulder injury during his ALCS start in Baltimore. Over the winter, the Twins had dealt Dean Chance to Cleveland for Cuban righthander Luis Tiant, who had suffered a hairline fracture in his right shoulder blade during a late-May start against Milwaukee.

When Tiant was sidelined, the Twins recalled Bert Blyleven, a nineteen-year-old righthander who had yet to pitch a full year in the minor leagues but who was striking out hitters at an impressive rate for Minnesota's Triple-A Evansville affiliate. In his big league debut on June 5, Blyleven survived a rocky start, allowing a leadoff home run to Washington's Lee Maye at RFK Stadium, but he scattered five hits over seven innings and fanned seven in a 2–1 victory. The teenager provided a huge boost to Minnesota's pennant push, showing remarkable poise and even better stuff. He allowed two runs or fewer in ten of his first thirteen starts, and despite a late call-up and some rough spots in August, Blyleven posted ten wins in his rookie season.

Despite Rigney's concerns, the pitching staff soon improved, and the rotation finally came together in July. Blyleven was not the only rookie hurler to step up. Both Tom Hall and Bill Zepp joined the rotation during the second half and pitched effectively in the pennant race. The lefty Hall, who was phenomenal working out of the bullpen for most of the season, went 5–0 with a 1.84 ERA in seven September and October starts. Three of those wins came against California and Oakland, the other AL West contenders.

After an impressive first half, Oliva headed to Cincinnati's shiny new River-front Stadium for the All-Star Game, which came just two weeks after the park had hosted its first major league contest. After missing the annual affair because of chicken pox in 1969, Oliva was eager to test the artificial turf of the game's newest cookie-cutter stadium. Jim Perry and Harmon Killebrew, selected as the American League's starting third baseman, were along for the fun. Rod Carew had been asked, but he was rehabbing his surgically repaired knee in Minnesota. With a glut of AL outfielders having fine years, César Tovar, who led the league with seventy-one first-half runs, was not on the AL roster.

Frank Howard, Frank Robinson, and Carl Yastrzemski started in the out-field for the American League, but Oliva was on the field for the dramatic conclusion that has become one of the Midsummer Classic's most lasting memories. The National League had scratched back from a 4–1 deficit to force extra innings, during which it survived AL rallies in three straight frames before the game's defining moment in the twelfth.

After Angels righthander Clyde Wright retired Joe Torre and Roberto Clemente on groundballs to start the bottom half, hometown hero Pete Rose popped a single up the middle. Dodgers infielder Billy Grabarkewitz moved Rose to second with a single to left, and the Cubs' Jim Hickman delivered a third straight hit off Wright, this one headed toward Amos Otis in cen-ter. Few remember Hickman's clutch hit; what is remembered is Rose's dash around third base, chugging for home. Otis's throw and the hard-charging Rose reached Cleveland catcher Ray Fosse at the same time, a few feet up the third-base line. Rose, who always lived up to his "Charlie Hustle" nickname, solidified his reputation as an aggressive, hard-nosed player by bowling over the catcher. The ball popped loose, and Rose scored to give the National League its eighth consecutive All-Star win.

After the Rose–Fosse collision, Oliva continued his hot hitting in the second half, embarking on a nine-game hitting streak that even one of the league's best lefties could not stop. A July 28 visit to Cleveland began with a double dose of mechanical problems. The charter flight scheduled for that morning was the first victim, and the team was 0 for 2 when a hastily pro-cured commercial flight was stranded in Chicago for a few hours of servicing. The Twins reached Cleveland roughly two hours before the Tuesday night opener with the Indians.

The night's assignment was hitting Sam McDowell, the rocket-launching, six-foot-five lefty who was just wild enough to inspire dread in anyone stand-ing in the batter's box. He eventually finished 20–12 for an under-.500

Cleveland club, leading the majors in strikeouts *and* walks in 1970, a testament to his ability to miss both bats and the strike zone. His wicked curve made him especially tough on lefthanded hitters, and he backed it up with heat. "Riding airplanes all day is no way to prepare to hit against Sam McDowell," Oliva told the *Minneapolis Tribune*'s Tom Briere after the Twins claimed a 5–2 win. To this day, Oliva insists McDowell gave him as much trouble as any pitcher, and it was no picnic standing firm when the flamethrower snapped off a high-and-tight pitch that broke back sharply over the plate. If the pitch was a fastball, a hitter did not have much time to get a read on it and duck.

But on this day, Tony O, in the midst of his nine-game streak, singled twice off Cleveland's starter. When discussing McDowell, Oliva gives the impression he never had the upper hand, but according to the Baseball Cube Web site, he batted .356 in fifty-nine career at-bats against the lefthander. McDowell certainly does not believe *he* ever had the edge with Oliva in the batter's box. "I thought he was probably one of the most difficult individuals for me to face," says McDowell. "He was a lefthander, and lefthanders usually did not raise much of a challenge. In fact, a lot of them begged out of the lineup so they didn't have to face me, but Tony never did. And Tony, I would say, hit me as well as any righthander in the major leagues."

When Oliva collected three more hits in a 9–8 loss to Dean Chance and the Indians the next day, July 29, he took over the lead in the AL batting race for the first time, at .327. Just two points behind was Boston's Carl Yastrzemski.

On July's final day, the Twins finished on the wrong end of a 10–9 decision, wasting a late lead and a towering home run by Tony O. Facing Tigers ace Denny McLain in Minnesota's six-run sixth inning, Oliva powered a 470-foot shot that hit the roof of Tiger Stadium's right-field upper deck and caromed onto Trumbull Avenue. Oliva collected two more hits in the loss to finish July with a league-leading .326 mark and ignited a ten-game hitting streak with his three-hit performance.

Sunday, August 2, was Al Kaline Day in Detroit. The Tigers were honoring their future Hall of Famer. Kaline's friend Harmon Killebrew addressed the Tiger Stadium crowd of 40,000 during the pregame ceremony. "I hope Kaline hits two home runs today," Killebrew told reporters before the tribute, "and the Twins win." A short time later, he took the lead role in getting his second wish, powering a 475-foot home run into Tiger Stadium's upper deck in center field, producing a 4–3 victory.

Oliva collected three more hits, including an opposite-field homer, on the day the Tigers honored a player whom he had admired from his earliest days in the majors. Kaline, at his peak when Oliva arrived on the scene, set the standard for what the young Twin wanted to be. Both right fielders hit for average and power, excelled at most aspects of the game, and were known for having the prototypically strong throwing arm seen as ideal for the position. Both, by coincidence, also wore number 6, and Oliva had been thrilled to find it on his jersey when he arrived in camp for his rookie year.

After leaving Detroit, Oliva continued to make solid contact, though not always bat to ball. In a 5–2 win over Milwaukee on August 4, the Twins had nine hits, plus a hit that Killebrew took in the on-deck circle: Oliva sent a bat flying on an inning-ending third strike in the seventh, and it struck Killebrew on the right arm. Killebrew remained on one knee briefly after absorbing the blow, but he finished the game. Oliva had two other hits on the day, but he and the Twins slumped in mid-August. The Twins lost nine in a row, briefly allowing the Athletics and the Angels back into the AL West chase. During the skid, Oliva batted just .206. This was his only slump of the season, and when the Twins finally ended their slide with a 9–6 victory at Fenway Park on August 16, he trailed Yastrzemski by eleven points in the batting race.

Yaz went 6 for 13 in Minnesota's four-game set with the Red Sox. He was batting just .268 in late June, but he had hit .410 in a span of fifty-four games to grab the league lead at .332. Yaz's surge resembled that of Oliva's in 1965, when the young Twin went on a similar second-half run to overtake Yastrzemski. This time Yaz was turning the tables.

When the Twins closed August by losing three of four at Yankee Stadium, Oliva was held hitless in four consecutive games for the only time all season. His hit-free series in the Bronx allowed Boston center fielder Reggie Smith to take the league batting lead. Yastrzemski and California's Alex Johnson also had leapfrogged over Oliva, who still was just five points behind Smith.

The Twins were in Anaheim for the Labor Day weekend, beginning a critical stretch with sixteen games against the Angels and Athletics. In the Friday night opener, Bert Blyleven and Ron Perranoski pitched a five-hit shutout and Oliva, mired in a 2-for-26 slump, bounced back by going 4 for 4. The 4–0 victory kicked off a 9–1 Twins surge, and Tony O's perfect day ignited one final hot streak.

Oliva hit safely in twenty-two of his final twenty-seven games, batting .398 over the last four weeks of the season. His hitting acumen impressed Brewers catcher Phil Roof, who would join the Twins in a 1971 trade. Roof was behind the plate at the Met on September 8, when Milwaukee stuck the Twins with their only loss in a ten-game span. Roof remembers an Oliva home run that epitomized what the Twins star could do with the bat, regardless of pitch location. With Blyleven and Brewers righty Marty Pattin locked in a 1–1 pitchers' duel, Oliva, already with two hits, stepped to the plate with two outs in the eighth. Pattin had retired six Twins in a row.

"Marty's on. He's got good stuff that night," Roof recounts. "Tony came up and took his bat and tapped me on the shin guards and he said, 'Roofy, I'm going to hit a home run here.' And I said, 'No, you're not in *this* game. Maybe another time, but not in this game.' I called for a slider, and any time I tapped the inside of my thigh more than once, that meant I wanted it in off the plate and down. He threw the ball. I know it was probably eight or ten inches in and probably six or eight inches off the ground. Tony golfed it for a homer." He adds, "Marty had some of the best stuff, especially a slider. Tony had zeroed in on that breaking pitch and he was looking for it and hit it."

The chip shot into the bleacher seats went for naught as the Brewers erased the Twins' 2–1 lead in the ninth. Mike Hegan stroked a one-out single off Blyleven, and after Perranoski took the hill, Roof caved in on the Twins. He powered a home run to left field, lifting Pattin and the Brewers to a 3–2 victory. "He just wears us out," Rigney said of Roof after the game. He was right. Roof, a .215 lifetime hitter, batted .429 with four homers in fourteen games against the Twins in 1970. The next July, the Twins acquired him from the Brewers. Instead of roughing up Minnesota pitching, he spent five years tutoring Blyleven and a host of young Twins hurlers.

By hitting .398 from Labor Day weekend through the end of the season, Oliva stayed in the thick of the AL batting race. One of the rare days he did not get a hit was Monday, September 21, with the Twins one win away from clinching their second AL West crown. That night *no* Twin got a hit. At Oakland–Alameda County Stadium, twenty-one-year-old Vida Blue, with two career wins and five big league starts under his belt, threw a no-hitter against a red-hot club that had won fourteen of its last nineteen games. The Athletics lefty retired the first eleven Twins before allowing a fourth-inning walk to Killebrew, the only blemish on the pitching line in a 6–0 win.

On Tuesday, the Twins had an easier time facing the Athletics' Chuck Dobson. César Tovar, the last Twin retired by Blue the night before, walked to open the game. He was retired at second base on shortstop Jose Cárdenas's infield grounder, but Cárdenas then advanced to second on a wild pitch with Oliva at the plate. Up 3–1 in the count, Oliva must have been anticipating a breaking pitch. He waited back nicely, turned on a curveball and drove it into the right-field bleachers for a quick 2–0 lead.

When Oliva crossed the plate on Rich Reese's two-out double in the seventh, the Twins were up 5–2 and needed only nine more outs to claim a second AL West crown. Jim Kaat, who had pitched the pennant clincher against Washington in 1965, worked five-plus innings before giving way to Perranoski, the AL saves leader, who recorded the final eleven outs. The Athletics scratched for a ninth-inning run to close the gap to 5–3, but with two down, Perranoski induced a weak grounder from Felipe Alou, which Cárdenas carried across second base for the final out. The Twins stormed onto the field to congratulate one another before retreating to the clubhouse. They broke open five cases of champagne that had been on ice, awaiting that one win in Oakland. The Twins had brought six cases west, but had given one to Vida Blue the previous night after his brilliant no-hit performance.

After collecting a single, a double, and a homer in the AL West pennant clincher, Oliva was at .324, a single point behind Alex Johnson. Carl Yastrzemski loomed at .320, and White Sox shortstop Luis Aparicio, hitting .316, was a legitimate contender with eleven days left in the season. The day after the Twins sealed the pennant, Oliva stroked three more hits and scored three times in a 7–4 win over the Athletics. He delivered six three-hit games and a 4-for-4 performance in September. When he stroked his league-best thirty-ninth double and tripled in the season finale, he finished at .325—to that point the highest single-season average of his career.

That kind of season-closing surge would normally be enough to nail down a batting title, but both Johnson and Yastrzemski had their way with AL pitchers down the stretch. Yaz batted .406 over his last twenty-one games and closed the season with a six-game hitting streak in which he was 12 for 20. By hitting .600 in those final six games, he finished four points ahead of Oliva at .329.

Johnson hit safely in twenty-eight of his final thirty games and closed his fine year with a twelve-game hitting streak in which he batted .468. Even with twenty-two hits in twelve games, he trailed Yaz by a single point going into the Angels' final game of the season on October 1. Yaz and the Red Sox had finished their season a day earlier, so the batting title hinged on Johnson's performance. The Angels left fielder went 2 for 3 in a 5–1 win over Tommy John and the White Sox to close at .329. He took the batting title by four-tenths of a percentage point. It did not matter that Oliva finished by going 6 for 11 against Kansas City in the final three games of the season.

For Oliva and the Twins, the American League Championship Series was a return engagement with the formidable Baltimore Orioles. The defending AL champions had posted a 108–54 record, the best in the majors, after winning 109 games in 1969. American League MVP Boog Powell and Frank Robinson were again the big boppers of a balanced attack that featured six regulars with seventeen or more homers. And the Orioles' pitching staff now included three twenty-game winners, including southpaws Mike Cuellar and Dave McNally, both of whom tied Jim Perry for the league lead in victories with twenty-four. Jim Palmer, a budding ace at twenty-four, became a twenty-game winner for the first time.

The Twins would have to be on their game to avenge Baltimore's sweep in the 1969 ALCS. There was reason for optimism. The Twins had taken the season series, seven games to five, and this time the showdown for the American League pennant opened in Minnesota. Two twenty-four-game winners, Cuellar and Perry, took the hill at the Met in Game One, but the bats took center stage on that blustery Saturday afternoon.

Neither Cuellar nor Perry survived the fifth inning in the Orioles' 10–6 win, but Cuellar stuck around long enough to lift a fourth-inning fly into a strong wind, which carried the ball into the right-field bleachers for a grand-slam homer. The wind did more than blow the ball beyond the fence; without the stiff breeze, Cuellar's fly would have been a foul ball. That was apparent to Orioles shortstop Mark Belanger, who was standing on first when Cuellar put the ball in play. "When the ball went by, it was 15 feet foul," Belanger told *St. Paul Pioneer Press* writer Patrick Reusse. "The wind blew it back in." Baltimore starter Dave McNally was in the clubhouse watching the game on television when his rotation mate made contact, and he told Reusse that NBC broadcaster Jim Simpson's immediate response was "There's a long foul ball to right." Thinking the ball was foul, Perry did not even follow its flight. Cuellar did not start running until it had tucked inside the foul pole. Oliva, tracking the ball on the run, suddenly thought he had a play, but it dropped into the seats three rows behind him.

Baltimore scored seven runs in the inning to take a 9–2 edge. The Twins chipped away at the deficit and managed eleven hits, but only one after a three-run uprising in the fifth. That was a seventh-inning single by Oliva, his third hit of the day.

Sunday was a beautiful fall day with temperatures in the seventies, but not much changed in Game Two. The Orioles jumped on rookie starter Tom Hall for four runs before Rigney yanked him with one out in the fourth.

Minnesota rebounded, however, scoring three runs off McNally in its half of the inning. After Leo Cárdenas drew a leadoff walk, Harmon Killebrew and Oliva powered back-to-back home runs into the left-field bleachers. With the Orioles leading 4–3, the pitching staffs took over, keeping both teams off the scoreboard as the game moved into the ninth. But for a second time in the series, Baltimore scorched Twins hurlers for a seven-run inning. Ron Perranoski retired only one of the six batters he faced. Boog Powell's bases-loaded double down the left-field line lifted the Birds to a 6–3 advantage, and two batters later, Davey Johnson provided the big blast, with a three-run homer off Luis Tiant.

With their 11–3 romp, the Orioles had won their thirteenth straight game and put the Twins on the brink of elimination again. The AL West champs did not have long to ponder their predicament, as the series resumed in Baltimore on the following afternoon.

The Orioles called on Jim Palmer to pitch Game Three, against Jim Kaat, bypassed by Billy Martin in favor of Bob Miller the year before. As they had in the first two games of the series, the Orioles scored early and quickly forced the Twins starter from the game. Boog Powell's run-scoring single, his sixth RBI of the ALCS, gave the Orioles a first-inning lead, and Paul Blair singled home another run in the second. Aided by a Twins error, the Orioles blew the game open in the third, tallying three unearned runs to go up 5–0. Palmer dodged trouble in the middle innings and fanned twelve Twins in a 6–1 series-clinching victory.

Once again the season ended in disappointment for Oliva, who was 6 for 12 with two doubles and a homer in the ALCS. Personal success did not take the sting out of losing, but the seven-year veteran had been extremely productive in 1970. Despite failing to win the AL batting title, Tony O had collected a league-high 204 hits and set personal highs with a .325 average and 107 RBIs.

Family Reunions and the Career-Changing Knee Injury

After the Orioles swept the Twins in the American League Championship Series for the second straight season, Oliva headed to Mexico again to play winter ball. His return to Los Mochis was motivated less by the opportunity to play than by the possibility of reuniting with his family, as he had tried to do the previous winter. The efforts of Los Mochis club owner Martín Estrada to bring Oliva's mother and sister to Mexico had run into bureaucratic snags, and Oliva had returned to Florida for spring training in 1970 with the paperwork still not in place. But by that summer, Estrada and club officials had passports and visas in the works. At the close of the 1970 campaign, Oliva drove directly to Los Mochis, then flew to Mexico City for the highly anticipated reunion.

By then, Oliva had been cut off from his loved ones in Cuba for nearly a decade. The plan was to have Gordette and their two toddlers, Anita and Pedro, fly from Minnesota to Mexico City to join the festivities after Oliva's mother and sister had arrived. They would then all fly together to Los Mochis, where the baseball team had arranged the rental of a home large enough for everyone to stay.

On a November afternoon in 1970, Oliva stood on an observation deck at Mexico City's airport, waiting excitedly for a plane to arrive from Cuba. The reunion was well documented by Bob Fowler, the longtime Twin Cities sportswriter who collaborated with Oliva on the 1973 biography, *Tony O! The Trials and Triumphs of Tony Oliva*:

My mother walked down the steps from the plane, and I recognized her right away. I waved and yelled, but she couldn't hear me over the noise. As she was walking to the airport, a woman grabbed her shoulder, pointed up to me, and said, "Mama, mama, I think that's Tony."

When we met inside the airport, my mother kissed me and said, "You look the same as when you left home. You're a little heavier, but you haven't changed at all."

She hadn't changed either, except she looked a little older. As for my baby sister, well, I didn't recognize her; she had grown up.

Gordette and the kids arrived a short time later, and we got rooms at a local hotel. That night we went out to dinner, and I was so happy, I forgot everything I was going to tell my mother and everything I wanted to ask her.

The reunion lasted several weeks before the ladies returned to Cuba. After some sightseeing in Mexico City, the Oliva clan settled into life in Los Mochis, a small town reminiscent of the Oliva family's surroundings in Piñar del Río. Anita fell in love with her grandchildren and quickly grew close to Gordette. When the two mothers were not shopping with Felicia or playing with the children, they were watching Tony play for Los Mochis.

Oliva wanted Anita and Felicia to travel to Minnesota with his family. The visas were good for fifty days, but long before they expired, he was thinking about extensions that would allow them to stay longer. When he asked his mother about it, she said that she was happy that she had finally seen her son and his family and gratified that they had spent several weeks together, but that it was time to go home. The rest of the family awaited her return, and she was beginning to feel homesick.

Oliva dreaded saying goodbye. That his mother was ready to return home made it easier, but parting this time was more difficult for him than it had been a decade earlier. When Oliva had left Cuba in the spring of 1961, he expected to play baseball for six months and be back home for the winter. This time, he did not know when—or if—he would see his mother again. As much as the unknown was disconcerting, it helped that his mother left happy.

Returning to Florida to prepare for a new baseball season was always an uplifting experience for Oliva, but the family reunion for which he had waited so long heightened his sense of renewal. Although nothing that happened between the lines could make him as happy as he was after seeing his mother and sister, Minnesota's consecutive American League West titles sparked optimism heading into the 1971 campaign. Despite a controversial managerial change the previous winter, the Twins had enjoyed a successful 1970 season and expected to continue winning under Bill Rigney.

It was not meant to be. In 1971, the team began a sudden and rapid decline, a dry spell that lasted most of two decades. The Twins won just seventy-four games and finished fifth in the AL West in 1971, and even getting over .500 became a struggle for years to come. César Tovar and Rod Carew were again effective tablesetters in 1971, but other than Oliva and Harmon Killebrew, the team lacked the firepower associated with the 1960s teams.

Killebrew, who turned thirty-five near midseason, was showing the wear and tear of a succession of injuries, including the dislocated elbow in 1965 and the ruptured hamstring in 1968. But the injury that took the biggest toll late in Killebrew's career was an old one. He had torn cartilage in his left knee as a young man, and most of the torn cartilage was removed surgically. By the 1970s, he was enduring the pain of bone rubbing on bone, compromising his power and eventually forcing him to retire. Killebrew's homer total dropped to twenty-eight in 1971; he would never hit thirty in a season again.

By 1971, Minnesota's farm system was rarely producing the big-impact talent needed to keep the team competitive. Plus, the core veterans were on the downside of the age curve; Carew was the only cornerstone position player not yet thirty years old. And the team's downward spiral became more pronounced on a fateful day in June.

When the Twins gathered in Orlando for spring training, the unfortunate turn of events awaiting the team would have been hard to fathom. The Twins had won ninety-seven and ninety-eight games the previous two summers, with their star right fielder turning in two of his best seasons. Although Oliva was thirty-two years old, an age when player performance often begins to slip, he was not showing signs of decline. The proof was in the numbers. Heading into the 1971 campaign, he had led all American League players over the two previous seasons with 401 hits, and no major leaguer could match his seventy-five doubles. He batted .317 in this span, the fourth-highest average in the majors, and slugged .505. Among all players with a thousand plate appearances over those two seasons, only twenty-one players posted a .500-plus slugging percentage.

Although Oliva was not a prototypical slugger, he powered 133 extra-base hits in 1969 and 1970, the same number as Killebrew, the 1969 American League MVP. In the American League, only Red Sox stars Carl Yastrzemski (139) and Rico Petrocelli (137), based in the doubles paradise known as Fenway Park, had more. Tony O also delivered his first two 100-RBI performances in Minnesota's conquest of the new AL West. He generated 208 RBIs over those two seasons, and only four players in the league recorded more: Killebrew, Boog Powell (the 1970 AL MVP), Frank Howard, and Yaz.

Despite his consistent production at the plate, Oliva was always experimenting with adjustments. He had changed to a more upright stance with great success in 1970. While practicing with other Cubans in Miami before the start of spring training in 1971, he tweaked his stance again. In response to discomfort he was experiencing in his left heel, he tried lifting the heel as he positioned himself at the plate, so that he was standing on the ball of his back foot. To his surprise, he pulled the ball more often and hit it with even more authority. He tried his new approach in spring training games, and it worked so well that he stuck with it.

As productive as Oliva was in 1970, he was even better in early 1971. He hit everything in sight that spring, following a protracted contract battle with Calvin Griffith. Oliva rarely encountered problems settling on a dollar amount during the annual spring ritual, but talks hit a wall when the Twins star attempted to negotiate a $100,000 salary for 1971. Killebrew had joined the $100,000 club a month earlier, and undoubtedly Griffith was not thrilled with the notion of paying six-digit salaries to *two* of his players. Paying his entire roster $200,000 probably did not sit well with him.

Seven years earlier, Oliva had made just $7,000 in his rookie season. By quickly developing into one of the league's best hitters, he had bumped his pay to $78,000 in 1970. By the next spring, more than a dozen players had crossed the $100,000 barrier, and Oliva, coming off what was arguably his best season, thought he deserved to join this select group. But Oliva grew frustrated at being in Miami working on a deal with the owner rather than being in Orlando preparing for the new season. He had negotiated all his previous contracts on his own, but this time he hired an attorney to represent him. Eventually the two sides came to a compromise. Oliva did not get his six-digit payoff in 1971, but he did sign a two-year contract that pushed him over the $100,000 mark in the second season. The deal was noteworthy for another reason: Griffith loathed multiyear contracts and rarely negotiated one. With a deal in place, Oliva headed to Orlando and took any lingering frustration out on the baseball.

While the team dropped a 7–2 decision to Milwaukee on Opening Day and struggled offensively in the early going, Oliva hit safely in nineteen of his first twenty games, a red-hot start reminiscent of his rookie year. He began 1971 with a nine-game streak, batting .361, and it was not until the tenth game, when California Angels lefties Rudy May and Dave LaRoche held Oliva hitless, that he finally struck out for the first time. Tony O fanned three times that evening in a 4–1 loss, but he then countered with a ten-game hitting streak that pushed his average to a league-leading .398 on May 1. The high point of Oliva's fast start was a trip to Yankee Stadium during the last week of April. He collected six hits in thirteen at-bats, including a double and four home runs, and the Twins took two of three from New York.

The Twins got off to a disappointing 9–12 start in April, but for the month, Oliva led the league with thirty-one hits, seven homers, and a .769 slugging percentage that was more than a hundred points higher than any other AL regular. He was on one of his classic tears.

Meanwhile, Oakland's first trip to Metropolitan Stadium in April foreshadowed difficult times ahead. The Twins had won twenty-six of thirty-six games between the clubs over the two previous seasons, but the Athletics turned the tables on their AL West rival. They held the Twins to four runs and won the first two matchups. In 1971, the Athletics claimed ten of eighteen games—their win total over Minnesota the two previous seasons combined—en route to their first of five straight AL West crowns.

The Athletics emerged as a powerhouse for the first time in forty years. They featured a power-laden lineup built around Reggie Jackson, Sal Bando, Joe Rudi, Gene Tenace, and Bert Campaneris. The starting pitching improved when twenty-one-year-old Vida Blue joined Catfish Hunter at the top of the rotation in 1971. Blue's emergence coincided with the Twins' sudden fall. The young southpaw departed early and lost in Washington on Opening Day but then won ten consecutive decisions in his next eleven starts. Blue finished 24–8 with a league-leading 1.82 ERA. Sparking the Athletics to their first AL West title, he claimed both MVP and Cy Young honors.

Unlike Blue, the Twins could not string together wins and never worked their way into the AL West race. All the while, Oliva kept pounding the ball like a man possessed. He produced multiple hits ten times in a twelve-game stretch, including three early-May contests at Fenway Park.

Oliva's new stance caught the attention of Red Sox great Carl Yastrzemski, who had competed with the Twins star for batting titles for several seasons. It was unusual for an established run producer to make mechanical changes when his career was going extremely well, but Oliva did just that, and did it far more successfully than could have been anticipated. "When I first saw Tony use that new stance with his back heel raised, I couldn't believe it," Yaz told Bob Fowler, Twins beat writer and the author of the 1973 Oliva bio. "To me, it was a radical change. I consider dropping my hands a little a major change, and here he was lifting his heel. Someone told me he had started lifting his heel because he had injured it. But that still didn't explain the change to me. That man could go to the plate with a broken leg and stand on his head and hit a line drive."

On May 8, an upright Oliva executed his first four-hit performance of the season, the twentieth of his career. He singled off Senators ace Dick Bosman his first two trips to the plate before lifting a three-run homer into the Met's bleachers to give the Twins a 5–1 lead. Oliva finished the game with three runs and four RBIs in a 9–2 victory.

Hall of Famer Ted Williams, one of the game's greatest hitters, was in his third season as Washington's manager. Early in Oliva's career, Williams had often praised the up-and-coming star to his former teammate and longtime friend Sam Mele. After Oliva's big day against his club, Williams spoke highly of him in a clubhouse conversation with *Minneapolis Tribune* writer Jon Roe. "He's a real good hitter," Williams kept repeating to Roe. "Maybe the best in the league. He's unorthodox, but that makes him tough to pitch to. What might not be a good pitch to somebody else he'll hit. There's no way you can defense him either. He hits the ball all over."

When Oliva finished his May 8 assault on Senators hurlers, he led the league with a .395 average. His ninth homer put him at the top of the leaderboard. He pushed his average to .407 with three more hits in a Mother's Day matinee the following afternoon, including a pair of doubles off longtime Twins nemesis Denny McLain, now with Washington. Oliva had recorded multiple hits in seventeen of twenty-eight games to start the season. He could not possibly maintain a .400 batting clip, but even when his average dropped to .370 at the end of May, it still topped AL regulars by a wide margin. So did his .659 slugging percentage.

The league leader opened June with a torrid 14-for-31 run that jumped his average to a major league–high .383. An eight-game hitting streak stalled in Detroit on June 11, but Oliva drilled a two-run homer off Mickey Lolich the following afternoon to spark a 5–4 victory and kick off an eleven-game hitting streak. The towering blast landed on the roof of Tiger Stadium's upper deck in right field.

The Twins, losers of eight of ten, moved on to Cleveland, where Oliva homered twice more and recorded two hits in each of the three games. They swept the series and returned home, where Oliva collected two hits in each of the four games of a weekend series with Chicago. In the Saturday matinee, the Twins trailed 1–0 in the bottom of the ninth when Oliva teed off on knuckleballer Wilbur Wood for his league-leading sixteenth home run. One inning later, George Mitterwald singled him home to complete a 2–1 comeback victory.

First-place Oakland followed Chicago into town. The Athletics were 44–22, well ahead of second-place Kansas City and 10.5 games in front of the third-place Twins. The series lacked its typical urgency. Oliva was limited to a single hit off Vida Blue in the June 21 opener, a 3–2 Athletics victory in which the twenty-one-year-old southpaw struck out thirteen and improved to 15–2. In the second game, Tony O stroked three hits, including a three-run homer, to spark a 10–1 Twins romp.

With the win, the Twins, at 35–34, were better than .500 for the last time in 1971. They dropped the rubber game to Oakland the following day, when Athletics righty Blue Moon Odom put an end to Oliva's eleven-game streak, his longest of the year. Then the Twins lost three of four at home to Milwaukee before heading to Oakland for a return engagement with the Athletics to close out June. Oliva, batting .375, doubled and homered in the first game, but the Twins finished on the short end of a 6–4 decision and fell 14.5 games behind the front-running Athletics. The second game on June 29 went much better, as the Twins tallied four runs off Vida Blue over seven innings and claimed a 5–3 win that dropped Oakland's ace to 16–3.

The Twins, however, were not celebrating. After Oliva caught Bert Campaneris's looping fly for the first out in Oakland's half of the ninth, Athletics left fielder Joe Rudi sent another soft, sinking liner in the right fielder's direction. Oliva charged the ball as it tailed toward the foul line, debating whether to dive for it. He almost never dove for balls, but this time, at the last second, Oliva left his feet in an effort to record the out. His right foot slipped as he lunged forward and he landed hard on his right knee.

Oliva got back on his feet, retrieved the ball, and held Rudi to a double. Initially Oliva did not believe he was seriously hurt, but quickly realized he could not stay on his feet. By the time a few teammates had helped Oliva off the field and Doc Lentz had ushered him into the clubhouse, the knee had begun to swell. "I started feeling pressure there right away, and swelling, but there wasn't a lot of pain at first," Oliva says of the moments immediately after suffering the career-changing injury. "Later I had a lot of pain because I had a lot of loose bodies in the knee."

Still, at first he was not convinced that the knee was a major concern. He put an ice pack on it for the swelling and kept it iced throughout the night in his hotel room. The ice pack was to become a nightly ritual for years on end to combat pain and swelling. Despite the ice treatment that night, the swollen and tender knee was even worse the next morning.

On June 30, hobbled stars Oliva and Killebrew—with his bad knee and an injured toe suffered playing the Brewers—returned to Minnesota to be examined by team doctors. Oliva experienced his first helicopter ride, as they were transported to the San Francisco airport on an air ambulance. Oliva recalls that the injuries kept both players from being able to rest comfortably on the long flight home. X-rays revealed cartilage damage in Oliva's knee, but doctors determined that he could return to the field if he rested it until the swelling and discomfort subsided. Killebrew also had to play the waiting game, hoping that rest would alleviate the pain and improve his mobility.

The injuries laid waste to the team's run production. Oliva went down leading the league with a .375 average and eighteen home runs. Killebrew, despite a power drop-off that summer, still topped the circuit with 55 RBIs. With 104 RBIs between them, they had accounted for more than a third of the Twins' total.

Although still hurting, both players missed only a few days. Oliva returned on the Fourth of July as a pinch hitter in Milwaukee. He got the call in the ninth with Leo Cárdenas on first, one out, and the Twins trailing the Brewers 4–0. Oliva slapped a grounder in the direction of first baseman John Briggs, and as he started out of the batter's box, his knee collapsed on him. He was unable to run more than a couple of steps. After Briggs easily executed the game-ending double play, a forlorn Oliva sat quietly in the clubhouse with an ice pack on his aching knee. Killebrew also played in pain, limping badly as he returned to the dugout after flying out in the eighth. After the game, manager Bill Rigney decided that it made no sense to play either of his stars as long as they were hobbling.

For Oliva, the decision meant missing the All-Star Game in Detroit, for which fans had selected him as the starting right fielder. He had hoped he might feel well enough to go, but he had to settle for watching the game at home. Oliva missed a 6–4 slugfest, the American League's first win in the Midsummer Classic since 1962. All ten runs came via the longball. Oakland's Reggie Jackson served up the biggest blast, a 520-foot drive off Pittsburgh's

Dock Ellis, which struck a light tower on Tiger Stadium's roof in right-center field. In the sixth, Killebrew hit a shot off Cubs ace Fergie Jenkins that brought in the winning runs. With Al Kaline aboard, the ailing slugger slammed a 3–2 slider into the left-field seats, overcoming a strong crosswind blowing from left to right.

Although Oliva was not ready to play regularly again, he was with the Twins when they opened the second half at Fenway Park. On July 16, he pinch-hit in the ninth and grounded out, as he had in his last plate appearance on the Fourth of July. This time, at least, he could run the ball out.

Today, a player with Oliva's injury spends a significant stretch on the disabled list. Instead, he returned to the starting lineup on July 18, just twenty days after his ill-fated dive in Oakland. "I kept playing because when you had torn cartilage, doctors thought you weren't going to hurt it more," Oliva explains. "It's already torn. It hurt to play and run, but I kept doing it. I think I hurt it more. I think if I would have taken care of my knee right away, who knows, maybe I would have saved my career." But that was not how players of the era looked at injuries, even one as serious as Oliva's. Getting back on the field took precedent over long-term health.

So Oliva was back in the lineup on July 18 for a three-game series with the Senators in Washington. Despite a layoff of nearly three weeks, he singled to center in each of his first two at-bats and drove in a run in a 3–2 loss. In the fifth inning, though, after grounding back to Washington starter Bill Gogolewski, he failed to run to first. That was uncharacteristic of Oliva, a clear sign that he was still far from healthy.

Nevertheless, he hammered out five hits in his first nine at-bats after returning to the lineup, pushing his league-leading average to .379. That included a 2-for-4 performance at Yankee Stadium on July 20, his thirty-third birthday. But playing with cartilage damage began to take its toll. He managed just three hits in a six-game stretch and saw his average slip to .359 in the final days of July.

Twins fans witnessed a classic Tony O moment, however, in a 4–2 walk-off victory over Washington on July 27. With the game knotted 2–2, Killebrew led off the ninth with a single off reliever Paul Lindblad. The lefthander seemed to have the advantage with Oliva coming to the plate, but Tony O jumped on an inside pitch up in his eyes and drove it into the Met's bleacher seats in right field. It was Oliva at his best as a bad-ball hitter. "It was a bad pitch, a really bad pitch," Oliva told *Minneapolis Tribune* writer Jon Roe after the game. "But I swing at anything, because that's my habit. But I still can't believe I hit it out." Although Oliva added that he did not usually hit that pitch, it was not exactly a surprise to his teammates, who had seen him go outside the strike zone frequently and still hit the ball on the money.

Oliva's skills as a bad-ball hitter often inspire comparisons to Yankees great Yogi Berra, another player who excelled at fishing outside the zone. Jim Bouton, who pitched for the Yankees in the 1960s, says Oliva and Berra shared a swing that "I don't want to say is primitive, but just natural, an almost unschooled swing." Bouton adds that Oliva's ability to hit any pitch in any location made it difficult to stay with a single approach. "There was no formula. There was no known weakness," Bouton notes. "You couldn't throw a waste pitch. He would hit that."

A pitch that bounces in front of the plate certainly qualifies as a waste pitch, and apparently Oliva even hit a home run on one bounce. Former Twins hurlers Bert Blyleven and Bill Campbell remember it, though research failed to locate the "chip-shot" homer. Hitting the ball on a bounce is against the rules, so the umpires would have had to miss the call as well.

For the 1971 Twins, the highlights were few down the stretch. Two days prior to Oliva's walk-off shot, Killebrew powered his 499th career home run in a 6–2 loss to Boston. Still bothered by knee and toe injuries, he had played through a stretch of twenty-two games without a homer, one of the longest such skeins of his career. Thirteen games later, on August 10, the ailing slugger became the tenth player in big league history to reach the 500 plateau. With two out in the opening frame, he connected on a Mike Cuellar curveball for one of those typical Killebrew shots that everyone knew would leave the yard as soon as it was hit. Killebrew, known to stoically circle the bases with his head down, treated number 500 no differently, despite the rousing ovation from the 15,881 fans at the Met.

When Killebrew returned to the Twins dugout, manager Bill Rigney light-heartedly told the slugger, "Don't let it be so long between 500 and 501." Killebrew obliged. In the sixth, he belted a Cuellar fastball into the left-center-field seats, a two-run blast to tie the game 3–3. Unfortunately for the man who had meant so much to the franchise, he delivered his milestone homer in a 4–3 loss. Despite his injuries and a substantial power drop-off, Killebrew still topped the league with 119 RBIs in 1971.

On July 30, three days after his walk-off blast against Washington, Oliva kicked off a nine-game hitting streak with two hits in a loss to the Yankees.

Despite running more like a catcher than a top-flight outfielder, he recorded multiple hits in each of the nine games, including his twentieth home run in a 10–7 win over New York on August 1. During his streak, Oliva batted .541 in thirty-seven at-bats. His average climbed to .374, which was nearly forty points higher than anyone else in the league.

Oliva could make hitting look effortless, but it did not come easy that summer. Staying in the lineup required some ten cortisone shots in his aching knee, and he still needed two or three pills, either Darvon (propoxyphene) or aspirin, before each game to kill the pain. Even with the aid of painkillers, the cartilage damage made it impossible to run hard, and no amount of medication could dull the pain when he tried to run all out. By September, the injury was beginning to affect Oliva's swing. His power all but disappeared, and his lofty batting average began to plummet. Swinging became increasingly painful, and after weeks of discomfort every time he took a cut, it became difficult to *not* think about it when he was at the plate. His concentration was as compromised as his knee.

Oliva managed to hit safely in all three games of a mid-September series with Oakland during the team's final West Coast swing. But less than a week later, on September 15 in Milwaukee, Tony O went 0 for 4 in what proved to be his final start of 1971. He went without a hit in three pinch-hitting appearances over the next few days, and he shut it down for the season on September 19 after going hitless in his last eleven at-bats. By then, team doctors were recommending knee surgery, and he finally relented. He had accepted that he could not run well, but he refused to quit playing until he was convinced his bat was no longer helping the team. Although he had managed to play nearly two full seasons with a bone chip in his knuckle, the knee injury had been devastating.

By the time Oliva played his last game, his batting average had dropped to .337, still the highest single-season mark in Twins history to that point. Despite hitting just .289 after he was injured, he finished with a seven-point lead over New York's Bobby Murcer, his only competition in the AL batting race. In addition to winning his third batting title in eight seasons, Oliva led the league in slugging for the first time at .546. His power took a big hit playing on just one healthy leg, yet his first-half performance had been so dominant that he still outslugged his peers.

Oliva probably would have topped the league in several raw-numbers categories had he stayed healthy. The lost playing time and his struggles to produce before being shut down worked against him when it came to

Behind the batting cage before a game, Oliva greets Vice President Hubert H. Humphrey, the longtime U.S. senator from Minnesota and a devoted Twins fan. Courtesy of the Minnesota Twins.

Oliva's accommodating nature made him a fan favorite. He is still a Twins icon nearly forty years after his retirement because of his warmth and openness in greeting those he meets. Courtesy of the Minnesota Twins.

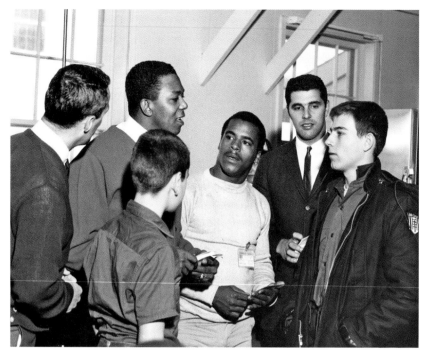

On a trip orchestrated by the Minnesota Twins to promote baseball and the team's commitment to the fan base, Oliva visits Job Corps trainees at Fort McCoy in central Wisconsin. Courtesy of the Minnesota Twins.

Oliva is off and running, with Harmon Killebrew kneeling in the on-deck circle. For most of their decade together, Oliva batted third and Killebrew held down the cleanup spot. Courtesy of the Minnesota Twins.

During one of many pregame events at Metropolitan Stadium in the 1960s, Oliva and teammates enjoy a leisurely game of horseshoes. Courtesy of the Minnesota Twins.

Occasionally the Twins hosted a fishing contest on a nearby lake, featuring Twins stars with rods and reels. Courtesy of the Minnesota Twins.

Oliva and his wife, Gordette, became parents with the birth of their daughter Anita in 1968. After seven years of isolation from his family in Cuba, Oliva took great joy in starting a family of his own. Courtesy of the Minnesota Twins.

Oliva and daughter Anita take in the sunshine while sitting on the Metropolitan Stadium turf before a game in 1970. Seated directly behind Oliva is fellow Cuban and mentor Minnie Mendoza. Courtesy of the Minnesota Twins.

César Tovar *(left)*, a Triple-A Dallas–Fort Worth Rangers teammate of Sandy Valdespino and Oliva in 1963, was a dynamic leadoff man for the division-winning Twins clubs of 1969 and 1970. Courtesy of the Minnesota Twins.

The Twins added another Cuban player in 1969, shortstop Leo Cárdenas *(left)*, a defensive standout. Here he talks with his double-play partner, second baseman Rod Carew. Courtesy of the Minnesota Twins.

Oliva greets fans and shows off his Louisville Slugger bat on the field before a game at Metropolitan Stadium. Courtesy of the Minnesota Twins.

After sixteen years in the minor leagues, Minnie Mendoza arrived at the major league camp in 1970. Already a veteran nearly a decade earlier when he assisted Oliva and other Cuban players adjust to a new culture and professional baseball, Mendoza finally made the Twins that spring at age thirty-six. Courtesy of the Minnesota Twins.

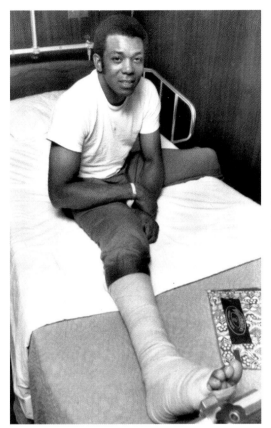

Oliva recuperates from major knee surgery in September 1971, three months after suffering the injury that changed the course of his baseball career. AP Photo/Robert Walsh.

Nearly eleven years after leaving his home in Piñar del Río, Cuba, Oliva reunites with his father Pedro and sister Felicia at Mexico City International Airport on January 4, 1972. Felicia had accompanied her mother, Anita, to a similar reunion with her brother a year earlier. AP Photo/Hdo.

Players came and went, but for most of a decade Harmon Killebrew followed Oliva in Minnesota's batting order. Courtesy of the Minnesota Twins.

Sharing a light moment are perennial All-Star Rod Carew and longtime Minneapolis sportswriter Sid Hartman. Courtesy of the Minnesota Twins.

Oliva assists his son Pedro, who takes his hacks during the annual Twins father–son game at Metropolitan Stadium in 1972. Courtesy of the Minnesota Twins.

Tony and Gordette Oliva with their children, Anita, Pedro, and Ric, in the late 1970s. Courtesy of the Minnesota Twins.

Both as a player and as a coach, Oliva frequently greeted fans and signed autographs along the walls at major league stadiums. Courtesy of the Minnesota Twins.

Yogi Berra and Tony Oliva were two of the game's best bad-ball hitters in the 1960s. Both went on to long coaching careers, serving with the Yankees and the Twins, respectively, at the time of this photograph in the late 1970s. Courtesy of the Minnesota Twins.

Oliva and Yankees star Reggie Jackson pose during spring training. Courtesy of the Minnesota Twins.

Oliva plays with Liam Killebrew, the great-grandson of Harmon Killebrew, while riding the light rail to a Target Field memorial for the late Twins slugger on May 26, 2011. Liam is held by his father, Todd Killebrew. *Pioneer Press/Star-Tribune.*

postseason awards. Despite being the American League's dominant hitter for the first three months of the 1971 season, Oliva finished a distant tenth in the league's MVP vote. Vida Blue took both MVP and Cy Young honors, and two other hurlers, Mickey Lolich and Wilbur Wood, also finished ahead of Tony O in MVP voting.

On September 22, eight days before the season ended, Oliva underwent surgery to remove torn cartilage from his right knee—the knee's third operation. Carew had suffered a ligament tear in his knee in 1970, and team doctors considered the severity of the two injuries and the cleanup procedures comparable. Carew came to camp in 1971 ready to run all out and to start the regular season at full strength. He struggled at the plate over the first two months, but he batted .335 in the second half to prove he was all the way back. Twins officials and doctors, therefore, believed Oliva would be ready for spring training in 1972.

To prepare for his return, Oliva took on a rigorous rehabilitation program, working with weights to build strength in the joint and stretching to break adhesions that had developed in the scar tissue. Both at home and during three-times-a-week physical therapy sessions, Oliva executed hundreds of leg lifts wearing a weighted boot on his right foot. Initially he could only work with a few pounds on the boot, but by diligently following the program, he was lifting thirty pounds by December. Although encouraged by the strength he had regained in his right leg, Oliva discovered that the pain returned when he tried even light running. As discouraging as that was, he continued to build leg strength, hopeful that he would be ready to go in the spring. But the weight training mostly benefited the thigh and did nothing to heal the knee.

Although Oliva could not play winter ball, the offseason was still memorable. He became a U.S. citizen in December. His wife and children were U.S. citizens, and after eleven years in the country, it seemed only right that he take the oath of citizenship. Then, in early January 1972, Felicia returned to Mexico for another visit, this time bringing along Oliva's father, Pedro. Oliva flew to Mexico City for the reunion, and he recalls his father greeting him just as his mother had a year earlier. Upon seeing each other for the first time in nearly eleven years in the airport's immigration area, Pedro, who went by Pirico, told his son that other than being a bit heavier, he looked the same as he had when he left home.

Pirico, now sixty-seven years old, looked older as well. Even at that age, however, the son discovered that his father had not lost the undying source of energy that had been his trademark. No matter where they went or what they did in Mexico, Pirico was always ready for more. When Oliva asked him if he would like to have his visa extended beyond fifty days, Pirico said yes without hesitation.

Unable to play for Los Mochis, Oliva was free to sightsee and spend more time with his visitors. Once the visa extensions were in place, Tony, Felicia, and their father departed warm and sunny Mexico for the late-January deep freeze of Minnesota. Temperatures were below zero when they arrived, and snow blanketed everything. Pirico and Felicia had never experienced such extreme weather, but the harsh climate did not stop them. Oliva owned a snowmobile, which Gordette and the children enjoyed. So did Felicia, who proved to be a speed demon when given the opportunity to drive.

Although Pirico was not fond of the cold weather, he took part in an ice-fishing expedition to Lake Minnetonka. After they had arrived and were bundled up for the trek onto the ice, Pirico looked out of the car window and asked, "Where's the lake?" He had not anticipated a frozen body of water covered with snow. The notion of opening a hole in the ice and fishing was an alien concept, and Pirico was even more surprised when the first fish surfaced from the cold waters. Father and son participated in a second ice-fishing trip and watched several University of Minnesota basketball games, but soon it was February and time to head to spring training.

Oliva did not enjoy driving cross-country to Florida, but he usually drove anyway so that he had a car available. This time he looked forward to the 1,700-mile drive, which provided an opportunity to spend more time with his father. The trip also gave his father a chance to see the countryside, though Minnesota was still covered in snow. Oliva's teammate Jim Holt, who was from North Carolina but had spent the winter in Minnesota, rode along for part of the trip. He was heading home before spring training began and shared the driving. It was not until they neared Indianapolis that Pirico saw American soil for the first time. At that point Oliva recalls his father joking, "I thought dirt here in the United States was white."

The temperature slowly climbed and the world turned green again as they approached Florida. A trip highlight was a stopover in Miami, where the Olivas met up with the Morales family, who had lived near the Oliva farm in Piñar del Río. The family had relocated to Miami, but years earlier the Morales boys had played baseball and fished with Tony and his brothers.

The family hosted a large group of Cuban friends and roasted two pigs. The experience was memorable for the Olivas, energized by the warm weather and the reunion with familiar friends. It was as if father and son were back in Cuba for a day.

The Extremes of 1972

For reasons both good and bad, spring training in 1972 was like no other for Oliva. When he made the annual sojourn to Florida, his father Pirico was with him. They had spent the winter together in Minnesota with Tony's family, and now Pirico would see his son take the field as a major leaguer for the first time.

Oliva had waited for more than a decade for this opportunity, but his surgically repaired right knee had not responded as expected. It was bothersome all spring, as fluid collected in the joint whenever Oliva stepped up his running. The pain and swelling, which caused him to run with a limp, kept him out of exhibition games deep into the spring. Finally, on a sunny day in late March, Pirico watched from the grandstand at Orlando's Tinker Field as his son took the field against the White Sox. Tony lined out in the first inning, later hit into a force play, and capped the memorable day by tucking a long drive just inside the right-field foul pole for a home run. "His father didn't clap or cheer," Bob Fowler reported in the *Sporting News,* "but just watched and beamed."

After the game, Pirico told Fowler, through an interpreter, "I wondered if I would see him play before I had to go back to Cuba." His son had wondered, too, as his ailing knee failed to improve and allowed only a brief opportunity to play. Oliva took part in only a few exhibition games before he had to shut down. Not only did his right knee remain swollen and sore, but he sprained his *left* knee soon after his father had seen him play. The frustrated batting champ returned to Minnesota to have the right knee drained and his rehab program revamped. Opening Day was out of the question.

Tests ruled out more surgery, an overly optimistic finding that was a great relief to Oliva, who had feared his season would end before it even started. Yet no adjustment in his rehab routine kept the fluid from returning. Good days—when he could stand the pain—were few. A cortisone shot numbed the discomfort, and the fluid buildup sometimes subsided, but after a few days, the pain and swelling would return. Oliva estimates that he got roughly ten cortisone shots during the summer of 1972. "They put so much cortisone in that knee, sometimes it changed the color of the skin," he recalls. Neither the multiple injections nor weight training, however, stabilized the weakened joint. Sometimes when he was simply walking, his right knee buckled and he would have to catch himself to avoid falling. It simply was not strong enough to run on, yet he faced pressure from the front office to return. At one point, a local newspaper reported that team officials believed Oliva was ready to play and that his hesitancy to return was in his head.

Such comments irked Oliva, who had always played through injuries, beginning with the knuckle ailment during his first two big league seasons. Only *he* knew how his knee felt, and he remembers the sensation of feeling moving parts in the joint. All the X-rays in the world might say his knee was sound, but he knew better. "One thing that bothered me that year was that I had a two-year contract," says Oliva. "This was the first time I signed for two years, and some of the media people said, 'Tony doesn't want to play because he has a two-year contract. The doctor said his knee is okay because the ligament is okay.' Yeah, my ligament was good, but I was the one feeling my knee. My knee was full of fluid and swollen. One time when they took fluid out of the knee, there were pieces of cartilage in the needle."

Although Oliva traveled with the team, he was on the disabled list, limited mostly to batting practice. At one point, team doctors decided he needed to push himself harder, but that approach only led to another draining of the knee. Yet the Twins looked to have Oliva back on the field in early June. After weathering a long, mostly unsuccessful rehabilitation, Oliva was excited to return. Pirico and Felicia were still in Minnesota, for another week, so they would get to see him play in a regular-season game before they returned to Cuba.

Oliva managed to hit well with his father in attendance, though from the moment he made his 1972 debut it was clear he was hobbled, a compromised player. As meaningful as it was to have his father there, Tony could not flash the array of skills that had made him a premier run producer in his first eight seasons.

When Oliva returned on June 11, a Sunday afternoon in Cleveland, nine months had passed since he had last appeared in a regular-season game. Earlier, manager Bill Rigney had pulled Oliva aside behind the batting cage. "That's home," the skipper teased as he pointed toward the plate. "And that's first base, and second, and third." Harmon Killebrew picked up on Rigney's light-hearted jab. "Careful," he said. "Don't tell him too much. He might get confused." Not too confused to pick up a single in three trips in a 5–3 victory. Rigney, demonstrating caution, removed Oliva after he flied out to deep center with the bases loaded to end the top of the fifth. For good measure, Oliva had to handle only one flyball.

When the Twins returned home for a nine-game homestand, Pirico finally saw his oldest son play in a big league game. Tony responded with six hits in his first seven contests, an impressive performance for one playing on a gimpy knee after such a long layoff. Seeing his son perform in a major league stadium was a source of immense pride for Pirico. "I thought he was a good ballplayer. I thought he had a chance to make it," Pirico reminisced in an interview with Fowler, speaking through an interpreter. "But I sure didn't think he'd become such a star."

Pirico also admitted that he and Anita missed their son. The politically enforced separation was an unfortunate aspect of Tony's career, though his father said it was worth it, knowing how successful their son had become in the United States. "If I knew in 1961 what I know now, I'd still want Tony to leave his home," Pirico explained. "It was a great opportunity for him to do what he loved." Finally, even if only for several days, they were able to share his success on the field.

With his father watching, Oliva went hitless in the homestand's opener against Detroit's Joe Niekro. As in Cleveland, Oliva played five innings and handled the one fly hit to him. Not a single ball was hit his way in the next game, but after singling home a run and playing five frames for a third straight day, the swelling and pain in his knee were as bad as ever. Oliva pressed on, encouraged by his hitting. Making his fifth start on June 17 with the Orioles at the Met, Oliva collected his first extra-base hit of the season—a double off Pat Dobson that he hit so deep that he arrived at second base with ease. He also singled and played eight innings.

After starting two games in a row, Oliva sat out the next day. Though pleased with his hitting, he admits he wanted most to homer with his father in the park. Surprisingly, Rigney started him in both games of a June 20 doubleheader with Cleveland. With his knee as sore as ever, Oliva began swinging for the fences. He hit a ball with authority to left early in the second game, and in the fifth he powered a pitch to straightaway center field. The ball probably would have gone out had Oliva turned on it and pulled it to right, but instead, Del Unser caught the drive on the warning track.

The Twins squared off against future Hall of Famer Gaylord Perry to close the homestand on June 21. Pirico and Felicia were booked to fly home to Cuba the following morning. They had enjoyed a remarkable reunion, sharing a harsh winter and the joys of ice fishing in Minnesota, driving cross-country together to spring training, and meeting up with old neighbors from Piñar del Río in Miami. Oliva hoped to generate one more lasting memory with a home run in the series finale. Early in the game, he jumped on a Perry offering, but once again lined the ball to deep center, where Unser hauled it in. In his final at-bat in the eighth, he was thinking home run when Perry gave him a waist-high pitch he thought he could drive. However, Oliva was on the receiving end of what he remembers was "one of the best spitters I had ever seen."

The pitch from Perry, who openly admitted to doctoring the ball, looked like it dropped off a table as Oliva swung through it. Its movement also fooled catcher Ray Fosse: the diving pitch bounced past him, allowing Oliva to reach first base on strike three. Oliva had been completely fooled by Perry's wet one. Rod Carew remembers his good friend's quirky take on facing spitters: "One time he said, 'Oh roomie, I'll just hit it on the dry side.' I looked at him and I laughed. That was Tony."

That at-bat against Perry, though, was his last chance to hit a long one for his father. The following day, Pirico and Felicia flew to Mexico City and the Twins boarded a plane for Kansas City to begin a weekend series. On his flight, Oliva could not help wonder if and when he would see them again.

Even with his right knee compromised, Oliva was hitting the ball hard. He had not been a defensive liability, thanks to some luck, so he was fully committed to playing as long as he could help the team. But despite Oliva's success and Rigney's conservative approach to playing time, keeping the star on the field simply was not realistic. That he faced only a few balls hit his way merely postponed the inevitable. And the inevitable quickly closed in on him in Kansas City.

Oliva was in right field at Kansas City's old Municipal Stadium for the Friday night opener. His night started well, as he singled off Royals lefty Paul Splittorff his first two times up. Splittorff and Jim Perry pitched shutout ball into the sixth, when the Royals' Richie Scheinblum slapped a two-out loop-ing flyball into short right. The ball should have been caught, but Oliva was not able to get to it. When the ailing right fielder failed to pick up the ball cleanly, Scheinblum pulled into second. The next batter, slugging first base-man John Mayberry, singled to give the Royals a 1–0 lead. Two innings later, left fielder Lou Piniella lofted a lazy fly down the right-field line, again with two outs. Again, a healthy Oliva would have executed the catch easily, but instead Piniella landed at second with another double. This time the extra out opened the door to a four-run rally, and the Royals rolled to a 5–0 win.

The game was Oliva's tenth and last of 1972. No matter how much rehab work he did, or how tightly Doc Lentz wrapped his knee, he always limped and could barely run. Pain was a constant, both on and off the field. The experiment to see how he would hold up under game conditions did not have a happy ending. Oliva remained on the roster, but Rigney and the Twins' brass now accepted that he could not play. Now that the front office had come around to his point of view, however, Oliva, still driven by his intense desire to play, was disappointed to be on the bench.

Though barely able to run, Tony O had batted .321 in ten games. While he generated little power playing on one healthy leg, the opportunity to play for his father made all the rehab work worthwhile—even if it could not keep him on the field. Now he faced the likelihood of a second knee operation in ten months. He was not keen on midseason surgery, dreading the notion that he would be out until the next spring. But on July 5, he went under the knife again—for the fourth time in eight years—in a far more extensive procedure than what had been performed the previous September. Dr. Harvey O'Pha-len removed roughly a hundred cartilage fragments and two bone spurs in the one-hour operation, and he refashioned the cartilage that remained to offer the best chance for a successful recovery.

Oliva turned thirty-four on July 20 with his career in jeopardy. O'Phalen admitted that the surgery might not be a success, and Oliva pondered that possibility frequently. Only time and a lot of rehab work would tell. With the knee severely weakened by two procedures in such a short span, the only certainty was that Oliva would be sidelined until 1973. However, there was reason for hope. Surgery reduced Oliva's discomfort to a far-less-substantial ache, and the roughly one hundred bone chips that had caused so much pain were now contained in a jar given to him by O'Phalen. For Oliva, that jar of cartilage validated the severity of his injury. After all, it took only one bone chip to lock up the knee or cause discomfort.

At first Oliva could not walk following the procedure, but he quickly kicked his post-op rehabilitation into action. He diligently maintained his rehab work throughout his final years as a player, a daily regimen that often lasted longer than the time required to play a baseball game. The rehab grind involved hundreds of hours of weight work, water pool exercises, massages, and physical therapy. Yet running continued to be difficult. After returning in 1973, Oliva endured regular pain and occasional bouts of fluid buildup. At least a few times each season, the knee required the needle—either to deliver a cortisone shot or to drain the joint, which required a much thicker version.

The suffering was a curse that Carew, Oliva's road roommate, witnessed firsthand. He remembers frequently hearing his friend moaning in pain even as he slept. Just as often, the knee kept Oliva awake at night. "I have never see a grown man cry as much as I used to, being his roommate—late at night and his knee is just killing him," Carew recalls. "He'd go get some ice or I'd get him some ice, and he'd pack his knee in it. But he never complained when he went out on the field. We'd stay up all night talking, and he'd talk about how bad his knee hurts. Then the next day, he'd go out to play. It's what he wanted to do. And for him to be able to go out and play on that bad knee and never complain—it's different today. Back then, we wanted to play even if we were hurt."

Carew added, "Tony tried just about every remedy you can think of. Snake oil. I saw him with a can of STP oil treatment one time. He was rubbing it on his knee with some other stuff. I said, 'Roomie, what is that for?' He said, 'Oh, somebody told me that if I took this and rubbed it in.' I said, 'Yeah, but you're not a car.' But he tried just about everything to see if that knee would get better." By the end of his career, Oliva had undergone seven right-knee surgeries. The knee continued to be problematic long after he quit playing, but the discomfort was far more manageable once he quit running on it. Finally in 1991, Oliva had his right knee replaced. The joint was replaced again in 2005, and a year later, he had the left knee done.

It is difficult to imagine a player today—or in any era—doing what Oliva did to stay in the game. To him, the reasons were simple. "I went through it for two reasons," he explains. "I enjoyed what I was doing, but I also needed a job. It wasn't my plan what happened to me. I was in my prime. It's a lot different if you're from America because you know the language. Maybe you went to college or learned a skill, so people will give you a job. I needed a job."

Oliva's absence in 1972 was just one of several challenges facing the Twins. César Tovar mostly played in right field with Oliva out for all but ten games, and Harmon Killebrew, who played the rest of his career with knee troubles, returned to first base. The Twins had All-Star second baseman

Rod Carew, who won his second batting title, but the makeup of the rest of the lineup was uncertain from the start of spring training. The Twins had pitching concerns as well, even with the offseason acquisition of dependable relievers Dave LaRoche and Wayne Granger. When Leo Cárdenas was dealt for LaRoche, Danny Thompson took over at short.

A rare bright spot in 1972 was Bobby Darwin, a twenty-nine-year-old rookie who had moved from the mound to the outfield two years earlier. He drilled homers in his first two games and finished his first big league season with twenty-two home runs and eighty RBIs.

But the team's performance could not save Bill Rigney's job. After the Twins lost eleven of fifteen games to start June and fell 9.5 games behind first-place Oakland, Griffith fired him little more than two seasons after he had taken over.

Oliva underwent extensive knee surgery that same day, and Griffith announced that Frank Quilici—one of Oliva's first friends in the United States—would be the new manager. Quilici was seen as a Billy Martin protégé, which would play well in Minnesota. He had already won over Twins fans and was warm, outgoing, and funny interacting with the local press, which had embraced him. He was a face of the franchise despite playing only 405 games in five big league seasons. With Twins attendance in steady decline, perhaps a well-liked manager could soften the public relations blow for a club that could no longer contend after a long winning stretch. The owner wanted his new skipper to both turn things around and draw fans back to the park.

With no previous managing experience, Quilici, who had just turned thirty-three, was the youngest manager in the majors. He mixed energy and fire with an attention to detail and an emphasis on communicating effectively with the players. His pleasant nature and good humor still shone through, but players soon learned that Quilici was a disciplinarian. He called more practices, pushed fundamentals, crusaded against mental mistakes, and insisted on an honest effort from everyone. Despite the new energy Quilici brought to the job, the Twins finished 77–77 in a strike-shortened 1972 season. It was a tough time to manage the club. The farm system was no longer producing premier talent, and the top two run producers of the previous decade, Oliva and Killebrew, were hurting.

How Oliva's knee would respond following two surgeries was uncertain. And Killebrew, approaching his thirty-seventh birthday, had played with a host of injuries that had caused his power to decline. "I really, really felt bad when I managed that Tony was practically on one leg," says Quilici. "And so was Harmon. That was the most difficult part of managing that ball club, to see your two really, really good friends suffer through those injuries." A dozen years after Quilici and Oliva had started pro careers together in Wytheville, Virginia, Oliva's playing days were in limbo.

Following the failed 1972 campaign, Oliva headed to Venezuela for another reunion. During his parents' visits, he had learned that his two youngest brothers, Reynaldo and Juan Carlos, were elite ballplayers in Cuba. Reynaldo, a center fielder, was a righthanded hitter, unlike both his father and his more famous brother. But like Tony, he had joined the country team in Piñar del Río as a teenager, playing against men of all ages. Reynaldo married, had children, and gave up baseball while he was still young.

Juan Carlos, the youngest and a seventeen-year-old in 1972, had pitched his team to Cuba's amateur championship that summer. He was chosen to represent Cuba in a junior-level international tournament held in Caracas, Venezuela. Juan Carlos, six when his big brother left home in 1961, had grown into a young man with a promising baseball career. He pitched two complete-game victories and hit a homer, and the Cuban team won all twelve of its games to claim the tournament title.

Oliva says the club, made up mostly of sixteen- and seventeen-year-old kids, was loaded with major league prospects, none of whom ever had an opportunity to play on the mainland. Juan Carlos spent nearly a decade on the Cuban national team, an honor bestowed on the island's best players, and traveled all over the world. But after the Bay of Pigs fiasco in April 1961, decades passed before Cuban players began to defect and make their way to North America.

After Oliva left Cuba, twelve years passed before he finally returned to the island. He applied for a visa during the 1973 season, and to his surprise, Cuban officials granted one. Only he could make the trip because of travel restrictions, so in mid-November he boarded a plane for Mexico City, where he made arrangements for a month-long stay in Cuba. His anticipation of a long-awaited reunion grew during the drive from Havana to Piñar del Río. He had expected to make this trip through western Cuba in the fall of 1961, following a six-month baseball season, but he now returned home wondering if he would recognize his younger siblings, who were now adults.

Oliva had reunited with Felicia in Mexico and with Juan Carlos in Venezuela, but he had not seen his other seven siblings in twelve years. He also met their children for the first time, including young nephews he did not know he had. "It was hard to describe," Oliva says of reconnecting with everyone that day. "I was there, yet it was like I was dreaming. It was like I was floating on air, because I don't think my feet were touching the ground."

Although the family had grown, the family farm had shrunk. The Castro government had confiscated and divided up most of the land, leaving the Oliva family a much smaller plot to cultivate. By then, Pirico was up in years, and the children had moved him and Anita to nearby Consolación del Sur, one of the larger towns in the province, where Juan Carlos had settled during his baseball career.

Even if the family's land had not been divided into smaller plots, Oliva doubts that his brothers would have continued to farm after their father retired. He, Reynaldo, and Juan Carlos had baseball careers as young men, and his two other brothers pursued other work options to generate income. As much as he loved the farm, Oliva says it was a difficult way to make a living. His family farmed without the help of machinery, and crops—and thus the family's income—were always vulnerable to drought and hurricanes.

Oliva's return to Cuba was also an opportunity to see the country, something neither he nor his family could previously afford to do. He found Cubans to be as baseball-crazy as ever. New baseball stadiums had sprouted up all over the country, some as nice as the American League parks in which he played. Oliva attended several games and discovered a host of Cuban players who could have been on major league rosters, and numerous other prospects who would have had promising futures if they could have left the island.

In a tournament featuring top talent from several Latin American nations, a Panamanian pitching prospect caught Oliva's attention. A hard-throwing teenager named Juan Berenguer pitched seven innings for Panama against the Cuban team. The righthander had just started pitching and was quite raw, but his talent was apparent. Oliva approached the young man after the game. "He told me a lot of good things about my pitching and to work hard," Berenguer recalls of the meeting with Oliva, a three-time batting champion who was a hero to baseball fans throughout Latin America. Oliva told the teen that he could reach the major leagues if he continued to progress as a pitcher. These words of encouragement inspired Berenguer, who later noted, "I took pride in myself and worked so hard after that, so that I could get there."

Soon scouts began paying attention to Berenguer, who signed with the New York Mets in 1975 and debuted as a starting pitcher three years later. With the Mets and the Twins training close to one another in Florida,

Berenguer and Oliva frequently met during spring training early in the young man's career. He remembers that Oliva always encouraged him to keep working hard—that he would get his big chance if he kept plugging at it.

Oliva was right, though Berenguer eventually shifted to the bullpen during big league stints with New York, Kansas City, Toronto, Detroit, and San Francisco, before the Giants released him in December 1986. Berenguer, who had just turned thirty-two, signed with the Twins. Fans, taken by his long hair, bushy mustache, hard-as-nails demeanor on the mound, and mid-nineties heat, called him "Señor Smoke." He immediately became a key man out of the pen for the 1987 World Series champions.

Shortly after that first meeting with Berenguer, Oliva departed Cuba for Minnesota. Saying goodbye was no easier than saying goodbye to his parents had been after their recent visits. Says Oliva, "You never knew if you'd be able to come back because of the rules and regulations."

Oliva did not return to Cuba again until 1981, though his parents visited the United States together in 1976. Pirico and Anita also ventured west to Hitchcock to meet Gordette's parents, Bob and Lura DuBois. Although language was a barrier, Gordette says the gathering was festive and often transcended language. She remembers Tony's parents joyfully dancing together in her parents' home.

"They had so much fun together," Gordette recalls. "We all had a lot of fun. You don't have to understand words to be able to dance to music. Then my mom taught his mom how to crochet. We sent a bunch of yarn back with her. That's one thing my mom could show her even though they couldn't speak." Anita crocheted an entire blanket before she returned home to Cuba.

The 1976 visit marked the only time Pirico and Anita traveled to the United States together. As always, when it was time to part ways, goodbyes were difficult. By then, Pirico, much older than Anita, was in his seventies. He was healthy and spry, but time was fleeting when political borders isolated loved ones.

As much as Oliva would have loved to have his parents stay permanently, living in Minnesota was never a realistic possibility for them. Both Tony and Gordette believe Pirico was open to the idea, but Anita, on the other hand, was always ready to go home when the time came. "She would get so lonesome for the others," Gordette explains. "Tony was the only member of his family here, and nine more siblings still there. They were all having families, too. She never wanted to stay, never."

When Anita died unexpectedly in 1981, Oliva quickly set up a return trip to Cuba. Arranging travel continued to be laborious, but with the assistance of Juan Carlos—who, as a member of the Cuban national team, could work political channels—Oliva set up a visa and returned for the funeral. He would have liked his family to travel with him, but time did not allow it. He stayed only a few days.

Anita's sudden death at age sixty-three was not only a painful lesson in how fleeting life can be, but also a sad reminder of the decades of family time lost to political realities. Those years could never be regained. Oliva had been fortunate enough to spend time with his mother during three separate visits over the previous decade, but he had missed out on twenty years of family gatherings for holidays. He had not witnessed the big events in his siblings' lives, missing their weddings and the births of their children. His parents were not able to be part of their grandchildren's lives, and his children barely knew the grandmother they had just lost.

Within a year of Anita's passing, Pirico, now in his late seventies, made one final visit to the United States. Despite his age, he still was full of energy, always game to try new experiences and to meet new people. Although he never left the island again after his 1982 visit, Pirico lived into his nineties and saw his son several times in his remaining years. Travel restrictions were minimized for Cuban émigrés in 1986, and suddenly, after some twenty-five years, it became relatively easy for Oliva to take his family to Cuba.

Even making a phone call to the island had always been problematic. Connecting to the one line serving the only public phone in Consolación del Sur had been a hit-or-miss proposition; he would dial the phone number dozens of times to get through. Gordette says he might sit for three or four hours attempting to complete a call. "And then the line would be so bad, you couldn't hear," she recalls. "I felt so bad for him in those days. He had more patience than a saint."

When Oliva made his third trip home in 1986, he took his eldest child, Anita. A year later, the entire family traveled together to Cuba. The three children never experienced the family farm that held so many fond memories for their father. By then, the family owned just a couple of acres, and only one sister lived on the tiny plot that remained in the family. The small home in which Pirico and Anita had raised their ten children, by now an uninhabited little shack, would soon be torn down. The baseball field that had been the center of Oliva's life as a young boy was gone. "It's a pasture now," Oliva says. "I still go there. I go to the spot where there used to be home plate. There used to be a tree there, too. It's nice to go there. It brings back some memories."

Anita fondly remembers that 1986 trip with her father. As a high school senior, she was beginning to embrace her heritage, and although she spoke very little Spanish at the time, her first visit to Cuba meant the world to her. She says it was hard to leave. "The sky is a different shade of blue, the stars are brighter in the sky," she explains. "There is this culture out there and it's part of me. I kind of had that validation of some of the culture that I knew I always had in me and longed to be able to share. It was like it filled a big empty hole that I had, that I knew was in me."

When the entire family traveled to Piñar del Río in 1987, youngest son Ric was eleven, an age when boys are often consumed by baseball. He had plenty of cousins and family friends with whom to strike up a game. He was less aware of the cultural significance of the experience at the time, yet that first trip had a lasting impact on his worldview. "I started not caring as much about material things because I was aware of the stark difference between how all my relatives there live versus how I live," Ric explains. "It wasn't an all-of-a-sudden overnight process, but I know I don't need as much when I go to a relative's house and they don't have running water. My attitude just shifted in what I thought was important. What do I really need?"

"It didn't matter if there was no electricity," adds Anita. "If there was no electricity, we just stood outside and the stars lit up the sky. We'd sit there and [the parents] would tell stories by moonlight." She reflects, "Being there in the moment, it slows down life." She says that although many of her father's siblings were living without toilets, running water, and other basic amenities, there were "joys in simple pleasures that they have that we don't have. I came back feeling I needed to slow down my high-paced life."

Today Cuba is a far cry from the land that Oliva and his ball-playing countrymen left behind when they were cut off from their homeland in 1961. In the years leading up to the revolution, Cuba had a substantial middle class, concentrated mostly in the largest cities, but rural Cubans were markedly poorer. Few homes in the countryside had electricity or plumbing, and since the sugar crop was seasonal, a significant percentage of the rural population lacked year-round employment.

The poverty that Cuban émigrés see when returning after so many years can be unnerving. Poverty certainly is not new to Cuba. Prior to Castro's taking power in 1959, the disparity in wealth was substantial. Although Havana was a tourist mecca in the pre-Castro years, with luxurious hotels and casinos, the concentration of wealth among those who owned businesses and large agricultural plantations spurred the revolution that brought Castro to power. Because there has been little foreign investment in Cuba since the revolution, particularly since the collapse of the Soviet Union in the 1980s, the island's infrastructure is in tatters. The disparity in wealth is less significant among working people, but Cubans as a whole are poorer today. Food and goods remain in short supply, now more than ever.

If the failures of the Castro regime were not enough, many former major leaguers from Cuba already harbored bitter feelings toward the dictator for his part in creating and maintaining the country's leave-and-no-return policy. When Castro disbanded Cuba's prestigious professional baseball league in 1961, players with established careers in both countries were forced to choose between sacrificing their livelihood to stay on the island, and permanently abandoning the homeland to continue their careers in the United States.

Many former players have never returned to Cuba. The families of Camilo Pascual and his wife Raquel were rooted in Spain, and once Camilo's parents and a few other family members joined him in the United States in the mid-1960s, he had little reason to return to the island. "I love Cuba, no question about it," Pascual explains. "I was born there. I made my life there. [But] I don't have anybody over there. If the situation with this government changes, maybe I will visit Cuba."

Other Cubans who came to the United States to play in the 1950s are more vehement in refusing to return as long as the current government, now run by Fidel's brother Raúl, remains in power. That includes José Valdivielso, who spent parts of four seasons with the Senators and retired after the franchise's first year in Minnesota in 1961. A promising shortstop from Matanzas, a port city on Cuba's north shore, Valdivielso spent his winters playing alongside Minnie Miñoso and Julio Bécquer with Marianao. He could see that the future of professional baseball in Cuba was bleak in late 1960, when the revolutionary government banned American players from what proved to be the final season of the Cuban Winter League.

By then, Valdivielso's career was winding down. Three years earlier, Triple-A Indianapolis teammate Sam Mele had helped him tweak his hitting mechanics, and Valdivielso believed he was better prepared to stick in the majors. But after the 1957 season with Indianapolis, he contracted an eye infection playing for Marianao, which caused permanent damage. He could no longer judge the speed of pitches and groundballs, and he struggled to play in bright sunlight.

Valdivielso was also on the roster when the Bay of Pigs invasion put Cuba and the United States on a collision course. It took six years for him to relocate his entire family in the United States. During those years, the Valdivielso clan, like other well-to-do families in Cuba, saw its property confiscated by the government. With no family on the island, Valdivielso has no interest in returning as long as the current regime maintains control. "I love my country," Valdivielso says of his homeland, "and I would never say never, but I could not live under any circumstances like that." He hopes for regime change in his lifetime, but he has made a wonderful life for himself in America. He and his wife Rosa raised three daughters in the New York City area. The recently retired Valdivielso enjoyed a broadcasting career covering the Yankees and Mets for Telemundo, and for a stretch he also reported on baseball and boxing for ESPN.

Politics never factored into Oliva's decision whether to return to Cuba. To this day, it is a topic he refuses to address. He will not discuss Castro and Cuban politics, or how the revolution affected his family after he left in 1961. The one thing he makes clear was his desire and commitment to see Piñar del Río again. "I knew I wanted to go," Oliva says. "My family is important to me. My brothers, sisters, my mother and father—nothing was more important to me than family. When I go there, you can see how happy they are, how much they care. I go to see family. I go to see friends."

Gordette adds that they and the children do not stay in hotels or eat in restaurants when they visit Piñar del Río. The nearly annual sojourns are all about family. And Oliva's commitment to loved ones in Cuba remains steadfast.

"My dad has built a home for each one of his siblings," notes Anita. "He provided all the materials and the work, so that they each could have a habitable home." Oliva had never mentioned that fact in our many hours of conversation, and he was reluctant to reveal details when pressed, but he said it was the least he could do to have something good come out of the years of separation.

"I don't like to talk about it a lot because I just wanted to help my family," Oliva explains. "I was lucky to be able to get a good job and be able to help them."

In the early 1960s, Oliva debated the validity of his decision to stay in the United States. Despite all the time with loved ones lost, he knows the difficult choice he made was the right one. "If I had to do it all over again, I'd do it in a minute," Oliva says. "I have nothing to regret. I love that I had the opportunity, that I was able to help my family and help some other people close to my family. I wish I could help more, but you only can help so much."

Oliva has reconnected with his Cuban family in a meaningful way, more than five decades after he and his fellow Cubans became men without a country. Political events had forced them to choose between a promising career in the United States and their families.

"It was pretty hard," recalls Julio Bécquer, who had been playing professional ball in the United States for a decade when he was forced to make that decision in 1961. "If I would have gone back to Cuba, that meant I probably would have been doing something else. But at the time, I was a baseball player and I was making a good living playing baseball. I was not necessarily thinking about myself; I was thinking about my family."

That included his parents and siblings. Bécquer was the oldest of eight children. When he faced the decision whether to continue a professional baseball career, his father had already retired and his younger brothers were still teenagers. He had been able to bolster his family's income, but the political fallout of the Bay of Pigs fiasco affected his ability to help out and led to his separation from family.

Over the years, three of Bécquer's brothers moved to the United States, but two brothers, two sisters and a host of cousins remain on the island. He has not seen them in more than fifty years. "A few times I did get close to going back," Bécquer explains, "and one of my regrets is that I didn't go back home with my wife. My wife [Edith] and my daughter [Frances] went twice."

Bécquer, who had a long post-baseball career as a buyer for the Dayton–Hudson Corporation in Minneapolis, says that work made return trips to Cuba difficult. He frequently traveled on the job, often to New York and Europe, and somehow never made it back before Edith passed away in 2007. For years, Frances has prodded her to father to make the trip, and more recently his sons, José and Pedro, have expressed interest in going. Bécquer hopes the long-awaited reunion with siblings and their families will take place soon.

"This was real, real hard for everyone," Minnie Mendoza says of the forced isolation. He had been instrumental in helping Oliva adjust to his new life and faced the same difficult decision when Cuban–U.S. relations deteriorated. "I had my family. I had a wife and two daughters," says Mendoza. "And my father told me, 'You don't have no future here. You better leave. It's the best thing for your family. As soon as possible.' And that's what I did."

Mendoza never again saw his father Ricardo, who died in 1969 while his son was playing winter ball in the Dominican Republic. Mendoza says the news evoked "tremendous pain, because I didn't have a chance to ever see him or go to the funeral." He reunited with his mother, Carlota Carreras, and five siblings in Cuba in 1979, after nearly two decades away, and he returned for Carlota's funeral in 1984, his last trip to his homeland. He still has a sister and two brothers in Cuba, as well as a new generation of family born since his 1984 visit.

Encouraged by his wife Julia and two daughters, Mendoza has not closed the door to another return trip. But like so many of his fellow Cubans who played with him fifty years ago, he has had a rewarding career here—as a player, coach, and scout—and is firmly rooted in the United States. "People here in the United States made us feel like family," Mendoza says. "This is my country. I have two daughters here. I have five grandchildren." Married for more than fifty years, Mendoza still scouts for the Cleveland Indians, working as a field coordinator for Latin American prospects.

Another Cuban with Hall of Fame credentials, Luis Tiant, returned to Cuba for the first time in 2007, more than forty-six years after the Bay of Pigs invasion. In *The Lost Son of Havana,* director Jonathan Hock documented the return of the colorful Marianao native with the bushy Fu Manchu mustache and ever-present cigar. "I want to see my country before I die," Tiant says on film. "I have to go to Cuba before I die. That will complete my life."

The film is filled with quiet yet expressive moments: Tiant looking out the window of the small plane as it lands in Havana, riding in the back of a cab as he observes what decades of Castro's rule has done to Cuba, and the first meeting with family members. Few words are needed when Tiant heads to a small home to reunite with his aunts—his father's sisters—not actually knowing who in the family is still alive. They embrace at length, with tears flowing down their cheeks. It is a scene of unspoken sadness after forty-six years of separation. The joy of reuniting does not erase the memory of all that lost time.

In one of the final meetings of family and friends, a tearful Tiant admits that he regrets having stayed away so long. A successful baseball career in the United States came with a price. "Things could have been different," he tells them. When it is time to say goodbye, Tiant and his aunts share a common concern: whether they would ever see each other again. During his stay, Tiant also met with Oliva's youngest sibling, Juan Carlos, who bears a strong resemblance to his big brother. Juan Carlos teared up when he discussed the forced separation his family had experienced in 1961, forty-six years earlier.

The Final Years as a Player

Amerian League owners, looking for more scoring, voted to begin using the designated hitter in 1973. Lowering the mound and adding four expansion teams after 1968, the Year of the Pitcher, helped shift Major League Baseball away from an overly pitcher-friendly era, but run production still lagged in the junior circuit. Through the late 1960s and into the '70s, the National League outscored the American League—significantly in some seasons—and NL hitters frequently posted gaudier numbers. The National League was also considered the faster league, with Lou Brock, Bobby Bonds, Joe Morgan, Pete Rose, César Cedeño, and Roberto Clemente among those providing dazzle and flash.

"The American League was kind of a dull league, and the National League was *the* league," Jim Kaat said of those years in a 1992 interview with *Minneapolis Star-Tribune* sportswriter Steve Aschburner. Fans seemingly agreed with Kaat's perspective, as the National League outdrew the American League by 36 percent in 1972. Several AL franchises experienced significant attendance drop-offs in the early '70s.

After drawing more than one million fans in each of their first ten years in Minnesota, and following consecutive AL West titles, the Twins saw attendance slip to 941,000 in 1971, as an aging club in desperate need of pitching failed to be a contender. Attendance dipped to less than 800,000 in 1972, another lackluster season on the field, and owner Calvin Griffith fretted publicly about the decline in fan support and what he considered the suddenly perilous state of the franchise.

Free agency and player arbitration were on the horizon, and they were sure to fuel higher salaries, but Griffith supported the designated hitter rule. Even though the rule threatened to add another run producer's salary to the budget, the DH concept was tailor-made for his team. Both Oliva and Harmon Killebrew, rehabbing from surgical procedures and facing long-term health issues, fit the new role perfectly. The timing of the new rule was perfect. Oliva was not ready to play in the outfield that spring, so the DH was the only way to keep both him and Killebrew in the lineup. Neither player liked the prospect of only hitting, but second-year manager Frank Quilici was not complaining. He could use both veterans as long as they could stay healthy.

Quilici hoped to have his top two run producers anchor a lineup of largely young, untested talent, but Killebrew, returning from operations for varicose veins and a bone growth in his big right toe, continued to be plagued by injury. His troublesome left knee, where little cartilage remained, soon gave the Twins *two* players who were best suited for DH duties. That scenario became an ongoing concern for the Twins and created an uncomfortable situation for Oliva when he was asked to pinch-hit for Killebrew. "We were both hurt," says Oliva. "Killebrew started the game as the DH and later I pinch-hit for him. I said to Harmon, 'I'm sorry. I don't want to pinch-hit for you.' But when the manager said something in those days, you better do it."

Killebrew's health took a turn for the worse when he tore cartilage in the knee while taking a swing at Comiskey Park on June 25, 1973, four days shy of his thirty-seventh birthday. He attempted to rehab the injury, but after a month of making little progress, he underwent surgery. He returned in September and finished with five home runs and thirty-two RBIs. His bad knee further compromised, Killebrew's future with the Twins was less certain at season's end.

Oliva, who never again took the field wearing an outfielder's glove, faced the same doubts about his ability to perform. He had endured two major procedures on his right knee and appeared in just ten games in 1972, spending the summer rehabbing after having dozens of bone chips removed in July. He arrived in Florida knowing his only option was to adjust to this new DH role. Assuming, of course, he still had a big league job. "I thought Minnesota was going to release me in spring training '73," Oliva says, "because I was making a lot of money in those days and I was only going to be the DH. I knew I could hit, but I was concerned. I didn't know who I could sign with. If the Twins released me then, I might have to go to Mexico. A lot of guys did that because they had to make a living."

Oliva not only stayed but proved he could still hit. Despite the long lay-off and a balky knee that robbed him of much of his power, Oliva was one of the league's most productive DHs in 1973. In 146 games, he delivered a team-high ninety-two RBIs, which ranked eleventh among all AL hitters. Twins pitchers appreciated his contribution. "I didn't have to hit any more as a pitcher. I loved that," Bert Blyleven says of the rule change. "I would much rather have Tony hit for me and take my chances against their best hitter. Because we had the best hitter in Tony."

The only designated hitter with more RBIs in the rule's inaugural season was future Hall of Famer Frank Robinson, who at age thirty-seven signed with the California Angels and drove in ninety-seven runs. He was the premier power threat among the DH crowd, chipping in twenty-nine doubles and thirty home runs. Oliva collected twenty doubles and sixteen home runs. His doubles total fell far short of the thirty-five he had averaged over his first eight seasons, which reflects the power lost to his ailing knee. Still, he batted .291, good for eleventh in the league.

Also among the DH elite was another future Hall of Famer, Orlando Cepeda. He had been released by Oakland after the 1972 season, not long after weathering two knee surgeries. His legs were shot, and he went home to Puerto Rico thinking his career was over. Expecting to retire, Cepeda did not keep up with offseason news and was unaware of the new DH rule. "The day they make the rule, I was on the phone asking Tony how he was feeling," Cepeda told the *New York Times* years ago. "He told me about this new rule and told me to sign with Boston." Soon the Red Sox came calling.

Cepeda was a good fit for Fenway Park. After two difficult years side-tracked by injury, the thirty-five-year-old slugger enjoyed one last productive summer, batting .289 with twenty home runs and eighty-six RBIs. As a former Cardinal, he remembers the year fondly for the opportunity to play *with* 1967 World Series opponents Carl Yastrzemski, Reggie Smith, and Rico Petrocelli.

Oliva and Cepeda were friends going back to their close batting race in the Puerto Rican Winter League in 1964. Oliva, in the weeks leading up to his first major league season, had competed with two established stars from the island, Cepeda and Roberto Clemente. While Oliva and Clemente went on to win their leagues' batting titles in each of the next two big league seasons, Cepeda came out ahead that winter in Puerto Rico. In time, Cepeda and Oliva became known as two of the best curveball hitters of their era.

When Oliva and Cepeda met in Florida in 1973, Cepeda had a gift for his friend: a bandage containing two magnets, which Cepeda said had done wonders for his ailing knees. He had been given the bandage by Dr. Ralph Sierra, a San Juan chiropractor and electrical engineer, who believed the separate and distinct energies of a magnet's north and south poles had healing properties. (The field of magnetic therapy, practiced more widely in parts of Europe and Asia today, has never taken root in the United States.)

Oliva was receptive. He had tried dozens of home remedies to counter the discomfort and fluid buildup in his right knee. If wrapping the knee with a magnetic bandage had worked for Cepeda, it was worth a try. Once he began wearing the bandage, he says fluid no longer accumulated in the joint. He strapped it on for team workouts and even occasionally wore it during games. The magnetic bandage sparked hope that one day he might be able to return to right field. Oliva believes he would not have been a productive hitter without it. His damaged knee held up through the six-month grind of a season, boosting his confidence in the knee's ability to withstand regular play. And right from the start, he showed a knack for this new DH thing.

On April 6, the Twins opened the season in Oakland, where Oliva's career had run aground twenty-one months earlier. Blyleven made his second straight Opening Day start, and Catfish Hunter took the mound for the World Series champion Athletics, winners of a dramatic seven-game affair with Cincinnati the previous October.

Larry Hisle, acquired over the winter from the Cardinals, led off and greeted Oakland's ace with a looping single that dropped in front of center fielder Billy Conigliaro. Rod Carew then hit a perfect double-play grounder, which rolled through second baseman Dick Green's legs, putting runners on first and second for young Bobby Darwin, Oliva's replacement in right field. Darwin struck out with the runners in motion, though Hisle came around to score when Oakland catcher Ray Fosse rifled the ball into left field trying to throw him out at third. With Carew still aboard and one out, Oliva stepped to the plate for the first DH at-bat by a Twins player. He jumped on Hunter's first pitch and deposited it in the Coliseum's right-field bleachers. This was the first home run ever by a DH. Hunter did not finish the fourth inning, and the Twins rolled to an 8–3 victory.

Tony O hit safely in each of the first three games and in five of his first six. He found his groove in May, collecting at least one hit in eighteen of twenty-four starts. The multihit games and RBIs began to pile up, as Oliva was once again making consistent contact and hitting the ball hard. Extra-base hits were rare, but as the season progressed, Oliva showed flashes of the dangerous hitter who had frustrated AL pitchers for nearly a decade. Not only was he attacking the ball again, but he was aggressively rounding first base on hits to the outfield. Once he even broke up a double play with a slide at second base. He had always slid on his right side, which now was painful and risky, and training himself to slide on his left side at that point in his career was nearly impossible. He took his chances.

Twins coach Ralph Rowe worked with Oliva on running techniques that might alleviate knee pain and allow him to run harder. His progress spurred talk of a return to the outfield, but he remained a designated hitter.

Oliva executed a season-high nine-game hitting streak in June. It was not long by his standards, but he batted .432 during the streak and flirted with .300 the rest of the season. On July 3, with the Twins briefly in first place in a wide-open American League West race, Tony O stroked three home runs in a game for the first time.

The first was a two-out solo shot off Royals pitcher Mark Littell in the opening frame. With Kansas City up 4–3 in the sixth, Oliva led off the inning with a second drive to the sod bank beyond the right-field wall at newly opened Kauffman Stadium. The Royals tied the game in their half of the sixth and took a 6–5 lead into the ninth. Royals cocloser Gene Garber retired Carew and Jerry Terrell to start the inning. With the Twins down to their final out, Oliva drilled a liner into the seats in right-center for the first three-homer game in Kansas City's new park. There was little doubt about the game-tying shot; Royals right fielder Ed Kirkpatrick never moved as the ball sailed out of the yard.

Kansas City won in its half of the ninth, and the Twins' flirtation with first place ended soon after. A 3–13 skid that began in late July forced the Twins out of the pennant race, and only a September surge in which they won thirteen of their last twenty-one games secured an 81–81 finish—the second straight .500 season by the Twins. The young club had been prone to errors and mental mistakes.

Oliva finished 1973 with a flourish. He hit safely in thirty-one of his final forty starts, knocking in thirty-seven runs. September began with a seven-game hitting streak, and a six-game run stalled when he went hitless on the final day of the season. The last hitting streak was in full swing when Oliva took charge of a 9–4 victory on September 25. He drilled a two-run double off Athletics starter Chuck Dobson to put the Twins up 3–1 in the second inning. Then he put the game out of reach with a three-run blast off reliever Darold Knowles in the fifth. Oliva's five RBIs gave him ninety for the season.

In the final 1973 meeting between the clubs, Bert Blyleven tossed a one-hitter to secure his twentieth victory. He outdueled Oakland's twenty-one-game winner, Catfish Hunter, who also pitched into the ninth. With the score knotted 1–1, Oliva led off the ninth by powering Hunter's first pitch into the seats for his sixteenth and final homer of the year. The Twins touched Hunter for two more runs, and Blyleven worked a quick ninth for the 4–1 victory.

Oliva finished with ninety-two RBIs, a remarkable total considering that the knee injury had compromised his power. He collected 166 hits in 146 games, and the only Twin with more hits and a higher batting average was Carew, the American League batting champion. Carew, with a league-leading 203 hits, batted .350 to secure his second of four straight AL batting crowns.

When Carew made it four in a row in 1975, either he or Oliva had been the league's leading hitter in eight of the previous twelve seasons. The student had supplanted his teacher. After Oliva's retirement following the 1976 season, Carew capped his Twins career with batting titles in 1977 and 1978, his final two summers in Minnesota. That included a flirtation with .400 in '77, when he finished at .388 with career highs in runs (128), doubles (38), triples (16), homers (14), and RBIs (100).

The Twins' housecleaning began long before Rod Carew's departure. After the Twins went from contender to pretender in 1972, owner Calvin Griffith dealt César Tovar to Philadelphia and shuffled Jim Perry to Detroit. Then in August 1973, with the Twins struggling to play .500 ball, Jim Kaat was waived to the White Sox. None of those moves landed a major league regular, a serviceable starting pitcher, or a top prospect to build around. A smaller deal netted Larry Hisle, who took over in center field, but Frank Quilici's teams were light on talent and depth. A crop of untested pitchers endured on-the-job training and struggled to develop into dependable starters.

And 1974 was more of the same, including the sloppy defensive play and mental miscues that had plagued the Twins during the second half of 1973. The 1974 club made thirty-seven errors in its first twenty-eight games, leading to just twelve wins. The season was not a month old, and Quilici's patience and good-natured manner were being tested. "This isn't spring training," Quilici complained to players and sportswriters alike. "It's too late in the season to be doing some of the things we're doing." His club fell far behind the AL West contenders during a June swoon and could not get back into the mix.

Carew, the defending batting champion, was immune to the Twins' early-season difficulties. He stroked three hits in Kansas City on Opening Day, including the go-ahead single that sparked a 6–4 victory in the eleventh inning. Carew hit safely in forty of his first forty-five starts. With multiple hits in twenty-five of them, Carew was batting .411 at the start of June. He cruised to a third straight batting title, finishing far ahead of the competition at .364.

While Carew was the game's hottest hitter in the early going, Oliva also got off to a strong start. A week into the season, with the Twins hosting the Royals, Oliva delivered four hits in five trips, the twenty-third four-hit game of his career. He singled three times and powered a bases-loaded triple off Kansas City starter Marty Pattin, and he again drew attention with his baserunning.

In the third inning, with the bases full and one out, Oliva drove a Pattin pitch into the right-field corner. He was thinking double, but when Royals right fielder Vada Pinson was slow getting to the ball on a rain-soaked field, Oliva rounded second and slid safely into third. The triple was his first since June 1971, two days before he was injured. Equally rare was Oliva's slide. The moment called for it, though it had been unanticipated. "I surprised myself," Oliva cracked after the game. "After all that running, and the slide, my legs still feel good. My legs feel better than at any time last season." He was running pain-free early in 1974, and Quilici rested his DH more often to help keep him healthy. Oliva did not like sitting, but he knew the extra time off saved wear and tear on his knees.

Oliva delivered another triple on May 4 in a 10–0 romp over Detroit at the Met. He was busy on the bases again, falling a home run short of the cycle, scoring two runs and driving in three. His three hits pushed his average to .360 through sixteen games. Two more four-hit performances soon followed in a three-game span. Oliva had a seven-game hitting streak on May 28 after collecting four hits at Fenway Park, one of his favorite places to hit. The streak reached eight games the following night, when he went 2 for 4 with an RBI in an extra-inning win that closed out a road trip.

The Twins returned home to host the New York Yankees. In the series opener on May 31, Oliva bumped his hitting streak to nine games with another four-hit game. He ripped four singles in four trips, giving him ten hits in his last thirteen at-bats. He was on a Tony O tear, boosting his average to .339 after roughing up New York pitching. Two days later, his longest hitting streak of 1974 stalled at ten games.

In the midst of his hitting surge, Oliva learned of the death of Phil

Howser, the man who had paid for his housing and assisted him after his arrival in the United States. Thirteen years earlier, as the general manager of the Twins' affiliate in Charlotte, Howser had taken in the young Cuban after the Twins had released him. Oliva would probably not have had a big league career without his intervention. The sixty-three-year-old Howser, who left the affiliate in 1970 and spent his final years as a Twins scout, died after suffering two major heart attacks in a ten-month stretch.

From June 1 through the end of the 1974 season, Oliva batted .265 with little power. Quilici often used him in a lefty–righty platoon with Harmon Killebrew. They shared the DH role, with the lefthanded-hitting Oliva starting mostly against righthanded pitchers and Killebrew usually facing lefthanders. Neither player liked taking a part-time role, though neither was healthy enough to play full-time. As usual, Oliva had phenomenal runs of multihit games, but the low points became more pronounced and lasted longer than during his healthy years. Oliva finished with a .285 average, thirteen home runs, and fifty-seven RBIs.

In arguably his hottest stretch of 1974, Oliva stroked six of his longballs in a span of nine June contests. The power display began and ended with homers off White Sox knuckleballer Wilbur Wood. On June 20, with Wood working a 1–0 shutout in the eighth, Oliva came to the plate with two runners aboard and one out. He powered a fluttering pitch from Wood into the Met's bullpen in right-center field, lifting the Twins to a 3–2 win. Wood had his bread-and-butter pitch working that evening. He fanned Oliva twice with darting knucklers, and the rubber-armed southpaw said the pitch that left the yard "broke good for me. He just hit the heck out of it."

Tony O teed off on Wood twice at Comiskey Park on June 28, in a 10–3 Twins victory. The knuckleball specialist limited the Twins DH to an infield single in the opening frame, but Oliva led off the third by lining one of Wood's floaters into the lower deck in right field. Two innings later, after Carew drew a one-out walk, Oliva drilled another liner into the lower deck. "I know his knees were bothering him, so he was limited, but he could still swing the bat," Wood said in a 2012 interview. "You know a pitcher only makes so many good pitches to a hitter. If you made a good pitch on him, he had the knack of just making contact and fouling that ball off. When the next pitch you made wasn't quite as good, then he'd get his base hits."

Unlike most knuckleballers, Wood had an uncanny ability to locate the pitch. Ed Herrmann, his longtime catcher with Chicago, says Wood's command allowed him to work hitters in and out. But Wood notes that his control did not make it easier to retire Oliva. "He got the same pitch that everybody else got—the knuckleball. You throw it and pray."

Wood departed following Oliva's second homer. Later Tony O completed a 4-for-4 day with a single to center in the seventh—his fourth four-hit game of the year. Killebrew then joined the longball parade with a two-run shot that carried into the upper deck in left. He also doubled home a run; together, Killebrew and Oliva combined for six hits and six RBIs. It was just like old times. The pair wore huge smiles when sportswriters came calling after the game. "Hey, press conference!" quipped Killebrew, making light of the fact that he rarely drew the attention of writers in 1974. Injuries had sabotaged another season. He had suffered a partial dislocation of his right shoulder diving for a groundball in a spring-training game. He played through the injury, but between the shoulder and his compromised left knee, he also showed little power.

Injuries limited Killebrew to fewer than four hundred plate appearances. He and Oliva each finished with thirteen homers, and together combined for 101 RBIs—a total that each of them might have produced in his prime. Yet for one final time, Killebrew and Oliva, who spent most of their careers following each other to the plate, shared the spotlight for their contributions on the field. They had spearheaded so many wins over the years that even Wood admitted after the game that "it was like old times" losing to Oliva, Killebrew, and the Twins.

An era was coming to an end. Neither Oliva nor Killebrew could play a defensive position, so Calvin Griffith had two well-paid designated hitters on his roster as he looked to 1975. Although both Killebrew and Oliva had taken pay cuts, combined they made $180,000 in 1974, which was financially unacceptable to Griffith. He would not say so, but someone had to go. Oliva was two years younger than Killebrew—though the Twins thought the difference was five years—but trading either Minnesota icon would be unpopular. Griffith repeatedly told sportswriters that he had no idea who was going to be traded or released. As ten-year veterans, both were positioned to reject a trade under the collective-bargaining agreement, so Griffith faced the possibility of having to release an extremely popular player.

The perceived age difference made Oliva more valuable in trade, but perhaps Griffith had an inclination of who was leaving when he honored his top slugger with Harmon Killebrew Day on August 11, 1974. Killebrew initially balked at the idea, uncomfortable with the attention and gifts, but he relented when the event was set up to fund charities of his choice. Fans were able to pay tribute to the Twins great while contributing to his favorite causes. Griffith announced at the ceremony that Killebrew's number 3 would be the first Twins number to be retired, and he presented the future Hall of Famer with a camper to enjoy in retirement. Months later, the owner faced a tough business decision on the player he had honored before a large Metropolitan Stadium crowd. He faced an equally difficult one with Oliva.

"If Griffith trades Oliva, he alienates Tony's fans," beat writer Bob Fowler explained in a piece for the *Sporting News* late in the 1974 season. "If he trades Killebrew, he alienates Harmon's fans. If he trades both, he alienates everyone." If the situation was not complicated enough, only a few AL teams lacked a primary designated hitter. The market for either player was small.

Oliva's compromised right knee, which began acting up again after the All-Star break in 1974, further complicated Griffith's dilemma. Oliva continued to play in pain, but late in the season the knee began to lock up. In the fall he endured his fifth procedure to clean out cartilage and bone fragments. "I love Minnesota," Oliva told Fowler soon after he went under the knife. "The fans have been great to me, and my home is here. But I understand someone has to go, and it could be me. That's okay. It would be better than going through another season of being platooned." Tony O did not have to worry about that.

On December 11, Griffith called Killebrew to his office. The slugger assumed the meeting was to sign a new contract. But Griffith, who had failed to find a deal for either designated hitter, surprised Killebrew by offering him three options: a coaching job with the Twins, a minor league managerial assignment, or outright release. With the DH rule in place, the slugger wanted to play two more years, so he accepted Griffith's option to "make a deal for yourself." He quickly signed with Kansas City. The Royals offered a full-time job, which was important to him. By then, Killebrew had written his ticket to the Hall of Fame with 559 home runs over twenty-one seasons, and he was cherished in the Midwest for his character and humility.

The move to Kansas City shocked more than a few Twins fans. A day before the signing was announced, even Minnesota governor Wendell Anderson weighed in. Anderson urged a gathering of businessmen to support the Twins, "even though they're dumb enough to consider letting Harmon Killebrew get away." After the announcement, Griffith admitted that even his wife, Natalie, gave him a hard time.

When Frank Quilici and the Twins arrived in Florida in spring 1975, Oliva was the lone member of the 1965 World Series team still on the roster. Griffith was more optimistic than he had been in recent springs. Bobby Darwin had had his best season in 1974, delivering twenty-five home runs and ninety-four RBIs, and Larry Hisle had contributed nineteen homers and seventy-nine RBIs in his first year with the Twins. Plus Eric Soderholm and Steve Braun had had promising offensive seasons. Top outfield prospect Lyman Bostock debuted in 1975, and Dan Ford arrived in a trade with Oakland. The 1975 club was a more balanced mix of power and speed, but the young Twins pitching staff could not keep opponents off the scoreboard or keep the ball in the yard.

While the Twins sorely lacked pitching depth, the overabundance of outfielders provided insurance in case Oliva's offseason knee surgery limited his playing time and production. He did not run well in spring-training games, though he was encouraged because he did not require cortisone injections in his right knee, a spring ritual in recent years.

That might seem an odd premise for optimism, but Oliva was in the Opening Day lineup when the Twins squared off against the Texas Rangers. Bert Blyleven, starting his fourth straight opener, opposed Fergie Jenkins, who had defeated the Twins in the 1974 finale to claim his league-leading twenty-fifth win. This day, however, Jenkins did not survive the second inning and was torched for six runs in Minnesota's 11–4 victory. Oliva collected two hits and homered in each of the first two games in Texas. Facing Jenkins in the second inning of the opener, he slugged a towering four-hundred-foot home run with two runners aboard. He touched Rangers righthander Jim Bibby for a solo shot the following evening, when the Twins made it two straight with a 3–2 win.

Though the season had started well, Oliva's ailing right knee would be less cooperative in 1975. Pitchers took advantage of the weakened joint by working him inside, because he was unable to turn on inside pitches as he had earlier in his career. With pitchers increasingly taking that approach to the fourteen-year veteran, Oliva led the league with thirteen hit-by-pitches in 1975. He was plunked four times in the first five games, and in the finale of the season-opening series in Texas, Rangers starter Jackie Brown struck him on the right knee. After the game, Oliva returned to Minnesota to get the knee drained. He missed three games in Kansas City, where Killebrew faced his former teammates for the first time in a Royals sweep, but was back in the lineup for the home opener against the Angels on April 15.

The home portion of the schedule began on a sunny, fifty-degree day, decent mid-April weather in Minnesota. Yet only 11,909 fans showed up, the smallest crowd for the home opener in fifteen years of Twins baseball. Apparently Twins fans were less optimistic than the owner. They were right: the Twins finished 76–83, their first losing season under Quilici.

After the home opener, Oliva managed just four hits in his next thirty-seven at-bats over a five-week stretch. He was not running well, and by May Quilici was considering making Bobby Darwin the designated hitter and reducing Oliva to pinch-hitting duties. Oliva still managed to put together a decent first half, batting .290 with ten home runs, but he hit just .251 with only seven extra-base hits in sixty-four games after the All-Star break.

There had been a fair share of good days and bad days after Oliva returned to action as a designated hitter—at least until 1975, his last year as a regular. The pain had become constant, and he experienced a looseness in the joint that made the knee even less stable. "In 1975, most of the days were bad days," Oliva explains. "Sometimes I would have a decent day, but most of the time it was, 'Hey, why go to the ballpark?'"

On October 2, just days after the final game, Oliva again headed to the operating room for a now-commonplace cleaning out of the knee. He spent just two days in the hospital, but soon after he came home, the knee began to swell and he struggled with a persistent fever. He had developed an infection. Within days, he was back in the hospital, and the knee was cut open again to treat it.

During Oliva's second hospital stay, Gordette joined him and gave birth to their youngest child, Ric. Tony's medical condition made the second stay far from typical as well. He was hospitalized for nearly three weeks and dropped twenty pounds while battling the infection. When he returned home, he faced a taxing rehab program and questions about his ability to come back from the sixth and seventh medical procedures performed on his right knee. "The doctors are very optimistic," Oliva told Twins beat writer Bob Fowler soon after the ordeal. "They think my knee will be better next season than it has been the past few years." Realistic or not, Oliva fully committed to a winter-long program to strengthen the knee and headed to Florida early to get in shape.

While Oliva was contending with his rehabilitation, Griffith fired Quilici, who had spent three-plus seasons at the helm. Oliva did not agree with the decision and remains perplexed as to why his longtime friend never ran another club. "I don't understand how Frank disappeared from baseball after he managed the Twins, because he did everything in baseball," Oliva says. "He played. He managed. He worked on the radio for the club. He's smart, a good speaker, and good with public relations. The time he managed here, he didn't have the talent to win."

Griffith hired veteran skipper Gene Mauch to take over the club in 1976. Mauch, a baseball lifer, had managed the Philadelphia Phillies and the Montreal Expos for fifteen seasons before replacing Quilici. The new man, a former infielder, advocated "small ball," which made sense taking over a club that lacked sluggers.

By the time Oliva arrived in Florida for spring training, his knee had made little progress and he knew his days as a regular were over. He says prior to coming to camp, Griffith had offered him a coaching position, but he was not ready to never play again. He asked the owner if he could have until February 15 to make a decision, and at that time they agreed on a player-coach role for 1976. With Steve Braun taking over as the primary designated hitter, Oliva served as a part-time hitting instructor and first-base coach. When Oliva played, Mauch coached third and third-base coach Joe Nossek shifted to first. Four times early in the season, Mauch penciled in Oliva as his starting second baseman and leadoff hitter in road contests, and then replaced him with Jerry Terrell after he batted in the first inning.

Oliva made just thirty-two starts in his final season, batting 128 times in sixty-seven games. When he reached base, a pinch runner often took over, and he says there were times he left the first-base bag for the first-base coaching box. Highlights were few, as he hit .216 with just one home run—a two-run shot at Yankee Stadium off Doyle Alexander on August 24, giving him 220 for his career.

On July 20, 1976, Tony O celebrated his thirty-eighth birthday in grand style. Making just his ninth start of the season, he batted eighth with the Twins facing rookie sensation Mark Fidrych and the Tigers at the Met. The eccentric righthander—tagged "the Bird" for his Big Bird–like skinny six-foot-three frame and wild blond curls—had taken the baseball world by storm, talking to the baseball and painstakingly landscaping the mound en route to a 10–2 start and stellar 1.60 ERA. He had given up just two earned runs in his previous thirty-two innings.

With a crowd of 30,425 on hand—the Met's largest of the season—to watch the mound phenom, Oliva stroked four singles, though Fidrych went the distance for an 8–3 victory. "That was my birthday and I'll never forget it," Oliva says. "The fans gave me a standing ovation." His fourth hit, a hard-hit single off the glove of Tigers first baseman Jason Thompson in the final frame, brought the grateful crowd to its feet. Apparently Oliva's performance made quite an impression on Fidrych as well. To Oliva's surprise, the gangly twenty-one-year-old headed for first base after Oliva reached the bag in the ninth. Caught off guard at the time, Oliva now enjoys a hearty laugh about the unanticipated Fidrych encounter. He says Fidrych shook his hand and said, "I'll have to learn how to pitch to you next year."

There would be no next year for Oliva, but he had another memorable moment less than a week after facing the Bird. In June, the Twins had traded staff ace Bert Blyleven to Texas in a six-player deal that brought veteran infielders Roy Smalley and Mike Cubbage to Minnesota. After Fidrych and the Tigers left town, Blyleven and the Rangers came calling. On July 26, Blyleven was back in Minnesota facing his former teammates for the first time. Oliva was not in the lineup, but he came to the plate in the ninth as a pinch hitter with Blyleven working on a nifty two-hit shutout. Blyleven had one of the game's great curveballs, and Oliva had been one of the best breaking-ball hitters of his era. They knew each other's tendencies well, so would the cat-and-mouse game begin with a heater or bender?

"I only faced him once, and I started him off with a breaking ball," says Blyleven. "He hit a groundball to short for a quick out. I remember he was yelling at me going up the first-base line. He was saying something like, 'Challenge me! Challenge somebody!' I threw him a little breaking ball and got the groundball. So he's 0 for 1 against me. And I make sure I let him know that. But I've seen him too many times just have tremendous nights at the plate. Tony was born a baseball player. He could hit."

"Yeah, he tricked me," Oliva says and laughs. "I hit the curve better than the fastball, but I was looking for the smoker on the first pitch. Most of the time I don't like to swing at the first pitch. I knew that he's got a good curve but didn't think he was going to throw it to me. I was ready for the first pitch."

Fewer than 2,500 fans were on hand for the home finale on September 29. The Twins enjoyed a hefty 9–1 lead in the eighth inning, seemingly their final at-bat, when the small crowd began chanting "Tony! Tony O! Tony! Tony O!" As the chant grew louder, Mauch approached the longtime Twins icon: "Tony, do you want to hit?" Of course he did, so Oliva made his way to the plate one final time to face Rangers lefty Steve Barr. As Oliva emerged from the dugout, the crowd greeted him with a standing ovation. He fought off a tough two-strike curveball and lined another two-strike offering just foul before he was called out looking at a sinker on the outside corner. The crowd booed the call, but just as quickly began to cheer as Oliva tipped his cap and headed toward the dugout.

A young fan rushed onto the field to greet Oliva but was quickly intercepted by an usher. As the fan was led away, however, Oliva walked over and shook his hand. Then he slipped back into the Twins dugout for the last time as a player. Oliva still refused to admit he would retire and had thoughts of playing in 1977, when he says his knee was in better shape than it had been in his final season. But his playing days were over. Still, the love affair between Twins fans and Oliva would continue through the years.

Serving as a hitting instructor and first-base coach in 1976 set in motion the next phase of Oliva's life in baseball. He headed to Mexico that fall to manage the Los Mochis club he had played for several years earlier and returned as Minnesota's hitting coach in 1977. In a long and successful career teaching hitting to future generations of ballplayers, Oliva won World Series rings as Minnesota's hitting coach in 1987 and 1991.

Tony O

The Man

I used to ask Tony a lot of questions about growing up as a young kid in Cuba and then leaving his family and how that affected him. Because baseball is such a mental game, that if things are unsettled back home for whatever reason, it usually has a negative impact on your playing days. And obviously he was able to separate the two and turned himself into a tremendous, tremendous baseball player.

—GENE LARKIN, GAME SEVEN HITTING HERO
OF THE 1991 WORLD SERIES

Gene Larkin, whose tenth-inning single scored Dan Gladden to secure Jack Morris's Game Seven shutout and the World Series championship in 1991, touches on a remarkable aspect of Oliva's career in his comment above. In a bid to develop into one of the top baseball players in the world—in a highly competitive work environment—the Cuban émigré was able to overcome his sense of isolation and excel between the white lines. His ability to compartmentalize his alienation, however, did not dull its long-term effects. His early years in the United States shaped the man he is today. Immediate family is paramount, and he is equally committed to his siblings and their families in Cuba. He has made sure everyone there lives in a habitable home.

Oliva demonstrates a soft touch for people on the outside looking in. Growing up on a family farm, where one's labors determine how much there is to eat, shapes that sensibility, but so does feeling far from the mainstream while pursuing a challenging career. For Oliva, talent and perseverance won out.

Daughter Anita shared a quirky story from her youth. She and her father were in the family car, driving along Nicollet Avenue in Minneapolis. They came upon a family of four walking on a cold spring day, carrying a heavy load of groceries. "My dad pulls up next to them and he says, 'Hi. Do you guys have any plans tonight?' I mean he's talking to total strangers," recalls Anita, who laughs at the memory. "People sometimes don't really recognize him right away. And they were probably wondering, 'Who in the world is asking me if I have plans for tonight?' And he says, 'If you guys don't have any plans tonight, I think you should have some fun and go to a ballgame.' And he gets their name and information. He says, 'If you go down to the stadium and you go to will call, there will be four tickets in your name.'"

Anita says her father would stop to "talk to anybody and everybody everywhere." He is still well-known for greeting strangers with his gold-toothed smile, willing to gab about the 1960s Twins or today's version, for whom he remains a part-time hitting instructor.

In the early years, Oliva successfully masked loneliness, winning over teammates with his glowing smile and an upbeat take on everything he did. His closest friends in the Twins family—from Harmon Killebrew and Rod Carew to Julio Bécquer and Jim Rantz—say the true Tony came through even when he was hurting. "I've known him for fifty years and I have never heard that man complain," says Bécquer. "He's always positive. He always has that disposition." Carew says that he has never heard his longtime roommate utter a bad word about anyone, and this writer could not induce one in hours and hours of conversation.

"Rod Carew is the same," adds Bécquer, comparing him to Oliva. "They're very humble individuals. Where they come from, they're very humble. You come from little towns and all of a sudden you're in these big cities. And you don't speak the language. You don't know anything about food. It's very, very hard. It's survival. They demonstrated a tremendous ability to adjust. They made the adjustments and they're successful. They just have the 'I can' attitude."

"Tony was such a great teammate, a great player to play with, and even now we're great friends," Killebrew said in a 2010 interview. "One of the cute, cute stories—a couple years ago, Tony and I were at the Metrodome. When they played the National Anthem, we were standing on the top step of the dugout. And he was standing on my right side. "'Killy,' he says. He turned to me and says, 'Do you know, Killy?' I said, 'No Tony. What?' He said, 'Do you know, Killy, I've heard that song so many times, I should know the words to it.' Ya *think*? Must be 5,000 times that he's heard the Anthem—and the words are up on the board. I kid him. I said, 'Tony, you've been here forty-some years and still can't speak English.' Great guy. Just a wonderful guy."

Oliva's take on English is part of his charm. In all his years crossing the Midwest with the Twins Winter Caravan, longtime Twins broadcaster Dick Bremer has seen Oliva captivate audiences with his off-kilter storytelling and a "comedic quality" that transcends his trouble with language. Tony has learned to make it work, and at the same time he has a sense of humor about his English. "He was in the office a few years ago when I was trying to get ahold of someone in Mexico or Latin America," recalls Jim Rantz, recently retired from the Twins' top player development post. "I would give him the phone to get the person on, because you have to go through the operators. A lot of the operators are bilingual, but you never know. So this one particular time I gave him the phone. He's talking in English and the operator is talking back. Then he had to repeat himself and he says to her in English, 'You don't understand English?' He looks at me and he laughs. Then he started speaking in Spanish and everything was fine. But it was funny: *'You don't understand English?'*"

Oliva added a little Cuban spice to the lexicon. Teammates and friends have labeled his flashes of linguistic creativity "Tonyisms," and most have heard him talk about getting the "Cuban sandwich" at the plate. (No pork, ham, cheese, or Cuban bread involved.) At the major league level, a batter is fortunate to see a mistake pitch—delivered right where he likes it—even once during an at-bat. Major league hurlers rarely cough up the groove pitch. It's the pitch a hitter *can't* miss, Oliva says, and a good big league hitter rarely does. "Pitch it right there, it looks like a Cuban sandwich!" Oliva says and laughs. It's that hittable pitch. Tony O feasted on the Cuban sandwich.

As a coach for the World Series–winning teams in 1987 and 1991, Oliva introduced a new generation of Twins to another Cuban import. It's made of mahogany—"we call it *mahogwa*," he notes—a dark, dense, heavy wood not normally associated with baseball. But when he traveled home after his first trip back to Cuba in 1973, Oliva was carrying a bat cut from mahogany. And the bat had a name: this bat was called "Thunder." "It's a Cuban wood that brings back some memories," says Oliva, who explains that he and his father and brothers sometimes made bats from whatever kind of wood was available. A bat made from *mahogwa* was not unusual in Cuba, though none were quite like Oliva's bat. "Thunder is a little bit heavy," he admits.

"I don't think anybody could have possibly swung it except for Tony, because Tony was so strong in the hands and the forearms," insists Rick Stelmaszek, who spent thirty-two years coaching in the Twins organization and was part of Tom Kelly's staff in both 1987 and 1991. "That was his baby. Yeah, I know Thunder."

As the club's hitting coach, Oliva says he brought Thunder to the Metrodome in 1987 at a point when the club was struggling offensively. The bat was illegal for major league play, but he encouraged players to hack away with it during batting practice. So the players had a little fun and took their minds off their batting woes. "It's the most dense piece of wood," recalls Tim Laudner, 1980s Twins catcher and clubhouse cutup. "The bat was green and it was probably a thirty-five-, maybe thirty-six-inch bat. That's bigger than the bat I use, and it had to weigh anywhere from thirty-eight to forty ounces. It was just a monster piece of wood."

Twins hitters took their cuts with Thunder with mixed success and good humor. By then, Oliva, nearly fifty, could not swing Thunder like he used to, but Laudner says his hitting coach could still put a good swing on the ball when coaches took batting practice. Laudner remembers Tony O "one-hopping the baggie in the Metrodome. Just hanging out these line drives and giggling like a school girl."

Did Laudner ever use Thunder? "I couldn't pick it up," he quips. "I got a hernia just looking at it."

"It was like the Roy Hobbs 'Wonderboy' bat," says Tom Brunansky, the right fielder for the 1987 Twins and Minnesota's current hitting coach. "We'd swing it in batting practice sometimes. But in [Tony's] mind, he was making a point of saying, 'C'mon boys, let's go swing the bat.' That was who we were as a ball club. We struck out. We weren't guys that go up there looking for walks. We were an aggressive, fastball-hitting team. And that's what Tony wanted us to be." He adds, "Tony wasn't a real mechanical hitting coach. He wasn't a philosophical hitting coach. He just wanted us to be aggressive. He wanted us to swing the bat. Most of the time, guys that get to this level, your swings are pretty good. The thing you really need to do at times is to work upstairs, because you lose your concentration, you lose your confidence. When you start to struggle, you're not aggressive. You start taking pitches. And Tony's big thing was just go swing the bat."

Sabermetricians and the new baseball statistics be damned! Oliva was not a proponent of plate patience or an advocate of on-base percentage, but he was a student of the game in a number of other ways. When he played, he knew what nearly every pitcher threw and how those pitches moved. He believed in tailoring his approach at the plate based on the game situation and the count. Those adjustments were critical to his success, he says, but when it came to hitting itself, he kept it simple and encouraged an aggressive approach.

"Tony's philosophy is 'see the ball, hit the ball.' Try to hit the ball hard every time you make contact," says Larkin, also part of both championship teams. "Then, understand the game situations, the counts, and understand yourself as a hitter—your strengths and weaknesses. He did a lot of work with me early on in my career as far as understanding situations, where to drive the ball based on pitch location. Tony made it real simple, and he brought a lot of humor to it."

"Every major league ballplayer goes through periods that could be described as a slump," notes Laudner, "periods when you're not seeing the ball very well, periods when you're a little too anxious, periods when you don't relax as much as you should when you go to the plate. To me, the good hitters are the guys that can go to the plate and relax and allow their abilities to take over. Tony worked very hard to try, from an example standpoint, to teach it. So, he says, 'Hey, you have to have confidence. You have to go to the plate and erase everything from your mind and know that you're capable of doing the job.'"

Oliva won two World Series rings as a Twins coach, and more than two decades later, hitting remains a passion. His eyes light up when discussing the craft that spawned a lifelong career.

After he retired as a player in 1976, Oliva served two stints as Minnesota's hitting coach—one at the start of his post-baseball life and the other during a seven-year stretch that began with a core of promising young players in 1985 and culminated in two World Series titles. He has been an adjunct hitting instructor for the organization throughout the years and continues to be available to Twins hitters at Target Field.

Early in his retirement, Oliva also gained experience managing winter ball teams in Mexico and Colombia. The managerial gigs meant more time away from family, but they generated income, kept him in the game, and fueled a flicker of hope that he might manage at higher levels someday. "I managed nine years and liked it," Oliva says. "It was a lot of fun. I knew I could do the job. I could handle the players, but I didn't have confidence in my English. So I never applied for managing jobs in the big leagues. I think that was a mistake. I should have applied." It was difficult enough for Hispanic candidates to get a legitimate shot at a major league managing job in the late 1970s and early 1980s. Oliva says that because of his language difficulties, he had virtually no chance of landing one. He considered a front-office job just as unlikely.

He admits there have been times when he has regretted not going to school in the United States, which might have opened doors for him professionally after his baseball years. He says he was encouraged to take classes by friends when he first joined the team in 1964, but it did not make sense to him at the time. He still anticipated that one day he would be allowed to travel freely between Cuba and the United States. "My goal was to go back to Cuba anyway," Oliva explains. "My goal was to play here six months of the year, and spend six months in Cuba. I could set up a business in Cuba with my family. I didn't expect to stay here fifty years." He flashes a grin. "Everything worked out all right anyway."

Although a big league managerial career was not in the cards, Oliva made a mark as a coach and mentor. His inclination to assist young players took root early in his career, motivated by the guidance he had received as a young man. Phil Howser, Minnie Mendoza, Nestor Velazquez, and Julio Bécquer had been instrumental to his very survival during his first few months in North America. Vic Power and other veterans stepped up when he joined the Twins. "When I first came here, Harmon Killebrew was a superstar. I didn't speak much English, but he helped me a lot," Oliva explains. "So did many of the others: Jim Kaat, Jim Perry, Mudcat Grant, Earl Battey. Earl spoke Spanish and he was like our godfather. We also had Zoilo Versalles, Camilo Pascual, and Pete Ramos. All those people helped me. You learned to appreciate what they did for you, and you tried to do the same for the young players."

Oliva became a mentor to twenty-one-year-old Rod Carew when he joined the Twins in 1967. That spring, Calvin Griffith insisted that the talented prospect have a spot in the Minnesota lineup, just as he had with Oliva in 1964. Oliva stepped up and counseled Carew, who remains genuinely touched by the constant guidance he received to this day. "For an established player to do something like that with a kid," explains Carew, "it was just an amazing thing. Just being with him and talking about the game, talking about how to handle myself away from the game, going out and taking extra batting practice, and him sitting on the bench with me and telling me about pitchers. I think that's why I was able to have so much success."

Oliva says he took to Carew immediately and that they quickly became friends. "He was like my little brother. He could be moody and not talk much for two or three days, but I didn't care. I was able to talk to him." Both Oliva and Carew excelled at making adjustments at the plate, and the elder says it was something they worked on during practices. A batter who does not work on adjusting to pitches in practice probably will not be adapting to pitches in the course of game action. "Watch the good hitters," Oliva notes. "You'll see them crouch down a little or stand up a bit, sometimes open up their stance or close it a little bit."

Tony O mentored other young players as well. Both he and Carew assisted Lyman Bostock when he joined the Twins in 1975. At that time, the two veterans between them had taken seven of the previous ten American League batting titles, so they offered the outfield prospect a wealth of knowledge about hitting.

Bostock might not have seemed like the ideal student. Rookies of his era were expected to be seen and not heard; Bostock, who joined the Twins in 1975, would not shut up. Teammates dubbed him "Abdul Jibber-Jabber," but Bostock, the talkative, good-natured son of a former Negro leagues star, did not let chatter get in the way of making the most of Oliva's and Carew's advice.

Oliva taught Bostock the art of setting up pitchers. For instance, a hitter wanting a fastball might move closer to the plate to entice a pitcher to think he is looking for a breaking ball that moves away from him. Likewise, a hitter getting "busted inside" consistently might back off the plate to force the pitcher to change tactics and then look for a pitch on the outer half of the plate.

In 1976, his first full season in the majors, Bostock finished fourth in the American League batting race with a .323 average, six points behind Carew and ten behind the batting champ, Kansas City's George Brett. In 1977, the twenty-six-year-old Bostock batted .336 and might have won the AL batting title if Carew had not flirted with .400 for much of the season and finished at .388. One of the game's first big-money free agents, Bostock left the Twins for the California Angels before the 1978 season. When he struggled and batted just .147 in April for the Angels, he attempted to return his April salary to owner Gene Autry. The offer was refused, so Bostock donated his first month's earnings to charitable organizations.

Bostock rebounded nicely as the season wore on, but in late September, during a road trip to Chicago, he was murdered while riding in a car with an uncle and two family friends in Gary, Indiana. He was the victim of a shotgun blast, fired into the back seat by the estranged husband of one of the woman in the vehicle. It was a senseless act that shocked Oliva. "He was a very nice kid. I can't believe what happened to him," Oliva says. "It was hard to understand what happened that day. I had worked with him a lot. He was a very easy guy to work with, willing to listen and take advice about hitting." Oliva adds that he was touched when, during an interview before a nationally televised game early in the 1978 season, the struggling Bostock said that he missed not having his mentor and teacher with him. "That was nice what he said about me."

Carew was not the only Hall of Famer to benefit from Oliva's experience. In the early 1980s, Oliva met a young Twins prospect named Kirby Puckett, who excelled with a hitting approach similar to his own. Puckett favored an inside-out swing, one that drives the ball to the opposite field, and he hit for average. Although he was just five-foot-eight, Puckett had a thick, muscular build. Long before the future Hall of Famer reached Minnesota, Oliva suggested he could hit twenty home runs a year in the big leagues with a few adjustments to his approach. Puckett did not buy into the idea initially, knowing that hitting for power usually meant having a longer swing than the quick, short stroke that had worked for him his whole life.

Puckett joined the Twins in 1984 and batted .296 as a rookie. He did not hit a single home run in nearly six hundred plate appearances, and he collected just four in 1985. Still, Puckett resisted focusing on pulling the ball more frequently. "Kirby didn't believe he could pull the ball, but if you saw him in batting practice, he hit the ball farther than Kent Hrbek," Oliva recalls. "If he hit the ball in batting practice like that, it's a good sign that he could pull the ball and hit a lot of home runs, too."

Puckett was concerned that altering his stroke would hurt his batting average, but Oliva eventually convinced him hitting for more power would *boost* his average. Outfielders would have to play him deeper, and they would have to spread out if he was not predictably going to right field on a regular basis. That would open up more holes in the outfield, which Oliva believed would make the young prospect a consistent .300 hitter. And that is exactly what happened.

During spring training in 1986, Oliva and Puckett spent a few weeks developing the high leg kick that would become the young man's trademark. The Mel Ott–style kick, which involved shifting his weight to his back leg and then transferring it forward, allowed Puckett to stride into the ball more forcefully without altering his basic swing. Timing was everything, and getting the leg kick and swing synchronized with the pitch's arrival required a lot of batting practice. Oliva encouraged Puckett to turn on pitches that were on the inner half of the plate. Slowly it all came together, and by the end of spring training, Oliva says Puckett had powered nearly a dozen home runs in exhibition games and no longer had to think about his timing. Pleased with the early results, Puckett was prepared to use his new approach in games that mattered.

How ready was he? He led the majors with eight home runs that April, and only three regulars could top his .396 average in the opening month. Puckett went on to bat .328 and stroke a career-high thirty-one homers in 1986. He set new personal bests in nearly every offensive category and remained a multidimensional threat at the plate, much like Oliva, for the rest of his career.

These days, Oliva still lends a hand when a young hitter is looking for help. He is at Target Field before every home game. "He's got a way of making his rounds," notes longtime Twins exec Jim Rantz, "talking to everybody, giving someone a little tip—what to look for in different hitting situations, different things that worked for him." Rantz adds that Oliva is available as a hitting instructor each spring in Florida and participates in the Twins' organizational meetings in the fall, when the just-finished season is assessed and decisions are made concerning the team's future. If he is not busy enough in his retirement years, Oliva also teams with Alfonso Fernández for fifty Spanish-language broadcasts of Twins games each year.

Oliva is inspired most by what happens in the batter's box. He has coached a couple of generations of hitters since retiring and still enjoys working with kids. He does not buy into the notion, perpetuated by each aging generation of major leaguers, that today's players are not as motivated or committed because of the money being made. He has no trouble relating to players in this era of long-term contracts for tens of millions of dollars. "I don't care how much they make," Oliva says. "Players, if they have any pride, want to do well. They don't want to make a mistake or look silly. They may make millions, but they still dive for a ball. They still run into the wall. They still try to run over catchers. They have the same goal. They play hard."

"I loved working with him," 1991 Game Seven hero Larkin says of Oliva. "He's a guy who was always very positive with me. Tony was always willing to talk and listen and make adjustments with me, and try to make me a better hitter. I was one of the last guys on the team, but he still gave me the same amount of time he was giving the top-echelon players, like a Hrbek or a Puckett or a Brunansky, which, as a player, that's what I really respected."

Not only did Oliva's humble origins fuel a work ethic to succeed as a player, they contributed to his makeup as a coach. "He was a young man from a poor country, and he was hungry to make a living," notes longtime big league catcher Phil Roof, who managed for nearly two decades in the Twins organization. "He educated himself in the game of baseball, in all facets of it—hitting and fielding, and building up the individual by patting him on the back and telling him that he was doing the right things. I just gained a lot of respect for him because of what I saw—the results of working with our young kids in the minor league system."

By 1991, when the Twins were in pursuit of their second World Series title in five seasons, both of Oliva's knees were troublesome and he had developed back problems that have persisted over the years. His ailments prevented him from throwing batting practice or doing the other physical tasks a coach must do. Terry Crowley had taken over many of Oliva's responsibilities that summer, and the lifelong Twin—approaching his fifty-third birthday and in his thirty-first year with the organization—was set to retire as a full-time coach at season's end.

The 1991 World Series championship season, which generated a lifetime of memories, included a special day for Oliva. On July 14, a Sunday afternoon with the Red Sox in town, the first-place Twins paid tribute to Tony O by retiring his number 6 before a crowd of 38,066. The honor came almost exactly thirty years to the day after the raw, unheralded prospect's first professional game in Wytheville, Virginia. "That was beautiful, especially when you don't expect anything," Oliva says. "I didn't expect something like that was going to happen to me. When they retire your number, that's a big honor. Because you see how many ballplayers play and only a few got their number retired."

Twins owner Carl Pohlad, who had purchased the team from Calvin Griffith in 1984, presented Oliva a key ring during the pregame ceremony, which seemed insignificant. Then Roberto Fernández Tápanes, the Cuban native who had discovered Oliva after a long minor league career spent mostly in the Washington Senators system, drove a new Chevy Lumina minivan onto the field, to the surprise of its new owner.

Also on hand for Tony Oliva Day were Gordette and the children, other family members, and a host of friends and former teammates, including Rod Carew, Frank Quilici, Zoilo Versalles, Sandy Valdespino, and Jim Perry. The Metrodome's scoreboard featured career highlights, and when it came time to retire Tony O's number, Twins star and Oliva protégé Kirby Puckett had the honor of unveiling the number 6 positioned next to the retired numbers of Carew and Harmon Killebrew on the outfield wall. "It was pretty emotional for me. Tony's a guy who taught me quite a bit," Puckett told *St. Paul Pioneer Press* writer Gregg Wong later that day. "It was really classy to show him how much the people of Minnesota care for him."

The Metrodome crowd showered him with love and several standing ovations in the course of the ceremony. Speaking to reporters after the ceremony, Oliva said he fought to keep his composure, knowing that if he broke down he would never be able to speak. He kept it together and returned the love. "I'd like to thank you, the fans. I love you," Oliva told a captivated audience. "I'll never forget all those wonderful moments that I played baseball in front of you. Minnesota fans are the best in the world. Thank you and God bless you." The crowd erupted again as Oliva stepped away from the microphone. He waved to fans and walked off the field with family and friends to the classic "Thanks for the Memories."

Carew made the trip from his California home to honor his longtime friend. The very next weekend, Oliva traveled to Cooperstown to reciprocate, as his road roommate with the Twins entered the Baseball Hall of Fame. With Carew's induction just days away, Oliva's own candidacy was a hot topic among reporters on Tony Oliva Day.

While Carew made it to Cooperstown on his first try, Oliva had fallen far short of the necessary votes in his ninth year of eligibility. As much as he believed he belonged in the Hall, he was not going to make the Cooperstown discussion about *him*. "It was a privilege to see Rod Carew make it in his first shot," Oliva responded. "He deserved to get in his first year. Maybe I'll get in there soon, too, along with Rod Carew and Harmon Killebrew." When pressed by another reporter, Oliva quipped, "If they put me in [the Hall of Fame], they wouldn't be embarrassed."

In 2000, Oliva and Carew joined Killebrew, Puckett, Hrbek, and the late Calvin Griffith in the inaugural class of the Minnesota Twins Hall of Fame. The first inductees were announced as part of an August weekend celebrating forty years of Twins baseball.

The very next August, in 2001, Puckett paid tribute to his mentor again. Glaucoma had forced him to retire following the 1995 season, and now Puckett stood at the podium in Cooperstown as the newest member of the Hall of Fame. He saluted his loved ones, the Twins family, and players who assisted or inspired him along the way. "To my good friend, Tony Oliva, an awesome hitter who helped me to become a better hitter with his tremendous knowledge of this game," Puckett said. "I hope to be here next year listening to you give your induction speech, Tony. I love you." Sadly, Puckett suffered a stroke and died five years later, a week shy of his forty-sixth birthday.

With his number retired and with his admittance into the Twins Hall of Fame, Oliva hit the trifecta when the Twins honored him with a bronze statue on the Target Field plaza on Opening Day 2011. They had paid similar tribute to Twins icons Harmon Killebrew, Rod Carew, and Kirby Puckett when Target Field opened, and they began the park's second season by unveiling Oliva's image, striding into a pitch with his arms extended, outside the appropriately numbered Gate 6.

The ceremony was bittersweet. Countering the celebratory mood was the absence of Killebrew, who had been diagnosed with esophageal cancer the previous winter. The close friends had spent time together during Killebrew's brief stay in spring training that March and had anticipated reuniting in Minnesota. They hugged before Killebrew left the Twins clubhouse in Fort Myers to return to his Arizona home. Oliva said he would see him on Opening Day.

Killebrew had been slated to throw out the first pitch before the April 8 opener with Oakland and to attend the pregame ceremony for his good friend. But he was too ill to travel to Minnesota. Following the statue's unveiling, Oliva stepped in for his longtime teammate and tossed the ceremonial first pitch to Killebrew's grandson Casey. Five weeks later, on May 13, Killebrew announced that he was forgoing further cancer treatment. A few days later he was gone.

Oliva and Julio Bécquer visited Killebrew in his final days. Tony movingly discussed their final visit with Steve Aschburner, the author of the 2012 biography *Harmon Killebrew: Ultimate Slugger*. "I was thinking I would go see him in very bad shape," Oliva told Aschburner. "When I saw him laughing and talking, it was a big surprise for me. That was Saturday, and I was happy for me to have the opportunity to get there and see him in person. Sunday was a different story. I came back and was visiting and he was very down. You could see he was hurting. He said, 'You know I love you.'"

One week later, Oliva, Carew, Quilici, Paul Molitor, Ron Gardenhire, Michael Cuddyer, Justin Morneau, and Joe Nathan were pallbearers at Killebrew's funeral. They had lost a friend whose real power had been not as a premier slugger but as a man who touched people's lives with his kindness and humility. "Killebrew was the perfect gentleman," Oliva said a year after his friend's death. "I never saw him mad. He never said a bad word and treated everybody nice. He was a great human being."

Carew, Bécquer, and many others who shared a baseball clubhouse with Oliva ascribe those same traits to him. So does at least one longtime opponent. "I enjoy being around Tony," says Hall of Famer Brooks Robinson. "I see him three or four times a year in Florida or somewhere. He never changes, and the guy is loved by all anywhere he goes. He's just got a great, outgoing personality." Minnesotans are familiar with Oliva's warm, welcoming smile and his willingness to engage in conversation almost anywhere. If you have had the opportunity, you may have experienced having your paw disappear in his large right hand as he greeted you. The twinkle in his eye is still there; talk of hitting a baseball, the Twins, or family ignites the spark.

The man projects an upbeat, can-do attitude—the approach to life that fueled him along the path from small family farm to major league star. Both at home and in his coaching career, he plays the role of motivator and confidence-builder. The Twins not only tap into Oliva's expertise as a hitting instructor but also draw on his enthusiasm for life. He still goes on the road with the Twins Winter Caravan and makes frequent public appearances, ranging from corporate speaking engagements to youth ballpark dedications. For a man in his seventies, he stays extremely busy and seemingly works full-time for stretches of the summer.

Oliva has little time for hobbies—at an age when hobbies are often a person's primary focus—though he squeezes in some golf when his back cooperates. He took up the game late in life, but when time permits, he and Gordette will get in a round with Quilici and his wife Lila. Quilici says his friend's swing is unorthodox, much as in baseball, but he adds that Oliva "hits the hell out of [a golf ball]. And he's a good putter, too."

When asked about his hobbies, Oliva said he is most likely to spend his free time with his five grandchildren. His children all live nearby, but busy schedules sometimes mean he goes several days, or a week, without seeing them and their kids. He was forced to miss a lot of time with his own young children as a player and does not like having several days pass without seeing the grandchildren. "I miss the little one a lot," Oliva says of son Ric's youngest, born in 2012. "You can see her change. Every time you see her is different."

Today Oliva radiates the warmth of the grandfather we always loved. He lives without regrets, though there are a few things in life he would still like to do. "I had the opportunity to come to the United States, meet so many great people, and travel to so many places and a lot of different countries," Oliva says. "There are only a couple more places that I would like to go and see. I'd like to go to Spain. And maybe Italy. I'd like to go to Spain because my mother's family came from Spain many, many years ago. I want to go soon, because people wait and wait and wait, and then never make it."

That remains a dilemma, as Oliva's summers are consumed by baseball and he travels to Cuba each winter. Even still, he does not feel he sees enough of his siblings and their families. "I'd like to spend more time with my family in Cuba," he says. "Ten days, two weeks is not enough. This year I stayed three weeks. When I go again, maybe I could stay a month or two. But sometimes you postpone, postpone, postpone. And hey, this is life. You never know when your last day is."

When asked how he would like to be remembered, Oliva appeared surprised at the question, but then a smile crossed his face. "I wish that I will be remembered as a person that gets along—or tried to get along—with everybody. I speak to everybody. My wife and kids, they think I cannot stop talking sometimes. But I hope people remember me as the way I am, as somebody who would like to be buddy-buddy with everybody."

Epilogue
The Hall of Fame Question

From a remote family farm in Cuba to a Hall of Fame–caliber career, Tony Oliva has led a remarkable life. It was rare for a young man growing up far from Havana to make it to the United States at all. Then, after never being away from home, Oliva persevered through the political turmoil resulting from the Bay of Pigs invasion, which left him without a country soon after his arrival on foreign shores.

For the latter half of Oliva's life, baseball writers and Hall of Famers have debated whether his career was worthy of the game's ultimate honor: a place in Cooperstown. After all, the successful Twins teams of the 1960s featured Hall of Famers Harmon Killebrew and Rod Carew, and Oliva was the most-gifted all-around player on those clubs. Oliva and Carew were two of the era's best pure hitters. They shared an uncanny knack for putting lumber squarely on the ball: Carew was a study in discipline, while Oliva aggressively attacked all types of pitches in any count or location. Both won their share of batting titles, but Tony O also was a power threat.

Over his first eight big league seasons, 1964–71, Oliva ranked first in doubles and tenth in slugging among the 105 major leaguers with at least 3,000 plate appearances in this span. Eight of the nine players with higher slugging percentages are in the Hall of Fame—Dick Allen is the exception—and Oliva's .507 mark in this stretch exceeds those of Hall of Famers Carl Yastrzemski, Ron Santo, Tony Pérez, and Orlando Cepeda. So Oliva had a pretty good 1960s.

"Everybody that I've ever talked to about Tony thinks he was one of the best hitters that ever came down the pike," says Gary Bell, who pitched for Cleveland, Boston, Seattle, and Chicago and saw plenty of Oliva. "I remember he had that wide stance and he could hit the ball anywhere. He spread the ball around, but he had power. He was just a good, solid hitter. It's just a shame. You could put him in a category with Mantle, because Mickey was the same—bad legs. I'm sure Tony would be in the Hall of Fame by now if he hadn't had that problem."

Oliva was a threat to drive almost any pitch deep for extra bases. And like a healthy Mantle, a healthy Oliva was just as likely to beat out an infield hit or take an extra base on an unsuspecting outfielder. Until he was hurt in pursuit of his third batting title in 1971, he was a complete hitter and seemed well on his way to Cooperstown.

"Tony belongs," Killebrew said during a 2009 interview. "You look at certain players who don't have the stats necessary to get in the Hall of Fame, but during the period that they played, they were a dominant player or pitcher. To me, that's a criterion. Tony was a dominant player in his era. Three batting championships and just over a .300 lifetime average. Just a great, great hitter. He was the best offspeed hitter that I've ever seen."

As a power threat, Oliva was not in the class of his longtime friend Killebrew, Mantle, or the era's other sluggers. But he powered his share of home runs: 177 in his eight relatively healthy seasons, an average of twenty-two a summer. That may not seem like many, but during this pitching-friendly era, only fourteen players had more homers. Hank Aaron (297) and Killebrew (292) ranked first and second. When it comes to Hall of Fame qualifications, Killebrew and Carew clearly have more impressive career totals than Oliva. Killebrew stroked 573 home runs, which ranked fifth all-time when the baseball writers voted him into the Hall in 1984. Carew batted .328 and captured seven batting titles in nineteen seasons, and only nine players had topped his 3,053 hits when he gained admission in 1991.

Unfortunately, Oliva failed to reach even 2,000 hits before he retired in 1976, which probably hurt his Hall of Fame chances dramatically with both baseball writers and the various Veterans Committees that have weighed in on his candidacy. If you look at the Hall of Fame membership, however, you will find numerous players who finished with fewer than 2,000 hits. Just since 1920, the end of the dead-ball era, this group of Hall of Famers includes Jackie Robinson, Larry Doby, Ralph Kiner, Hank Greenberg, Monte Irvin, Roy Campanella, Phil Rizzuto, Tony Lazzeri, Mickey Cochrane, Lou Boudreau,

Gabby Hartnett, Rick Ferrell, Freddie Lindstrom, Travis Jackson, Hack Wilson, Earle Combs, and Chick Hafey.

Undoubtedly the ill-fated dive for the sinking liner that Joe Rudi hit on June 29, 1971, played a key role in subverting Oliva's career. The devastating knee injury compromised his run production when he returned and shortened his career by several years.

Another factor beyond Oliva's control—where he was born—affected his career. As a native of Piñar del Río, where no scouts ventured in search of young talent, he went undiscovered into his twenties. Otherwise, he might have reached the majors at a much younger age.

Eventually Oliva came to the attention of the Minnesota Twins via Cuban native and former Senators prospect Roberto Fernández Tápanes. Tony signed his first professional contract on July 24, 1961, four days after his twenty-third birthday. He did not join the Twins for good until 1964, when he was nearly twenty-six. Most of the game's best hitters become major leaguers in their early twenties. Several Hall of Famers from Oliva's era, including Al Kaline, Hank Aaron, Brooks Robinson, Frank Robinson, Joe Morgan, Johnny Bench, Reggie Jackson, and Rod Carew, were big league regulars at age twenty-one.

Despite a lack of pro-level coaching in rural Cuba, Oliva needed only three minor league seasons to reach Minnesota. In his first exposure to the professional game in 1961, he batted .410 in the Appalachian League, the highest average in all of pro ball. In 1962, Oliva jumped two levels and batted .350 with thirty-five doubles, seventeen home runs, and ninety-three RBIs in 127 games for Class-A Charlotte. He advanced to Triple-A ball in his third minor league season in 1963. On the brink of the majors, Tony O batted .304 with thirty doubles and twenty-three homers in 146 games. Then he won batting titles in his first two years with the Twins.

What if scouts had discovered Oliva five years earlier? Had he grown up in or near Havana, he would have been playing professionally as a teenager. With his ability as a pure hitter and with his physical tools, Oliva might have executed the same rapid rise to the majors had he signed at eighteen or nineteen. Perhaps it would have taken an extra year to reach Minnesota, but one could argue that Oliva lost as many as four major league seasons simply by growing up on a remote part of an island. Had Oliva reached the majors a few years earlier, his rookie season may not have been the astounding success that it was at age twenty-six in 1964. As it was, Oliva collected 402 hits in his first two years with the Twins. He might have accumulated another

500 hits over his career, perhaps considerably more, had he been scouted as a teen.

Those lost years dramatically affected Oliva's Hall of Fame candidacy. For instance, if Oliva had flirted with 2,500 career hits rather than 2,000, or 1,500 RBIs instead of 1,000, when he was forced to retire in 1976, baseball writers would have taken him more seriously as a candidate.

Let's consider the career paths of Oliva and Hall of Fame outfielder Billy Williams, born five weeks before Oliva in June 1938. Cubs scout Ivy Griffin, on a scouting mission to Alabama to watch Tommie Aaron, Hank's younger brother, saw Williams's picture-perfect lefthanded swing. Williams, just shy of his eighteenth birthday, signed with the Cubs in 1956. Two days after he graduated from high school, he left home to start his career. Williams played five seasons in the minor leagues before taking over left field for the Cubs in 1961. Despite spending two more years in the minors than Oliva, Williams had a three-year jump on a big league career.

Both outfielders turned twenty-six in 1964, during the summer Oliva exploded onto the scene. They were approaching their prime years as hitters. Williams clearly had more power, though he played half his games in what was arguably the most hitter-friendly park in the National League. He was more durable than Oliva, missing only seven games between 1964 and 1971. Oliva was a doubles machine, a faster runner, and a better defensive player.

In those eight years, leading up to Oliva's career-changing knee injury in June 1971, these two premier lefthanded hitters compared favorably to the game's elite (Table 3). Not only was Williams durable, playing more games than anyone during this stretch, but he was consistently productive. Oliva, who played through a remarkable number of injuries, lost enough playing time to cut into his raw numbers. But if their production is converted into what they delivered per 162 games in these years, little separates them (Table 4).

Table 3. Billy Williams and Tony Oliva, 1964–71

	Plate appearances	Hits	Total bases	Batting average	Slugging percentage
Billy Williams	5,665 (2)	1,516 (3)	2,601 (1)	.298 (9)	.511 (9)
Tony Oliva	5,069 (10)	1,455 (5)	2,356 (3)	.313 (4)	.507 (10)

Note: MLB rank in parentheses; minimum 3,000 plate appearances for batting average and slugging percentage.

Table 4. Billy Williams and Tony Oliva per 162 games, 1964–71

	Hits	Doubles	Home runs	Total bases	RBIs
Billy Williams	190	31	31	326	100
Tony Oliva	200	38	24	324	99

Williams had accumulated 524 hits by the time Oliva settled into a major league role. When both retired following the 1976 season, Williams had 2,711 hits. Oliva, who lost out on those early years, missed the 1972 season to injury, and played hurt his last four years, finished with 1,917. Williams outdistanced Oliva in nearly every offensive raw number. We will never know if those lost years might have closed the statistical gap. Whatever numbers were lost, they may be keeping Oliva out of Cooperstown.

Once he finally joined the Twins, Oliva ranked among the best hitters in the game. With his trademark knock-kneed stance, feet spread far apart, Oliva attacked the ball with a quick, fluid swing and immediately established himself as a run producer. He became the only player in major league history to win batting titles in his first two seasons, and he led the league in hits in five of his first eight seasons.

Only four big leaguers generated more hits over those eight years: Pete Rose, Lou Brock, Billy Williams, and Roberto Clemente. Among players with 3,000 plate appearances in this span, Oliva ranked fourth in hits per game (Table 5). Oliva batted .313 over those eight seasons, a noteworthy feat considering the paucity of .300 hitters in the 1960s. In Oliva's first six seasons, 1964–69, American League hitters produced just twenty-two .300 seasons—on average, fewer than four each summer. Oliva had four of those twenty-two seasons—1964, 1965, 1966, and 1969—and among AL hitters, only Carl Yastrzemski matched his total.

Table 5. Most hits per game, 1964–71

Roberto Clemente	1.31
Pete Rose	1.27
Lou Brock	1.24
Tony Oliva	**1.23**
Curt Flood	1.19

Note: Minimum 3,000 plate appearances.

Then there are those three batting titles. Oliva is one of only seventeen Hall of Fame–eligible players who have won three or more in the modern era, which began with the startup of the American League in 1901. Fourteen are in the Hall, with only Oliva, Bill Madlock, and Larry Walker on the outside looking in. Of course, Oliva was much more than a singles hitter. Leaderboards for 1964 through 1971 (Table 6) show four key offensive categories—doubles, total bases, batting average, and slugging percentage—all heavily populated by Hall of Famers. No major leaguer collected more doubles during those eight summers, a result of Oliva's speed as well as his bat. He is in good company on the leaderboards. At least five Hall of Famers appear on each one, though Hank Aaron, Frank Robinson, Billy Williams, and Oliva are the only four on every list. During these years, Tony O ranked fifteenth in home runs, tenth in runs, and thirteenth in RBIs.

Table 6. Offensive leaders, 1964–71

Doubles	
Tony Oliva	**278**
Lou Brock	266
Pete Rose	257
Carl Yastrzemski	254
Billy Williams	246
Hank Aaron	241
Brooks Robinson	229
Vada Pinson	222
Rusty Staub	222
Frank Robinson	214

Batting average	
Roberto Clemente	.334
Matty Alou	.314
Pete Rose	.313
Tony Oliva	**.313**
Joe Torre	.309
Hank Aaron	.305
Frank Robinson	.300
Curt Flood	.300
Billy Williams	.298
Lou Brock	.298

Note: Minimum: 3,000 plate appearances.

Total bases	
Billy Williams	2,601
Hank Aaron	2,542
Tony Oliva	**2,356**
Lou Brock	2,288
Dick Allen	2,287
Ron Santo	2,267
Roberto Clemente	2,249
Carl Yastrzemski	2,244
Frank Robinson	2,223
Pete Rose	2,214

Slugging percentage	
Hank Aaron	.564
Willie McCovey	.553
Dick Allen	.544
Frank Robinson	.543
Willie Mays	.529
Harmon Killebrew	.528
Willie Stargell	.526
Roberto Clemente	.514
Billy Williams	.511
Tony Oliva	**.507**

Note: Minimum: 3,000 plate appearances.

From 1964 through 1971, Oliva averaged a major league–high thirty-five doubles, twenty-two homers, and ninety RBIs a season—impressive numbers in the pitching-friendly 1960s. They compare favorably to the numbers posted by the best hitters in his day. The same is true if we factor in time lost to injury and generate averages per 162 games (Table 7). Oliva's production matches up well to the others. Although the Twins star showed less power than many of the Hall of Famers of his era, no big leaguer could top Oliva's 117 game-winning RBIs in those eight years.

Table 7. Tony Oliva and Hall of Fame players, 1964–71

	Runs scored	Doubles	Home runs	RBIs	Batting average	On-base percentage	Slugging percentage
Hank Aaron	111	32	40	113	.305	.379	.564
Lou Brock	110	34	13	60	.298	.347	.439
Roberto Clemente	102	30	20	98	.334	.383	.514
Al Kaline	91	28	23	86	.288	.388	.478
Harmon Killebrew	93	20	41	114	.266	.396	.528
Willie McCovey	91	24	38	109	.283	.398	.553
Tony Oliva	**98**	**38**	**24**	**99**	**.313**	**.360**	**.507**
Brooks Robinson	82	30	22	93	.273	.332	.437
Frank Robinson	109	30	34	107	.300	.398	.543
Willie Stargell	86	27	35	109	.280	.353	.526
Billy Williams	103	31	31	100	.298	.363	.511
Carl Yastrzemski	96	33	30	92	.293	.397	.504

Note: Raw numbers are averages per 162 games during this span.

The shortcoming of Table 7 is that it compares Oliva in his prime years with players not necessarily in *their* prime years. For instance, both Hank Aaron and Al Kaline, born in 1934, are four years older than Oliva. Both Hall of Famers became everyday players in 1954—Kaline as a teenager and Aaron soon after he turned twenty—and spent a decade in the majors before Oliva debuted in 1964. Kaline's power began to drop in 1968, though he remained a productive player through 1972 before retiring in 1974. Aaron, of course, remained a prolific power hitter throughout his thirties. His last season was 1976, the same as Oliva's.

Clemente also was born in 1934, and he debuted in 1955, a year after Aaron and Kaline. The Pirates outfielder, who arguably matched Oliva's 1964–71 production as closely as anyone in Table 7, died on New Year's Eve in 1972, flying a relief mission to Nicaragua following a devastating earthquake. He collected his 3,000th hit in his final regular-season game.

Harmon Killebrew and Frank Robinson were born in 1935; Brooks Robinson, two years later in 1937. Billy Williams, Willie Stargell, and Oliva all were born in 1938, with Tony O the youngest of the three. Among the players shown in Table 7, only Stargell, Lou Brock, and Carl Yastrzemski were born after Oliva, though none were as much as two years younger.

If we provide eight-year statistics for the group and match their ages with Oliva's age from 1964–71, he still compares favorably to the era's best players (Table 8).

Oliva played his entire career in Minnesota, far from the nation's media centers, and appeared in just one World Series. He may have been less well-known than most of the players featured in Tables 7 and 8, but his peers knew the challenges of facing the free-swinging star, who could put nearly any pitch in play and hit it hard.

"For the period that I played against him in the 1960s, he was, I would say, one of the top five hitters in baseball," recalls Jim Bouton, a twenty-game winner and a key member of the Yankees rotation in the final years of their American League reign. "There was no set way to get him out because there was no formula. He had no known weakness. You couldn't throw a waste pitch. He could hit that!"

Catfish Hunter agreed with that assessment. In a 1995 interview with *Baseball Digest,* when asked who his toughest opponent had been, the Hall of Fame righthander singled out "Tony Oliva of the Twins, because he could hit any pitch anywhere. He did not have a weakness."

"Tony Oliva was the best hitter I ever saw, bar none," former Tigers ace

Table 8. Hall of Fame players at same age as Tony Oliva

		Runs scored	Doubles	Home runs	RBIs	Batting average	On-base percentage	Slugging percentage
Hank Aaron	(1960–67)	119	32	40	121	.311	.376	.569
Lou Brock	(1965–72)	107	34	12	58	.297	.347	.430
Roberto Clemente	(1960–67)	102	30	19	97	.330	.373	.498
Al Kaline	(1960–67)	102	32	27	97	.299	.384	.505
Harmon Killebrew	(1962–69)	96	20	44	114	.263	.385	.539
Willie McCovey	(1964–71)	91	24	38	109	.283	.398	.553
Tony Oliva	**(1964–71)**	**98**	**38**	**24**	**99**	**.313**	**.360**	**.507**
Brooks Robinson	(1963–70)	81	30	21	89	.271	.328	.432
Frank Robinson	(1961–68)	112	35	35	114	.305	.399	.559
Willie Stargell	(1966–73)	93	31	38	113	.286	.369	.552
Billy Williams	(1964–71)	103	31	31	100	.298	.363	.511
Carl Yastrzemski	(1965–72)	98	33	28	94	.290	.396	.499

Note: Raw numbers are averages per 162 games during each player's eight-year span.

Denny McLain told *St. Paul Pioneer Press* columnist Charley Walters during a 2013 interview. "I don't care who they talk about today, but imagine Tony Oliva hitting against the pitching quality now. Just imagine! He would hit .450 in this day." He added, "I think it's awful Tony's not in the Hall of Fame. Three batting crowns, and he can't even get mentioned! Geez. If Carl Yastrzemski got in the Hall of Fame, gosh darn it, Tony Oliva belongs right along side of him."

Oliva made an immediate impression on the American League's two award winners in 1964, MVP Brooks Robinson and Cy Young honoree Dean Chance. Oliva and Robinson competed for the batting title that summer. "Really, you had no place to pitch this guy," Robinson says of Oliva. "He was the type of hitter that you just tried to keep the ball down, but he was going to get his base hits no matter who pitched against him. I don't care if it's Palmer or Cuellar or McNally—you're going to have to deal with Oliva. He's just a great hitter. Absolutely in the top two or three guys I played against, hitting-wise." And, Robinson notes, "I think he's really been slighted in his career. For some reason, he just doesn't get the support that he deserves. I put him in a class almost by himself as far as a guy who could hit your line-drive singles but also hit with power. Just a terrific all-around player."

When the twenty-three-year-old Chance won twenty games and posted a league-low 1.65 ERA for the Angels in 1964, the major leagues named a single Cy Young Award winner. And Chance was the only Cy Young winner not named Sandy Koufax in the four-year span of 1963–66. The six-foot-three righthander was tough on hitters. Once he took the sign, Chance never again looked at the plate, turning his back to the batter before snapping off an electric fastball. And he could be a little wild. Somehow Oliva wasn't intimidated. "Without a doubt, Tony Oliva was the best hitter I ever faced in the majors," recalls Chance. "No one could hit like him. Carl Yastrzemski was a close second, but Tony was the toughest. There's no way he shouldn't be in the Hall of Fame."

Lee Stange, who mostly pitched for Minnesota and Boston in a ten-year career, was teammates with both Oliva and Yastrzemski. He concurs with Chance when it comes to the American League's two premier lefthanded hitters of the era. "Both attacked the ball, but I think on average, Tony was a better hitter," Stange says. "I think Yaz was a better hitter when he was younger, when he hit a lot of balls to left field. And then as he got older, he pulled the ball a little bit more. Tony never really was what you'd call a real pull hitter."

"I would say that Tony was the toughest lefthanded hitter I ever faced," says Sam McDowell, the southpaw who threw hundred-mile-per-hour fast-balls and was slightly wilder than nearly any of his peers. Managers often gave their lefthanded hitters a rest when McDowell was the opposing pitcher. Perhaps a few hitters begged off from facing the hard-throwing lefty, but not Oliva. McDowell won twenty games in 1970, and posted thirteen or more victories in five other seasons, pitching for mediocre Cleveland clubs between 1962 and 1971. He led the American League in strikeouts five times, twice fanning more than three hundred batters in a season. He also issued more than a hundred walks in eight consecutive years. "The difficulty with Tony was," says McDowell, "I didn't know, and I still don't know, of any weakness that he had. He was a fantastic hitter, and quite frankly, I think he should be in the Hall of Fame."

With an up-close look from behind the plate, a catcher is in the unique position to learn a hitter's strengths, weaknesses, and tendencies at the plate. Phil Roof, who caught parts of fourteen big league seasons, including five with the Twins in the 1970s, came to the same conclusion many pitchers did. "There was no way to pitch him," Roof says. "He was smart enough to make adjustments. You just had to make quality pitches and hope that if he hit it hard, it was at somebody. He could hit the ball to left field as hard as most righthanders could hit the ball to left field."

The ability to drive the ball equally hard to left, center, or right is a rare skill, and was even more so in an era when players were less muscle-bound and not enhanced. Oliva's quick wrists and strength to drive the ball the opposite way impressed another catcher, Ed Herrmann, who caught three knuckleballers— Hoyt Wilhelm, Eddie Fisher, and Wilbur Wood—as a member of the White Sox in the late 1960s and early '70s. "I still don't think that anybody was as good as Oliva going the other way on the inside pitch," says Herrmann. "He had Hank Aaron wrists. Quickness *and* strength. Tony's wrists were so quick that he could get the barrel of the bat through on an inside pitch or drag his hands through the ball and hit it with power to left field."

Roof says that Oliva was so successful going the other way that he would frustrate pitchers by driving their best pitch into the left-field corner. "We had good righthanded sinkerball pitchers," Roof says of his stint with the Milwaukee Brewers during Oliva's prime years. "He would drill the sinker to left field. He would hit it and he would have the same pull spin as if a righthander hit it. You thought you made a good pitch and he's hitting it to left field." Herrmann adds that Oliva was "a lot like Clemente. No matter where the ball was, he could drive it. There really wasn't a true way to pitch to him."

Back-to-back surgical procedures on his right knee left Oliva physically compromised by 1973. He somehow managed to be productive at the plate, but playing on just one healthy leg took its toll. His power took the biggest hit in the post-injury years (Table 9). Former Twins closer Bill Campbell, a 1973 rookie who spent four years with Minnesota, remembers that pitchers would regularly bust Oliva inside. Pitchers discovered that he could no longer open his front hip to turn on pitches with authority, a movement he once made easily. Pitchers could now take advantage, retiring him by pitching inside.

Table 9. Oliva's per-season averages, before and after injury in 1971

Years	Games played	At-bats	Hits	Doubles	Home runs	RBIs	Batting average	Slugging percentage
1964–71	147	581	182	35	22	90	.313	.507
1973–75	135	495	140	15	14	69	.283	.401

Hall of Famer Bert Blyleven, who joined the Twins in 1970, says the loss of power was to be expected. "Hitting is from the waist down," he notes, adding that even with his knee problems, Oliva "still had the great hand-eye coordination and he could hit with the best of them." Harmon Killebrew agreed in a 2010 interview, saying, perhaps only half-jokingly, "even today I think Tony could get out there and hit line drives all over the place."

Remarkably, Oliva batted .291 in 1973 with sixteen homers and a team-leading ninety-two RBIs while playing on one healthy leg. Serving as Minnesota's designated hitter in the first year of the DH rule, he ranked eleventh in the American League in both batting and RBIs. His performance, according to one former teammate, furthers his case for the Hall of Fame. "I think definitely he should be in the Hall of Fame," says 1960s hurler Lee Stange, always cordial and quick with a quip. "He hit nearly .300 when he could hardly walk to first base. He didn't beat out any hits. He *hit* it."

Over time Oliva's knee became more problematic and his playing time declined. Still, he batted .285 in 127 games in 1974, and .270 in 131 games in 1975, his final season as a regular. Over those two seasons, American League hitters collectively batted .258. He also managed thirteen homers each year.

It took a great pure hitter to perform as Oliva did. In any sport, no matter the task, executing consistent mechanics on one good leg is extremely challenging, even for a professional athlete. That is certainly true of hitting a baseball, widely regarded as among the most difficult athletic undertakings to execute successfully. "If you've got a knee injury like that, it's obviously going to affect your balance," notes longtime Twin Jim Kaat, "and most good hitters have good balance." For Oliva, who successfully went out of the strike zone and adjusted well to offspeed stuff and still hit the ball hard, balance was critical to his success.

Although Oliva ground it out for four final seasons, he might have made a run at 3,000 hits had he not lost a few years on each end of his career. He was thirty-four years old when he returned in 1973, an age by which most major leaguers show signs of decline. We cannot possibly know how long a healthy Oliva would have played or how productive he would have been, but he was in the midst of the longest, most productive stretch of his career when he blew out his knee in Oakland in 1971.

In 1969 and 1970 combined, Oliva batted .313, the fourth-highest average among all batting qualifiers. He also slugged .505 over those two summers, one of only twenty-one players with a slugging percentage of .500 or higher. Among all players, Tony O ranked first in doubles, third in hits, and fifth in total bases. After falling short of one hundred RBIs in each of his first five seasons, he had cleared the century mark in both '69 and '70.

And in 1971, Oliva was having his best season when he went down on June 29. He led the majors in batting (.375) and topped the American League in hits (101), homers (18), total bases (176), and slugging (.654). He had such a commanding lead in the two hitting percentages that despite a decline in production after he returned in July, he still finished first in the league in both categories. His .337 average, a personal high, secured his third batting title. He slugged .546, a mark he had only surpassed in his rookie season. For half a season, he was the game's best hitter. Oliva was clearly at the top of his game prior to the injury. He had posted 401 hits in 1969 and 1970 combined, and in 1971 he had 101 in seventy-six games at the time he was hurt. Tony O, on course for a single-season high of 215 hits, might have set new personal standards in several offensive categories.

If not for his right knee, Oliva might have had several excellent seasons beyond 1971, but he retired with a career severely compromised and eventually cut short by injury. Others have been elected to the Hall of Fame based on excellence over a similar number of years.

Sandy Koufax is the most deserving of this group. He was wildly inconsistent his first six years with the Dodgers before emerging, in the second half of his career, as the game's most dominant lefthander. Koufax was the planet's best pitcher over his final four summers with Los Angeles, following the Dodgers' move to Chavez Ravine. But after pitching nearly seven hundred innings and winning fifty-five games in 1965 and 1966 combined, including World Series play, Koufax's arthritic elbow could take no more. He retired after the 1966 Series, two months shy of his thirty-first birthday. The Hall of Fame came calling in 1972, his first year of eligibility.

Two other premier pitchers, Bob Lemon, a key member of Cleveland's dominating postwar rotation, and Dodgers righthander Don Drysdale, were forced to retire early due to injury. Lemon suffered a leg injury and retired in 1958. The righthander won just 207 games, but he enjoyed seven twenty-win campaigns between 1948 and 1956, when the Indians were perennial contenders. In a breakout 1948 season, his first as a twenty-game winner, Lemon finished with a pair of postseason wins for Cleveland's 1948 World Series champions. His 1976 admission to the Hall, courtesy of the Veterans Committee, was based on nine impressive seasons.

Drysdale went 209–166 (.557) before retiring at thirty-three in 1969 because of a torn rotator cuff. He managed to pitch a dozen full seasons in the majors before shoulder trouble set in. He had a few more healthy years than Oliva or Lemon, but Drysdale figured prominently on pitching leaderboards in only six or seven of his fourteen seasons. The six-foot-six righthander's career year came in 1962, when he went 25–9 with a 2.83 ERA and led the National League in wins and strikeouts. The power pitcher had his only other twenty-win season in 1965, when he was 23–12, and his performance was critical down the stretch in a tight pennant race between the Dodgers and the Giants.

If you take away his 1962 and 1965 numbers, Drysdale was 161–145 (.526) for Brooklyn–Los Angeles clubs that were 1,105–883 (.535). Although for his last eight years he pitched in what was arguably the majors' most pitcher-friendly park, he finished with one of the five best ERAs in the National League just four times. He did win three World Series rings. He tossed a three-hit shutout of the Yankees in the Dodgers' four-game sweep of the 1963 Fall Classic, en route to a 3–2 career record in World Series play. He also started five All-Star Games for the National League.

The point here is not to judge whether Drysdale should be in the Hall but, rather, to demonstrate that his induction reflects favorably on Oliva's credentials for *his* eight excellent seasons. It seems fair to say that Drysdale's high-profile career in Brooklyn and Los Angeles, and winning three World Series, loomed large in his 1984 Hall of Fame election by the baseball writers.

It is easier to compare hitters to hitters, of course, and there are two Hall of Famers with injury-shortened careers who seem similar to Oliva in their Hall of Fame credentials. The first is longtime Pirates slugger Ralph Kiner, who was elected to the Hall by a single vote over the minimum in 1975, his final year of eligibility with the baseball writers. As hitters, Oliva and Kiner were different animals. Kiner, the National League's premier slugger in the early postwar years, topped the league in home runs for seven consecutive seasons beginning in 1946. He ranked eighth in slugging as a rookie in '46, but otherwise he finished in the top five in the six other seasons he won or shared the home-run title.

Forced out of the game by a back injury in 1955, Kiner had powered 369 home runs over ten seasons. Over his nine healthy years, Kiner posted homer totals similar to Oliva's annual doubles totals, and Oliva's home-run numbers were similar to Kiner's doubles production. Over those seasons, Kiner averaged twenty-three doubles and thirty-nine home runs a year; Oliva averaged thirty-five doubles and twenty-two homers. When you look at where Kiner and Oliva ranked on league leaderboards in their healthy years—in several key offensive categories—they seem quite comparable in their production (Table 10).

Table 10. Tony Oliva and Ralph Kiner: Number of seasons leading league or in top five

First or tied for first in league		
	Tony Oliva	Ralph Kiner
Batting average	3	0
Slugging percentage	1	3
Runs	0	1
RBIs	0	1
Hits	5	0
Doubles	4	0
Home runs	0	7
Extra-base hits	1	1
Total bases	1	1

Among top five in league		
	Tony Oliva	Ralph Kiner
Batting average	7	2
Slugging percentage	4	6
Runs	3	5
RBIs	3	6
Hits	5	0
Doubles	7	0
Home runs	0	8
Extra-base hits	7	5
Total bases	6	5

But the Hall of Famer with an injury-shortened career whom Oliva may resemble most closely is the man he mentored as a Twins coach in the 1980s: Kirby Puckett. The spark plug of Minnesota's championship clubs in 1987 and 1991, Puckett was forced to retire in 1995 at age thirty-five because of glaucoma. He was enshrined in the Hall in 2001, the first year he was eligible. Like Oliva, Puckett was an immediate success putting the bat on the ball as a rookie in 1984. Unlike his mentor, who had stroked thirty-two home runs as a rookie twenty years earlier, Puckett was initially a singles hitter, but he developed into a productive blend of contact hitter and power threat when he began using a high leg kick with Oliva's tutoring. He consistently featured the doubles pop that was a trademark of his hitting coach.

When his eyesight failed him, Puckett retired with 2,304 hits in twelve healthy seasons, a total Oliva may have exceeded had he been scouted in Cuba as a teenager. Over their careers, Puckett appeared in 107 more games than Oliva. Puckett finished with a .318 average, an .837 on-base plus slugging percentage (OPS), and nearly 1,100 runs and RBIs. Oliva, playing in a far more pitcher-friendly era—and on one healthy leg for four seasons—batted .304 with an .830 OPS, and roughly 900 runs and RBIs. Their league-leading rankings also are similar, though Oliva actually won two more batting titles and finished near the top of leaderboards more times in fewer healthy seasons. Puckett celebrated two World Series titles in Minnesota (Table 11).

Table 11. Tony Oliva and Kirby Puckett: Seasons leading league or in top five

First or tied for first in league		
	Tony Oliva	**Kirby Puckett**
Batting average	3	1
Slugging percentage	1	0
Runs	0	0
RBIs	0	0
Hits	5	4
Doubles	4	0
Home runs	0	0
Extra-base hits	1	0
Total bases	1	2

Among top five in league		
	Tony Oliva	**Kirby Puckett**
Batting average	7	2
Slugging percentage	4	2
Runs	3	3
RBIs	3	1
Hits	5	5
Doubles	7	5
Home runs	0	0
Extra-base hits	7	3
Total bases	6	4

Oliva had just turned thirty-eight when he retired following the 1976 season, while Puckett was a few months shy of thirty-six when he hung 'em up. Both were still remarkably productive when health issues sabotaged their careers, though Oliva suffered his career-altering injury a month shy of turning thirty-three and hobbled along for another four years. Both Oliva and Puckett, as well as other Hall of Famers with injury-shortened careers, might have bolstered their raw numbers significantly if not for health problems in their thirties. But only Oliva also lost years at the start of his career.

Oliva—like Jackie Robinson, other Negro leagues stars, and numerous players drafted into the military during World War II—had his major league career sidetracked by realities beyond his control. The lost time might have made the difference in a number of close Veterans Committee votes. He, Ron Santo, and Gil Hodges have been the top finishers for years, always short of the 75-percent requirement until Santo was elected posthumously in 2012. "Everybody I talk to who votes on the old-timers' part of the voting, everybody tells me, 'Yeah, I think Tony should be in there,'" said Killebrew. "But then when the voting comes out, we don't get it done."

In his fifteen years of eligibility with the baseball writers, when 75 percent of the vote is required to gain admittance, Oliva topped out at 47.3 percent in 1988—his seventh year on the ballot. Interestingly, in nine of the ten years that both he and Bill Mazeroski were on the ballot, Oliva finished ahead of the Pirates second baseman, who was inducted into the Hall by the Veterans Committee in 2001. Only in Mazeroski's final year before the writers did he get more votes than Oliva. Likewise, in eleven of the twelve years that Oliva and Ron Santo were on the ballot together, Oliva finished ahead of the longtime Cubs third baseman. The Veterans Committee inducted Santo a little more than a year after his death.

The fact that Oliva played his entire career in the Midwest may have hurt his cause with both the baseball writers and the Veterans Committee. So might the fact that he played in only one World Series in a career spanning fifteen seasons, at a time when there were fewer opportunities to make a mark on the national consciousness in October. "There wasn't as much postseason," notes Jim Kaat. "I think that hurt all of us in those days. Now you've got wild-card games. You've got all that postseason play. A guy like Bernie William, they'll say he's got more postseason home runs than anyone. Well of course. Mantle hit all his in a World Series. Now you've got all the games on TV. We didn't get that kind of exposure."

Not everyone is convinced that Oliva did enough in his eight healthy years, including longtime baseball writer Bill James. In his 1995 book

Whatever Happened to the Hall of Fame? the sabermetrics pioneer ran Oliva through what he calls the "Keltner List," his systematic though non-numerical method for assessing players' candidacies. The list is made up of fifteen questions, several focusing on whether the player was ever the best in his league or in the majors, the best on his team, or the best at his position who is not in the Hall. Other questions addressed how many times the player affected pennant races, assembled MVP-type seasons, appeared in All-Star Games, and had All-Star seasons. And did Oliva stack up? Although James concluded Oliva was a "viable" candidate and gave him the nod as the best right fielder not in the Hall at that point, ultimately he did not support Oliva's induction.

One argument against Oliva is that he did not draw walks and reach base as frequently as other elite players of his era. He walked more than forty-five times in a season only once—in 1965, when he drew fifty-five free passes and posted a single-season high .378 on-base percentage (OBP). Still, his .353 career OBP was well above the league average, though inflated by his .304 lifetime average. That makes Oliva's hitting profile quite similar to another right fielder with speed and a strong arm: Hall of Famer Roberto Clemente. The Pirates star retired with a .317 average and .359 OBP, winning four NL batting titles in eighteen seasons. His highest walk total was fifty-one, in 1959.

Both players averaged roughly one hundred runs and one hundred RBIs per 162 games from 1964–71. Clemente held a slight edge in slugging, .514 to .507, attributable to his huge edge in batting average. No one topped his 1.31 hits per game in this span, though Oliva was not far behind at 1.23. Tony O demonstrated significantly more power, but otherwise he and Clemente look quite similar when you stack their numbers from 1964–71 (Table 12). In the home-run department, Oliva probably benefited from his home park. With just bleacher seats running along the left-field line and no upper deck sheltering the right-field bleachers, Metropolitan Stadium was open to the elements and the ball carried well in warm weather. At the same time, Clemente played in the league that consistently tallied more runs per game and posted higher leaguewide hitting percentages. National League leaderboards frequently featured gaudier numbers.

Table 12. Roberto Clemente and Tony Oliva, 1964–71

	Games played	Runs scored	Doubles	Home runs	RBIs
Roberto Clemente	1,118	702	207	138	675
Tony Oliva	1,179	711	278	177	719

	Total bases	Walks	Strikeouts	Hitting percentages[1]
Roberto Clemente	2,249	352	658	.334/.383/.514
Tony Oliva	2,356	328	503	.313/.360/.507

[1]The three hitting percentages are, in order, batting average, on-base percentage (OBP), and slugging percentage.

In my many evenings spent at Metropolitan Stadium years ago, I witnessed Tony Oliva manipulate a bat in seemingly impossible ways. He solidly hit pitches just inches off the ground, driving them into the seats with what resembled a golf swing. He could pound the ball in on his hands with authority, as well as yank an outside pitch into the right-field seats. A few times in his career, he put bat on the ball as the bat left his hands. Tony O could hit any pitch in any location. That kind of pure hitter is rare, and given enough playing time, such a hitter is often celebrated in Cooperstown.

In his eight big seasons, Oliva ranked with the great hitters of his era. While he lacked the milestone numbers accumulated over a long career, his brilliance over his healthy years deserves recognition. He was widely perceived as one of the most dangerous hitters in the game, a more multidimensional threat than Harmon Killebrew or Rod Carew. "I think probably the best compliment he got was from catchers who caught in that era," notes Kaat, "because as I got into broadcasting and as my career moved around to other teams, I'd cross paths with guys like Bill Freehan, who caught for the Tigers, and Andy Etchebarren, who caught for the Orioles, and Duane Josephson. They all talked about how respectful they were for Harmon's ability and Rod's. But Tony was the guy they feared more than any of them."

Perhaps his teammates' dominance as American League batting and home-run leaders hurt the way baseball writers perceived Oliva when he became eligible for induction in 1982. He may have been overlooked by writers who had not seen him play regularly. Nearly forty years after Oliva retired, however, he remains beloved by Twins fans. Not only do they appreciate that he made the most of his gifts in the time that he had, but they are equally taken by the warmth and magnetic personality of the man they will always know as Tony O.

Table 13. Tony Oliva versus top pitchers of his era

Righthanders	At-bats	Hits	Doubles	Home runs	RBIs	Hitting percentages[1]
Gary Bell	33	14	5	1	6	.424/.525/.788
Jim Bouton	37	11	0	1	6	.297/.308/.378
Dean Chance	35	15	3	4	10	.429/.500/.857
Pat Dobson	54	20	4	2	5	.370/.414/.556
Eddie Fisher	44	16	6	1	9	.364/.417/.568
Joe Horlen	86	28	5	6	18	.326/.368/.593
Catfish Hunter	93	31	8	8	19	.333/.356/.699
Fergie Jenkins	32	6	2	2	5	.187/.235/.437
Jim Lonborg	32	14	5	0	3	.437/.486/.594
Denny McLain	80	26	6	6	12	.325/.357/.625
Andy Messersmith	35	13	2	1	7	.371/.405/.514
Jim Palmer	61	21	5	0	4	.344/.375/.426
Milt Pappas	23	6	2	1	3	.271/.320/.478
Dick Radatz	11	5	3	0	5	.455/.538/.909
Robin Roberts	20	7	1	2	3	.350/.350/.700
Nolan Ryan	40	5	0	0	2	.125/.314/.125
Sonny Siebert	71	19	7	0	9	.268/.293/.366
Mel Stottlemyre	112	33	6	7	18	.295/.319/.571
Luis Tiant	97	31	6	4	15	.320/.362/.505
Hoyt Wilhelm	31	6	1	1	2	.194/.242/.323
Earl Wilson	63	21	5	5	8	.333/.394/.714
Clyde Wright	51	16	0	2	3	.314/.352/.431

Lefthanders	At-bats	Hits	Doubles	Home runs	RBIs	Hitting percentages[1]
Steve Barber	42	13	3	0	2	.310/.370/.381
Vida Blue	31	5	0	0	2	.161/.235/.161
Mike Cuellar	58	15	1	2	9	.259/.318/.414
Al Downing	42	9	1	0	2	.214/.255/.286
Whitey Ford	22	5	1	0	1	.227/.261/.273
Tommy John	74	27	3	1	4	.365/.373/.446
Bill Lee	28	10	1	1	5	.357/.357/.500
Mickey Lolich	109	23	5	2	19	.211/.233/.349
Sam McDowell	59	21	1	0	8	.356/.424/.441
Dave McNally	62	23	1	1	14	.371/.403/.435
Gary Peters	79	18	6	1	9	.228/.235/.342
Wilbur Wood	67	18	3	6	13	.269/.290/.582

Note: Career stats from *The Baseball Cube* (www.thebaseballcube.com).

[1] The three hitting percentages are, in order, batting average, on-base percentage (OBP), and slugging percentage.

Acknowledgments

Tony Oliva's ability to hit a baseball inspired me to consider a biography of one of my childhood heroes. After I discovered the profound impact of the Bay of Pigs incident on his life, I definitely wanted to pursue this project. The project became a reality when Tony agreed to sit down over lunches to talk about his life. I will always appreciate that he gave his time to a complete stranger, who soon probed into the cultural difficulties and emotional pain of his early years in the United States. My stirring up old memories of tough times may not have been an enjoyable experience for him, but Tony stuck with it to the end, telling me his story.

Tony's wife, Gordette, and their children Anita and Ric also shared their stories, which were instrumental in understanding how the isolation caused by Cuba's "closing" affected entire families. Ampy Versalles-Curtis, the daughter of Zoilo Versalles, shed light on the complicated man who was her father and described the ways political events of the times affected her family. Their insights were priceless.

That isolation was an experience that Tony shared with the other Cubans playing for the Twins in the 1960s. They amicably gave me their time, and among the highlights of working on this book was engaging with Minnie Mendoza, Julio Bécquer, Camilo Pascual, Sandy Valdespino, and José Valdivielso. I learned a great deal about Cuban baseball from them, as well as from Roberto González Echevarría, the author of *The Pride of Havana: A History of Cuban Baseball*.

I thank former Twins players, the major league pitchers and catchers of Tony's era, and Hall of Famer Brooks Robinson, all of whom took time to discuss Tony's career with me. They are too many to mention, though a special thanks goes to Frank Quilici, who spent many hours with me early in the project.

As this book developed, no one gave me more time than Stuart Shea, good friend, musician, and author of *Wrigley Field: The Long Life and Contentious Times of the Friendly Confines*. Even as he prepared his own book, he was always there for me with ideas, feedback, and much-needed encouragement. His editing skills were invaluable.

Thanks also to Ken Goldberg, Bill Miller, Ron Thompson, and James Bailey, friends who offered to read the manuscript and who provided key suggestions and edits. Chuck Miller, another friend and a longtime colleague at STATS LLC, gave me IT support and statistical assistance. Also contributing help with numbers were STATS buddies Aaron Charlton, Ethan D. Cooperson, and Jim Henzler. I enjoyed seventeen years covering sports at STATS LLC, based in Northbrook, Illinois, and the company's vast databases allowed me to include revealing statistics throughout the text.

Through it all, Barb Loescher, who transcribed dozens of interviews, was a valuable contributor. Her attention to detail, timely work, and knowledge of the game are very much appreciated.

Twins curator Clyde Doepner took an early interest in the book and paved the way for me to receive photographs from the Minnesota Twins and to reprint them here without permission fees. Clyde's assistance and storytelling will long be remembered. Thanks also to Twins communications executives Dustin Morse and Bryan Donaldson and to the broadcast team of Dick Bremer and Bert Blyleven. I offer my sincere thanks to the Minnesota Twins.

Also deserving a big shout-out is Stan Dickman, who runs a terrific Twins fantasy camp in Fort Myers. He graciously opened the camp to me so that I could interview the former Twins who gather each January for the event. I had as much fun as the campers.

Others helped along the way, offering ideas, resources, and leads. They include Dr. Jorge Iber, Tom Shea, Terry McMahon, Joe Stillwell, Kaari Beaver Kohn, Galen Wagner, Ron Durner, Lou Galgano, Dave McCarthy, and Bill Nowlin of the Ted Williams Museum; Gina Ciganik and Teresa Skaar of Aeon in Minneapolis; and Jake Zimmerman, Bob Kuenster, and all my colleagues at *Baseball Digest*.

The research process was made far easier by Retrosheet.org, the Web site housing box scores and play-by-play accounts of nearly all major league games of Oliva's era. Baseball-Reference.com was another useful research tool. Add to that the years of impressive baseball coverage from beat writers covering the Twins for St. Paul and Minneapolis newspapers, from Arno Goethel, Glenn Redmann, Pat Reusse, and Gregg Wong to Sid Hartman, Jim

Klobuchar, Dwayne Netland, Jon Roe, Tom Briere, and Steve Aschburner. Their work not only provided valuable information and inside stories but hours of enjoyment.

Hats off to another former Twins beat writer, the late Bob Fowler, who penned *Tony O! The Trials and Triumphs of Tony Oliva* with Tony in 1973. His work provided insights and filled a few gaps involving events that happened nearly fifty years ago. Fowler was one of several authors with informative books about the Twins, offering little-known facts and perspective to a fascinating time in the team's history. Their fine research and writing should be acknowledged: Dave Mona and Dave Jarzyna, *Twenty-Five Seasons: The First Quarter Century of the Minnesota Twins* (1986); Jim Thielman, *Cool of the Evening* (2005); Dennis Brackin and Patrick Reusse, *Minnesota Twins: The Complete Illustrated History* (2010); Jon Kerr, *Calvin: Baseball's Last Dinosaur* (1990); Rod Carew with Ira Berkow, *Carew* (1979, reprinted 2010); Dean Urdahl, *Touching Bases with Our Memories: The Players Who Made the Minnesota Twins, 1961–2001* (2001).

Several national magazines covered baseball during Oliva's era, and a few were valuable research tools. They include *Baseball Digest,* the sport's oldest active publication, and *Sporting News, Sports Illustrated,* and *Sport.*

I offer my gratitude to the University of Minnesota Press staff for its fine work, guiding the book from its beginning through the final touches. Working with the editorial team of Erik Anderson, Kristian Tvedten, and Erin Warholm-Wohlenhaus was constructive, enjoyable, and gratifying, and the book is better for it. The production skills of Laura Westlund, Rachel Moeller, and Kathy Delfosse whipped the manuscript into shape, and a big thanks also goes to Heather Skinner, Emily Hamilton, and the marketing crew for their promotional efforts.

I would like to acknowledge my family. My father, Richard Henninger, shared his passion for baseball with me when I was young. My mother, Bette Lentsch, inspired my love of learning and the arts. My stepfather, Louie Lentsch, taught me that success requires hard work. Thanks as well to Jim Sherman and my father-in-law, the late Jack McMahon, an early believer in my writing career. I also express gratitude to my brother Dale and his wife, Lisa: they opened their home and took me in during my many research trips to Minnesota. And thanks to my sister, Monica Kelly, who hosted me during working trips to Florida.

Finally, I thank my wife, Kathy McMahon, and my daughter, Meara Henninger-McMahon. They endured my strange hours, as I often worked on this book in the hours leading to sunrise, and they held the fort during my frequent absences to pursue research or interviews in Minnesota and Florida. We all have our own passions, and they allowed me to chase mine.

Thanks to all.

Index

Aaron, Hank, 49, 65; All-Star Game appearances, 71, 91; Oliva compared to, 228, 229, 232, 236, 238
Abernathy, Ted, 55
Adair, Jerry, 127, 128
Adcock, Joe, 65, 120
Aguirre, Hank, 74
AL. *See* American League
ALCS. *See* American League Championship Series
Alexander Doyle, 210
Allen, Bernie, 16, 37, 109, 113
Allen, Dick, 49, 109, 122, 227
Allison, Bob, 14, 19, 28, 38, 87; in 1965 AL batting race, 72; in 1965 World Series, 101, 104; in 1967 AL pennant race, 114, 128–29; in 1969 ALCS, 152; All-Star Game appearances, 71–72; batting statistics, 51–52, 54, 66; encouraging Oliva, 86–87; at first base, 7, 53–54, 55; home runs by, 54, 65, 76, 134; Oliva as tablesetter for, 56; Rookie of the Year Award, 54
All Sports Stadium (Oklahoma City), 42
All-Star Games: in 1964, 71–72; in 1965, 91; in 1967, 121–22; in 1968, 135, 137, 140, 145; in 1970, 161; in 1971, 175–76; Oliva's consecutive appearances record, 149–50
Alou, Felipe, 165
Alston, Walt, 104

American League (AL): expansion teams in, 144, 198; league-wide batting averages, 48, 109, 239. *See also* All-Star Games; batting titles; Cy Young Award winners; Gold Glove Award winners; pennant races; Rookie of the Year Award winners; Triple Crown winners; World Series; *and individual teams*
American League batting races, Oliva competing in: in 1964, 68, 72-74, 77-78; in 1965, 86-87, 94-96; in 1966, 108-9; in 1967, 124, 125, 130; in 1968, 136, 137, 138; in 1969, 146, 150; in 1970, 159, 162, 163, 164, 165; in 1971, 172, 173, 175, 176, 178
American League Championship Series (ALCS), 151–55, 166–67
Anderson, Wendell, 207
Andrews, Mike, 129
Aparicio, Luis, 165
Appalachian League, 32, 33; Oliva plays for, 51, 229
Arcia, Oswaldo, 66
Arrigo, Gerry, 41–42, 55, 72, 75
Azcue, Joe, 120

bad-ball hitters, 64, 176–77
Bailey, Steve, 120
Baker, Floyd, 56

255

Baltimore Orioles: in 1966 World
Series, 109, 117; in 1969 ALCS,
151–55; in 1969 World Series, 154;
in 1970 ALCS, 166–67; Oliva's
hitting success against, 124, 125. *See
also individual team members*
Bando, Sal, 139, 172
Banks, George, 38, 71
Barber, Steve, 60–62
Barr, Steve, 211
bases, total: Oliva's annual, 78, 87–88,
130; Oliva's ranking for, 233, 240;
Versalles's annual, 98
Batista, Fulgencio, 8
bats, mahogany, 215–16
Battey, Earl, 19, 61, 62, 87, 109, 133; in
1965 AL pennant race, 97; in 1965
World Series, 101, 102–3, 104; All-
Star Game appearances, 91; Oliva's
friendship with, 35, 115, 218
batting averages: AL overall, 48, 109,
239; Bostock's, 219; Carew's, 203,
204, 219, 228; Clemente's, 109,
246; Puckett's, 220, 221, 243; Ted
Williams's, 124; Yastrzemski's, 48,
63, 130, 138, 145
batting averages, Oliva's: annual, 47–48,
68, 77, 130, 138, 145, 146, 165, 167,
200, 205, 239; against Baltimore,
124; career, 228, 231, 246; major
league, 49; minor league, 32, 34, 35,
40, 51, 64, 229; ranking of, 233, 240;
during September call-ups, 50. *See
also* hitting ability, Oliva's; slugging
percentages, Oliva's
batting titles, AL: Carew's, 188, 203,
204, 219, 228; Alex Johnson's, 165;
Puckett's, 243; Frank Robinson's, 47,
108–9; Yastrzemski's, 48, 63, 130,
138, 145
batting titles, NL: Clemente's, 246
batting titles, Oliva's, 45, 49, 200,
229, 231, 232, 237; in 1964, 28,
44, 46, 55, 63, 68, 72–73, 77; in
1965, 95–96, 98; in 1971, 48, 178;

compared to Hall of Fame members,
229, 231, 232, 237
Bauer, Hank, 121
Baumann, Frank, 19
Bay of Pigs invasion, 9, 18;
complications resulting from, 24,
28, 75, 82, 83, 196; effects on Oliva's
career, 12, 13
Bécquer, Julio, 27, 43, 83, 196; in
Cuban Winter League, 18–19, 23,
194; Dayton-Hudson Corporation
job, 20, 196; and Killebrew's death,
224–25; Oliva's friendship with,
21–22, 35, 214, 218; Twins career,
19–21
Belanger, Mark, 17, 152, 153, 154, 155,
166
Bell, Cool Papa, 14
Bell, Gary, 127, 228
Bench, Johnny, 229
Berenguer, Juan, 190–91
Berra, Yogi, 64, 73, 177
Berry, Ken, 137
Bethea, Bill, 81
Bibby, Jim, 208
Blair, Paul, 153, 167
Bloomington, Minnesota, 84; Oliva
living in, 132, 139–40, 141–42
Blue, Vida, 174; MVP and Cy Young
awards, 172, 179; no-hitter by, 164,
165
Blyleven, Bert: comments on Oliva,
177, 239; on DH rule, 200; pitching
performances of, 160, 163, 164, 201,
203, 208; trade of, 211
Bonds, Bobby, 198
Border League (minor leagues), 22
Bosman, Dick, 173
Bostock, Lyman, 208, 219–20
Boston Red Sox: in 1967 AL pennant
race, 47, 122, 123, 125–26, 127,
128–29. *See also individual team
members*
Boswell, Dave, 87, 108, 151, 160; in
1969 ALCS, 153–54; bar fight with

Martin, 147, 156; Oliva's argument with, 120–21

Boudreau, Lou, 228

Bouldin, Carl, 56, 57, 59

Bouton, Jim, 64, 73, 76, 177, 236

Braun, Steve, 208, 210

Bressoud, Eddie, 66, 76

Brett, George, 219

Briggs, John, 175

Bristol, Dave, 10

Brock, Lou, 49, 198, 231

Brophy, George, 156

Brown, Jackie, 208

Brown, Larry, 65, 120

Brunansky, Tom, 216

Buford, Don, 37, 152

Bunker, Wally, 78

Bunning, Jim, 14, 24, 71

Burdette, Lew, 118

Burgmeier, Tom, 159

California Angels: in 1967 AL pennant race, 122, 129; in 1970 AL pennant race, 159, 160, 163. *See also* Los Angeles Angels; *and individual team members*

Callison, Johnny, 71

Cambria, Papa Joe: death of, 35; signing Cuban players, 18–19, 22, 26, 27, 43–44; signing Oliva, 4, 10

Campanella, Roy, 228

Campaneris, Bert, 139, 172, 174

Campbell, Bill, 177, 239

Canseco, Jose, 26

Cárdenas, Jose, 164

Cárdenas, Leo, 146, 149, 151, 153, 165, 167, 175

Carew, Rod, 16, 45, 156, 170, 179, 224; and 1968 AL batting race, 136, 137; in 1969 ALCS, 153, 155; in 1969 season, 145–46, 150, 151; in 1970 season, 159, 160; in 1973 season, 201, 202; All-Star Game appearances, 122, 161; batting titles,

188, 203, 204, 219, 228; comments on Oliva, 46, 121, 148, 185, 187, 214; in Hall of Fame, 223, 227, 229; hit totals, 203, 228; Oliva's friendship with, 114–15, 141, 218–19, 220, 222; rookie year, 114, 117; stealing home, 145–46

Carreon, Camilo, 67

Casanova, Paul, 125

Cash, Norm, 116

Castro, Fidel, 8; disbanding of Cuban Winter League, 14–15, 18, 194

Cater, Danny, 138, 139

Cedeño, César, 198

Cepeda, Orlando, 43, 200–201, 227

Chance, Dean: in 1969 ALCS, 155; All-Star Game appearances, 122; with Cleveland Indians, 160, 162; comments on Oliva, 237; Cy Young Award, 78, 94, 107, 113, 237; with Los Angeles Angels, 78, 94, 107–8; with Minnesota Twins, 113, 114, 118, 128, 129, 134; no-hitter, 123

Charlotte Hornets (minor leagues): Oliva plays for, 9, 10–12, 32, 36–37, 51, 229

Chicago White Sox: in 1967 AL pennant race, 122, 123, 125–26

Cimino, Pete, 113

Clark, Ron, 139

Clarke, Horace, 47, 117, 119

Clemente, Roberto, 11, 71, 161, 198; All-Star Game appearances, 91; batting titles, 109, 246; Oliva compared to, 49, 200, 231, 236, 246–47

Cobb, Ty, 45, 106–7, 146

Cochrane, Mickey, 228

Colavito, Rocky, 54, 55, 61, 67, 98

Combs, Earle, 229

Conigliaro, Tony, 78–79, 122, 201

Cottier, Chuck, 56

Crowley, Terry, 222

Cuba: absence of prejudice in, 5, 31; breakdown of relations with United

States, 8–9, 12, 13, 14, 16, 18, 83; closing of, 13, 28, 31; contemporary situation in, 193–97; love of baseball in, 2–3, 190; Oliva's trips to, 189–93, 195–97, 226; travel restrictions lifted for citizens, 140. *See also* Bay of Pigs invasion

Cuban players, 7, 10, 21, 189; Cambria's signing of, 18–19, 22, 26, 27, 43–44; cultural adjustments for, 11–12, 13, 27, 28, 39; cut off from homeland, 22, 31, 75, 82, 194, 196; decisions to return to Cuba, 194–97; favorite foods, 11, 21–22, 27, 85; media images of, 81, 82, 83; playing in New York City, 88–89

Cuban Revolution, 8–9, 194

Cuban Winter League: Castro's disbanding of, 14–15, 18, 194; Twins players in, 23

Cubbage, Mike, 211

Cuddyer, Michael, 224

Cuellar, Mike, 17, 152, 166, 177

Cunningham, Joe, 67

Cy Young Award winners: Blue, 172, 179; Chance, 78, 94, 107, 113, 237; Perry, 159

Dallas–Fort Worth Rangers (minor leagues): Oliva plays for, 39–42, 51

Dark, Alvin, 109, 110

Darwin, Bobby, 188, 201, 208, 209

Davis, Willie, 100

dead-ball era, 109, 133, 144, 228

DeBusschere, Dave, 37

designated hitter (DH), 198; Oliva as, 199, 200, 201, 205, 206, 239

Detroit Tigers: and 1967 AL pennant race, 122, 125–26, 127–28, 129; and 1968 championship season, 133, 139

DeWitt, William, 108

Dihigo, Martín, 14–15

Dillman, Bill, 124

DiMaggio, Joe, 124, 149–50

Dobson, Chuck, 164, 202

Dobson, Pat, 184

Doby, Larry, 6, 228

Dodger Stadium (Chavez Ravine, Los Angeles), 102, 144

Dominican Republic: winter ball in, 32, 132, 158, 197

Donovan, Dick, 38

doubles, Oliva's, 124, 170, 229; annual totals, 37, 40, 78, 130, 138, 139, 145, 146, 165, 200; compared to Hall of Fame players, 227, 232, 234, 242; ranking for, 233, 234, 240

Downing, Al, 73, 117

Dropo, Walt, 124, 149

Drysdale, Don, 24, 71, 241; in 1965 World Series, 26, 28, 99–100, 101, 102, 104

Ellis, Dock, 176

English (language): Cuban players' struggles with, 39; Oliva's difficulties with, 5, 8, 11, 21, 29, 30, 31, 36, 56, 63, 106, 215, 217–18; Versalles's difficulties with, 81, 84

Ermer, Calvin Coolidge: as Twins manager, 119, 121, 132, 138, 144

Estrada, Martín, 158, 168

Etchebarren, Andy, 247

extra-base hits, 49; AL leaders, 49; Oliva's, 58, 63, 130, 170–71; Versalles's, 87. *See also* doubles, Oliva's; home runs, annual totals; home runs, Oliva's; triples, annual totals

Fairly, Ron, 101, 104

farm, Oliva family, 1–4, 190, 192; Oliva's work on, 3, 29, 30, 45, 131, 214

Fenway Park (Boston), 171, 204

Fernández, Chico, 11

Fernández Tápanes, Roberto, 4, 222, 229

Fernandina Beach, Florida, 5, 7, 8

Ferrell, Rick, 229
Fidrych, Mark, 210, 211
Fingers, Rollie, 132
Fischer, Bill, 66
Fisher, Eddie, 119, 238
Fitz Gerald, Ed, 58
Flick, Elmer, 138
Flood, Curt, 135
Florida. *See* Fernandina Beach, Florida; spring training, Oliva at; spring training, Twins
Florida International League (minor leagues), 23
Ford, Dan, 208
Ford, Whitey, 24, 54, 90
Fosse, Ray, 161, 185, 201
Foytack, Paul, 65
Francona, Tito, 65
free agency, 46, 199, 219
Freehan, Bill, 66, 247
Fregosi, Jim, 74, 135

Garber, Gene, 202
García, Silvio, 14–15
Gardenhire, Ron, 224
Gibbs, Jake, 117
Gibson, Bob, 24, 91, 133
Gibson, Josh, 14
Gilliam, Jim, 100, 104
Gladden, Dan, 213
Gladding, Fred, 76
Gogolewski, Bill, 176
Gold Glove Award: Oliva, 34, 46, 111–12
Gordon, Joe, 148–49
Grabarkewitz, Billy, 161
Granger, Wayne, 188
Grant, Jim "Mudcat," 14, 42, 121, 218; in 1965 AL pennant race, 97; in 1965 World Series, 99, 100, 104; All-Star Game appearances, 91; with Twins, 55–56, 71, 114, 132
Green, Dick, 201
Green, Lenny, 19, 25, 35, 37, 38, 54, 70

Greenberg, Hank, 228
Griffin, Ivy, 230
Griffith, Calvin, 9, 198, 199; assigning Oliva to Dallas–Fort Worth, 39, 40; assistance to Cuban players, 18–19, 20–21, 24, 25; comments on Oliva, 61, 64; contract negotiations, 4–5, 36, 106–7, 171, 183, 229; firing managers, 118–19, 144, 156, 157, 188, 209–10; in Minnesota Twins Hall of Fame, 223; moves Senators to Minnesota, 4, 96; trades made by, 70, 113–14, 132, 203; on Versalles, 32, 133
Griffith, Clark, 4
Guerra, Julio, 10
Gwynn, Tony, 45

Hacker, Warren, 19, 20
Hafey, Chick, 229
Hall, Halsey: suit jacket fire, 134–35
Hall, Jimmie, 55, 93, 94; All-Star Game appearances, 91; batting statistics, 51–52; home runs by, 65, 66–67, 89, 110; Oliva as tablesetter for, 55, 56; trade of, 113
Hall, Tom, 139, 160, 166
Hall of Fame: Minnesota Twins players in, 20, 93, 207, 220, 223–24; Oliva's qualifications for, 45, 48, 49, 200, 227–49. *See also individual members*
Hamilton, Steve, 76–77, 121
Handrahan, Vern, 65
Hannan, Jim, 56
Hansen, Ron, 67
Harper, Johnny, 131
Harrelson, Ken, 136, 137
Hartnett, Gabby, 229
Hatcher, Mickey, 124
Havana Sugar Kings (minor leagues), 4
Hegan, Mike, 160, 164
Held, Woodie, 65
Hendricks, Elrod, 17, 153, 155
Herrmann, Ed, 205, 238

Hershberger, Mike, 160
Herzog, Whitey, 18
Hickman, Jim, 161
Higgins, Pinky, 124
Hinton, Chuck, 72, 111
Hisle, Larry, 201, 203, 208
hits, Oliva's: annual totals, 37, 77, 98, 108, 130, 145–46, 167, 229; career, 49, 170, 228, 231, 240; trying for consecutive hits record, 124, 149. *See also* doubles, Oliva's; extra-base hits: Oliva's; hitting ability, Oliva's; home runs, Oliva's; triples, annual totals: Oliva's
hitting ability, Oliva's, 3, 33, 58, 62, 66, 236–39; as bad-ball hitter, 64, 176–77; batting stances, 157–58, 159, 171, 172–73, 231; as breaking ball hitter, 44–45, 148, 164, 165, 200, 211; digging-in process, 59, 61; hitting all types of pitches, 72, 107–8, 227; hitting to all fields, 28, 37, 51, 57, 93, 228, 247. *See also* American League batting races, Oliva competing in; bases, total; hits, Oliva's; hitting streaks, Oliva's; RBIs, Oliva's; slugging percentages, Oliva's
hitting streaks: Alex Johnson's, 165; DiMaggio's, 124; Mantle's, 72; Yastrzemski's, 137, 165
hitting streaks, Oliva's: in 1964, 58, 59, 62–63, 64–65, 67, 73–74, 78; in 1965, 92–93; in 1967, 119, 124, 125; in 1968, 135, 136; in 1969, 147–48, 149, 150; in 1970, 159, 161–62; in 1971, 172, 173–74, 177–78; in 1973, 202; in 1974, 204. *See also* hitting ability, Oliva's
Hodges, Gil, 245
Holt, Jim, 180
home runs, annual totals: Aaron's, 228; Allison's, 54, 55, 76, 134; Carew's, 203, 228; Jimmie Hall's, 65, 66–67, 89, 110; Mincher's, 38, 53, 75–76, 109; Puckett's, 221, 243; Versalles's, 89–90

home runs, Killebrew's: annual totals, 51–52, 54, 65, 90, 110, 127, 134, 145, 151, 162, 170, 206; career totals, 207, 228; five-hundredth, 177; inside-the-park, 20; longest at Metropolitan Stadium, 118
home runs, Oliva's: in 1964, 55, 57, 77; in 1965, 107, 110; in 1968, 138, 139; in 1969, 151; in 1973, 200, 203, 205; against Baltimore, 124; career totals, 205, 210, 240; compared to Hall of Fame members, 228, 232, 234, 239, 242, 243; first by a DH, 201; inside-the-park, 73, 76; longest, 42, 148; minor league, 37, 40, 64, 229
Horlen, Joe, 123, 136, 149
Horton, Willie, 98
Hotel Maryland (Minneapolis), 89, 107
Houston Colt .45s, 8
Howard, Elston, 77, 78
Howard, Frank, 96, 135, 136, 151, 161, 171
Howser, Phil, 9–11, 27, 32, 204–5, 218
Hrbek, Kent, 220, 223
Humphrey, Hubert H., 24, 25, 75
Humphreys, Bobby, 37
Hunter, Jim "Catfish," 107, 109, 122, 134, 172, 201, 203, 236

injuries, Oliva's: in 1964, 69–70, 75–76; in 1965, 86, 95; in 1966, 106, 107; in 1967, 111, 117, 119–20, 130; in 1968, 135, 137–38; in 1969, 145, 154–55; in 1971, 176, 178; in 1972, 183, 188; in 1974, 207; bat-throwing incidents, 46, 70, 75, 77, 92, 100, 122, 163, 247; knee problems, 47, 48–49, 51, 78, 92, 174–75, 182–88, 201, 208, 222, 229, 240; minor league, 35, 46; surgeries, 99, 105–6, 108, 179, 186–87, 188, 199, 207, 209, 239. *See also* Killebrew, Harmon: injuries
Irvin, Monte, 14, 228

Jackson, Larry, 24

Jackson, Reggie, 139, 151, 172, 175–76, 229

Jackson, "Shoeless" Joe, 77

Jackson, Travis, 229

James, Bill: *Whatever Happened to the Hall of Fame?*, 245–46

Jenkins, Ferguson, 122, 176, 208

John, Tommy, 165

Johnson, Alex, 163, 165

Johnson, Davey, 154, 155, 167

Johnson, Lou, 100–101

Jones, Dalton, 128

Josephson, Duane, 247

Kaat, Jim, 14, 27, 35, 124, 127, 198, 203; in 1965 World Series, 100, 101, 104; in 1967 AL pennant race, 114, 119, 120, 125, 126, 129, 167; in 1969 ALCS, 152, 155; in 1970 season, 160, 165; assistance to Oliva, 88, 218; comments on Oliva, 34, 62, 63, 240, 245, 247; pitching performances, 56, 96–97, 110

Kaline, Al, 47, 116, 162, 176; Oliva compared to, 229, 236; Oliva's admiration for, 71, 163

Kansas City Royals: Killebrew plays for, 207, 208

Keltner List, 246

Kemmerer, Russ, 19

Kennedy, John F., 9, 50

Killebrew, Harmon, 17, 25, 35, 61, 96, 218; in 1965 World Series, 101, 102, 104; in 1967 AL pennant race, 120, 124, 127, 128, 129; in 1969 ALCS, 152; in 1970 ALCS, 167; in 1970 season, 159, 160, 162, 164; in 1971 season, 179; All-Star Game appearances, 71–72, 91, 122, 135, 145, 161, 176; batting statistics, 49, 51–52, 77, 145, 149, 171, 177, 206; comments on Oliva, 108, 123, 184, 214–15, 228, 245; death of, 224–25;

as DH, 199, 205, 206; easy-going personality, 46; at first base, 19, 114, 151, 187; in Hall of Fame, 223, 227; honoring, 206–7, 224; injuries, 87, 93, 94, 98, 117, 135, 137, 145, 170, 175, 188–89, 199, 206; jersey number retired, 207, 223; on Kansas City Royals' team, 207, 208; MVP Award, 145, 146, 171; Oliva as tablesetter for, 56; Oliva compared to, 236; and Oliva's bat-throwing incidents, 70, 163; six-digit salary, 171; at third base, 16. *See also* home runs, Killebrew's

Kindall, Jerry, 54

Kiner, Ralph, 228, 242, 243

Kirkpatrick, Ed, 202

Kline, Ron, 113–14

Kling, Johnny, 124

Klippstein, Johnny, 111, 113

Kluszewski, Ted, 19

Koch, Al, 76

Koplitz, Howie, 58

Kostro, Frank, 54

Koufax, Sandy: in 1965 World Series, 26, 28, 99, 100, 101, 102, 103, 104–5; comments on Oliva, 237; in Hall of Fame, 22, 24, 240–41

Kralick, Jack, 20

Kubek, Tony, 77

Landis, Jim, 20

Larkin, Gene, 213, 217, 221

LaRoche, Dave, 172, 188

Larsen, Don: perfect game by, 134

Latino players. *See* Cuban players

Laudner, Tim, 216, 217

Lavagetto, Cookie, 20

Lazar, Danny, 151

Lazzeri, Tony, 228

Lefebvre, Jim, 101

Lemon, Bob, 241

Lemon, Jim: as coach, 108, 116, 133; comments on Oliva, 44, 46; as manager, 134; as player, 19, 35

Lentz, George "Doc," 48, 69, 86, 110, 120, 186
Lindblad, Paul, 107, 109, 110, 176
Lindstrom, Freddie, 229
Littell, Mark, 202
Lock, Don, 56, 96
Lolich, Mickey, 59, 62–63, 75, 159, 173, 179
Lonborg, Jim, 128
Lopat, Eddie, 64
López, Al, 19
López, Héctor, 73
López, Marcelino, 148
López Oliva, Anita Petrona (Oliva's mother), 1, 5, 29; death of, 191–92; reunions with, 158, 169, 190, 191
Los Angeles Angels, 102. *See also* California Angels
Los Angeles Dodgers: and 1965 World Series, 99–105
Los Mochis, Mexico: winter ball in, 158, 168–69, 212
Los Palacios, Cuba: Oliva plays for the team from, 3–4
Lost Son of Havana, The (documentary), 197
Lumpe, Jerry, 18

Madlock, Bill, 232
magnetic therapy, 201
Mantilla, Felix, 55, 94
Mantle, Mickey, 54, 61, 72, 73, 78, 89, 91, 109; Oliva compared to, 64, 228, 245
Manuel, Charlie, 148
Maraniss, David, 11
Marichal, Juan, 24, 71, 122
Maris, Roger, 54
Martin, Billy: in 1969 ALCS, 152, 153, 154, 155–56, 167; bar fight with Boswell, 147, 156; firing of, 156, 157; as Twins coach, 81, 87–88, 97, 144; as Twins manager, 144–47, 151
Martinez, Buck, 151
Mathews, Eddie, 65

Mauch, Gene, 210–11
May, Rudy, 172
Mayberry, John, 186
Maye, Lee, 160
Mays, Willie, 49, 71, 91
Mazeroski, Bill, 245
McAuliffe, Dick, 139
McCarver, Tim, 122
McDowell, "Sudden Sam," 38, 91, 117, 120, 161–62, 237–38
McKeon, Jack, 40
McLain, Denny, 87, 116, 129, 133, 162, 173; comments on Oliva, 236–37
McLish, Cal, 20
McMullen, Ken, 96, 129
McNally, Dave, 117, 152, 166, 167
Mele, Sam: in 1965 World Series, 102, 104; comments on Oliva, 60, 63, 92, 111; fines given out by, 70, 116; firing of, 118–19; friendship with Ted Williams, 173; lineup changes by, 117; as Twins manager, 19–21, 37–39, 87, 97, 114, 117, 194
Mendoza, Minnie: and disbanding of Cuban Winter League, 15–16; hosting parties for Cuban players, 7, 27; Oliva's friendship with, 17–18, 27, 36, 218; plays for Charlotte Hornets, 16–17; return to Cuba, 196–97; in Twins organization, 9–11
Merritt, Jim, 127, 146
Metropolitan Stadium (Bloomington, Minnesota), 63, 91, 118, 246
Mikkelsen, Pete, 76, 90
Miller, Bob, 132, 133, 154, 155–56, 167
Miller, John, 25
Mincher, Don, 93, 113; in 1965 World Series, 101, 103; at first base, 19, 54; home runs by, 38, 53, 75–76, 109
Minnesota Twins: and 1962 season, 51; and 1963 season, 39–43, 51–52, 54; and 1964 season, 49, 50–79; and 1965 season, 80–98; and 1965 World Series, 99–105, 113; and 1966 season, 106–12; and 1967 season, 46,

113–30; and 1968 season, 133–39; and 1969 ALCS, 151–55; and 1969 season, 144–56; and 1970 ALCS, 166–67; and 1970 season, 157–67; and 1971 season, 169–79; and 1972 season, 182–89; and 1973 season, 198–203; and 1974 season, 203–7, 208; and 1975 season, 208–9; and 1976 season, 210–12; and 1991 World Series, 213, 222; arrival in Minnesota, 4; attendance figures, 90, 188, 198, 209, 210, 212; consecutive home runs in one inning record, 64, 109–10; fantasy camp, 143; farm system, 170, 188; Hall of Fame, 223, 224; meeting with LBJ, 75; Winter Caravans, 106, 215, 225. *See also* Griffith, Calvin; spring training, Twins; *and individual team members*

Minnesota Twins career, Oliva's: in 1964 season, 28, 29, 50–79, 88, 229, 240, 243; in 1965 season, 44, 80–98; in 1966 season, 47, 99, 106–12; in 1967 season, 47, 113–30; in 1968 season, 133–39; in 1969 ALCS, 151–55; in 1969 season, 144–56, 240; in 1970 ALCS, 166–67; in 1970 season, 157–67, 240; in 1971 season, 48, 169–79, 240; in 1972 season, 182–89, 199; in 1973 season, 187, 188, 198–203, 239; in 1974 season, 203–7, 239; in 1975 season, 208–9, 239; in 1976 season, 210–12; All-Star Game appearances, 71–72, 91, 121–22, 135, 140, 161; Boswell's argument with, 120–21; as broadcaster, 221; contracts, 4–5, 36, 106–7, 171, 183, 229; defensive game, 7, 58, 76, 111–12, 185–86; as DH, 199, 200, 201, 205, 206, 239; Gold Glove award, 34, 46, 111–12; Hall of Fame qualifications, 48, 49, 200, 227–49; hit-by-pitch incidents, 59–62, 208; as hitting coach, 143, 216–22, 225; jersey number retired,

222, 224; on Martin, 145, 156; in Minnesota Twins Hall of Fame, 223; pitchers' performance vs., 248–49; as player-coach, 210–12; retirement, 203, 217, 225, 244; Rookie of the Year award, 29, 46, 71, 78–79; running game, 57, 98, 145, 204, 232; September call-ups, 21, 35, 37–38, 42–43, 50–51; sliding plays, 47, 69, 117, 202, 204; tablesetter role, 56–57, 76; Target Field statue, 224; tribute to, 222–23; in Twins Hall of Fame, 224; on Winter Caravans, 106, 215, 225; in World Series of 1965, 44, 99–105; and World Series of 1987 and 1991, 212, 215, 217. *See also* injuries

minor league career, Oliva's, 13–49; annual batting averages, 32, 34, 35, 40, 51, 229; Appalachian League play, 51, 229; Border League, 22; Charlotte Hornets, 9, 10–12, 32, 36–37, 51, 229; Dallas–Fort Worth Rangers, 39–42, 51; defensive game, 8, 33–34, 42–43; instructional league play, 21, 34, 36, 38, 43, 60; MVP award, 38; playing through injuries, 35, 46; Silver Louisville Slugger award, 35; spring training, 5–8, 26–27, 36, 39; Wytheville, Virginia, 32–35, 57, 189, 222

Miñoso, Minnie: in Cuban Winter League, 14, 15, 23, 194; playing against Twins, 20; rookie season batting average 77

Mitterwald, George, 153, 174

Molitor, Paul, 224

Monbouquette, Bill, 69

Monday, Rick, 136, 137

Morales, Rich, 149

Morgan, Joe, 198, 229

Morneau, Justin, 224

Morris, Jack, 213

Most Valuable Player (MVP) Award winners, AL: Blue, 172, 179;

Killebrew, 145, 146, 171; Brooks Robinson, 77; Frank Robinson, 109; Versalles, 87–88, 94, 98; Yastrzemski, 128–29, 130, 133
Motton, Curt, 153
Murcer, Bobby, 178
Musial, Stan, 45

Nathan, Joe, 224
National League (NL), 144, 198, 246. *See also* All-Star Games; World Series; *and individual teams*
Nen, Dick, 96
Nettle, Graig, 139
New York Mets, 155
New York Yankees, 51, 73, 87, 88, 89–90, 98. *See also individual team members*
Niekro, Joe, 184
Nixon, Richard, 9
NL. *See* National League
Northey, Scott, 151
Norwood, Red, 32
Nossek, Joe, 100, 210

Oakland Athletics: in 1969 AL pennant race, 147, 149, 150–51; in 1970 AL pennant race, 159, 160, 163; in 1971 AL pennant race, 172; 1972 World Series championship, 201. *See also individual team members*
OBP. *See* on-base percentage
Odom, Blue Moon, 174
Oliva, Anita (daughter), 140, 141, 142, 168, 169, 195, 214; trip to Cuba, 192–93
Oliva, Antonio: birth certificate used by Oliva, 5, 13, 43–44, 150
Oliva, Damion, 142
Oliva, Felicia, 158, 169, 179–81, 183, 185, 189
Oliva, Gordette Dubois (wife): children, 140–42, 158, 209; marriage, 131–32; meets Oliva,

29–31; on Oliva's age discrepancy, 43–44; travel to Cuba, 142–43, 195; visits with Oliva family, 168, 169
Oliva, Juan Carlos, 189, 190, 192, 197
Oliva, Pedro, Jr. (Peter, son), 140, 141, 142, 168, 169
Oliva, Pirico Pedro, 1, 5; baseball skills, 2, 3; genetic knee condition, 48; reunions with Oliva, 179–81, 182–85, 186, 190, 191
Oliva, Reynaldo, 189, 190
Oliva, Ricardo (Ric, son), 140, 142, 193, 209
Oliva, Tony: on amateur and country teams in Cuba, 3–4; car accident, 47, 99, 110–11, 115; chicken pox bout, 149–50, 161; childhood, 1–4; cut off from family, 15, 97, 140, 196, 213; easy-going personality, 46, 106, 114–15, 141, 214, 225, 226, 248; family life, 46, 139–43, 225–26; generosity, 18, 142, 195, 213–14; and Killebrew's death, 224–25; loneliness of, 12, 13–14, 29, 31–32, 36, 46, 107, 214; marriage, 131–32; meets Gordette, 29–31; reunions with parents and siblings, 158, 168–69; trips to Cuba, 189–93, 195–97, 226; U.S. citizenship, 179; uses brother's birth certificate, 5, 13, 43–44, 150; winter ball experiences, 14, 31, 32, 43, 51, 132, 140, 158, 168, 200, 212, 217–18; work ethic of, 2, 45–46, 111–12, 222. *See also* hitting ability, Oliva's; injuries, Oliva's; Minnesota Twins career, Oliva's; minor league career, Oliva's; spring training, Oliva at
on-base percentage (OBP): Oliva's, 217, 246
on-base plus slugging percentage (OPS): Puckett vs. Oliva, 243
O'Neil, Buck, 14
OPS. *See* on-base plus slugging percentage

Orsino, John, 61
Osinski, Dan, 108
Osteen, Claude, 25, 102
Otis, Amos, 161

Palmer, Jim, 87, 152, 154, 166, 167
Pappas, Milt, 61, 108
Parker, Wes, 101
Pascual, Camilo, 22–26; in 1965 World
    Series, 25, 102; and closing of Cuba,
    22, 75, 194; Cuban Winter League
    play, 14, 15; curveball, 22, 23, 24,
    134; injuries, 25–26, 87, 93, 96, 147;
    Oliva's friendship with, 35, 57–58,
    218; pitching performances, 55, 69;
    retirement, 26; trade of, 26, 113
Pattin, Marty, 164, 204
Paul, Gabe, 120
Paula, Carlos, 14
pennant races, AL: in 1965, 44, 80–98;
    in 1967, 47, 113–30, 132; in 1969,
    146, 147, 149; in 1970, 159, 160,
    163, 165; in 1971, 172; in 1973,
    202. See also American League
    Championship Series; World Series
Pepitone, Joe, 91
Pérez, Tony, 10, 15, 122, 227
Perranoski, Ron, 132, 133, 152, 153,
    155; in 1970 season, 163, 164, 165,
    167
Perry, Gaylord, 185
Perry, Jim, 208, 222; in 1969 ALCS,
    151, 152; in 1970 ALCS, 166; in
    1970 season, 160; All-Star Game
    appearance, 161; comments on
    Oliva, 72, 218; Cy Young Award
    winner, 159; pitching performances,
    17, 127, 147, 160, 185
Peters, Gary, 78
Petrocelli, Rico, 171, 200
Pfister, Dan, 65
Phoebus, Tom, 120
Pierce, Billy, 19
Piñar del Río, Cuba, 1, 2, 169, 195

Piniella, Lou, 186
Pinson, Vada, 204
pitching mound height, 102, 144, 198
Pizarro, Juan, 67
Plaskett, Elmo, 37
Pohlad, Carl, 222
Powell, Boog, 109, 152, 153, 166, 167,
    171
Power, Vic: benching of, 57; at first base,
    52–53; hitting performances, 38, 62;
    mentoring Oliva, 39–40, 55, 60, 128;
    response to prejudice, 6–7; trade of,
    54, 70
Puckett, Kirby: batting titles, 220, 221,
    243; comments on Oliva, 222–23;
    death of, 224; in Hall of Fame,
    223–24; Oliva's mentorship of,
    220–21, 243; retirement, 243, 244;
    Target Field statue, 224
Puerto Rican Winter League: Oliva
    plays for, 6, 43, 49, 51, 200

Quilici, Frank, 33, 85; in 1965 AL
    pennant race, 96, 97; in 1965 World
    Series, 99–100; comments on
    Oliva, 34, 35, 45–46, 120; firing
    of, 209–10; at Killebrew's funeral,
    224; in minor leagues, 189; Oliva's
    friendship with, 222, 225; as Twins
    manager, 188, 199, 203, 205, 208,
    209; on Twins Winter Caravan, 106

racism, U.S., 5–6, 31, 33. See also
    segregation, U.S.
Radatz, Dick, 69, 71
Ramos, Pedro, 65; in Cuban Winter
    League, 14, 15, 23; Oliva's
    friendship with, 35, 218; pitching
    performances, 18, 89–90
Rantz, Jim, 41, 60, 106, 214; comments
    on Oliva, 215, 221
RBIs, annual totals: AL leaders, 171;
    Carew's, 203; Killebrew's, 145, 177,

206; Puckett's, 243; Yastrzemski's, 130

RBIs, Oliva's: annual totals, 40, 98, 130, 138–39, 146, 151, 167, 200, 203, 205; against Baltimore, 124; career, 171, 232, 234; compared to Hall of Fame members, 239, 240; game-winning, 49; minor league, 37, 229; during September call-ups, 50; single-game highs, 65

Reed, Howie, 104

Reese, Rich, 146, 159, 160, 165

Regan, Phil, 59

Reniff, Hal, 89

Repoz, Roger, 37

Richert, Pete, 96

Ridzik, Steve, 56

Rigney, Bill: as Angels manager, 66; firing of, 188; and Oliva's knee problems, 184, 185, 186; as Twins manager, 157, 159, 160, 166, 170, 175, 177

Rizzuto, Phil, 228

Robertson, Sherry, 32, 118

Robinson, Brooks: in 1966 AL pennant race, 109; in 1969 ALCS, 152, 153; and AL batting title races, 74; All-Star Game appearances, 122; comments on Oliva, 124, 225, 237; Hall of Fame member, 14, 229; MVP Award, 77; Oliva compared to, 236

Robinson, Frank: in 1969 ALCS, 152, 154, 166; All-Star Game appearances, 91, 161; batting statistics, 49; batting titles, 47, 108–9; as DH, 200; MVP Award, 109; Oliva compared to, 229, 232, 236; Triple Crown winner, 47, 109, 127

Robinson, Jackie, 6, 228, 245

Rollins, Rich, 88, 116; hitting performances, 56, 62, 76, 89, 90, 109; at third base, 16, 55, 93

Roof, Phil, 163–64, 222; comments on Oliva, 238

Rookie of the Year Award winners: Allison, 54; Oliva, 29, 46, 71, 78–79

Rose, Pete, 37, 45, 49, 161, 198, 231

Roseboro, John, 132, 133, 153

Rowe, Ralph, 202

Rudi, Joe, 172, 174, 229

runs batted in. See RBIs, annual totals; RBIs, Oliva's

runs scored: AL, 144, 198; Carew's, 203; Minnesota Twins, 133, 175; Oliva's, 57, 98, 232; Puckett's, 243; Tovar's, 147; Versalles's, 87, 98

Ruth, Babe, 133

Sain, Johnny, 111–12

Salmon, Chico, 111

Sanford, Jack, 118

Santiago, José, 127

Santo, Ron, 91, 227, 245

Schaal, Paul, 151

Scheinblum, Richie, 185, 186

Schilling, Chuck, 94

Scott, George, 47, 108, 125

Seaver, Tom, 135

segregation, U.S., 5–6, 7, 11, 33, 40. See also racism, U.S.

Siebert, Sonny, 88

Silver Louisville Slugger Award, 35

skin color. See racism, U.S.; segregation, U.S.

slugging percentages, Oliva's: annual, 48, 130, 170, 178, 240; against Baltimore, 124; career, 49; compared to Hall of Fame players, 227, 243, 246; ranking for, 233, 234

Smalley, Roy, 211

Smith, Reggie, 150, 163, 200

Snyder, Russ, 93

Soderholm, Eric, 208

South Atlantic League (minor leagues), 36–37

Splittorff, Paul, 185

Spring, Jack, 66

spring training, Oliva at: in 1964, 43,

51–54, 58; in 1965, 80–86; in 1966,
106–7; in 1967, 115–16; in 1970,
157–58; in 1971, 169–71; in 1972,
180–81, 182; in 1975, 208; during
minor league years, 5–8, 26–27, 36,
39; segregated housing for, 5, 6, 7, 11
spring training, Twins: in 1961, 5–8;
in 1964, 51–54; in 1965, 80–85; in
1966, 106–7; in 1967, 115–16; in
1969, 145, 157–58; in 1971, 169–71;
in 1972, 179, 180–81, 182; in 1975,
208; Oliva as hitting instructor at,
143. *See also* spring training, Oliva at
Stange, Lee, 33, 41, 59, 70, 108;
comments on Oliva, 34, 36–37, 237
Stargell, Willie, 91; Oliva compared to,
236
Stelmaszek, Rick, 216
Stevenson, Adlai, 9
Stiehm, Farrell, 82
Stigman, Dick, 38, 46, 63, 72, 88, 108
stolen bases, 135, 145–46
Stottlemyre, Mel, 89, 136
Stroud, Ed, 125
Stuart, Dick, 53
surgeries. *See* injuries, Oliva's
Suzuki, Ichiro, 45, 77

Talbot, Fred, 107
Target Field (Minneapolis) statues, 224
Tenace, Gene, 172
Terrell, Jerry, 202, 210
Thomas, Frank, 65
Thomas, Lee, 19, 76
Thompson, Danny, 188
Thompson, Jason, 211
3M Company, 135
Tiant, Luis, 150, 160, 167, 197
Tiger Stadium (Detroit), 37
Torre, Joe, 161
Torriente, Cristóbal, 14–15
Tovar, César: in 1965 AL pennant race,
97; in 1969 season, 146–47, 151;
in 1970 season, 159, 160, 164; car

accident, 47, 110; on Dallas–Fort
Worth Rangers team, 41, 42; fielding
performances, 124, 138, 187; Oliva's
friendship with, 40; playing all
positions, 114, 139; running game,
116, 145; tablesetter role, 147, 170;
trade of, 203
Tresh, Tom, 89
Triple Crown winners, 47, 109, 127, 130
triples, annual totals: Allison's, 54;
Carew's, 203; Oliva's, 78, 130
Trosky, Hal, 78
Tuttle, Bill, 18, 19–20
Twins. *See* Minnesota Twins

Uhlaender, Ted, 114, 121, 136, 137, 138
United States: relations with Cuba, 8–9,
12, 13, 14, 16, 18, 83. *See also* Bay of
Pigs invasion
Unser, Del, 185

Valdespino, Sandy, 15, 26–28, 97, 109,
120; comments on Oliva, 93, 125;
on Dallas–Fort Worth Rangers team,
39, 41, 42; Oliva's friendship with,
27–28, 114, 115, 139, 158, 222;
trade of, 132
Valdivielso, José, 14, 18, 35, 194–95
Valentine, Fred, 125
Velazquez, Nestor, 7, 10, 36, 218
Versalles, Zoilo, 21, 76, 81–86, 96; in
1965 AL pennant race, 93, 96; in
1965 World Series, 28, 100, 103,
104; in 1967 AL pennant race, 127;
All-Star Game appearances, 91;
brings family to United States, 82,
83; children of, 83, 84, 85, 142; and
disbanding of Cuban Winter League,
15–16; inside-the-park home run,
89–90; Martin's coaching of, 81,
87–88, 144; mentoring Oliva, 39–40;
MVP Award, 87–88, 94, 98; Oliva's
friendship with, 21–22, 35, 114,

218, 222; running game, 87, 88; at shortstop, 16, 33, 54; trade of, 132–33
Versalles-Curtis, Ampy, 83, 84, 85

Wagner, Leon, 66
Walker, Larry, 232
Walker, Todd, 124
Walters, Charley, 156
Waner, Lloyd, 77
Ward, Pete, 129
Washington Senators (expansion team), 26
Washington Senators (original team), 4, 7, 23–24, 53; all-Cuban triple play, 18, 19
Weaver, Earl, 152, 153
Whitfield, Fred, 111
Wickersham, Dave, 59, 148
Wilber, Del, 34, 58, 60
Wilhelm, Hoyt, 24, 136, 238
William, Bernie, 245
Williams, Billy: batting statistics, 49; Oliva compared to, 230–31, 232, 236
Williams, Dick, 122, 128
Williams, Ted, 52, 124; comments on Oliva, 173; Oliva compared to, 74–75
Wills, Maury, 103
Wilson, Earl, 110
Wilson, Hack, 229
winter baseball leagues. See Cuban Winter League; Los Mochis, Mexico; Los Palacios, Cuba; Oliva, Tony: winter ball experiences; Puerto Rican Winter League
Wood, Wilbur, 174, 179, 205–6, 238

Woodson, Dick, 154
World Series: of 1965, 25–26, 28, 44, 99–105, 113; of 1966, 109, 117; of 1969, 154, 155; of 2003, 40; playoff rounds, 144, 245. See also American League Championship Series
Worthington, Al, 76, 108, 113, 126–27, 128, 151
Wright, Clyde, 161
Wyatt, John, 110
Wynne, Billy, 151
Wytheville, Virginia (minor leagues): Oliva plays for, 32–35, 57, 189, 222

Yankee Stadium (New York City), 73, 88, 89
Yastrzemski, Carl, 76, 79, 91, 200; in 1967 AL pennant race, 128–29; AL batting titles, 48, 63, 133, 138, 145; All-Star Game appearances, 91, 122, 161; comments on Oliva's new batting stance, 172–73; competition with Oliva for batting titles, 86–87, 92, 94–95, 124–25, 136–38, 145, 162, 163, 164, 165; extra-base hits, 171; MVP Award, 128–29, 130, 133; Oliva compared to, 231, 236, 237; slugging percentage, 227; Triple Crown win in 1967, 127, 130
Year of the Pitcher (1968), 133, 135, 138, 198

Zepp, Bill, 156, 160
Zimmer, Don, 96–97
Zimmerman, Jerry, 102, 111

Thom Henninger is the associate editor of *Baseball Digest* magazine in Evanston, Illinois. He was a contributing author to *Play It Again: Baseball Experts on What Might Have Been,* edited by Jim Bresnahan. He contributed to several baseball annuals published by STATS LLC.

Patrick Reusse is a sports columnist for the *Star Tribune* and a radio personality in the Twin Cities of Minnesota.